Charity and Lay Piety in Reformation London, 1500–1620

To my families

Charity and Lay Piety in Reformation London, 1500–1620

CLAIRE S. SCHEN

ASHGATE

Published by
Ashgate Publishing Limited
Gower House
Croft Road
Aldershot
Hants GU11 3HR
England

Ashgate Publishing Company
131 Main Street
Burlington
Vermont 05401–5600
USA

Ashgate website: http://www.ashgate.com

British Library Cataloguing in Publication Data

Schen, Claire S.
  Charity and lay piety in Reformation London, 1500-1620. -
  (St Andrews studies in Reformation history)
  1. Charitable bequests - England - London - History - 16th
  century 2. Charitable bequests - England - London - History
  - 17th century 3. Charity 4. Piety 5. Reformation - England -
  London
  I. Title II. University of St Andrews. Institute for
  Reformation Studies
  253'. 094212'09031

Library of Congress Control Number: 2001098618

ISBN 0 7546 0098 X   9007295509 X

Typeset in Sabon by Manton, Typesetters, Louth, Lincolnshire, UK and printed in Great Britain by MPG Books Ltd, Bodmin, Cornwall.

Contents

St Andrews Studies in Reformation History

The Magnificent Ride: The First Reformation in Hussite Bohemia
Thomas A. Fudge

Kepler's Tübingen: Stimulus to a Theological Mathematics
Charlotte Methuen

'Practical Divinity': The Works and Life of Revd Richard Greenham
Kenneth L. Parker and Eric J. Carlson

*Belief and Practice in Reformation England: A Tribute to
Patrick Collinson by his Students*
edited by Susan Wabuda and Caroline Litzenberger

*Frontiers of the Reformation: Dissidence and Orthodoxy
in Sixteenth-Century Europe*
Auke Jelsma

*The Jacobean Kirk, 1567–1625:
Sovereignty, Polity and Liturgy*
Alan R. MacDonald

John Knox and the British Reformations
edited by Roger A. Mason

*The Education of a Christian Society:
Humanism and the Reformation in Britain and the Netherlands*
edited by N. Scott Amos, Andrew Pettegree and Henk van Nierop

Tudor Histories of the English Reformations, 1530–83
Thomas Betteridge

*Poor Relief and Protestantism:
The Evolution of Social Welfare in Sixteenth-Century Emden*
Timothy G. Fehler ·

*Radical Reformation Studies:
Essays presented to James M. Stayer*
edited by Werner O. Packull and Geoffrey L. Dipple

*Clerical Marriage and the English Reformation:
Precedent Policy and Practice*
Helen L. Parish

Usury, Interest and the Reformation
Eric Kerridge

The Correspondence of Reginald Pole:
1. A Calendar, 1518–1546: Beginnings to Legate of Viterbo
Thomas F. Mayer

Self-Defence and Religious Strife in Early Modern Europe:
England and Germany, 1530–1680
Robert von Friedeburg

Hatred in Print: Catholic Propaganda and Protestant Identity
during the French Wars of Religion
Luc Racaut

Penitence, Preaching and the Coming of the Reformation
Anne T. Thayer

Huguenot Heartland:
Montauban and Southern French Calvinism
during the French Wars of Religion
Philip Conner

List of figures and tables

Tables

Figures

Acknowledgements

This book began as a Ph.D. dissertation at Brandeis University, under the direction of Samuel K. Cohn. I would like to thank him, first of all, for having seen me through that process and for having remained a mentor and teacher to me. I cannot say, though, to have made a better pair of shoes than the cobbler. I would also like to thank the other members of my dissertation committee, Antony Polonsky and Susan Staves, for their thoughtful comments and advice. Thanks to another former member of the History Department at Brandeis, Bernard Wasserstein, for having been a collegial guide through graduate school. And, to go back to my undergraduate days when I thought I wanted to be a nineteenth-century historian, I owe special gratitude to David Underdown who first piqued my interest in the time period that has become my intellectual home. The staffs of the Guildhall Library, Public Record Office, Corporation of London Record Office and the staff of the library at Wake Forest have made my work much easier. The Rare Books Room at Wellesley College kindly allowed me access to Thomas Tanner's *Notitia Monastica*. I have enjoyed crucial financial assistance from Brandeis University and from the Archie Fund, funded by an endowment from the Mary Reynolds Babcock Foundation.

I must especially thank the anonymous reader for his or her thoughtful comments on my original manuscript. The editors of the Series and the Publishers, particularly Thomas Gray, Jo Jones and Barbara Pretty, have helped to make this a better book.

I also have new mentors and colleagues to thank for their interest in my teaching and research career. Judith Bennett, Paul Fideler, Craig Harline, Barbara Harris, Cynthia Herrup, Caroline Hibbard, Mark Kishlansky and Robert Tittler have all been generous to me with their time and their expertise. The members of the Feminist Women in History Group and of the North Carolina Research Group on Medieval and Early Modern Women have been models of scholarly enthusiasm. I would also like to thank Paul Slack and Ian Archer for having discussed my project with me at an early stage. Caroline Barron and Vanessa Harding, and those who attended the Medieval and Tudor London Seminar, especially Clive Burgess, have been most kind and generous and have helped me to understand London and its sources much better. I am deeply indebted to Lynn Botelho, Michael Braddick, Francis J. Bremer, Eric Carlson, Katherine French, Gary Gibbs, Fiona Kisby, Beat Kümin, Marjorie McIntosh, Malcolm Smuts, Pat Thane, Barbara Todd and Joe Ward for the questions and comments they have offered about my research and written work. I owe special thanks to a group of people I had the good fortune of meeting in the Institute of Historical Research in London who helped me to maintain enthusiasm for the early (and later) research: Glenn Wilkinson, Tim Wales, Keith Surridge, Fiona Kisby, Charles Littleton, Jonathan Harris and Daniel Page. Rupert and Mary Wilkinson opened their home to me on the vaguest of recommendations from a mutual friend – I cannot thank them enough.

Most recently, my colleagues at Wake Forest University, especially the members of the Department of History and the Medieval Studies Group and its leaders Gillian Overing and Gale Sigal, have been most supportive to me. Simone Caron, Soledad Miguel-Prendes, Anthony Parent and Susan Zayer Rupp took great care in reading my work and Robert Beachy, Michele Gillespie, Michael Hughes and Sarah Watts were always willing to discuss it with me and to encourage me. I would like to thank Julie Cole and Julie Edelson in Research Programs and Partnerships and Janice Walker in the History Department for all their help.

Any errors or faults remain my own.

Last, but most certainly not least, I give my love and thanks to my families, who have always supported me in my endeavours. My parents, Jane and Charles Schen, and my siblings Walter, Andrea and Lisa, have given material and spiritual aid for many years now, making so much possible for me. My husband, Gregory Cherr, and now, too, baby Madeleine, have made my life all the richer. It is to these people that I gratefully dedicate this book.

                                                    Claire S. Schen

Abbreviations and notes

Chantry Certificate	C.J. Kitching (ed.), *London and Middlesex Chantry Certificate, 1548*, London Record Society 16 (London, 1980)
CLRO	Corporation of London Record Office
DNB	*Dictionary of National Biography*
Fraternity Register	Patricia Basing (ed.), *Parish Fraternity Register: Fraternity of the Holy Trinity and SS. Fabian and Sebastian in the Parish of St. Botolph without Aldersgate*, London Record Society 18 (London, 1982)
GL	Guildhall Library
JBS	*Journal of British Studies*
Morley	John Stow (Henry Morley, ed.), *A Survay of London* (*London under Elizabeth: A Survey*) (London, 1890)
OED	*Oxford English Dictionary*
PaP	*Past and Present*
The Parish	Katherine French, Gary Gibbs and Beat Kümin, *The Parish in English Life, 1400–1600* (Manchester, 1997)
PRO	Public Record Office
PROB	Prerogative Court of Canterbury Probate Records
Rep.	Repertory Book
SCJ	*Sixteenth Century Journal*
Somers	Baron John Somers, *A Collection of Scarce and Valuable Tracts* (London, 1809)
TED	R.H. Tawney and Eileen Power, *Tudor Economic Documents* (3 vols, London, 1951)
Thoms	John Stow (William J. Thoms, ed.) *A Survay of London*, written 1598, increased 1603 (London, 1876)
TRHS	*Transactions of the Royal Historical Society*
TRP	Paul L. Hughes and James F. Larkin (eds), *Tudor Royal Proclamations* (3 vols, New Haven and London, 1969)
VAI	Walter Howard Frere and William McClure Kennedy (eds), *Visitation Articles and Injunc-*

tions of the Period of the Reformation (3 vols,
Alcuin Club, 1910)

VCH   *The Victoria History of the Counties of Eng-*
land

I have followed the dating used in manuscripts but, where possible,
have taken the year to begin on January 1. I have retained the spelling
of the original documents, except to use one form of a given personal
name. Not all of the sources are foliated. I have followed the idiosyncratic foliation of the Public Record Office, by which the pages are
numbered left and right, not verso and recto. Hence, '117L' is the
equivalent of '116v'.

CHAPTER ONE

Introduction

In St Botolph's Aldersgate in 1601, the scribe drew upon a verse from Proverbs to begin the new volume of vestry minutes: 'He that hath mercy upon the Poore, rendeth unto the Lord. And the Lord will recompence him that w[hi]ch hee hath given.'[1] A list of benefactors to the poor followed the verse, with their names and details about their donations. The churchwardens in St Botolph's used Scripture to sanction the idea of charity and celebrated the exemplary donations of parishioners to encourage the act of giving. Before the Reformation, parishioners understood that salvation came through good works, including charity, and the intercession of priests, saints and Christians who prayed for the souls of the dead. Without denying the selfless motives for giving, the selfish components, from securing salvation to perpetuating the family name, helped to spur late medieval women and men to charitable acts. After the Reformation, even with purgatory abolished and Catholic acts of mercy or good works discredited, charity remained an important act of faith, beneficial to the individual, useful to society, and pleasing to God. Religion, before and after the Reformation, shaped parishioners' views of poverty and poor relief. Protestant ideas, however, were only part of the powerful influences on London's inhabitants; the spectacular growth of the city and the growth in poverty, whether real or perceived, also shaped responses to the problem of the poor.

'Charity' in the sixteenth century encompassed God's love of humankind, humankind's love of God and neighbour, the specific act of almsgiving, and benevolence to the poor.[2] I use the term in this study to represent the relief of the poor and the kindness shown to needy kin and neighbours and being 'in charity' to refer to the love between God and humankind, and among humankind. In speaking of the poor, I include the abject poor, their poverty being structural, with the occasionally impoverished, theirs being conjunctural.[3] Informal charity and formal poor relief functioned together to alleviate poverty, an ideal

---

[1] Proverbs 19:17; GL, MS 1453, Vol. 1, fol. 1.

[2] *OED*; Judith Bennett urges consideration of the complexity of the term: 'Reply', *PaP*, 154 (Feb. 1997), p. 241.

[3] 'In medieval and early modern England, poverty was something that could befall all but the most fortunate ... ', ibid., p. 236.

encapsulated in the 1598 poor law calling on the parents and children of the lame, blind, impotent and aged to maintain them while also solidifying the formal national law.[4] Neither alms nor statutory relief were intended to negate social inequality, however. Instead, gifts and formal relief acknowledged, even reified, social distinctions.

Marcel Mauss's theory of the 'gift' demonstrates how charity marked social difference even though it allowed the temporary transcendence of the divide between rich and poor. Mauss described the power of the gift, and the giver, in this way: 'To give is to show one's superiority, to be more, to be higher in rank, *magister*. To accept without giving in return, or without giving more back, is to become client and servant, to become small, to fall lower (*minister*).'[5] For testators, whose personal returns on charity came only with death, charity elevated the social status of their survivors and imbued their parish or city with the family name. In pre-Reformation London, the poor were likened to Christ and, with testators' salvation linked to almsgiving, impoverished men and women 'repaid' testators with prayers and remembrance. When the poor prayed and processed in black mourning gowns, they returned some of the monetary and other gifts in spiritual 'superiority'. The Reformation, however, succeeded in recasting the poor as client or servant, ornaments at funerals whose own devotions no longer helped testators to pass through the eye of the needle into heaven.[6]

The Reformation did not, however, destroy charity, nor did the imposition of rates for parochial relief undo altruism. Commentators and preachers still urged charity as an example of Christian love and a way to preserve 'community'. As Mauss wrote about gift exchange, 'To refuse to give, to fail to invite, just as to refuse to accept, is tantamount to declaring war; it is to reject the bond of alliance and commonality'.[7]

---

[4] 39 Eliz. c.3.

[5] Marcel Mauss, *The Gift: Form and Reason for Exchange in Archaic Societies* (New York, 1990), orig. 1950, trans. by Mary Douglas, p. 74. Recent uses of Mauss's theory: Miri Rubin, *Charity and Community in Medieval Cambridge* (Cambridge, 1987); James G. Carrier, *Gifts and Commodities: Exchange and Western Capitalism since 1700* (London and New York, 1995); Maria Moisà, 'Debate', *PaP*, **154** (1997), pp. 223–34; Jane Fair Bestor, 'Marriage Transactions in Renaissance Italy and Mauss's *Essay on the Gift*', *PaP*, **164** (1999), pp. 6–46.

[6] Rubin sees this as a slow process beginning in the medieval period. 'Yet, in the realignment of ideas, which took place over a long period and in different forms in different social groups, the poor were no longer lodged, fed and cared for but rather, they were appended to funerary and commemorative occasions, almost external to the act, just as the clergy was hired and the bells rung': Rubin, *Charity and Community*, p. 299.

[7] Mauss, *The Gift*, p. 13.

The connection between parish relief and the stability and governance of metropolitan London has been noted.[8] Although historians once used 'community' un-self-consciously, recent works have questioned the appropriateness of the term. Robert Tittler's summary of the useful elements of the word – emphasising mutual identity and obligation and yet not precluding 'conflict and disharmony' – accords with the sixteenth-century practice of using charity to blur and mark social difference.[9] Further, no single community existed in sixteenth-century London where parish, court, guild and neighbourhood intersected and members overlapped. London's history and various communities have been the subject of renewed interest, especially in relation to its companies and its seventeenth-century Puritanism.[10] Despite continuity in the motives behind charity, compassion and Christian love as well as a desire to maintain order, the developments of the sixteenth and early seventeenth centuries did bring real change in the relationship between donors and recipients. The 'artificial yet intimate link between members of the Christian community'[11] of the late medieval period grew even weaker as the poor remained in a secondary role, lacking even the power to promise prayers to generous donors.

---

[8] Ian Archer, *The Pursuit of Stability: Social Relations in Elizabethan London* (Cambridge, 1991), pp. 198–203; Valerie Pearl, 'Change and Stability in Seventeenth-Century London', *The London Journal*, V, No.1 (May 1979), pp. 3–34; Susan Brigden, 'Religion and Social Obligation in early Sixteenth-Century London', *PaP*, **103** (May 1984), pp. 67–112.

[9] Robert Tittler, *The Reformation and the Towns in England: Politics and Political Culture, c. 1540–1640* (Oxford, 1998), pp. 13–17. See also Maryanne Kowaleski (ed.), 'Village, Guild, and Gentry: Forces of Community in Later Medieval England', *JBS* **33**, 4 (Oct. 1994); Joseph P. Ward, *Metropolitan Communities: Trade Guilds, Identity, and Change in Early Modern London* (Stanford, CA, 1997), pp. 1, 7–8; Keith Thomas on breakdown of community and witchcraft: *Religion and the Decline of Magic* (New York, 1971), pp. 520, 552.

[10] Archer, *Pursuit*; Steve Rappaport, *Worlds within Worlds: Structures of Life in Sixteenth-Century London* (Cambridge, 1989); Susan Brigden, *London and the Reformation* (Oxford, 1989); Jeremy Boulton, *Neighbourhood and Society: A London Suburb in the Seventeenth Century* (Cambridge, 1987); Gervase Rosser, *Medieval Westminster, 1200–1540* (Oxford, 1989); Julia Frances Merritt, 'Religion, Government, and Society in Early Modern Westminster, c. 1525–1625', unpublished Ph.D. thesis, Royal Holloway and Bedford New College, University of London, 1992; Ward, *Metropolitan Communities*; Fiona Kisby, 'Music and Musicians of Early Tudor Westminster', *Early Music*, **23**, 2 (1995), pp. 223–40 and 'Royal Minstrels in the City and Suburbs of Early Tudor London: Professional Activities and Private Interests', *Early Music*, **25**, 2 (1997), pp. 199–219; Laura Gowing, *Domestic Dangers: Women, Words, and Sex in Early Modern London* (Oxford, 1996); Peter Lake and David Como, ' "Orthodoxy and Its Discontents: Dispute Settlement and the Production of "Consensus" in the London (Puritan) "Underground"', *JBS*, **39**, 1 (Jan. 2000), pp. 34–70.

[11] Rubin, *Charity and Community*, p. 289.

Although elements of the English case set the country apart, and London's special problems with poverty and charity distinguished it from the rest of the country, reform of poor relief spread across Europe's confessional and geographical lines in the sixteenth century. Catholic and Protestant countries alike fixated on social disorder and saw older notions of charity, particularly indiscriminate almsgiving, slowly erode.[12] The Protestant criticism that first attacked the mendicant orders developed into an attack on begging that most Catholic policy also incorporated.[13] In general, reform meant relying on a community chest, administering relief through secular leaders, ending unregulated begging, and regulating the poor, though all elements of this reform were not present throughout Europe.[14] While Catholic and Protestant charity exhibited similarities, Protestant relief tended to greater centralization than did Catholic efforts.[15] Paul Slack has noted the special English contributions to widespread reform: rates and workhouses.[16] Historians of England agree that poverty was redefined and that the nascent differentiation between deserving and undeserving poor matured in the sixteenth century, but they disagree on the roots or agents of this historical development.[17] Compared to Continental stud-

---

[12] Sampling of literature on poverty and charity: Paul Slack, *Poverty and Policy in Tudor and Stuart England* (London, 1988) and *From Reformation to Improvement: Public Welfare in Early Modern England* (Oxford, 1999); Felicity Heal, *Hospitality in Early Modern England* (Oxford, 1990); Paul A. Fideler, 'Poverty, policy and providence: the Tudors and the Poor' in Fideler and T.F. Mayer (eds), *Political Thought and the Tudor Commonwealth* (London and New York, 1992), pp. 194–222; Brian Pullan, 'Catholics and the Poor in Early Modern Europe', *TRHS*, 5th Series, 26 (1976), 15–34; Robert M. Kingdon, 'Social Welfare in Calvin's Geneva', *American Historical Review*, 76, 1 (1971), 50–69; Olwen H. Hufton, *The Poor of Eighteenth-Century France, 1750–1789* (Oxford, 1974); Samuel K. Cohn, *Death and Property in Siena* (Baltimore, MD, 1988) and *The Cult of Remembrance and the Black Death: Six Renaissance Cities in Central Italy* (Baltimore, MD, 1992); Kathryn Norberg, *Rich and Poor in Grenoble, 1600–1814* (Berkeley, CA, 1985); Christopher F. Black, *Italian Confraternities in the Sixteenth Century* (Cambridge, 1989); Philip Gavitt, *Charity and Children in Renaissance Florence: The Ospedale degli Innocenti, 1410–1536* (Ann Arbor, MI, 1990); Maureen Flynn, *Sacred Charity: Confraternities and Social Welfare in Spain, 1400–1700* (Ithaca, NY, 1989); Robert Jütte, *Poverty and Deviance in Early Modern Europe* (Cambridge, 1994); Anne McCants, *Civic Charity in a Golden Age: Orphan Care in Early Modern Amsterdam* (Urbana and Chicago, 1997); Thomas Max Safley, *Charity and Economy in the Orphanages of Early Modern Augsburg* (Atlantic Highlands, NJ, 1997).

[13] McCants, *Civic Charity*, p. 7.

[14] As summarized in Safley, *Charity and Economy*, p. 3.

[15] Jütte, *Poverty and Deviance*, pp. 100–42.

[16] Slack, *From Reformation*, p. 21.

[17] For the interpretation of 'puritan' or bourgeois influence, see W.K. Jordan, *The Charities of London, 1480–1660: The Aspirations and the Achievements of the Urban Society* (London, 1960); Christopher Hill, 'William Perkins and the Poor' in *Puritanism*

ies, the spectre of Max Weber's puritan ethic is largely absent in English historiography.[18]

The similarities across geographical and confessional boundaries are mirrored by the comparisons across the chronological divide between medieval and early modern society. An historiographical tendency to study either pre- or post-Reformation society and culture has exacerbated the problem of seeing sixteenth-century developments as novel.[19] Notions of the deserving and undeserving poor originated in the medieval period, although the dichotomy was formalized by the developing poor laws.[20] Fraternities and religious guilds permitted medieval men and women to balance the obligation to give with the desire for control and discrimination. Donors' fears of the potentially disruptive poor and their resentment of the idle poor existed alongside this emphasis on almsgiving.[21]

Across time and place, the reform of relief and charity sprang from common problems of economic distress, demographic stress and religious or cultural change, but local conditions also influenced the response to these problems. Ingredients for unrest existed in London and the other towns of England in the sixteenth century: sporadic economic crises, a decline in civic ritual, religious uncertainty and rapid population growth. Economic decline in English cities and towns resulted in decay, and less civic ritual in turn exacerbated social difference.[22] London's stability in the sixteenth century, despite expansion, economic

---

and Revolution: Studies in the Interpretation of the English Revolution of the Seventeenth Century (London, 1958), pp. 215–38. On the power of social control, see Archer, *The Pursuit*; Paul Slack, *Poverty and Policy*; cf. Margaret Spufford, 'Puritanism and Social Control?' in Anthony Fletcher and John Stevenson (eds), *Order and Disorder in Early Modern England* (Cambridge, 1985), pp. 41–57.

[18] For example, see: McCants, *Civic Charity*, p. 14; Safley, *Charity and Economy*, pp. 11–13.

[19] Notable exceptions in Marjorie K. McIntosh, *A Community Transformed: The Manor and Liberty of Havering, 1500–1620* (Cambridge, 1991) and *Controlling Misbehavior in England, 1370–1600* (Cambridge, 1998); Beat Kümin, *The Shaping of a Community: The Rise and Reformation of the English Parish, c. 1400–1560* (Aldershot, 1996).

[20] Michel Mollat, trans. by Arthur Goldhammer, *The Poor in the Middle Ages: An Essay in Social History* (New Haven and London, 1986), orig. 1978, pp. 133–4; Rubin, *Charity and Community*; Lorraine Attreed, 'Poverty, payments, and fiscal policies in English provincial towns' in Samuel K. Cohn and Steven Epstein (eds), *Portraits of Medieval Living: Essays in Memory of David Herlihy* (Ann Arbor, MI, 1996), pp. 337–8; Slack, *Poverty and Policy*, pp. 23–5.

[21] Rubin, *Charity and Community*, p. 98.

[22] Peter Clark and Paul Slack (eds), *Crisis and Order in English Towns, 1500–1700: Essays in Urban History* (Toronto, 1972); Charles Phythian-Adams, *Desolation of a City: Coventry and the Urban Crises of the Late Middle Ages* (Cambridge, 1979).

crises and religious turmoil, has been the object of recent studies.[23] Steve Rappaport emphasizes the crisis of the 1590s, while Ian Archer downplays the extent of economic crisis in that decade. In his study of craft guilds, Rappaport states that the opportunities for social mobility within them lessened the threat of serious unrest. Although the crisis of the 1590s may have brought London closer to riot than at any other time, he paints a picture of a quiet city.[24] Archer counters this view, suggesting that an absence of riots after 1595 'may reflect tightened social control rather than the restoration of social calm'. Elites crafted a careful balance among social groups that balanced the 'rulers and ruled', but articulated greater social polarization. Broad-based social involvement in parishes, wards and companies, if not on the court of aldermen, and social policies overseeing the poor promoted stability, Archer argues.[25] Bouts of the plague, natural disasters, minor disturbances about the city, and increasing numbers of poor, however, coloured contemporaries' perceptions of increasing urban poverty and disorder. These perceptions encouraged and justified further discrimination in charity and poor relief to relieve the sufferers and punish the idle. The opinions of contemporaries, even if quantitatively incorrect, made a real impact on policy and practice.[26]

Charity was not just a means to keep civic order, but also an expression of piety. Bequests and poor relief reflected Catholic and Protestant beliefs, providing another way of analysing the course and impact of the English Reformation. Revisionist historians have dismantled the traditional interpretation of the event, or series of events: a popular Protestant Reformation driven by anti-clericalism and popular piety. Revisionists' careful study of lay piety revealed the vitality of and lay enthusiasm for late medieval Catholicism, the traditional or 'old' ways. Eamon Duffy and Ronald Hutton have revealed the richness of late medieval piety, but have perhaps over-emphasized its monolithic nature

---

[23] Cf. Rappaport, *Worlds* and Archer, *Pursuit*.

[24] Rappaport, *Worlds*, pp.13–19; cf. Archer's claims that fiscal pressures were lower in the 1590s than the 1540s, or than those on the Continent in the 1590s, but that the numbers of poor had risen and created stronger perceptions of crisis: *Pursuit*, pp. 12–13.

[25] Archer, *Pursuit*, p. 9; Archer, 'The nostalgia of John Stow' in David L. Smith, Richard Strier and David Bevington (eds), *The Theatrical City: Culture, Theatre and Politics in London, 1576–1649* (Cambridge, 1995), p. 25; for explanation of vestries, wardmotes, and city organization, also see Pearl, 'Change and Stability', p. 15.

[26] Gertrude Himmelfarb, writing about poverty in the nineteenth century, describes the 'pessimistic' contemporary reality with which statistical data could not 'compete'. She blames the difference between 'reality' and historians' statistical interpretations on the 'cultural lag' between experience and memory: *The Idea of Poverty: England in the Early Industrial Age* (New York, 1985), p. 137.

in pre-Reformation England. Despite the great attention paid to lay people, in the end revisionist historiography falls back on high politics.[27] Christopher Haigh called for a new view 'from below', but his *English Reformations* often overlooked lay piety, although his notion of stages of reform helps to reintroduce the urgency and uncertainty that was so much a part of the lives of sixteenth-century adherents to the 'new' or 'old' ways.[28] Caroline Litzenberger offers a new view 'from the pews', but her analysis of popular piety rests on the standard mid-century periodization.[29] Nicholas Tyacke specifies the weaknesses of the historiography of the English Reformation compared to the historiography of Continental reform: that it is studied in the confining middle decades of the sixteenth century and treats the Reformation as a 'succession of legislative enactments' rather than as a 'religious movement'.[30]

In arguing for a re-thinking of the reform movement in England along the lines of Continental historiography – and therefore of a 'Long Reformation' – Tyacke points to lacunae in our studies, particularly how England became Protestant, not just stopped being Catholic. His emphasis on divisions among Protestants, earlier noted by Patrick Collinson, also reminds us of the complexities and varieties of religious beliefs.[31] Muriel McClendon's study of Norwich shows the tolerance for varied religious beliefs within segments of reforming society.[32] Studying the evolution of lay piety through the long stretch of the period 1500 to 1620 unites pre-Reformation England with that which followed, to help us understand how 'Reformations' or a 'Long Reformation' happened in

---

[27] The traditional interpretation: A.G. Dickens, *The English Reformation* (New York, 1964); Claire Cross, *Church and People, 1450–1660: The Triumph of the Laity in the English Church* (Atlantic Highlands, NJ, 1976). Revisionist interpretations: Christopher Haigh (ed.), *The English Reformation Revised* (Cambridge, 1987) and *English Reformations: Religion, Politics, and Society under the Tudors* (Oxford, 1993); J.J. Scarisbrick, *The Reformation and the English People* (Oxford, 1984); Eamon Duffy, *The Stripping of the Altars: Traditional Religion in England, 1400–1580* (New Haven and London, 1992); Brigden, *London and the Reformation;* Susan Wabuda, 'Revising the Reformation', *JBS*, 35, 2 (1996), pp. 257–62.

[28] Haigh, *English Reformations*, pp. 16–17.

[29] Caroline Litzenberger, *The English Reformation and the Laity: Gloucestershire, 1540–1580* (Cambridge, 1997).

[30] Nicholas Tyacke, 'Introduction: re-thinking the "English Reformation"' in *England's Long Reformation 1500–1800* (London and Bristol, PA, 1998), pp. 1–2.

[31] See Patrick Collinson, 'Popular and Unpopular Religion', in *The Religion of Protestants* (Oxford, 1982), p. 189.

[32] Muriel McClendon, 'Discipline and punish? Magistrates and clergy in early Reformation Norwich' in Eric Josef Carlson (ed.), *Religion and the English People 1500–1640: New Voices, New Perspectives*, Sixteenth Century Essays and Studies, Vol. 45, pp. 99–118.

London. Evidence from wills and testaments and parochial records show the persistence through the long sixteenth century of old Catholic forms and the resonance of new Protestant functions. The charity of sixteenth- and early seventeenth-century Londoners opens a window on to their attitudes towards the old and new religious ways. In Protestant doctrine and in puritan godliness Londoners found reasons for more stringent discrimination in charity.

The parish provides the key to studying religious, social and urban change through the Reformation and the long sixteenth century, and has provided fertile ground for a number of recent studies on religious and social identity.[33] Parochial-based studies bridge the artificial divides between medieval and early modern, between pre- and post-Reformation, between religious and secular change in the sixteenth century. Parishes were the centres of religious change – the churches implemented new religious policies with varying speed and enthusiasm – and were the foci of social change, particularly relating to charity and the relief of the poor. As a result of increased administrative responsibilities, parochial officials assumed more authority over many aspects of urban life, from seating within the church to the regulation of morality to poor relief.[34]

Part of re-thinking the Reformation and the reform of poor relief, and therefore of life in the parishes of London, needs to encompass considerations of gender, as women and men had different social, legal, political and religious opportunities in the medieval and early modern periods. In her overview of the state of women's history in early modern studies, Merry Wiesner remarks that gender has not been integrated into general studies of the Reformation. 'The groups that have been the focus of Reformation scholarship over the last decade, such as peasants, city populations, and clergy', she writes, 'remain male groups, though not explicitly so, for the only scholars of the Reformation interested in

---

[33] Ian Archer calls the parish the 'cockpit of local government', choosing the parish as the central unit of his comprehensive study of Tudor London because the parish vestry was the foundation of civic organization: *Pursuit*, pp. 63–74. Growing historiography of parishes: Katherine French, Gary Gibbs and Kümin (eds), *The Parish in English Life, 1400–1600* (Manchester, 1997); Kümin, *The Shaping*; Andrew Brown, *Popular Piety in Late Medieval England: The Diocese of Salisbury, 1250–1550* (Oxford, 1995); Daniel C. Beaver, *Parish Communities and Religious Conflict in the Vale of Gloucester, 1590–1690* (Cambridge, MA, 1998); French, *The People of the Parish: Community Life in a Late Medieval English Diocese* (Philadelphia, PA, 2001); N.J.G. Pounds, *A History of the English Parish: The Culture of Religion from Augustine to Victoria* (Cambridge, 2000); Clive Burgess, 'Shaping the Parish: St Mary at Hill, London, in the Fifteenth Century' in J. Blair and B. Golding (eds), *The Cloister and the World: Essays in Medieval History in Honour of Barbara Harvey* (Oxford, 1996), pp. 246–86.

[34] 'English revolutions are bloodless because they are always led by English church-wardens': quoted in Pearl, 'Change and Stability', p. 27.

the very new research area of masculinity are those who have already focused on women'.[35] The revisionist history of the English Reformation has by and large not considered women, or, more broadly, gender, as a distinct category of analysis, although the works are considered synthetic histories of the events we have come to place under the 'Reformation'. The much-needed recent studies of women in early modern England in turn have not directly addressed the debates surrounding Reformation revisionism or poor relief studies.[36] Eric Carlson's history of marriage and the Reformation offers a tantalizing contrast between English and Continental Protestant theology in that England did not hurry to reform its marriage law, a change that could have brought greater egalitarianism between the sexes.[37] No piece, however, offers a definitive statement on the impact of the Reformation on women, or women's influence upon it, in contrast to research on women on the Continent.[38] Protestant women lacked opportunities for emulating saints,

---

[35] Merry Wiesner, *Gender, Church, and State in Early Modern Germany* (London and New York, 1998), Series: Women and Men in History, pp. 202–3. She first made this general point in a 1987 article, showing how little has changed in the history of women and the Reformation in the last decade or so: 'Beyond Women and the Family: Towards a Gender Analysis of the Reformation', *SCJ*, 18 (1987), pp. 311–21. See also debate over effective studying and writing of the history of women: Bridget Hill, 'Women's history: a study in change, continuity or standing still?', *Women's History Review*, 2, 1 (1993), pp. 5–22; reply from Judith Bennett, 'Women's history: a study in continuity and change', *Women's History Review*, 2, 2 (1993), pp. 173–84.

[36] Barbara Harris discusses women and the Reformation, but in relation to aristocratic women and nunneries: 'A new look at the Reformation: aristocratic women and nunneries 1450–1540', *JBS*, 32 (1993), 89–113. Recent studies of women and religion: Patricia Crawford, *Women and Religion in England 1500–1720* (New York, 1993); Claire Cross, 'The religious life of women in sixteenth-century Yorkshire' in W.J. Sheils and D. Wood (eds), *Women in the Church, Studies in Church History*, 27 (Oxford, 1990), pp. 307–24; Susan Wabuda, 'Shunamites and nurses of the English Reformation: the activities of Mary Glover, niece of Hugh Latimer' in ibid., pp. 335–44; Diane Willen, 'Godly Women in Early Modern England: Puritanism and Gender', *Journal of Ecclesiastical History*, 43, 4 (October 1992), pp. 561–80. Histories of women or women and the family in early modern England: Susan D. Amussen, *An Ordered Society: Gender and Class in Early Modern England* (Oxford, 1988); Sara Mendelson and Patricia Crawford, *Women in Early Modern England, 1550–1720* (Oxford, 1998); Anthony Fletcher, *Gender, Sex and Subordination in England, 1500–1800* (New Haven and London, 1995); Gowing, *Domestic Dangers*. The exceptional women of seventeenth-century sects: Phyllis Mack, *Visionary Women: Ecstatic Prophecy in Seventeenth-Century England* (Berkeley, CA, 1992); Bonnelyn Young Kunze, *Margaret Fell and the Rise of Quakerism* (Stanford, CA, 1994).

[37] Eric Joseph Carlson, *Marriage and the English Reformation* (Oxford, 1994), p. 8.

[38] Including my own 'Women and the London Parishes 1500–1620' in French, Gibbs, Kümin (eds), *The Parish in English Life*, pp. 250–68. Cf. Lyndal Roper, *The Holy Household: Women and Morals, in Reformation Augsburg* (Oxford, 1989); Wiesner, *Gender, Church and State*; Natalie Zemon Davis, 'City Women and Religious Change', in *Society and Culture in Early Modern France* (Stanford, 1975 edn; orig. 1965), pp. 65–95.

joining nunneries and participating in Tridentine confraternities, some of the signs of female agency that have fuelled scholars' interest in Catholic women. English women's involvement in parishes, in charitable giving, and in reform and recusant activities make them significant actors, however, in the history of the Reformation in England.

The roles of women, as both donors and recipients of charity and relief, should be considered in the study of European-wide changes in attitudes about the poor and poor relief. Analysing the testamentary charity of (largely elite or at least of middling status) female donors provides another way to access the mental world of sixteenth-century women, although testamentary practice and law limited their wills' scope. Few single women made wills, wives needed their husbands' permission to make them, and widows had limited property to distribute after their husbands' bequests were fulfilled. Scholarship on English women has often concentrated on the lives of women exceptional for their talent, personality or wealth, in part due to the survival of records.[39] The 'gender crisis' of the sixteenth century also has a 'class' dimension, by which social status became entangled with gender issues that shaped the lives of poor women and modified their place in the early modern parish.[40]

The poor, although discussed by contemporaries and glimpsed in interaction with churchwardens, testators and executors, remain an elusive focus against this background of historical change. Individuals received charity, but the faceless or unknown poor embodied greater social concerns for contemporaries. The common themes of deservingness evoked by the pleas of the poor to parishes only downplayed individual characteristics. The roving bands of vagabonds and idle poor described in chronicles and pamphlets were likely exaggerated, but they became emblematic to city inhabitants who saw their parishes spending more time and money on the problem of poverty by the late sixteenth century. Female recipients can be even harder to see individually, rather than as part of the groups of deserving poor widows or women victimized by absent husbands or fathers. Even female vagabonds have largely escaped study.[41] Churchwardens' accounts indicate the circumstances of

[39] Sara Mendelson, *The Mental World of Stuart Women: Three Studies* (Brighton, 1987) and 'Stuart Women's Diaries and Occasional Memoirs' in Mary Prior (ed.), *Women in English Society 1500–1800* (London and New York, 1985), pp. 181–210; Joel Rosenthal, 'Aristocratic Widows in Fifteenth-Century England' in Barbara J. Harris and JoAnn K. McNamara (eds), *Women and the Structure of Society: Selected Research from the Fifth Berkshire Conference on the History of Women* (Durham, NC, 1984), pp. 36–47; D.M. Loades, *Mary Tudor: A Life* (Oxford, 1989); Mack, *Visionary Women*.

[40] Amussen, *An Ordered Society*.

[41] A.L. Beier, *Masterless Men: The Vagrancy Problem in England, 1560–1640* (London and New York, 1985), pp. 124–5; Fideler, '*Societas, Civitas* and Early Elizabethan

the poor receiving parish aid, but always through the perspective of parochial officials and parsons who bore varying degrees of sympathy for the varied poor men and women who passed through their parishes. Rappaport disputes calculations that two-thirds of London's population lived below or near the poverty line, but poverty and vagrancy were perceived to be on the rise and apparently were in real terms. Archer follows Paul Slack's calculations for provincial towns in arguing that 4–5 per cent would be structurally poor and another 10–15 per cent might need relief occasionally.[42]

What sources best allow us to study lay responses to the Reformation and to the broader social changes of the sixteenth century? No source can offer an unadulterated view of individual thoughts or motives, though we can piece together a collective view of how London's inhabitants responded to religious and social transformation. Churchwardens' accounts and vestry minutes reveal what was spent within parishes, the people and projects on which these parochial officers desired or were compelled to spend money.[43] The accounts in particular detail receipts and expenditures within parishes: money collected for rented church property and graves, the profits from the sale of church plate and vestments during reform and restoration, and the payments to conform to religious policy, to meet the wages of all those hired by the parish, and to relieve the poor of the parish and the city more generally. Churchwardens' accounts and vestry minutes provide clues to the extent of *inter vivos* giving, a potentially significant, but largely unrecorded, source of charity and relief.[44] Vestry minutes, either separately bound or scattered throughout churchwardens' accounts, summarized other business related to property rental, parochial disputes, poor relief or suits of law in which the parish was embroiled. Needy individuals brought their petitions to vestries, although traces of the conversations behind written

---

Poverty Relief' in Charles Carlton, Robert L. Woods et al. (eds), *State, Sovereigns and Society in Early Modern England: Essays in Honour of A.J. Slavin* (New York, 1998), pp. 65–6; call for addition of gender analysis to study of vagrancy: Jodi Mikalachki, 'Women's Networks and the Female Vagrant: A Hard Case' in Susan Frye and Karen Robertson (eds), *Maids and Mistresses, Cousins and Queens: Women's Alliances in Early Modern England* (Oxford and New York, 1999), pp. 52–3.

[42] Rappaport, *Worlds within Worlds*, p. 172; Archer, *Pursuit*, pp. 152–4.

[43] J. Charles Cox, *Churchwardens Accounts: From the Fourteenth Century to the Close of the Seventeenth Century* (London, 1913); Andrew Foster, 'Churchwardens' accounts of early modern England and Wales: some problems to note, but much to be gained' in *The Parish*, pp. 74–93. Haigh argues that 'churchwardens' accounts tell us only what churchwardens spent, not what they thought, and certainly not what the rest of the parishioners thought': *English Reformations*, p. 17.

[44] Exception in the case of St Margaret Westminster, where the churchwardens listed extensive lifetime gifts: Merritt, 'Religion, Government, and Society', pp. 288, 292.

decisions rarely survived. At the end of the year, parochial officers presented the minutes and accounts to the whole or 'better part' of a parish, for the final audit and approval of expenditures.

The value of wills and testaments, like churchwardens' accounts, has been questioned for what remains hidden from historians, although the documents were once seen as windows into the minds of early modern men and women. Historians have used wills to trace attitudes towards the Reformation and Protestantism or Catholicism, towards burial in early modern England, and towards charity.[45] For W.K. Jordan, testaments portrayed the easy transition to Protestantism, though he proclaimed 'surprise' at bequests for chantries and prayers for souls and at the 'surprisingly stable' number of traditional endowments until 1540.[46] Margaret Spufford uses preambles, after identifying scribes and their favoured openings, to study the dissemination of piety dependent on the mediation and redemption of Christ.[47] Claire Cross depends on wills – 'the only reasonable comprehensive source from which to gauge religious trends' – to analyse the spread of Protestantism in Hull and Leeds.[48] Litzenberger developed a schema for evaluating the range of religious beliefs in preambles.[49] Historians have also used wills to un-

---

[45] I have used 'will' and 'testament' interchangeably in this work, although wills described the immovable goods or property of testators and testaments disbursed moveable goods. Claire Cross, 'The Development of Protestantism in Leeds and Hull, 1520–1640: The Evidence from Wills', *Northern History*, **18** (1982), pp. 230–38; Litzenberger, *The English Reformation*; John Craig and Litzenberger, 'Wills as Religious Propaganda: The Testament of William Tracy', *Journal of Ecclesiastical History*, **44**, 3 (1993), pp. 415–31; Vanessa Harding, 'Burial Choice and Burial Location in Later Medieval London' in Steven Bassett (ed.), *Death in Towns: Urban Responses to the Dying and the Dead, 100–1600* (Leicester, London, New York, 1992), pp. 119–35; Jordan, *The Charities of London* and *Philanthropy in England, 1480–1660: A Study of the Changing Pattern of English Social Aspirations* (Westport, CT, 1978); Rubin, *Charity and Community*; Clive Burgess and Beat Kümin, 'Penitential Bequests and Parish Regimes in Late Medieval England', *Journal of Ecclesiastical History*, **44**, 4 (1993), pp. 610–30. Other European studies: Cohn, *The Cult of Remembrance* and *Death and Property in Siena* (Baltimore, 1988); Norberg, *Rich and Poor in Grenoble*. On scepticism about wills: Scarisbrick, *The Reformation and the English People*; Duffy, *Stripping*, esp. pp. 504ff; Burgess, 'Late Medieval Wills and Pious Convention: Testamentary Evidence Reconsidered' in Michael Hicks (ed.), *Profit, Piety and the Professions in Later Medieval England* (Gloucester, 1990), 14–33; Christopher Marsh, 'In the Name of God? Will-making and faith in early modern England' in G.H. Martin and Peter Spufford (eds), *The Records of the Nation: The Public Record Office, 1838–1988, the British Record Society, 1888–1988* (Woodbridge, 1990), pp. 215–49.

[46] Jordan, *The Charities of London* p. 276.

[47] Margaret Spufford, *Contrasting Communities: English Villages in the Sixteenth and Seventeenth Centuries* (Cambridge, 1974), pp. 336–7.

[48] Cross, 'The Development of Protestantism', p. 230.

[49] Litzenberger, *The English Reformation and the Laity*.

derstand systems of inheritance and to research business, familial and friendly ties.[50]

Nevertheless, some historians have cautioned against using this historical evidence because of scribal and clerical influence and of 'missing' information.[51] Clive Burgess argues that the incompleteness of wills, without the lifetime thoughts and bequests of testators, renders them too problematic.[52] Eamon Duffy urges 'great care' in handling wills and their preambles as a test of religious inclination, especially as recusants dissembled to hide their views. Duffy alleges that wills became an unsuitable place in which to voice religious conviction, so will makers masked their beliefs and conformed to prevailing policy. Shifts in preambles only represented 'shifts in the limits of the possible and the approved'.[53] A strict reading of preambles or testaments as personal statements, however, takes wills out of their social and cultural context, as Samuel Cohn argues.[54] Other influences on testaments included the legislative changes that shaped the documents' form, but could not mandate new attitudes and practices. Royal injunctions in 1547, for instance, encouraged testators to leave money to the parish poor box rather than to the high altar, the nearly universal bequests for forgotten or negligently withheld tithes before the Reformation. The lack of bequests to the poor box after 1547 speaks to the individual choice still open to the testator, despite legislative limits. Testators chose, or were persuaded to choose, other charitable outlets.

The critiques question the individuality of expression in wills, often written in the presence of authority figures or articulated through formulaic or imitative styles, as though only 'individual' responses would

---

[50] Amy Louise Erickson, *Women and Property in Early Modern England* (London and New York, 1993); Lawrence Stone, *The Family, Sex and Marriage in England 1500–1800* (New York, 1979).

[51] French, Gibbs and Kümin (eds) in *The Parish in English Life* confidently write, 'Wills alone now seem riddled with too many questions to allow an unrestricted window into people's souls or to enable us to assess the attitudes of entire local communities': p. 9, and fn. 20. On scepticism about using wills: Scarisbrick, *The Reformation and the English People*; Duffy, *Stripping*, esp. pp. 504ff; Burgess, 'Late Medieval Wills and Pious Convention'; Marsh, 'In the Name of God? Will-making and faith in early modern England'.

[52] Burgess, 'Late Medieval Wills and Pious Convention', pp. 14–33.

[53] Duffy, *Stripping*, pp. 513, 523. Haigh warns that 'we would be wise not to attach much (perhaps not any) significance to will preambles': *English Reformations*, p. 200.

[54] In his study of six Italian cities, Samuel Cohn avoids the 'romantic presumption that these testamentary decisions could somehow be purely the desires of "the individual" late medieval man or woman; rather, the very fact that these testaments were socially determined "products" makes them all the more valuable for interpreting societal change and difference': *The Cult of Remembrance and the Black Death*, p. 16.

communicate *mentalités* to the historian.[55] Reducing wills to preambles in isolation from the rest of the document, in particular, ignores what the documents do tell the historian.[56] Wills do not provide unadulterated access to the early modern mind, but they do allow reasoned speculation about personal responses to local and national change, in the midst of, and as part of, wider parish and civic responses.[57] These documents show the impact of new ideas and practices on the nature of community relations and parish life. Ambiguity in wills, an evidentiary 'failing' stressed by some revisionist historians, instead should be seen as the rich texture of experience, in which uncertainty, the persistence of old ways, and the appeal of new pious ideas vied for pre-eminence in English society. Preambles' formulae, types of bequests in the whole testament, the testator's gender and other variables offer an extensive view of the practices and motives of Londoners. While writing or communicating a will was a private occasion in the circle of friends, masters, family and clergy, dispensing of bequests to one's own social group and to the destitute often occurred in a public setting. The performance of a will crossed boundaries between the individual and the community. Testaments melded personal and shared standards and beliefs, before and after the Reformation, and help to reveal the pattern of sixteenth-century beliefs. Wills are valuable and unique sources of the thoughts and practices of women and men, even considering their shortcomings. Indeed, a historian of the early modern period rarely has complete records; he or she must rely on critical use of available and 'imperfect' sources.

In this study, I have used testaments, parochial sources, records from the Court of Aldermen, chronicles and other published primary sources, including tracts on the poor and poverty, and statutes. My analysis includes 685 wills from 1500–1620, surviving in three courts: the Prerogative Court of Canterbury (PCC), the Commissary Court and the Archdeaconry Court.[58] These courts served varying social levels in Lon-

---

[55] Burgess, 'Late Medieval Wills and Pious Convention'; Duffy, *Stripping*, pp. 504ff; Haigh, *English Reformations*, pp. 199–203. Cf. Craig and Litzenberger, 'Wills as Religious Propaganda'.

[56] David Hickman, 'From Catholic to Protestant: the changing meaning of testamentary religious provisions in Elizabethan London' in Nicholas Tyacke (ed.), *England's Long Reformation* (London, 1998), pp. 117–19.

[57] While admitting to limitations of the source, Cross believes that wills 'can still disclose a trend in the religious thinking of a community': 'The Development of Protestantism', p. 237.

[58] Twenty-one women and 148 men wrote wills through 1538, 49 women and 248 men wrote wills between 1539 and 1580, and 39 women and 180 men wrote wills between 1581 and 1620. The total includes some wills without clear dating or sex identifiers.

don. The PCC, under the Archbishop of Canterbury, probated wills of those dying with more than five pounds in goods and holding property in more than one diocese. The Commissary Court, under the bishop, was a city court covering criminal cases and probate. It presided over the deaneries of Middlesex and Barking and was considered the probate court for London. After 1521, London's mayor and aldermen oversaw the work of the London church courts, including probate. The Archdeaconry overlapped with the Commissary Court, but was a lower court. While primarily responsible for the oversight of the parish church fabric, the caseload of London church courts meant that this court also probated wills.[59]

In analysing the wills, I have separated bequests into pious and non-pious categories, putting all charity to the poor under the heading 'pious'. For the sake of separating targets of charity, I have erected an artificial distinction between pious and non-pious targets, without taking them to be exclusionary categories. Pious provisions ranged from masses and prayers for souls to loans for poor apprentices, scholars' exhibitions and dowries for poor maidens. This heading also includes money or goods left to poor kin, when they were identified as such in the wills. Under 'non-pious', I included friends, family and neighbours to whom testators left gifts, unless those individuals were identified as poor. Parsons and priests occasionally fall under this heading if the will shows that the individual received the gift as a friend. Even non-pious bequests carried pious or charitable restrictions and non-pious bequests could default to pious purposes. Testators, in requests for prayers and by reminders to executors and supervisors to fulfil the will honestly since they 'will answer before God on Judgement Day', expected spiritual help from friends and family as well as priests and parsons.

Four parishes of London, analysed through parishioners' wills and parish records, comprise the heart of this study of charity and the Reformation. Burial location or similar clues in the documents identify parishioners' wills. The chosen parishes have substantial, though incomplete, runs of churchwardens' accounts and some vestry minutes between 1500 and 1620. The strengths and weaknesses of the surviving records for the parishes and their varied characteristics help to produce a representative picture of life in London across the Reformation. St Botolph Aldersgate, St Mary Woolnoth, St Michael Cornhill and St Stephen Walbrook differ in size, population, wealth and location in and around London (see Figure 1.1).[60]

---

[59] Richard M. Wunderli, *London Church Courts and Society on the Eve of the Reformation* (Cambridge, MA, 1981), pp. 16–17.

[60] Emrys Jones, 'London in the Early Seventeenth Century: An Ecological Approach', *The London Journal*, 6, 2 (Winter 1980), 123–33.

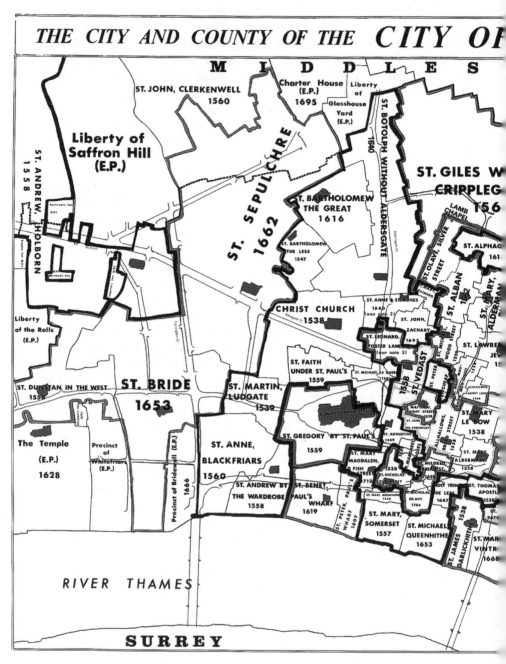

1.1   Map of London parishes taken from C.R. Humphery-Smith (ed.), *The*
      of the City of London is one of a series published by *The Institute of*
      of Cecil R. Humphery-Smith and the Trustees of the Institute.

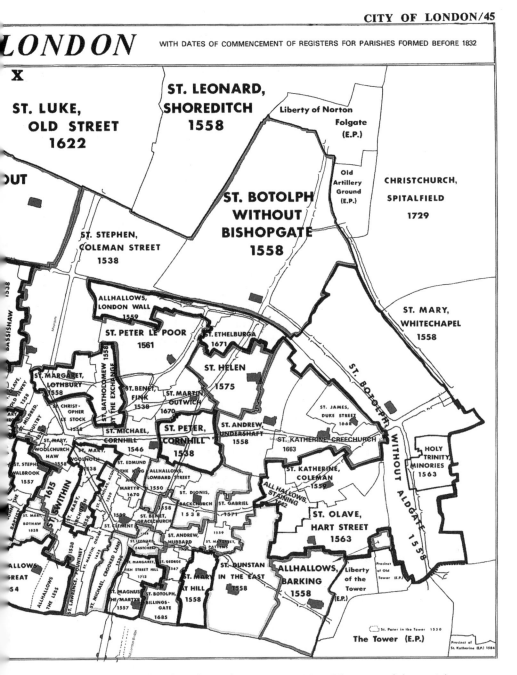

LONDON

WITH DATES OF COMMENCEMENT OF REGISTERS FOR PARISHES FORMED BEFORE 1832

X

ST. LUKE, OLD STREET 1622

ST. LEONARD, SHOREDITCH 1558

Liberty of Norton Folgate (E.P.)

Old Artillery Ground (E.P.)

CHRISTCHURCH, SPITALFIELD 1729

OUT

ST. BOTOLPH WITHOUT BISHOPGATE 1558

ST. STEPHEN, COLEMAN STREET 1538

ALLHALLOWS, LONDON WALL 1559

ST. PETER LE POOR 1561

ST. ETHELBURGA 1671

ST. MARY, WHITECHAPEL 1558

BASSISHAW

ST. MARGARET, LOTHBURY 1558

ST. BARTHOLOMEW 1558 THE EXCHANGE

ST. BENET FINK 1538

ST. MARTIN OUTWICH 1670

ST. HELEN 1575

ST. CHRIST-OPHER LE STOCK 1558

ST. JAMES, DUKE STREET 1668

ST. OLAVE OLD JEWRY

MILDRED POULTRY

ST. MICHAEL, CORNHILL 1546

ST. PETER, CORNHILL 1538

ST. ANDREW UNDERSHAFT 1558

ST. KATHERINE CREECHURCH 1663

ST. BOTOLPH WITHOUT ALDGATE 1558

HOLY TRINITY, MINORIES 1563

ST. MARY, WOOLCHURCH HAW

ST. MARY WOOLNOTH

ST. STEPHEN WALBROOK 1557

ST. EDMUND

THE KING MARTYR 1670

ALLHALLOWS, LOMBARD STREET 1550

ST. DIONIS BACKCHURCH 1538

ST. GABRIEL 1571

ALL HALLOWS STAINING 1642

ST. KATHERINE, COLEMAN 1559

ST. MARY BOTHAW 1538

ST. SWITHIN 1615

ST. MARY ABCHURCH

ST. BENET GRACECHURCH 1589

ST. ANDREW HUBBARD 1538

ST. MARGARET PATTENS

ST. OLAVE, HART STREET 1563

ALLHALLOWS THE GREAT 54

ALLHALLOWS THE LESS

ST. LAWRENCE POUNTNEY

ST. MARTIN ORGAR

ST. LEONARD EASTCHEAP

ST. CLEMENT

ST. MICHAEL CROOKED LANE

ST. MARGARET, FISH STREET HILL 1713

ST. GEORGE 1547

ST. DUNSTAN IN THE EAST

ALLHALLOWS BARKING 1558

Liberty of the Tower (E.P.)

Precinct of Old Tower (E.P.)

ST. MAGNUS THE MARTYR 1557

ST. BOTOLPH, BILLINGS-GATE 1685

ST. MARY AT HILL 1558

The Tower (E.P.)

St. Peter in the Tower 1550

Precinct of St. Katherine (E.P.) 1584

Phillimore Atlas and Index of Parish Registers (1995). The map of the parishes *Heraldic and Genealogical Studies*, Canterbury, and appears by kind permission

St Botolph without Aldersgate is a large parish outside the city walls that in 1548 had 1100 communicants.[61] For the assessment of 1638, this parish had over two hundred tithable houses.[62] Based on the mid-seventeenth-century assessment and sixteenth- and seventeenth-century parochial accounts, St Botolph's had a number of wealthy parishioners, but median rents of only £5–£10.[63] Running accounts of unpaid sixteenth-century rates on houses and buildings, however, showed that the parish had an absentee land-owning group that refused payment of parish assessments by claiming non-residence. In the accounts beginning in 1566, the churchwardens gathered £11 13s 2d for the wages and stipends of parish church officers, but could not collect the rest, 34s 8d. 'Some of them utterly refusyng the payement therof and dyv[er]s other their houses standyng shutt in by reason wherof the same can not be levyed yet here chardged as mony dew to the p[ar]ishe & hereafter dependyng upon the sev[er]all p[er]sons w[hi]ch oweth the same'. Those owing arrears included the Lord Chief Justice and another man for his stables.[64] Churchwardens' accounts from the late fifteenth and early sixteenth centuries showed theft of church goods and money, suggesting an unruly parish without strong governance. In the later period, the parish showed the signs of an extramural parish under the stress of an influx of poor women and men migrating to London. The presence of wealthy inhabitants, even if not always in residence, meant that the parish had the open space necessary for building large houses.[65]

St Mary Woolnoth had 300 communicants in 1548 and between sixty and one hundred tithable houses in 1638.[66] The parish exemplifies the distribution of wealth noted by Emrys Jones: part of the core running east and west through the middle of the city, the parish had median rents of more than £20 in 1638.[67] In the mid-seventeenth century, St Mary's had a number of substantial merchants and well-to-do craftsmen.[68] Even in the sixteenth century St Mary's showed a similarly

---

[61] C.J. Kitching, *London and Middlesex Chantry Certificate 1548* (London, London Record Society, 1980), p. 30. Kümin also studied this parish: *The Shaping*.

[62] Tai Liu, *Puritan London: A Study of Religion and Society in the City Parishes* (Newark, DE, 1986), p. 42.

[63] Jones, 'London', p. 124.

[64] GL, MS 1454, Roll 70.

[65] As Derek Keene describes, for the settlement of Walbrook ward in the later medieval period, some wealthy individuals moved into poorer areas of the city if those areas had open space for them to build substantial houses: *The Walbrook Study: A Summary Report, Social and Economic Study of Medieval London*, London University, Institute of Historical Research, 1987, p. 17.

[66] Liu, *Puritan London*, p. 30; Kitching, *Chantry Certificate*, p. 26.

[67] Jones, 'London', p. 124.

[68] Liu, *Puritan London*, p. 27.

well-off core of parishioners but, like other parishes in the city, it was not without poorer inhabitants. Before the Reformation, this parish church was known for its music and fraternities sponsoring music of the mass. In the later period, St Mary's accounts showed concern with the poor, but not with the urgency apparent in St Botolph's accounts or the Protestant zeal present in St Stephen's Walbrook.

St Michael Cornhill had between one hundred and two hundred tithable houses in 1638.[69] In the seventeenth century, it lacked extremely rich merchants and the median rents of less than £5 placed the parish outside the core of wealthy parishes in the inner City.[70] From 1503, the Drapers' Company endowed the church; the widow Elizabeth Peake gave the benefice to the Company.[71] This parish is located in Cornhill Ward, a marketplace with a number of drapers' homes and shops and the Royal Exchange, built in 1566.[72] The experience of St Michael's in plague years emphasizes the social mix within inner city parishes in the sixteenth century. In the 1563 plague year, contemporaries noted the progress of disease through the back streets and alleys of the parish. At the same time, the parish began to show a number of wealthier inhabitants.[73] Perhaps the presence of wealthier parishioners reflected the continuing influx of Drapers, possibly at the expense of the Upholders (dealers in second-hand clothing), and a social change in the parish and ward that brought in the Royal Exchange. Brett Usher has shown Cornhill Ward to be an important location for the survival of Protestantism under Mary and the development of puritanism in the 1560s.[74]

St Stephen's Walbrook was the smallest of the four with 250 communicants in 1548 and less than fifty tithable houses. In the period of the Civil Wars, it was one of the most puritan parishes.[75] By the early sixteenth century, 'learned and artistic services' had found a place in the parish.[76] The humanist Sir Thomas More lived in the area from 1505–

---

[69] Manuscript illegible for number of communicants: Kitching, *Chantry Certificate*, p. 7.

[70] Jones, 'London', p. 124.

[71] As noted in John Stow, William J. Thoms, ed., *A Survay of London*, written 1598, increased 1603 (London, 1876), p. 74.

[72] For a description of the participation of inhabitants in Cornhill ward in the early seventeenth century: Pearl, 'Change and Stability', p. 19.

[73] London did not seem to develop a defined 'social topography' until after the 1620s: Slack, *The Impact of Plague in Tudor and Stuart England* (Oxford, 1985), p. 153.

[74] Brett Usher, 'Backing Protestantism: The London Godly, the Exchequer and the Foxe Circle' in David Loades (ed.), *John Foxe: An Historical Perspective* (Aldershot, 1999), p. 112.

[75] Kitching, *Chantry Certificate*, p. 18.

[76] Keene, *The Walbrook Study: A Summary Report*, p. 15.

24, before he became chancellor. An organ maker asked for burial in the parish in 1455 and that occupational trend continued into the sixteenth century with the Howe family.[77] St Stephen's had less than fifty tithable houses in the mid-seventeenth century.[78] Although by the later sixteenth century the parish ran in debt for years at a time, financial worries seemed small. After running in the red, churchwardens called for 'loans' from parishioners to meet payments and to make repairs and alterations to the church. Not surprisingly, given this financial arrangement, this small parish averaged rents of more than £20 in 1638.[79]

New research on the Reformation answers questions, and raises more, about pious and secular concerns and Catholic and Protestant piety. The tendency to divide the sixteenth century into pre- and post-Reformation halves has reinforced the inclination to view the Reformation as a watershed between two intellectually and culturally opposed periods. Intense studies of more limited years have been, and still are, essential to understanding early modern England. A long stretch of 120 years, however, encourages us to look at a range of causes and consequences of change and continuity. The resilience of charity and its place within the context of shifting religious ideas about salvation and the nature and causes of poverty contributes to our knowledge of the social structure and popular piety of early modern London and England.

Charity provides a prism through which to view the individual, the parish and the nation. How did individuals alter their practice to fit religious change? Is Haigh right that, despite the noise of politicians and evangelicals, parishioners went to church, prayed, behaved, and went home again, whether in 1530 or 1590?[80] How were the experiences of women, as those giving and receiving charity in the midst of vast social and religious changes, different from those of men? What options existed for parishes to cope with and control growing poverty and population? Poor relief and charity have frequently been studied in relation to politics and legislation, but less often in relation to cultural change. How did shifting religious policy and social conditions in London shape the charitable practices and *mentalités* of city and suburban inhabitants?

---

[77] John Howe in particular worked in most parish churches about London, building and repairing their organs: Hugh Baillie, 'Some biographical notes on English church musicians, chiefly working in London (1485–1569)', *Royal Musical Association Research Chronicle*, 2 (1962), pp. 18–57. I owe thanks to Dr Fiona Kisby for this reference.

[78] Liu, *Puritan London*, p. 24.

[79] Jones, 'London', p. 124. GL, MS 593/4, unfol.

[80] Haigh, *English Reformations*, p. 295.

CHAPTER TWO

Prayers and purgatory: wills on the eve of Reformation, 1500–1538

Before the Reformation, and in the early years of reform, testators, who intended their bequests to help them gain salvation, endowed masses and prayers and performed good works, through the auspices of the parish. Charity to the poor, support for the parish church and its celebrations and organizations, and donations to other members of the social and religious community in London expressed lay piety. This exchange of material and religious aid through the giving and receiving of bequests cemented relations between testators and their fellow inhabitants by marking and temporarily easing social distinctions. Marcel Mauss explained the dynamics of gift exchange, in which donors must give, although their giving appears voluntary. The recipient likewise must reciprocate, and do so with a more valuable gift.[1] Pre-Reformation donors fulfilled an imperative to help the destitute and perform good works, while the prayers of the poor helped donors to reach salvation, a priceless gift in late medieval society.

Bequests to the poor secured prayers for worthy donors – powerful reciprocation – and helped those who hungered and suffered like Christ – obligatory generosity.[2] Testamentary charity, one form of pious bequests, ritualized aid to the poor as well as to other recipients, often by linking them to burial processions, services and anniversaries. 'Pious' testamentary bequests also maintained the 'church fabric' and services and sustained religious houses and organizations. 'Non-pious' gifts, by contrast, went to friends and family and were personal tokens, marriage or settlement portions and inheritances. These last bequests are not merely secular ones, as they carried an implicit, if not explicit, request for prayers and commemoration.

The cluster of acts and injunctions prior to and including 1538 makes that year pivotal to charitable giving and lay piety, as individuals altered wills and parishes reacted to religious change. The pre-1538 testaments and parochial records show a society traditional in religion and in almsgiving and exchange. Historians debate the impetus for reform

---

[1] Mauss, *The Gift*, pp. 5, 7, 65.
[2] Mauss, *The Gift*, p. 18.

under Henry VIII, whether for theological reform or for the confiscation of religious property for his coffers, as well as reform's cultural and religious changes.[3] Regardless of intent, Henry's religious reforms began with his attempts in 1527 to secure a divorce from Katherine of Aragon, though stirrings of protest and reform preceded this rupture. Efforts in the early 1530s to gain the divorce culminated in the break with Rome. In 1534, Henry proclaimed his Supremacy over the Church of England. The Ten Articles of 1536 began the reform of religious belief and practice for lay people and parishes in earnest, discussing only three sacraments: baptism, the Eucharist and penance. The Articles also affirmed justification through Christ's Passion, but maintained purgatory and the cult of saints. The First Royal Injunctions (1536) allowed images of Christ and saints to remain in churches, but distinguished commemoration from superstitious adoration. The Injunctions called for educating children and servants in the *Pater noster*, Articles and Ten Commandments. The new rules required Latin and English versions of the Bible in parish churches.[4] Henry VIII suppressed lesser monasteries and religious houses in 1536 and the rest in 1538. The Second Royal Injunctions (1538) would be more reformist than the first set issued through the King and Cromwell.[5]

Two noteworthy names in early sixteenth-century London were 'Percivale' and 'Lisle', wealthy benefactors whose bequests exemplified the power of purgatory and charity. Sir John Percivale was a knight and Lord Mayor who, with his widow Dame Thomasine Percivale, made a series of bequests for his soul and for the poor of London.[6] They were exceptional for their wealth, but their bequests nevertheless express common aims of charity and piety before the Reformation. That some of their gifts survived the Reformation, and therefore so did the Percivale name and fame, attests to the malleability of charity across the Refor-

---

[3] The terms of current debate on the English Reformation(s): Haigh, *English Reformations*; Duffy, *Stripping*; Kümin, *The Shaping*; Wabuda, 'Revising the Reformation'; Tyacke (ed.), *England's Long Reformation*.

[4] Walter Howard Frere and William McClure Kennedy, *Visitation Articles and Injunctions of the Period of the Reformation*, Vol. II, 1536–1558, pp. 1–11. Luther's approval of images and sermons to foster 'higher piety': Richard G. Cole, 'Pamphlet Woodcuts in the Communication Process of Reformation Germany', in Kyle C. Sessions and Phillip N. Bebb (eds), *Pietas et Societas: New Trends in Reformation Social History, Essays in Memory of Harold J. Grimm*, Vol. IV of Sixteenth Century Essays & Studies (Ann Arbor, MI, 1985), pp.108–9.

[5] VAI, II, pp. 34–43. Henry 'stopped the Reformation dead' in 1538 as his suspicion of Lutheranism grew: Haigh, *English Reformations*, p. 152.

[6] Robert Fabyan, *The Great Chronicle of London*, A.H. Thomas and J.D. Thornley (eds) (London: George W. Jones at the Sign of the Dolphin, 1938), orig. published 1516, p. 288.

mation. The Viscountess Lisle, widow of the late Lord Mayor Robert Drope and Edward Gray, the Viscount Lisle, who died childless, similarly left a legacy to her parish and her city. John Stow lamented the loss of her and Drope's name and fame, however, explaining that 'notwithstanding their liberality to that church and parish, their tomb is pulled down, no monument remaineth of them'.[7] Other inhabitants and citizens, not always so well known in their lifetimes, made pious and charitable contributions to institutions and people in the city.

Wills and the church fabric

Understood broadly, the church fabric linked lay piety and charity. The 'church fabric' refers to the ornaments, implements and even buildings of the parish but, taken as a metaphor, the church fabric means more. Testators were tied to the notion of parishes, the ones in which they were born, lived, or died, creating a sense of community not linked simply to a particular parish's borders.[8] Attention to the literal and metaphorical aspects of the parish church community marked testamentary bequests and parochial expenditures, for the support of Catholic services and for the welfare of the poor and impotent.

Testators began their wills by commending their souls to holy helpers. Until the late 1540s, most invocations in men's and women's wills recommended souls to God, the Virgin Mary and the Holy Company of Saints, and occasionally to a patron or named saint.[9] Although most addressed the usual group, in 1535 the widow Johan Devereux praised the Trinity and left her soul to Christ. Such an invocation melded aspects of Protestant and Catholic theology, suggesting a slow transition to new ideas.[10] For the mid-1530s, before the radicalism of Edwardian reform, introducing the Trinity broke with an older tradition of commending souls to Christ. This preamble and the few that

---

[7] John Stow, *A Survey of London*, (*London under Elizabeth: A Survey*), Henry Morley (ed.) (London, 1890), pp. 201, 205–6.

[8] See the growing historiography on parishes: French, Gibbs and Kümin, *The Parish*; Kümin, *Shaping*; Brown, *Popular Piety*, p. 77; Burgess, 'Shaping the Parish'; Pounds, *A History of the English Parish*; Litzenberger, *The English Reformation and the Laity*; Beaver, *Parish Communities and Religious Conflict*; French, *The People of the Parish*.

[9] For example, PRO, PROB 11/22, f. 190R; only four observations in database. 'Preamble debate': Marsh, 'In the Name of God?'. (Thanks to Dr Eric Carlson.)

[10] GL, MS 9171/10, f. 262. Slow emergence of recognizably Protestant form after 1560: Cross, 'The development of Protestantism', p. 232; cf. Litzenberger's use of 'ambiguous' as distinct from 'Traditional' or Protestant preambles, Litzenberger, *The English Reformation*, p. 172.

emphasized Christ's Passion reflected the gradual adoption of Protestantism's Christ-centred salvation over pre-Reformation reliance on saints
and mediators.[11]

Following the invocation, testators stated their plans for burial and
the location of their graves. Early sixteenth-century testators carefully
outlined gravesites after calling on the company of saints, acknowledging the social and spiritual community within which they lived and
died. Graves and burials, especially before the Reformation, occupied
an important place in Londoners' final plans. Most parishioners before
1538 requested burial within the parish.[12] Within their own parish,
individuals most frequently planned to rest in the churchyard or near a
family member. Fifteenth-century payments for church burial, 'the contributions a private person was expected to make for being allowed to
appropriate something which belonged to the community', shifted to
the sixteenth and seventeenth centuries' 'drawing of rigid social distinctions and indeed exclusions from church burial'.[13] In general, burial
within the church, subject to a higher fee, signified higher social status
than burial within the churchyard, though some testators deliberately
chose humble gravesites.

Nearly all testators made a customary bequest to the high altar for
'forgotten tithes', to present and former parish churches, that followed
preambles and burial requests. Gifts to church works and repairs, a
second customary bequest, often followed the token to the high altar.
These customary bequests reflected expectations held by the parish
church, but also reflected the attachment of parishioners to their home,
former and birth parishes, as personal wealth allowed. Principally, however, bequests to the church and church fabric centred on the saints and
a few popular devotions. Images of Christ and the saints, special helpers
and advocates for Christians, played a large part in lay piety.[14] Relics
held little appeal for many of London's testators, who instead bequeathed images or refurbished existing ones. Duffy has argued that in
the late medieval period images of saints drew the greater beneficence
from testators than did relics.[15]

---

[11] Under Mary, invocations to Christ's Passion also flourished as the Catholic Reformation emphasized Christ-centered doctrine in reaction to Protestant theology. Before
1538, 88.82 per cent (135) of preambles were dedicated to God and the saints.

[12] Until 1538, 84.62 per cent (143) of testators specified burial within their parish.

[13] Harding, 'Burial choice and burial location', p. 131.

[14] Parishioners '"adopted" specific saints in the hope that he or she would be adopted
and protected in turn': Duffy, *Stripping*, p. 161.

[15] 'Where early medieval devotion to the saints was focused on their relics, late
medieval devotion focused on images': Duffy, *Stripping*, p. 167. Yet parishes enjoyed
'financial advantages' from saints' relics: Brown, *Popular Piety*, p. 58.

The ties between testators and their parishes, literal and spiritual homes, remained continuous across the early Reformation, parishioners' gifts weaving the delicate netting of the communal parish. The gifts from goldsmith and citizen Robert Amadas in 1531 illustrate the common allegiance of testators to images of the saints and to the various parish churches that housed them. He left an image worth £10 in silver and gilt of the Lord at the Resurrection to the high altar of St Mary Woolnoth, the site of his obit and the same parish to which he left alms.[16] He left a like image of the same value to St Matthew Friday Street, perhaps where he once resided. Amadas's social and occupational standing enabled, even obligated, him to contribute sumptuous gifts that befitted his status and fostered parochial worship.[17] In 1534, Peter Cave asked that a tomb be made to his, his wife's, and his children's memory in the wall or window before St Margaret in St Michael Cornhill. Further, he left £10 to make and gild the saint's image.[18] He left a smaller bequest of £5 for the making and gilding of a picture of St Margaret in his birthplace of 'Crike'.[19]

Marian shrines, within parish churches or elsewhere, similarly attracted bequests and encouraged devotions and pilgrimages, irrespective of testators' social rank. Throughout Europe, women invoked saints and helpers in pregnancy and childbirth, especially the Virgin and Saint Margaret, as special patrons. Many late medieval English Catholics focused their piety on the Virgin Mary and on Christ, through images and devotions, services that will be discussed below.[20] The will of Elizabeth Massey, from St Botolph's, outlined a posthumous or vicarious pilgrimage to revered Marian shrines. She may have been a single woman, whose only relative mentioned in the will seems to have been a priest. In her will of 1510, she remembered images of Our Lady at Walsingham, 'Dunaste', Northampton and 'Coosforpe' with monetary bequests that, when distributed, would have allowed her soul's remembrance at the dispersed memorials. In Doncaster, the Carmelite church,

---

[16] PRO, PROB 11/25, f. 39L.

[17] Similarly, on the potlatch and sacrifice: Mauss, *The Gift*, pp. 15–16.

[18] PRO, PROB 11/25, f. 162R.

[19] PRO, PROB 11/25, f. 163L. 'Crike' may be Crich in Derbyshire, or Crick in Northamptonshire.

[20] See Davis, 'City Women and Religious Change', p. 76. Early sixteenth-century vision of Virgin at Ipswich: Norman Jones, 'Living the Reformations: Generational Experience and Political Perception in Early Modern England', *Huntington Library Quarterly*, **60**, 3 (1999), p. 284. '"New" shrines' and devotions: Ronald C. Finucane, *Miracles and Pilgrims: Popular Beliefs in Medieval England* (New York, 1995), orig. published 1977, pp. 195–202; popularity of new cult of Holy Name of Jesus in late-medieval urban areas: Brown, *Popular Piety*, p. 86.

established in 1350, held candles given by Henry VIII. Cokethorpe was another favourite devotional site of the royal family, with Elizabeth of York having made a donation there in 1502 for the Queen. Northampton was the site of Our Lady of Grace, with a 'Rood of the Wall'. Her gifts ranged from 3d to 5s, but an old gold noble (8s 4d) was left to Walsingham, the greatest shrine of all, only if the coin could be obtained from another man, Sir Robert White, who had perhaps borrowed from her. She also left 4d to each shrine in Canterbury. Her will made other pious bequests: for the great bell to ring for the memory of her soul and 20d to the church's 'best' cross. Her only other bequest was a gown to a female servant.[21] Dame Thomasine Percivale, widow of the Lord Mayor and of a far higher social status, also connected her bequests to worship of Our Lady, calling for services in her memory and leaving chalices to shrines to Our Lady, including the well-known one at Willesdon.[22] Male testators also recognized the efficacy of the Virgin Mary and certain female saints, especially for women in childbirth. In 1528, Jasper Shukburgh gave to every poor woman with child or in Our Lady's Bands in St Michael's 12d, 'to her comfort'.[23]

Other testators made the way to important shrines in England easier for pilgrims. Although social rank determined who could fund the construction, poorer women may have particularly benefited from easier routes to shrines.[24] Aiding pilgrims constituted an act of mercy that could be fulfilled even through a testamentary bequest for highway or bridge construction or repair. Wood and stone encouraged devotions to saints and showed testators' affection for them. The substantial gifts also ensured remembrance of prominent individuals and their families. The Viscountess Lisle put aside £20 for the repair of 'Rouchester Brigge in the worship of god and Seynt Thomas of Canterbury'.[25] John Weston donated £4 to highways in Ipswich for the good of the people and the 'relief and comfort of my soule'.[26]

---

[21] PRO, PROB 11/17, fols 262R–263L. See Edmund Waterton, *Pietas Mariana Britannica: a history of English devotion to the Most Blessed Virgin Marye Mother of God: with a catalogue of shrines, sanctuaries, offerings, bequests and other memorials of the piety of our forefathers* (2 vols, London, 1879), Vol. 1, pp. 78, 85, Vol. 2, pp. 15, 28, 106, 155; David Knowles, *The Religious Orders in England* (3 vols, Cambridge, 1961), pp. 76, 249; Samuel Lewis, *Topographical Dictionary of England*, 7th ed. (London, 1848). 'Surrogate pilgrimages': Waterton, *Pietas Mariana Britannica*, p. 110; Duffy, *Stripping*, p. 194.

[22] PRO, PROB 11/17, fols 218R, 221L–221R.

[23] GL, MS 9171/10, f. 116v.

[24] Crawford summarizes Finucane's findings that 39 per cent of pilgrims were women, and 86 per cent of those women 'were of the lowest social classes': *Women and Religion*, p. 23.

[25] PRO, PROB 11/12, f. 72R. Rochester, in Kent.

[26] PRO, PROB 11/12, f. 143L.

Testators could also support the worship of saints by contributing lights to burn before images or upon altars, or by contributing to funds for the same. Small donations from ordinary parishioners attested to shared piety, although the separate and more substantial endowments in money or left-over funeral wax highlighted the social status of wealthier benefactors. We must be careful not to overemphasize 'communal' harmony, since traditions of gift-giving to the church and to the poor were never predicated on earthly social equality.[27] In the early sixteenth century, St Botolph's parishioners made donations to sustain lights in the church.[28] Before the Second Royal Injunctions of 1538 these lights were acceptable ornaments in churches, and even after 1538 churches were allowed the rood light.[29] The St Stephen Walbrook churchwardens' accounts of 1522–23 noted payment of 31s to a man for making rood lights and other tapers in part from old wax obtained from the parish.[30] St Botolph's referred to their beam light as 'St Katherine's' and still supported it in the accounts of 1538–39.[31] Better-off testators who called for torches and tapers to be carried at their burial services often left the remnants to parish churches. Henry VII, for instance, bequeathed 20s and two torches to St Botolph's in return for the parish paying 8d for torchbearers at his burying.[32] Wealthy, but not royal, inhabitants like the knight John Skevyngton left what remained of 24 torches to the parish churches his corpse passed, to his own parish, and to the Crossed Friars, where he was buried.[33]

Testators sometimes explicitly linked devotion to and images of saints, the Virgin and Christ with commemoration of their souls at funerals or graves. Grave monuments and memorials could combine this holy imagery with Scripture or epitaphs to an individual. These seemingly permanent monuments exhibited the contradictory impulses of testators, between seeking remembrance and acknowledging the transitory nature of mortal life. Images invoked the special help of those saints and spurred the prayers of pious and charitable individuals who stopped to admire or meditate upon the monuments. The wealthier testators

---

[27] Mauss describes the evolution of the Hebrew word *zedaqa* or the Arab word *sadaka*, from 'justice' to 'alms', in the development of charity and in recognition of the disparity between rich and poor, a doctrine then 'spread around the world' by Christians and Muslims: *The Gift*, pp. 14–18, especially p. 18. Cf. danger in equating support for the church fabric with '"communal" piety': Brown, *Popular Piety*, p. 83.

[28] GL, MS 1454, Roll 21.

[29] *VAI* II, p. 38.

[30] GL, MS 593/1, f. 4v.

[31] GL, MS 1454, Roll 52.

[32] GL, MS 1454, Roll 29.

[33] PRO, PROB 11/21, fols 317L–319L.

who endowed these monuments memorialized themselves and honoured holy figures, while also encouraging pious reflection and prayer. William Babham asked for a 'scripture of remembrance of me' engraved on plate, set in marble stone and fixed to the wall by his burial in the Ambulatory of St Stephen's, near his mother and father.[34] In 1531, Lawraunce Eggylsfeelde, Yeoman Usher of the King's Chamber and chequer of the Guard, included an altar with an image of the Lord, standing, in his burial plans. He paid an 'honest' priest £7 per year to sing there for 21 years for his own soul, as well as those of parents, friends and all Christians.[35]

Not all epitaphs quoted Scripture or relied on saints, as Robert Fabyan's memorial shows. Stow recorded the chronicler's 1511 epitaph from St Michael Cornhill, destroyed in the Reformation:

> Like as the day his course doth consume,
> And the new morrow springeth againe as fast,
> So man and woman, by Nature's custume,
> This life to pass, at last in earth are cast,
> In joy and sorrow, which here their time do wast,
> Never in one state, but in course transitory,
> So full of change is of this world the glory.[36]

Robert Fabyan, former alderman and sheriff, saw life as fleeting, but left behind his substantial chronicle of England, published posthumously, and this verse for parishioners' reflection for years to come.[37]

Monuments and epitaphs provided models for derivative verses and ornamental styles, an indication of the power of imitation in late medieval piety.[38] A wealthy, married grocer without children and apparently without citizenship, perhaps because he was young, George Gowsell made arrangements for copying a burial monument in 1517. He willed that 'there be made in the wall ov[er] my burying place a convenient memory w[i]t[h] an image of Saint Anne and of our Lady a foot large w[i]thin the wall like unto the buriall place of maister mikloo in the ffrere Augustynes wherby may be the better rememb[e]red and praied for'. Gowsell used 'Mikloo's' grave as a model for the image of the two women, and he may have seen and experienced the image's effect on

---

[34] PRO, PROB 11/17, f. 215R.

[35] PRO, PROB 11/24, f. 60R. Organization of Court: D.A.L. Morgan, 'The house of policy: the political role of the late Plantagenet household, 1422–1485', in David Starkey, D.A.L. Morgan, John Murphy, Pam Wright, Neil Cuddy and Kevin Sharpe (eds), *The English court: from the Wars of the Roses to the Civil War* (London and New York: Longman, 1987), pp. 25–70, esp. pp. 32–33.

[36] Thoms, p. 75; Morley, p. 206.

[37] Fabyan, *The Great Chronicle of London*.

[38] Purposeful imitation in late medieval piety: Flynn, *Sacred Charity*, p. 70.

those who entered or lived in the friary. Besides carefully describing his monument and offering an example, Gowsell also detailed where he desired to be buried: on the north side of St Mary's, 'next a thisside' a gentleman and a skinner. Reinforcing the visual iconography of the Virgin Mary, he requested masses of Our Lady and Jesus 'by note' and other anthems sung by priests and children, for a twelve-year obit costing £7 yearly, with a total endowment of £120.[39]

Parochial monuments, not just those in the privileged burial locations within the city's friaries, provided patterns for mimicry. Rychard Acheley, a grocer from St Stephen's, in 1537 requested a plate of latten of the same size as 'Rauffe Whetton's', in the wall at the head of his grave, with Scripture and imagery at the executor's discretion.[40] Twenty years earlier, Rauff Welton or Wetton had asked to be buried near the grave of Master Foster in the south side of St Stephen's 'in the squared corner of the wall' and 'over my grave I wyll there stonde a Remembr[a]nce of our Lady and fyve verses that I have therefore appoynted'.[41] Acheley's imitation indicates the utility of Wetton's monument over the preceding two decades. William Dyxson, draper of St Michael's, likewise recognized the effectiveness of another's grave in producing prayers. He asked for a grave in the style of William Bradshaw's 'for a memoriall to have my soul praid for'.[42] Vanessa Harding has stressed social status in explaining widows' choices of burial location – by first or subsequent husband – but widows might also have considered the pious value of husbands' monuments. Elisabeth Warley, widow of the goldsmith Nicholas Warley, demanded burial under or near the marble stone that covered her husband in their parish church of St Mary's.[43]

For the most elite testators, burial in a religious house reinforced social status and prestige through the decoration of conventual churches

---

[39] PRO, PROB 11/21, f. 179L. Stow did not include a 'Maister Mikloo' in his list of people commemorated in the church of the Friars Augustinians: Morley, pp. 190–91. Importance of music in London parishes: Fiona Kisby, 'Urban Cultures and Religious Reforms: Parochial Music in London, c. 1520–c. 1580', presented at Leeds Medieval Conference, July 1998; Kümin, 'Masses, Morris and Metrical Psalms: Music in the English Parish, c. 1400–1600', in Kisby (ed.), *Music and Musicians in Renaissance Urban Communities* (Cambridge, 2001), pp. 216–41; Magnus Williamson, 'The Role of Religious Guilds in the Cultivation of Ritual Polyphony in England: the Case of Louth, 1450–1550', in ibid., pp. 242–70.

[40] GL, MS 9171/10, f. 305.

[41] PRO, PROB 11/18, f. 261L. See GL, MS 593/1 (1507–08), fols 5, 6 for variant spellings: 'Raffe Weton' heading to Lambeth about a suit over a priest or 'Raffe Wetton' paying the clerk's rate.

[42] PRO, PROB 11/21, f. 285R.

[43] PRO, PROB 11/24, f. 38L. (1531) Harding, 'Burial Choice and Burial Location', p. 127.

with lay people's tombs and memorials, grand 'remembrances'. Burial within the friars' church marked the prestige of the deceased and likely ensured the continuity of members' prayers on their behalf. John Skevyngton, wealthy knight, merchant of Calais and sheriff of London, asked his friends and executors to make a marble tomb over his sepulchre in the high choir of the Crossed Friars' conventual church. His own image or picture would adorn the tomb, with his wife's image if she chose to be buried there, and the images of their children around his feet.[44] Skevyngton left his wife's grave to her own discretion, just as he granted her the customary third without any rider prohibiting her remarriage. He might have rightfully expected a wealthy woman to remarry, or he might not have been her first husband himself, so her burial by another man might not have concerned him. A husband planning a monument in the prestigious resting place sometimes made provision for the inclusion of his widow, because widows apparently put husbands' relative social status before the chronological order of marriages when choosing burial locations.[45]

Testators must have planned for burial in these places prior to making last wills, especially when the monument was an elaborate one, though not many relate these lifetime arrangements in their testaments. In 1509, the goldsmith William Kebill described the lifetime provision he had already made for his burial within the church of the Grey Friars, although he was a parishioner of St Mary's. He asked to be buried before the altar of St Michael where

> there redy made of tymbre and pyked wt iron pykes ffro the which my burying place there soo to be hadde And the which to me ys graunted by the wardeyn and covent of the saide place I have redy contented paid and deliv[er]ed before hand unto m. doctor Cuttler nowe beyng there wardeyn and to M. Iver shall of the same place three angells of gold in value of xxs. — and a maser wt the bande and borsell of silv[er] and gilt ... wherof and wherwt they have knowleched to hold theym fully satisfied and contented.

His tomb in the Grey Friars' Church, which copied others there, aimed to encourage the prayers of friars and other lay people.[46]

Kebill's monument and testament exemplified the quandary for wealthy individuals who used their wealth to furnish ornaments, vestments, shrines and graves, but by doing so re-emphasized their social status and riches. Hence the gift, by which a wealthy individual donated

---

[44] PRO, PROB 11/21, f. 317L. Stow identified him as sheriff: Morley, p. 166.

[45] 'It is interesting that the [widow's] choice was not invariably to be buried with the last-deceased': Harding, 'Burial Choice and Burial Location', p. 127.

[46] PRO, PROB 11/16, f. 181R.

property to God and to the church to redeem him for salvation, called attention to the very abundance that necessitated magnificent gift-giving. Ostentatious tombs undermined acts of humility and charity, but they ensured testators' immortality in the hearts, minds and prayers of survivors. So, Kebill used language to emphasize the impermanence of his worldly fortune, a common device preceding pious and charitable bequests by wealthy testators who felt their obligation to give. In addition, he stated that his comfort in life had been a temporary gift from God. He humbly divided the 'litell substannce of the goods which god of his grace hath lent me in this transitory life' into three, minimizing the wealth that distanced him from Christ and Christ-like poverty.[47] He denounced common burial practices, the 'vanities of the world' – spice cakes, blacks and month mind – that sumptuous wills included and that ordinary testaments mimicked.

The striking post-Reformation description of destroyed monuments highlights the pre-Reformation significance of graves and reiterates the popularity of religious houses for the substantial tombs of heralds and other prestigious Londoners before the dissolution. The chronicler John Stow (1525–1605) described the fate of tombs in these religious institutions after the iconoclastic period of the English Reformation.

> All these and five times so many more have been buried there, whose monuments are wholly defaced; for there were nine tombs of alabaster and marble, environed with strikes of iron in the choir, and one tomb in the body of the church, also coped with iron, all pulled down, besides sevenscore grave-stones of marble, all sold for fifty pounds, or thereabouts, by Sir Martin Bowes, goldsmith and alderman.[48]

Sir Martin Bowes, later Lord Mayor, governor of hospitals and sheriff, colluded in the dismantling of pre-Reformation monuments. As an historical example, however, Bowes reminds the historian of the difficulty of assessing belief through action. Bowes sold the marble and iron that exemplified widespread pre-Reformation confidence in saints and prayers for the dead, but he would later cover the cost of rebuilding his parish church's rood loft, a key structure of the Catholic church, during Mary's reign.[49] Bowes participated in Reformation iconoclasm and Catholic restoration, contradictory actions that communicated little about his religious beliefs.

---

[47] PRO, PROB 11/16, f. 181R.

[48] Thoms, p. 120. While the tombs may have had unique details, they duplicated certain elements.

[49] This will be discussed in the next chapter. GL, MS 1002/1A, f. 1; significance of roods: Duffy, *Stripping*, pp. 157–9.

The wealthiest testators could fund more than the building of grave memorials; they could also endow major renovation or building projects.[50] These testamentary provisions combined testators' desire for remembrance of themselves and their lineage with their pious fervour to outfit the church with the structures and ornaments necessary for worship. Thomas Hobson, who said nothing of his occupation in his will, contributed toward the building of the steeple of St John's chapel in St Botolph's parish, although the probated copy of his will omits the amount. He explained: 'for I entende to be buried in the forenamed chapell and a stone to lye upon me and a scuptur' to be sett in the wall under the wyndow to shew that tyme I dyed and to desyre all men and women of their charitie to pray for me'.[51] In addition to hundreds of torches and thousands of masses in churches and friars' houses, the prominent widow Viscountess Lisle, in 1500, bequeathed £800 to St Michael's. She asked that the church use the funds to make and gild the crucifix and other images within the church and also put up both her husband's and her own arms to be remembered and prayed for by all in the church.[52] The centrality of the crucifix to mass and within the holiest space of the church emphasizes its importance as a bequest.

Jasper Shukburgh, who had also supported devotion to the Virgin Mary and female saints, in 1528 relied upon the worshipful parishioners of St Michael's to spend twenty marks to erect a cross in the new churchyard with five stone steps and a pulpit, modelled after one in St Paul's churchyard. Unsurprisingly for a pre-Reformation will, Shukburgh combined belief in holy helpers with dedication to sermons – a combination that would not be permitted by reformers. Stow claims in his chronicle that a Lord Mayor, John Rudstone, paid for construction of the pulpit. Rudstone wanted sermons said there after his decease, in 1531. His tomb under the pulpit had been removed, however, and the prescribed sermons discontinued by the time Stow wrote his history of London.[53] The endowment made under Catholicism withered in Protestant London, although a Protestant preacher might have still preached there, especially after the removal of Rudstone's body.

Other gifts for construction, what one historian called 'public works', had the same purpose as endowing religious buildings: soliciting prayers

---

[50] Cf. Pamela C. Graves, 'Social space in the English medieval parish church', *Economy and Society*, **18**, 3 (August 1989), pp. 312–13; Brown, *Popular Piety*, pp. 83ff.

[51] PRO, PROB 11/17, f. 50R.

[52] PRO, PROB 11/12, f. 72R.

[53] Morley, p. 207. Importance of pre-Reformation preaching: Robert Whiting, *The Blind Devotion of the People: Popular Religion and the English Reformation* (Cambridge, 1989), p. 237; Wabuda, 'Bishops and the Provision of Homilies, 1520 to 1547', *SCJ*, **25**, 3 (1994), pp. 551–66.

for souls, encouraging the remembrance of elite individuals and their families.[54] Highway repair or construction brought secular benefits to a community, but furthered the pious impulses of testators. London testators made a smattering of these bequests (14), mainly towards towns in which they had been born or where family still lived. The widow Elizabeth Berell made numerous charitable and pious bequests to parishes and religious institutions in and around London, and to towns near London that may have been family residences. She allowed the town of 'Okenton', her brothers' last names, to decide the best use for her £5: either to church 'werks' or for repair of highways.[55] Thomas Farande, a draper, who was married with a single child in his minority, left a straightforward will in 1536 with pious gifts principally directed to his parish. With gifts to his Company and to St Mary Overies, Farande provided for his brother. His only gifts not directed to parish, household or family went to repairing roads in London and the town where his father had lived. He provided 40s to make a 'kawsey' (causeway) in 'Sekypton' from the house in which his father died to the church, a gift that memorialized family, bettered a town's transportation, and facilitated attendance at church.[56]

Not only did parishes and parishioners work together to see churches built or rebuilt, often for the honour of saints and the glory of God and Christ, but they also outfitted the church fabric.[57] Parochial worship and celebration depended on devotion to images and relics. Testators donated vestments and ornaments for use in music, devotion and community celebrations, to make the holy images livelier and more respected. St Botolph's churchwardens paid for bread, ale and wine on St Botolph's Day as well as for coals on Easter evening, 'necessary expenses' in the parish.[58] St Stephen's celebrated the 'invention' of St Stephen as well as 'St Erkenwald's Day', with ringers and singers, and St 'Tantyllyns day' (St Antholin).[59] St Erconwald was a seventh-century Bishop of London,

---

[54] W.K. Jordan so named these bequests, classifying them with merchant company uses in the category of 'municipal betterments': *Charities of London, 1480–1660*, pp. 202–6. Cf. the construction and maintenance of bridges and highways as an act of mercy, helping the homeless, wayfarers and pilgrims: Flynn, *Sacred Charity*, pp. 56–7. Social status and piety: Whiting, *Blind Devotion*, p. 90.

[55] PRO, PROB 11/12, f. 28R. 'Okenton' would be Ockendon, either north or south.

[56] PRO, PROB 11/27, f. 102R. Seckington in Warwick? (Lewis, *Topographical Dictionary*.)

[57] Kümin, 'The English Parish in a European Perspective' in *The Parish*, p. 26; Brown, *Popular Piety*, p. 77; 'traditionalist activities and institutions': Whiting, *Blind Devotion*, p. 145, including fn. 1.

[58] GL, MS 1454, Roll 36, and surrounding years.

[59] The churchwardens may have meant St Antonin, the patron saint of the fraternity that gave rise to the Grocers' Company who held the advowson in St Stephen's: Ward,

buried in St Paul's and celebrated enthusiastically in the city of London.[60] In 1517, Rauff Wetton, who had also provided a grave monument worth imitating, left the parish a relic of the holy cross set in gold. The churchwardens were to make a case for it, 'my soule to be the more sp[e]c[i]ally remembered amongst the p[ar]isshen[er]s there'. In the next year, St Stephen's churchwardens paid Myles Gerred for the 'Juell off the crosse and a case ffor the same crose' and for paper and the entering of the accounts, all for a total of £4 2s 3d.[61] The next year the parish paid a joiner for repairs on the rood loft, including for 'mendyng of the Imygery'.[62] Further, vestments and altar clothes likely carried motifs relating to Christ and the saints, and perhaps also the heraldic arms of donors. The churchwardens of St Botolph's recorded a man's gift of a pair of 'offreyes' for vestment about 1503 and a widow's gift of two altar clothes in 1511–12, but gave no descriptions of either.[63]

Those who could not afford to donate ornaments, vestments or altar clothes could enable parochial worship in other ways, suggesting 'communal' piety coexisted with social inequality. Humble people, especially women, may also have been active in the parish through an extension of female domestic labour, what Katherine French has called 'holy housework'.[64] Like the male glaziers who made the stained windows, women who laundered clothes collected wages for their labour. Historians cannot uncover the emotions felt by these women and men during their work, but cannot preclude devotional attitudes, especially for lay people touching the lavish fabrics worn and used by priests and adorned with holy images. Parishes regularly paid for the washing of altar clothes and towels, as St Stephen's did in 1518 for 4s.[65] Around 1500, St Botolph's paid a small sum to a woman to wash and mend the clothes of the church, as well as 42s 11d to a widow who made tapers for the use of the parish.[66] Parishes also frequently paid for repairs of

---

Metropolitan Communities, pp. 101, 112–13; GL, MS 593/1, (1507–8), fols 2v–3; (1528–9), f. 3. [Note: in this volume each set of accounts has its own foliation.]

[60] Morley, p. 228; *The Catholic Encyclopedia*, orig. published 1913, entry by Columba Edmonds, transcribed to website by Michael C. Tinkler. http://www.csu.net/advent/cathen/cathen.htm

[61] PRO, PROB 11/18, f. 262L; GL, MS 593/1, (1518), f. 6v.

[62] GL, MS 593/1, (1519), f. 3v.

[63] GL, MS 1454, Rolls 23 and 32. Testators bequeathed 32 gifts of vestments, copes or altar clothes.

[64] French, 'Maidens' lights and wives' stores: Women's parish guilds in late medieval England', *SCJ*, **29**, 2 (1998), p. 402 and '"Where, Oh Where, Have the Lay Women Gone?"', unpublished paper presented at the American Historical Association Annual Meeting, 1997.

[65] GL, MS 593/1, (1518), f. 6.

[66] GL, MS 1454, Roll 20 (1499/1500–1500/1501).

vestments: St Stephen's paid an embroiderer 3s for mending copes with ostrich feathers and silk. St Stephen's also recycled old surplices once used by priests to clothe choirs of children.[67]

Reformation iconoclasts recognized the potency of monuments and articles of traditional faith and of images of saints, endowed by lay people, in encouraging prayers and 'superstitious' piety. Reformers attacked the relics, shrines and 'superstitious' practices, like repeated prayers or services, of the pre-Reformation church. Thomas ascribed a 'vast reservoir of magical power' to the medieval church, arguing that the pre-Reformation church disdained its simple followers for believing in superstitious intercessors and, at the same time, welcomed such ignorance since it fostered popular devotion.[68] Charles Wriothesley, herald and chronicler through the Reformations, related the exposé in 1535 of the relics of female saints, the girdle of Our Lady at Westminster and of Elizabeth and the relic of Our Lady's milk at St Paul's, 'with other reliques in divers places which they used for covetousnes in deceaphing the people'.[69] John Stow described the defacing of the tomb of William and (his godmother) Margaret Dyxson after the Reformation, an act that obscured its plea for prayers for the souls of the couple and other Christians.[70]

Bequests belied reformers' rhetoric about superstition and deception of simple people. Protestant reformers attacked saints' relics in an attempt to diminish the hold on lay people shown in the preceding testamentary examples. Londoners, however, believed in the efficacy of their provisions, whether made for pious or magical ends.[71] Their gifts of ornaments, fine linens, roadwork or stones strengthened the very fabric of their parochial communities, even as the gifts made a lasting monument to their social status. Self-interested and corporate-minded, pious and non-pious, testators' actions bridged motives seen as conflicting to twentieth-century minds, but not clearly so to sixteenth-century ones.[72]

---

[67] For instance, GL, MS 593/1, (1519), f. 3v; example of ostrich feathers, GL, MS 593/1 (1527–28), f. 4. GL, MS 593/1, (1534–35), f. 6v.

[68] Thomas, *Religion and Decline of Magic*, pp. 45, 49. That some practices 'Veered into magic': Robert W. Scribner, *For the Sake of Simple Folk: Popular Propaganda for the German Reformation* (Cambridge, 1981), p. 4.

[69] Charles Wriothesley (1508?–62, *DNB*), *A Chronicle of England During the Reigns of the Tudors, from AD 1485 to 1559*, W.D. Hamilton (ed.), Camden Society (London, 1875), Vol. I, p. 31; Schen, 'Women and the London Parishes', p. 252.

[70] Thoms, p. 75. His godfathers' tombs were also taken down: Morley, p. 206.

[71] Discussion of these English shrines and relics: Duffy, *Stripping*, pp. 384–5. Writing on the medieval mass, Thomas describes the 'magical efficacy of the Host [that] served to enhance respect for the clergy and to make the laity more regular church-goers': *Religion and the Decline of Magic*, p. 49.

[72] Cf. Graves, 'Social space', pp. 301, 305. She argues that the 'secular discourse' of

Prayers and services

Testators supplied and adorned the church fabric to encourage worship of the Virgin, Christ and the holy company of saints and to foster remembrance of individuals and their families. Testators also endowed prayers and services in their parishes, participated in lay fraternities, and, to a lesser degree, spread resources to religious institutions about London for devotion and memorialization. Masses and other services relating to remembrance of souls or celebrations of saints and Christ formed the core of pre-Reformation religious rituals and bequests for them were quite common.[73] The number, however, declined gradually after 1535, as the monasteries, nunneries and friaries that sang or said masses were confiscated and as reform slowly altered traditional services in parochial churches.

Bequests made by Londoners to religious houses before 1538 focused on masses and prayers for testators' and all Christian souls. Londoners willed plate, vestments, gowns, lights and occasionally a tenement or lease to religious institutions, but most often left money. Johane Sutton, mother of the priest John Sutton, in 1515 left 3s 4d to the Friars Observant in Greenwich to pray for her soul and the soul of her deceased husband, John. To the anchoresses without Bishopsgate and at Westminster she left 20d and linen 'kerchers' (kerchiefs).[74] Anchors frequently contributed to the church fabric and recited prayers for souls in return for support from the parish. Women left only five gifts to anchoresses, totalling less than £1, and one man left a bequest. Male anchorites drew even less testamentary support. Overall, no significant difference existed between the pious gifts left to women by men and those left by women before 1538.[75]

However, in the case of institutions and individuals representing aspects of the ascetic, separate, holy life, women left more gifts than did men, relative to the number of testators. This gender distinction likely relates to social status as well, with fewer women writing wills in the early sixteenth century and those who did enjoying fortunes. Support for monasteries and nunneries had declined before 1500, but the num-

---

patronage by wealthy families and testators 'defined' the 'space of religious discourse' in medieval churches. The dichotomy, however, between 'secular' and 'religious' may be an artificial, even twentieth-century construction.

[73] While 'rites' and 'ritual' have been used to belittle Catholic piety by reducing it to repetition of gestures or practices, this is not my meaning here. See Arnold van Gennep, *Rites of Passage* (Chicago, 1960), orig. published 1908; Graves, 'Social space', p. 306.

[74] GL, MS 9171/9, f. 48v. Stow described the anchoress in the churchyard wall of St Botolph without Bishopsgate: Morley, p. 179.

[75] Z-score of 0.61, showing no significant difference between the sexes' giving.

bers of bequests in London remained steady until 1535, peaking in a time of Church reform, 1520–25. Women concentrated on prayers and services in making bequests to the anchorites and the religious houses in and around London, with 17 per cent (13) of their bequests for repairs or remembrances. Women were less likely than men to establish obits and chantries in parishes, perhaps turning to extra-parochial outlets instead. Men who had served and perhaps identified themselves with parishes might have relied more on them for prestige, even after death. Men attended to repairs (3 per cent), remembrances, including anniversaries (7 per cent), processions at burials (13 per cent) and prayers and masses.[76] Bequests to repairs, or 'werks', covered the costs of renovations and additions to friars' churches and houses. Not unlike gifts to the poor, bequests to religious institutions served both recipient and donor. They sustained the institutions and memorialized the dead donor and his or her family.

Rarely did bequests exhibit testators' loyalty to particular orders or friars, especially without burial within one of their churches. Instead, elite testators often blanketed local houses with bequests, just as they tended to leave gifts to all prisons, not to a single one, to secure prayers. Testators may have indiscriminately utilized efficacious methods of salvation, like prayers from those taking vows, available before the Reformation. For instance, the widow Elizabeth Berell in 1500 endowed placebo, mass and dirige at the Syon, St Thomas, the four friaries in London, the sisters of St Mary and Elsing Spitals, and three friars' houses outside the city, before making gifts to the lazar houses and prisons of London.[77] Monasteries, nunneries and friaries allowed individuals to lead a contemplative, pious life and to serve the community with hospitality to the poor and travellers and intercessory prayers for the dead.[78]

Sisters and brothers in religious houses and anchors provided one point of contact with the church, but priests serving in parishes represented the church most intimately to common parishioners.[79] Priests and clerks were another aspect of the parochial community to which

---

[76] Forty-eight gifts from 27 women; 191 gifts from 196 men. Nine bequests for repairs, 20 for remembrances, 36 for processions. J.A.F. Thomson relates a decline in support for chantries: 'Piety and Charity in Late Medieval London', *Journal of Ecclesiastical History*, **16**, 2 (Oct. 1965), p. 191; Whiting, *Blind Devotion*, p. 263.

[77] PRO, PROB 11/12, f. 28L.

[78] Debate over attractiveness of nunneries to women: Crawford, *Women and Religion*, pp. 21–2; Davis, 'City women and religious change'; Harris, 'A new look at the Reformation', pp. 89–113.

[79] For the sake of brevity, I have used 'anchors' for both the men and women who lived in this way.

Londoners were attached, and therefore made important participants in burials. Before 1538, few testators commented upon their health and they seemed not to have been directed by clergy at their deathbeds. In 1503, Robert Hill, of St Olave's parish, ranked the clergy by his own parish affiliation. When he asked to be buried in St Stephen's, by his wife, he paid the priests from his latest church 8d, the other priests 6d, and the clerks and singing children 2d to convey his body.[80] Before 1538, of gifts related to burials, 29.5 per cent (52) went to priests, clerks, or the parish church. The bulk of such gifts (52.8 per cent, or 93) went to the poor and body bearers, with 17.6 per cent (31) of bequests reaching executors, neighbours, monks, nuns or friars.

In contrast to parishioners' hiring of priests, one pre-Reformation priest showed little allegiance to his parish, but instead loyalty to his fellows. John Molinars left a variety of religious books to priests and clerks for their prayers and remembrance in 1500, but none to the parish itself. The 'ortulus paradisi', perhaps a book of hours or primer (Ortulus or Hortulus Paradisi) went to the priest of St Swithin's. The Bible and 'Ortus Varbilore', possibly the Ortus Vocabulorum published by Wynkyn de Worde in 1500, went to Robert Marshe, clerk. Two great books went to Thomas Sheffeld, clerk. To Sir Richard Wilton, clerk, he left 'portius' and 'Sermones discipuli', the latter being a pre-Reformation preaching aid. To Sir Robert Thomson, he left 'dives et pauper', one edition of which had been printed in 1496 in Westminster by de Worde.[81] Molinars may have had a greater affinity for the priesthood than for the particular parish he served at his death.

Testators' donations to the church fabric demonstrated their attachment to parishes, even ones from which they had moved, and their gifts to priests, clerks and members of Catholic institutions exhibited their reliance on earthly intercessors. Processions and celebrations, important aspects of pre-Reformation piety, fostered and reflected parochial worship and participation and strengthened ties between Londoners and their parishes.[82] Corpus Christi processions were supported by individuals and by corporate bodies. While late medieval piety has been described as tending toward individual devotion, Corpus Christi still

---

[80] PRO, PROB 11/14, fols 56R–57L.

[81] GL, MS 9171/8, f. 226v. Susan Wabuda, 'Bishops and the Provision of Homilies', p. 555. Ortus Vocabulorum STC 13829; Diues et pauper STC 19213. Late medieval and early modern printed and manuscript books in parishes: Fiona Kisby, 'Books in London Parish Churches, c. 1400 – c. 1603' in C. Barron and J. Stratford (eds), *The Church and Learning in Late Medieval Society: Essays in Honour of Barrie Dobson*, Proceedings of the Harlaxton Symposium (Grantham, forthcoming).

[82] Ronald Hutton, *The Rise and Fall of Merry England: The Ritual Year 1400–1700* (Oxford and New York, 1994), esp. pp. 5–48.

emphasized a sense of community over individualism. The 'communal dimension' of Corpus Christi stressed unity even at the cost of social coercion.[83] Secular support and control of Corpus Christi introduced social tension into a religious ritual intended to unite the Christian community, and, according to Rubin, fostered 'competing visions of that community'. Control over and hierarchies within the processions organized by secular city leaders infused Corpus Christi with 'local political meanings'.[84]

Wealthy parishioners donated ornaments necessary for the celebration, displaying their fortunes and their largesse, but they benefited the whole of the parish with their gifts for the sacrament. For 'makinge and garnyshinge of the Bachellors torches of St Mary Wolnoth for the procession on Corpus Christi Day', Dame Percivale left 20 marks in 1512.[85] As an example of other ways to light the sacrament, Richard Amadas stipulated that five of the torches around his bier go to his church to be used at the 'sakeringe time' at the high altar and to pray for his soul.[86] Likewise, Richard Travis requested that immediately after his decease torches go to churchwardens in four parishes, including his birthplace, for the honour of God and ministration of the sacrament.[87] Testators supplied other elements of the procession as well. George Brigges gave a canopy to his parish to cover the sacrament, presumably as part of the Corpus Christi procession.[88] The canopy, like all other aspects of the 'church fabric', needed periodic repair to hold the instruments and the act of worship together.[89] By 1531 uncertainty of pending religious change altered some testators' support for traditional rituals, like Corpus Christi. Lawraunce Eggylsfeelde bequeathed 8s to be paid yearly, only as long as St Stephen's Walbrook kept that mass.[90] Perhaps his position in Henry VIII's court alerted him to the possibility of further change.

Although Michael Berlin has claimed that Corpus Christi played a small part in the pre-Reformation calendar in London, early sixteenth-

---

[83] Duffy, *Stripping*, p. 92.

[84] Rubin, *Corpus Christi: The Eucharist in Late Medieval Culture* (Cambridge, 1991), p. 248.

[85] PRO, PROB 11/17, f. 221R. Biographical information about and history of Dame Thomasine Percival: Barbara Hanawalt, *Growing Up in Medieval London: The Experience of Childhood in History* (New York, 1993), p. 187; Matthew Davies, 'Thomasyne Percivale, "The Maid of the Week" (d. 1512)' in C.M. Barron and A.F. Sutton (eds), *Medieval London Widows 1300–1500* (London, 1994), pp. 185–207.

[86] PRO, PROB 11/24, f. 39L.

[87] PRO, PROB 11/28, f. 53L.

[88] PRO, PROB 11/31, f. 164R.

[89] GL, MS 593/1, (1507–08), f. 2v.

[90] PRO, PROB 11/24, f. 61L.

century churchwardens' accounts suggest instead the importance of Corpus Christi to the city's inhabitants, and even its growing significance.[91] At the beginning of the Reformation, Corpus Christi did represent an integral part of religious life in early modern London. Although London's celebrations seem subdued in comparison with those of a city like Coventry, they were still worthy of consistent parish expenditures. St Stephen's paid 3s for garnishing the torches for Corpus Christi day.[92] Beginning in the accounts of 1525–26, the churchwardens collected £5 2s 8d for Corpus Christi, in the same way they collected £5 18s for the clerk's wage from the inhabitants of the parish. The collection for Corpus Christi lasted through 1537–38, though it fell to £3 9s 2d while the clerk's wage collection totalled £6 12s then. St Stephen's accounts through these years became more precise and expert, perhaps explaining the first notation of this collection, but the 'new' receipt may in fact signify a greater commitment to and interest in the celebration of Corpus Christi in at least one London parish. In that year the churchwardens paid for drink and bread for the singers of the mass, for dressing the torches, for coals and for the priest's singing at the same.[93] The following year's accountants named the clerks of St Anthony's responsible for the mass and the '*salve*' and paid the alewife for the singers' drinking, and made the usual payments relating to garlands and other elements of the service. The hiring of clerks from such a famous institution reinforces the interaction of parochial and broader ecclesiastical institutions within the city of London, mirrored in wills that spread bequests through parishes and religious houses. St Anthony's was a prominent hospital in St Benet Fink parish, with a renowned grammar school that had been founded in 1393.[94]

The celebration of the mass similarly emphasized community over individual devotion. The ritual meeting of parishioners in the context of the mass exemplified the notion of a harmonious community, which contemporaries in turn exploited to persuade or coerce neighbours to

---

[91] Michael Berlin, 'Civic Ceremony in Early Modern England', *Urban History Yearbook, 1986*, p. 20; cf. Gary Gibbs, 'New duties for the parish community in Tudor London in *The Parish*', p. 165. See also Phythian-Adams, 'Ceremony and the Citizen: The Communal Year at Coventry, 1450–1550', in Peter Clark and Paul Slack (eds), *Crisis and Order in English Towns, 1500–1700: Essays in Urban History* (Toronto, 1972), pp. 57–85.

[92] GL, MS 593/1, (1507–08), f. 3.

[93] GL, MS 593/1, (1525–26), fols 2v, 4, 6, 6v.

[94] GL, MS 593/1, (1526–27), fols 3, 3v. See Stow for explanation of school: Morley, pp. 100–101; description of its dissolution: Morley, pp. 194–5. The *Salve Regina*, known as the *salve*, was one of four anthems of the Blessed Virgin Mary: *The Catholic Encyclopedia (1913)*, H.T. Henry, trans. by John A. Scofield.

order. In London in 1529, a woman dragged her female neighbour from the Host, saying 'I pray you let me speke a worde with you for you have need to axe me forgyvenes, before you rescyve your rights'.[95] A most unusual bequest by Robert Yaxley covered the cost of priests to have the best red wine to celebrate mass. But, more importantly, Yaxley asked that the same wine reach women with children and the sick receiving the sacrament, widening the social scope of the 'best' in this religious meal.[96] His bequest emphasized the interconnected benefits to individual and community within the sacrament, as Duffy has argued: individual devotion, yet 'the source of human community'.[97]

Other devotions essential to belief on the dawn of reform similarly joined individual piety with communal activity and charity. Many centred on the pious numbers repeated in testaments and through late medieval devotions, like the fivefold devotions, prayers, services and attendants that sprang from attachment to the Five Wounds of Christ. The participants in the Pilgrimage of Grace of 1536–37 drew on this tradition, placing the image on their banners. Christ's Wounds expressed the 'essence' of his humanity and linked communicants to him.[98] Testators drew on the spiritual and visual potency of the Five Wounds of Christ, like Jasper Shukburgh did when he left five score pence (100) to needy people to say prayers for souls and for the honour of the Five Wounds.[99] The devotion encouraged charity to the poor by transforming 'the Wounds of Judgement into Wounds of Mercy' through help to 'Christ's wounded members, the poor'.[100] Shukburgh's hiring of the poor to remember the Five Wounds bound them with him in the remembrance of Christ's pain and of the good works necessary to salvation. Dame Percivale's bequest to the poor of St Mary's helped five poor men and women, apparently in imitation of the same wounds.[101]

Besides 'five', other numbers recalled holy events and people, layering devotional imagery in public displays of pious charity: the seven sacra-

---

[95] As told in Duffy, *Stripping*, p. 95; and in Brigden, *London and the Reformation*, pp. 18–19.

[96] PRO, PROB 11/28, f. 140L.

[97] 'The Host, then, was far more than the object of individual devotion, a means of forgiveness and sanctification: it was the source of human community': Duffy, *Stripping*, p. 93.

[98] Rubin, *Corpus Christi*, p. 303; Duffy, *Stripping*, pp. 238–48; D.M. Palliser, 'Popular Reactions to the Reformation during the Years of Uncertainty, 1530–70' in Haigh (ed.), *The Reformation Revised* (Cambridge, 1987), p. 97; Haigh, *English Reformations*, pp. 148–9.

[99] GL, MS 9171/10, f. 116v. (1528)

[100] Duffy, *Stripping*, p. 248.

[101] GL, MS 1002/1A, f. 2v.

ments and words on the cross, twelve apostles, thirteen for the apostles with Christ. Numbers signalled their meaning not only to the testator, but to observers and participants in the obit and services. Any pious reminder increased the efficacy of the action for the living and the dead. John Stow's grandfather, Thomas Stow, provided 5s for burning candles in worship of the seven sacraments, at seven altars, for three years.[102] Endowing lights on altars was a common practice, but since Thomas Stow was also a tallowchandler, the bequest became a self-referential act. Obits followed similar numerical patterns, with testators establishing five-, twelve- and thirteen-year obits.[103] In the wills from these London parishes, obits lasting two to five years, six to ten years, more than twenty-five, and into perpetuity occurred most frequently.

These obits and month minds remembered a person's death, re-enacted mourning and commemoration, and emphasized the need for prayers from the living. Far more men than women provided for obits, illustrating, first, men's economic advantage.[104] Second, men took responsibility for their and their family and friends' remembrance through prayer. Besides leading survivors through subsequent stages of mourning and invoking prayers for the dead, obits generally also included alms to the poor. Churchwardens' accounts carefully documented the performance of these anniversaries, encouraging other parishioners to establish them, by showing the faithful execution of testamentary requests. Clive Burgess and Beat Kümin have shown the significance of these services to the financial wellbeing of the parish, not to mention its spiritual vitality.[105]

Obits often followed the pattern outlined in an exemplary will of 1525. William Dyxson left £100 to the Drapers, the craft or company that held the parish's rectory, to see a perpetual obit performed 'by note' in St Michael Cornhill. His obit, costing 26s 8d yearly, began with 12d to the parson to attend the obit and to pray for Dyxson among other souls on the bead-roll, 'a list of benefactors for whose souls the people ought to pray, with the dates of their anniversaries'.[106] To priests of the church and his craft and to clerks, he left 4d each. Peals cost 2s, lights

---

[102] GL, MS 9171/10, f. 90.

[103] GL, MS 9171/10, f. 117; PRO, PROB 11/28, f. 289L; PRO, PROB 11/18, f. 36L. Ninety-three bequests directed to obits in wills written 1538 and earlier.

[104] Fifteen bequests came from women, 78 from men. Thirty-five testators (20.71 per cent) endowed at least one obit.

[105] Burgess and Kümin, 'Penitential Bequests', esp. pp. 614–15; importance of anniversary services: Brown, *Popular Piety*, pp. 101–4.

[106] 'At the "bidding of the beads" at Mass every Sunday the priest would read out the bead-roll from the pulpit': Brigden, *London and the Reformation*, p. 34. See also Duffy, *Stripping*, p. 116.

10d. Children of the choir received 4d. For their attendance, the master of the craft collected 3s 4d and each warden collected 20d. A potation (or drinking) among the fellowship followed, costing 6s 8d. The common clerk collected 8d. To prick his craft's memory, Dyxson left 4d for the beadle to warn the fellowship to the obit. The youngest (junior) warden of the craft had the obligation to distribute the residue among the poor householders of the parish at the *exequies*, the funeral rites or procession.[107]

Testators did fear that parishes, companies, friends or family might neglect testamentary obligations, to the peril of everyone's souls. Hence a testator who detailed a service also threatened and cajoled executors, craft wardens and churchwardens to ensure its performance. 'For the sure observing performyng and keping' of the obit, Dyxson advised his executors to seek legal advice and write a formal contract. He offered the late alderman John Wilkynson's contract as an example of how to bind the master and wardens of the craft and the parson and churchwardens of the parish to one another, to see the bequest fulfilled. If the craft refused to be bound, he asked that the money revert to highway repairs and poor maidens' dowries, a loss to the company and the parish. A 'wet' obit might be more faithfully kept, as some members of the Goldsmiths, for instance, complained of attending an obit once every twelve working days and hence combined 'dry' obits with 'wet' ones in 1497.[108]

London churchwardens' accounts yield examples resembling Dyxson's provision for an obit that show how services for the dead were central to parochial life.[109] In 1525/6, St Botolph's Aldersgate accounted for the 10s left for a man's perpetual obit: 12d to the parish priest, 12d among three other priests, 8d to the parish clerk, 8d to two other clerks, 8d for lights, 2s to the churchwardens to see the bequest fulfilled, 12d for a drinking, 1d for oblations or offerings, and 2s 11d for alms for the poor.[110] St Stephen's reported spending £5 4s 4d on obits during the accounting year 1522–23, an increase of £2 since the accounting year 1507–08, the earliest surviving churchwardens' account for the parish.[111] Like Dyxson, other testators directed their bequests for obits

---

[107] PRO, PROB 11/21, fols 285R–286R. On crafts fulfilling these bequests: Ward, *Metropolitan Communities*, p. 100. Brown, *Popular Piety*, p. 54.

[108] T.F. Reddaway, 'The London Goldsmiths *circa* 1500', *TRHS*, 5th series, **12** (1962), pp. 49–62.

[109] Brown, *Popular Piety*, p. 109; Kümin, 'The English parish', p. 21. Brown suggests that the office of churchwarden was bolstered by the need to oversee services connected to the dead.

[110] GL, MS 1454, Roll 45. [Alan Johnson] See *Chantry Certificate*, p. 30.

[111] GL, MS 593/1, (1522–23), f. 5v; (1507–08), f. 2.

through companies, warning them to see the services fulfilled or the endowment would be forfeited to another body, like the parish church itself. The draper John Toll left £100 to his company to hold an obit for fifty years in St Michael's with payments to priests, clerks and singing children in the parish church, as well as to attendant craft brothers and the clerk and beadle of the company. The residue belonged to the poor. If the company failed to perform it, the money went to St Michael's.[112]

An elaborate obit, drawing on familiar aspects of devotion to saints and illustrating the advantages of social privilege, comes from the testament of the Viscountess Lisle. She funded a weekly Saturday service over five years in the chapel of Our Lady and St Katherine in St Michael Cornhill. The length recalls the Five Wounds, a point of suffering for the Virgin Mary as well as Christ, or perhaps the Virgin's Five Sorrows or Joys.[113] Holding an obit 'where I am wonte to knele' associated this female testator more closely with devotion to Mary and attached her memory to the space she had occupied in life, in part a consequence of her social status.[114] Although she called it an 'obit', the service's attachment to a place within the church associated with her transformed it into an informal chantry provision and connected her memory with worship of the saints within the parish church, particularly of St Katherine. The devout mass of Our Blessed Lady to be performed at this obit, replete with singing children of the choir, playing organs, and ringing bells, started at eight o'clock. She set aside £5 per year for the event.[115] She established a separate obit by leaving a 'messuage' to the parish, asking for a placebo and dirige at night, followed by mass the next day. If the parish defaulted, the Drapers were to take on the responsibility. If they also defaulted, she asked that her friend, the alderman William White, see it properly done.[116]

Month minds were another anniversary that entailed meals, potations or services, even daily services through the thirtieth day after burial, but were not without critics. Thomas Oo, a citizen and grocer, in his 1495 testament, asked for 29 days of services after his burial in St Stephen's and for a perpetual obit.[117] Month minds, like obits, often included ritual charity to be distributed to paupers. In 1505, the draper William

---

[112] PRO, PROB 11/18, f. 236L.

[113] Duffy states that the Sorrows of Mary, encouraged in response to the plague in Europe and in the shared suffering of Christ's wounds, outweighed the celebration of the Five Joys in late medieval England: *Stripping*, pp. 257–9.

[114] PRO, PROB 11/12, f. 72L; Graves, 'Social space', p. 311.

[115] PRO, PROB 11/12, f. 72R.

[116] PRO, PROB 11/12, f. 73L.

[117] PRO, PROB 11/12, f. 4L. See St Stephen's churchwardens' accounts for this unusual spelling, written 'Hoo' in 1522/3. GL, MS 593/1, (1522–23), f. 5v.

Shukburgh left 20s for alms to the poor at month's mind.[118] In the early 1500s, however, some testators avoided the practice of establishing month minds and instead focused on charity, to undercut their privileged social status. Viscountess Lisle commanded,

> I will and charge myn executors that they shall in nowise doo hold or kepe for me any solempne moneth mynde in manner and forme as it is accustomed to be don in makyng of grete dyners drynkyngs ... don only to the pompe and vaynglory of the world.

A woman enjoying a substantial fortune could humbly downplay wealth, pomp and vainglory, yet leave sumptuous gifts, unlike a widow of lesser means who had no reason to excuse her own wealth and influence. Recipients of special gifts in Lisle's will included the King and his son and the Archbishop of Canterbury. Although Lisle used her great wealth to establish obits and to continue a chantry, she avoided a display that would have entertained mainly friends and neighbours, her select social level. Instead, she directed the foregone month mind expenditure to be spent on 'deeds and werks of pitie almesse deeds and charitie for the helth and comforte of my soule and of the other soules afternamed'.[119] Her gift to the poor, and her selective display of wealth in posthumous foundations, perpetuated social difference although she tried to scorn it.

Testators with sufficient resources supported chantries to ensure attention to their souls through purgatory, though few will writers in this sample made such endowments. Husbands, having more property to bequeath, were more likely to establish chantries than their widows were.[120] Men's wills referred to lifetime discussions with their wives about burial plans; perhaps couples similarly discussed the foundation of chantries. Lifetime discussions of pious legacies between a husband and wife possibly ensured that his endowment also reflected her wishes, or that she followed his orders carefully. Dame Percivale, for example, widow of a knight and lord mayor, charged her executor and cousin, John Dynham, to continue the chantry and grammar school in St Mary Week, Cornwall, patterned after the one begun by her last husband.[121] Elizabeth Berell established a chantry with an annuity of 40s, although she disdained the 'pompe or pride of the world'. Her lands, in the hands

---

[118] PRO, PROB 11/14, f. 277L.

[119] PRO, PROB 11/12, fols 72L–72R; for gifts, see PRO, PROB 11/12, f. 74R.

[120] Out of six bequests to chantries, men made five of them. Chantries: Brown, *Popular Piety*, p. 103; Alan Kreider, *English Chantries: The Road to Dissolution* (Cambridge, MA, 1979), pp. 2, 15. Chantry priests' roles in parochial ceremony: Burgess, 'Shaping', p. 248.

[121] PRO, PROB 11/17, f. 221R. Davies believes this foundation may be the first one by a non-noble woman: 'Thomasyne Percyvale', pp. 203, 206.

of William Wotton and his wife Elizabeth, Berell's cousin, generated the annuity. At their death, the remains would go to their daughter, Berell's goddaughter. Her burial cost 10s, in the middle range of charges, suggesting that she eschewed pomp and vainglory in her grave choice. Or, her request, to be buried by her husband in the St Nicholas chapel in St Stephen's, may have outweighed any desire for a more prestigious, and expensive, location in the parish church.[122]

For people of more modest means, guilds and fraternities, 'poor men's [and women's] chantries', performed a similar function of perpetuating prayer and remembrance.[123] The membership of medieval London parish fraternities was artisanal and feminine, in large part.[124] Parish fraternities and guilds, dedicated to the honour of God, Christ and saints, provided mutual help for living members. For deceased members, they ensured proper burials and prayers. Priests and clerks performed guild services and said prayers and collects for members, but lay people ran the fraternities and paid the clergy. Outside London, women controlled some single-sex guilds, but the wills in this sample do not refer to women's guilds.[125] Fraternities thus constituted the foundation of lay participation in the parish in the early sixteenth century. Barron has argued that the numbers and 'vitality' of lay fraternities indicated the dynamism of individual piety, the centrality of the parish in pre-Reformation London, and the liveliness in the parish.[126]

Few fraternity registers from London survive in the twenty-first century, perhaps as a result of compliance with mandates to destroy 'popish'

---

[122] GL, MS 593/1, (1507–08), f. 2 (burial); (1518), f. 3v. PRO, PROB 11/12, f. 27R. burial and statement, f. 28R chantry.

[123] Scarisbrick, *Reformation and the English People*, p. 20. See also Brigden, 'Religion and Social Obligation', pp. 94 ff. and her *London and the Reformation*, pp. 36–9; Caroline Barron, 'The Parish Fraternities of Medieval London' in Caroline M. Barron and Christopher Harper-Bill (eds), *The Church in Pre-Reformation Society: Essays in Honour of F.R.H. Du Boulay* (Woodbridge, Suffolk, 1985), pp. 13, 28; Burgess and Kümin, 'Penitential bequests', p. 613; on St Katherine and Sts Fabian and Sebastian guilds in St Botolph's Aldersgate: Joshua Toulmin Smith, *English Gilds* (London, 1870), pp. 6–11.

[124] Barron, 'The Parish Fraternities of Medieval London', p. 30.

[125] French identified women's guilds in Westminster and Southwark, but not in London: 'Maidens' lights and wives' stores', pp. 421–2.

[126] 'The increasing vitality of parish fraternities in London in the early sixteenth century may demonstrate, not so much an increasing commitment to the doctrines of what was to become "the old faith" but, rather, a rising tide of lay participation in religion fed, in its turn by rising prosperity and increasing literacy ... Perhaps we may look for the seed bed of the English Reformation, not in Lollardy, nor in anti-clericalism, but in the vitality of the parish community': Barron, 'The Parish Fraternities of Medieval London', pp. 36–7.

books.[127] For instance, in St Mary Colchurch the 'black booke of the brother hood of ye freternytie of St Katternes' survived in an inventory made in 1613 but, by 1616, the parish inventory no longer listed the book.[128] The register of the fraternity of the Holy Trinity and Sts Fabian and Sebastian in St Botolph's Aldersgate does survive, providing a glimpse into their activities. The register recorded the gifts to the fraternities, joined in the later fifteenth century, and the costs of holding obits for members. Memoranda listed members and the fraternity's possessions. The goods included numerous tablecloths, diaper napkins and table-cloths, 'a corporas casse with a scripture', a 'blake palle of blake damaske with a white crosse', a 'peyre of beedes', and a 'stayned bordere with the fyve Wondys of Owre Lorde'.[129] The goods illustrated the fraterni-ty's devotional attentions to saints and funereal obligations to members. No record of charitable work appears in this register, although fraterni-ties seem to have distributed alms informally and not recorded it.[130] For example, the fraternity lent the parish £4 to repair a tenement 'pertain-ing' to the church between 1496 and 1498, perhaps to help the parish use the building's rent for charitable purposes. The transaction ap-peared in the parish records, not those of the fraternity. The parish repaid the sum lent by the brotherhood out of the 'box' between 1515 and 1517, apparently with interest since the sum was then £10.[131]

Wills point to the significance of guild life to a social cross-section of London's parishioners. Gifts to make or gild images or to sustain lights at altars honouring saints, exhibited the donors' piety, and reminded parishioners and priests to pray for Christian souls. Men left greater monetary gifts to fraternities than did women, but proportionally women and men enthusiastically supported them. Five women (26 per cent of female testators) left ten gifts in money to fraternities, with a median gift of a little more than 1s 7d, a minimum of 1s and a maximum of £25. Forty-eight men (36 per cent) left 114 monetary gifts with a

---

[127] As demanded by the Royal Injunctions of 1559 and Lambeth Articles (1561); *VAI* III, pp. 7, 96.

[128] For 1613 inventory, see GL, MS 66, f. 7; for the 1616 one, see GL, MS 66, f. 17.

[129] Patricia Basing (ed.), *Parish Fraternity Register: Fraternity of the Holy Trinity and SS. Fabian and Sebastian in the Parish of St. Botolph without Aldersgate*, London Record Society 18 (London, 1982), p. 79. 'Diaper' refers to fabric woven of fine silk and gold threads.

[130] Barron speculates that fraternities favoured informal over formal charity and hence neglected to record aid, since chantry returns showed charity from fraternities: 'The Parish Fraternities of Medieval London', pp. 26, 27. Cf. Ben McRee 'Charity and gild solidarity in late medieval England', *JBS* 32, 3 (1993), pp. 195–225.

[131] GL, MS 1454, Rolls 17, 36. Example of fraternity lending to parish: Brown, *Popular Piety*, p. 145.

median gift of just more than 3s 4d, a minimum of just more than 4d and a maximum of £10.[132] The median gifts are humble ones, befitting the broad cross-section of parishioners involved in guilds. Men provided for more of the commemorative aspects of fraternity ritual in addition to devotion to saints, through prayers and lights. Women, however, concentrated on the honour of saints without targeting bequests for certain functions. Bequests to religious fraternities continued into the 1540s, preceding their destruction.[133]

These bequests may seem slight, but the majority of testators who remembered fraternities gave two or fewer gifts – one notable exception being John Stow's grandfather, who gave eight.[134] Thus, in wills drafted in or prior to 1538, fraternities comprise one of the most frequently cited pious targets, falling behind those to the parish church, priests, poor householders and dispersed gifts to friars and cloistered religious. The parishioners of St Michael Cornhill showed the greatest testamentary concern with fraternities, with 105 gifts in this period, but these parishioners also produced 40.5 per cent (62) of the wills. On the other hand, the survival of the Register Book of Sts Fabian and Sebastian and the Holy Trinity in St Botolph's reminds the historian that silence in wills does not signify a lack of interest on the part of parishioners. For lay people, the Reformation prohibition of fraternities would arguably have a greater impact on their lives than the confiscation of religious houses and chantries, despite the greater endowments of those institutions.[135] Testamentary bequests to fraternities were more evenly spread than those to parishes or parish churches and priests, where a handful of wealthy testators gave significant proportions of the total gifts.[136]

The gifts of William Waltham, citizen and upholsterer, emphasized the importance of guilds in the lives of members and of parishes before the Reformation. Waltham left music and music books to St Mary's and to his apprentice in 1520. 'To serve for the honor off o[u]r lady mass' Waltham willed his 'kerybooke with Allelmys and sequence' and old books of 'Antempnes' (anthems) of St John the Baptist. In the earliest surviving churchwardens' accounts of the parish (1539–40), the church-

---

[132] The average value of women's gifts was £2 8s, because of the outlying maximum, compared to the average value of men's gifts, slightly more than 12s 4d; 19 women's wills, 134 men's wills.

[133] See Jordan, *Charities of London, 1480–1660*, p. 276; Scarisbrick, *Reformation and the English People*, p. 54.

[134] Sixty-four per cent (34) of testators gave two or fewer gifts; GL, MS 9171/10, fols 116–17.

[135] Scarisbrick, *Reformation and the English People*, p. 19.

[136] Out of gifts to parishes, three wealthy women and four wealthy men gave 24.6 per cent (103); to priests, two of those women alone gave 19.6 per cent (30).

wardens noted the 20s received from the master and wardens of the Merchant Tailors to pay the conduct who kept the 'Antempne afore Sainte John with his Childern', one of Dame Percivale's provisions that honoured the saint after whom her husband was named.[137] Waltham might have owned the music for the service that was supported by Dame Thomasine Percivale's 1512 gift. One of the chapels in St Mary Woolnoth was dedicated to St John.[138] To the use of the choir, Waltham left his own great 'prycking' of ten masses and several 'Antempnes'. To another man's apprentice he gave five pricksong books with masses. To his son, a monk, he left the residue of his songbooks. To 'my childe' Nicholas Wyllslow, he left songbooks and a book of three parts of masses.[139]

While fraternities drew Londoners closer to their fellow parishioners and neighbours, trade guilds brought them together across parish boundaries for mutual benefit. 'Spiritual brotherhood' had been the foundation of the trade guilds and sixteenth-century testators relied on members of companies to carry their bodies to burial and to attend services. Companies comprised one of a number of 'artificial kinships' that 'owed obligations to dead brethren'.[140] Crafts provided or rented both lights and hearse cloths, the trappings of burial, to meet the spiritual needs of its members, as they had met their professional needs in life. In 1522, a cordwainer named John Buckler asked that his craft bring his body to earth 'w[i]t[h] theire lyght', for 3s 4d.[141] Gifts to associates, such as company brothers and sisters, masters, mistresses and journeymen, principally reflected a desire to secure remembrance and prayers for souls. Up to 1538, 23 per cent (14) of gifts left to such associates were gowns or cloth for gowns to wear when attending testators' burials and funeral or anniversary services. Testators left rings as well (13 per cent, or 8), a gift of affection and one that remained longer with the receiver.[142] Rings maintained a connection between living and deceased friends and kept the memory of former associates alive.

Parish guilds, as well as the masses and Corpus Christi processions, brought parishioners and neighbours together in common pious activi-

---

[137] GL, MS 1002/1A, f. 2v.

[138] GL, MS 1002/1A, f. 17.

[139] GL, MS 9171/9, f. 165.

[140] Brigden, *London and the Reformation*, p. 35; Scarisbrick, *Reformation and the English People*, pp. 122–4; Ward, *Metropolitan Communities*, pp. 99, 111–12. Need for greater attention to craft guilds when studying poor relief: Matthew Davies, 'The Tailors of London: Corporate Charity in the Late Medieval Town' in Rowena Archer (ed.), *Crown, Government and People in the Fifteenth Century* (New York, 1995), pp. 163–4.

[141] GL, MS 9171/10, f. 168.

[142] These gifts are distinct from gifts to companies themselves.

ties, although they may not have participated on equal footing. These modes of worship created excitement about and visceral reactions to traditional holy people and images and were bolstered by other means of theatrical presentation. Priests and lay people in pre-Reformation London led parishioners through the Lenten season and Easter, the most sombre time of the Christian sacred calendar. Parishes shrouded the rood with a violet or black cloth through Lent, revealing it only at the Palm Sunday procession. St Stephen's made regular payments for bread and wine on Palm Sunday and paid for a sermon that day, as well as various costs 'over Easter evyn'.[143] By the 1520s, the re-enactment of key biblical events had become increasingly elaborate and 'real', requiring the parish to hire 'heris' or hair (beards?) for the 'proffytts' (prophets) and to pay for their drink 'ov[er] palme Sundaye'. The churchwardens paid the parish clerk 'Gabriell' 4d for watching the sepulchre erected within the church on Good Friday. In the accounts of 1510–11, the churchwardens allotted 8d for bread and ale at the watching, and spent 1d on nails for the sepulchre. During Lent, the parishioners also consented to spend 10s for keeping an 'Antom' (anthem).[144]

Pre-Reformation parishes allowed dramatic performances of saints' plays, scriptural plays, morality plays and folk drama. In the early 1530s the churchwardens of St Botolph's collected 3s 4d from 'Walton and his fellows' for the hire of the churchyard for a play. Walton turned over an additional 11s 6d to the churchwardens in respect of a 'covenant' to donate part or all of the collection at the play to the church. Since Walton used the churchyard, the performance was probably a saints' or scriptural play, though folk plays also raised money for religious or civic ends.[145] The performances of biblical stories, acted out to awe and to educate parishioners provided another way of encouraging piety that did not require literacy or learning. In a similar vein, the Second Royal Injunctions distinguished between idols and images by stating that 'images serve for none other purpose but as to be books of unlearned men'.[146]

The sermon provided another mechanism for educating lay people in piety and even theology. Pre-Reformation preaching concentrated on

---

[143] GL, MS 593/1, (1507–08), f. 2v; (1510–11), f. 3v; (1527–28), f. 4. Information on rood from *Catholic Encyclopedia*, G. Cyprian Alston, transcribed by Lawrence Progel. See also Duffy, 'The parish, piety, and patronage in late medieval East Anglia: the evidence of rood screens' in *The Parish*, pp. 133–62, esp. 137.

[144] GL, MS 593/1, (1522–23), f. 3v; (1525–26), f.4v; (1527–28), f.4; (1507–08), f. 2v; (1510–11), f. 3v. (1528–29), f. 4v. Also see Duffy, *Stripping*, pp. 23–6.

[145] GL, MS 1454, Roll 47; Howard B. Norland, *Drama in Early Tudor Britain, 1485–1558* (Lincoln, Nebraska and London, 1995), pp. 3–61, p. 53 on collections.

[146] *VAI*, II, p. 38. Scribner notes the similar defence of images against Lollard attacks in the fifteenth century: *Simple Folk*, p. 4.

large, outdoor gatherings, usually linked to a feast day or procession, to educate the people in the sacraments or the saints.[147] Sermons on the saints and sacraments had been given at St Mary's Spital since 'time out of mind', according to Stow.[148] Some parishes also erected their own churchyard crosses for preaching, like the one Jasper Shukburgh funded, to be modelled on the one in St Paul's churchyard. In 1507–08 St Stephen's paid 4d for a 'great crose granet', perhaps intended for the churchyard or at one of the stopping points in Rogationtide.[149] As the Reformation evolved, however, these preaching crosses sometimes became the loci of contention and controversy, for the statement of orthodoxy and repudiation of heresy.[150]

Signs of contention do appear in the wills composed and probated on the eve of reform, despite many signs of traditional piety and bequests in Londoners' last plans and in their parishes' expenditures. For one, endowments for sermons began to mark Protestant leanings in the city, distinct from pre-Reformation preaching. A singular will of 1538, by a former churchwarden and business associate of the organ-making Howe family, outlined a new kind of piety and perhaps foretold puritanism's eventual hold in seventeenth-century St Stephen's. John Clymhowe, citizen and organ maker, asked for a sermon on the day of his burial in St Stephen's by a preacher of 'good, virtuous disposition' elected by the curate Robert Marsh.[151] He also asked for the *Te Deum laudamus* in English with the organs going, rather than the traditional *qui Lazarum* sung when the body went into the earth. He stressed the 'mercy' that called him to God and Christ: salvation through faith, not good works, and an insistence on English rather than Latin songs. From the same parish in 1541, John Bodnam's will illustrates how slowly *mentalités* shifted in Reformation London. He requested a person learned in divinity to preach the word of God to the people, at the mass of Requiem.[152] Unlike Clymhowe, however, he also provided for a trental of masses and for torches to burn before the Sacrament and at Corpus Christi, showing a clear attachment to traditional piety despite his interest in aspects of the new ways.

---

[147] Duffy, *Stripping*, p. 57; Scarisbrick, *Reformation and the English People*, p. 41; Whiting, *Blind Devotion*, p. 237; Wabuda, 'Bishops and the Provision of Homilies', pp. 551–66.

[148] Thoms, p. 63.

[149] GL, MS 593/1, (1507–08), f. 4v. Landmark crosses for Rogation: Duffy, *Stripping*, p. 139.

[150] Brigden, *London*, pp. 208, 335; Haigh, *Reformations*, pp. 123–5.

[151] PRO, PROB 11/27, f. 149R; churchwarden for 1534–35. See Baillie, 'Some biographical notes on English church musicians', pp. 18–57.

[152] PRO, PROB 11/28, f. 288R.

Clymhowe's burial plans emulated a new style of burial and devotion best illustrated in the description of the burial of the alderman and draper Humphrey 'Mommorth' (Monmouth), in 1537, by Wriothesley. Protestants copied models of new piety, just as late medieval Catholics had imitated monuments and acts.[153]

> ... having neyther herse, braunches [wax], nor dirige at his buriall, but onlye 6 staffe torches, and so to be buried in the churche yeard of All Hallowes Barkin, without anye bells ringinge or priestes singinge, but onelye a sermon at his buriall made by Dr. Cromer, and after that, insteed of a Trentall, to have 30 sermons, to be made by the Bishopp of Worcester, Dr. Barnes, Dr. Cromer, and Mr. Taylor, parson of St. Peeters in Cornehill, and after everie sermon Te Deum to be songen, to give laude and praise to God for the King that hath extinguished and putt downe the power of the Bishop of Rome, and hath caused the worde of God to be preached syncerlye and trulye, and that he may so proceed that we may have the verie true knowledge of scripture as Christe taught and left to his Apostles.

Despite dropping the usual trental of masses (thirty), the testator used the same number for a new devotion. Again in 1538, Wriothesley remarked upon the use of English in the mass and the *Te Deum* 'after the sermons made by Doctor Barnes, by Thomas Rooffe, and other of theyr sect, commonly called of the Papistes the newe sect'.[154] Provisions for English services or sermons remained rare, with only four examples from male testators before 1538.

Resistance to change within parishes offset these indications of new Protestant piety in some testaments. The hesitation to adopt English Bibles and services in some parishes reflected attachment to familiar Latin services, as well as the unevenness of Protestantism's dissemination through reading, preaching and edifying. The First Royal Injunctions called for providing the whole Bible in Latin and in English, though the Second Royal Injunctions repeated the order for the whole Bible of the 'largest volume' in English. A Royal Proclamation of 1541 noted many parishes still lacked the required volume, despite Protestantism's reliance on the knowledge and reading of the Bible.[155] By 1539, St Botolph's owned a Bible of some sort, paying 2d for a chain to keep it in the church that year.[156]

The prayers and services around which parochial life revolved focused on death and the remembrance of the dead. Services for the dead

---

[153] Craig and Litzenberger, 'Wills as religious propaganda', pp. 415–31.
[154] Wriothesley, *A Chronicle of England*, Vol. I, pp. 72, 83.
[155] *VAI*, II, pp. 9, 35; footnote 1, p. 35.
[156] GL, MS 1454, Roll 53.

and prayers for them for years after also benefited the parish church and the poor, however. The provision of goods and the worship of saints, all with an eye toward purgatory, meant the church fabric was embellished and repaired. These pious practices also linked aid to needy parishioners and neighbours to the wider goals of late medieval and early sixteenth-century lay piety.

Poverty and piety

Gifts to the parish made and mended the material of the church fabric, while alms to the poor wove together the socially divided community. The problem of the 'gift', as defined by Mauss, highlights the twin characteristics of charity: it reached across social difference, yet accentuated that difference for donor and receiver.[157] Benevolence bound needy recipients and donors in a reciprocal relationship that de-emphasized the disorderliness of the poor and emphasized their closeness to Christ, even if temporarily. Testators walked a fine line between vainglory and goodwill in their charitable and pious practices. Late medieval charity tended towards 'flamboyant excesses' in burials and chantry provisions and 'limited and closely watched' parish charity and almshouses. The 'display value' of charity and the extravagance of burials and related services conflicted with the 'recognized spiritual rewards' of 'selfless giving'.[158] Purely 'selfless' giving could not exist, as each gift cycled through the society and paid spiritual or even social benefits to the donor, whether in prayers or in the esteem of neighbours. Viscountess Lisle, for instance, balanced her pious endowments and personal gifts with generous charity to the poor. She also, however, donated vestments and 24 yards of cloth with her heraldic arms to any churches without sufficient 'gear' for their priests.[159] Patronage of the parish and the poor spread her name and fame through the city.

Nearly one-third of all pious bequests (32.6 per cent or 615) were directed to the poor before 1538.[160] Many of these bequests recom-

---

[157] Mauss, *The Gift*, p. 39.

[158] Rubin argues that this conflict had developed in the twelfth and thirteenth centuries: *Charity and Community*, pp. 291–97. Analysis of funeral extravagance among Trecento Florentines in reaction to the plague: Sharon T. Strocchia, *Death and Ritual in Renaissance Florence* (Baltimore and London: Johns Hopkins University Press, 1992), pp. 55ff.

[159] PRO, PROB 11/12, fols 73L, 74R.

[160] Almsgiving was part of the process of penance for medieval Catholics and penance and confession became increasingly important in the thirteenth century: Rubin, *Charity and Community*, p. 65.

pensed the poor for participating in services to the testator's benefit, in religious rites centred on the parish. Maureen Flynn points out that wearing those gowns long after the burial transformed their wearers into 'grim reminders' of burial and death for surviving city inhabitants.[161] Hiring paupers as mourners was a form of charity that persisted before and after reform. The widespread practice of giving black gowns obligated needy neighbours, as well as company brothers and sisters, family and friends to attend or participate in processions or services. Until the end of purgatory within the English church, impoverished men and women performed a further pious service for testators: recitation of prayers. The poor might conform outwardly (answer the call for body bearers or participants, obtain gowns, and recite or mumble requested prayers) and receive their food and money without understanding or caring. Donors, however, focused on their own motivations for giving and the form of recipients' actions.

The ostentation of elaborate processions and ornate memorials performed a necessary social function: to attest to the individual's and his or her family's prominence. Reluctance to pay the exorbitant cost of a funeral and to show such extravagance publicly sprang from the fundamental contradiction of reinforcing social status and maintaining humility before God and Christ. Public display ran afoul of personal piety, but elevated the person and his or her lineage. Testators may also have balked at consuming legacies in their own burials. Pre-Reformation protest against certain forms of funereal or memorial extravagance, from the size of burial processions to the performance of month minds, shows the long and slow growth of reform, not necessarily of Reformation. Testators wrestled with their desire for worldly remembrance and their repugnance for pomp and vainglory.

Burial processions and other services surrounding death elaborately demonstrated testators' piety and charity. Up to 1538, more than half of the bequests directed to the poor who were not confined in institutions had some connection to burial or funeral services. Those confined in institutions played a negligible funerary role, garnering no more than one per cent of these types of bequests before 1538. Poor mourners carried and followed corpses to burial and attended subsequent memorial services. In the 'manner and custom of London', a man asked for ten people to carry his body to the church and 14 poor men to carry the torches and tapers that offered further intercessory power.[162] George

---

[161] Flynn, *Sacred Charity*, p. 77. 'Wills made before the mid-fourteenth century also show that the use of the poor as liturgical appendages at funeral and anniversary services was a well-established practice': Brown, *Popular Piety*, pp. 198–9.

[162] PRO, PROB 11/12, f. 4L. See Clare Gittings, 'Urban Funerals in Late Medieval and

Lovekyn, despite pleading poverty when he set up his wife's son in training, in 1503 provided 16 torches. He asked that 16 poor men carry them, bringing his corpse to its burial place in St Mary, near the font under the chapel of St George. He also hoped, if it were 'convenient', that the four orders of friars within the city would accompany him as well.[163] In the same year, Robert Hill paid priests and children to convey his body from his own parish to his burial in St Stephen's, as outlined above. He also left 4d each to 16 poor men carrying 12 torches and four tapers at the burial.[164]

The Percivales' provisions illustrated the richness of burial ritual that depended on the poor. In 1502, John Percivale, knight and late mayor of London, asked for 24 poor men, householders of St Mary Woolnoth and the ward of Langborne, to carry 24 torches. He preferred that these poor householders come first from his own craft, the tailors. He chose the men and householders by their proximity and familiarity to him: people from his parish, ward and craft who shared a social or occupational bond. These individuals were not named, however, and he was not sure how many poor men would be found from within the company.[165] Corporate familiarity existed from location and occupation, but personal anonymity remained.

Percivale proposed paying for the funeral attire of and dole for the poor by selling his own clothing and jewels, a conscious exchange of his worldly goods for the benefit of the poor and the wealth of his own soul. Each householder received 12d for their pains. Percivale asked that each say the Lady's Psalter once a week for the year. In honour of Our Lady's Five Joys, five poor householders carried five tapers, wearing gowns and earning 12d. In return for acting as representative, grateful mourners, these poor householders received the traditional gowns. At a cost of 2s 4d a yard, russet gowns with hoods made of black lining, with '*Ihn*' in white wool on the right sleeve of each, clothed each man bearing a torch. Percivale asked that Jesus' name rise the space of a hand so 'that they may turne up the sleve and cove[r] the seid holy name if it please theym'.[166] In these striking gowns, the men bore torches about his body to the church and stood through the dirige, burial and Requiem. Each also held a pair of

---

Reformation England', in Steven Bassett (ed.), *Death in Towns: Urban Responses to the Dying and the Dead, 100–1600* (Leicester, London, New York, 1992), p. 171.

[163] PRO, PROB 11/14, f. 49L.

[164] PRO, PROB 11/14, fols 56R–57L.

[165] He asked for tailors, 'if so many be had'. In doles, Brown sees favouritism to the 'local poor': *Popular Piety*, p. 197.

[166] PRO, PROB 11/13, f. 193L.

beads. Five lights surrounded his body in emulation of the Five Wounds of Christ: one at the head, two at the feet, and two at the side. The men wore these gowns well after the burial, but Percivale's provision made a gesture toward disguising their funerary role in everyday life, and therefore their impoverishment. As Mauss argued, however, 'charity is still wounding for him who has accepted it', and this elaborate testamentary provision covered the divine name, but did not erase the recipient's social status.[167]

His widow's extensive pre-burial ritual outdid her late husband's plans in stretching the imagery and the sacred, significant number patterns. Her testament supports Gittings's argument that interment carried less significance than the services that preceded it in the early modern period.[168] Developing the strength of holy numbers, her body remained in her own home for three days, with five daily masses of the Five Wounds said by a priest for 20d a day. Each other priest in attendance, saying placebo, dirige, and commendation and sprinkling holy water about her body, received 12d. While night watching over that period, poor men and women 'sayinge sadly and discretely their praiers for my soule and other soules aforesaid' enjoyed bread, drink and meat. She required them to sit, stand or kneel about her body according to their physical capabilities. The mention of physical infirmities indicated her implicit definition of the deserving and most Christ-like poor as the elderly, sick and debilitated.[169]

Dame Percivale reinforced the pious significance of 'five' in further evocations of the Five Wounds at dirige, Requiem, burial and month mind, with five poor male householders at her head, sides and feet. These poor householders also said the Psalter and dressed like the torchbearers. She linked the potency of the repeated number with refreshment for and prayers from the poor. Food and drink for the poor and sick (imprisoned in their earthly misery) paralleled the spiritual refreshment they would later provide to her soul (imprisoned in purgatory) with prayer. Like her husband, Dame Percivale requested 16 torches born by 16 poor men, chosen first from the Merchant Tailors, to bear

---

[167] Mauss, *The Gift*, p. 65.

[168] PRO, PROB 11/17, fols 218R–222L; Gittings, 'Urban Funerals', p. 171.

[169] Sixteenth-century iconography plainly identified physical infirmities with poverty: Sir Henry Unton, c. 1596 narrative portrait with detail of funeral procession, passing in front of lame and diseased poor, National Portrait Gallery; reproduction of title page from John Taylor's *The Praise, Antiquity, and commodity, of Beggery, Beggers, and Begging* (1621) in William C. Carroll, *Fat King, Lean Beggar: Representations of Poverty in the Age of Shakespeare* (Ithaca and London, 1996), p. 65; Lee Palmer Wandel *Always Among Us: Images of the Poor in Zwingli's Zurich* (Cambridge, 1990), pp. 98, 101, 102.

her body to the church. Each received a black gown with black hood and a pair of beads to say the Psalter from burial to month mind.

She also celebrated the Five Wounds by gifts to prisons 'to have my soule by prayeres refreshed'. For five years on the anniversary of her death her executors were to provide beef and mutton or 'other vittels' to prisoners in London and Southwark. Susan Brigden believes that Londoners' guilt over and compassion for the victims of usury in prison motivated these kinds of bequests. Relief of prisoners, however, mimicked the ultimate refreshment of the soul in purgatory. Before 1538, 116 (6.15 per cent) pious bequests went to prisons in and about London. Prisons remained a small, but consistent, outlet for charity through the early stages of the Reformation.[170]

Dame Percivale's eventual salvation rested upon impoverished men and women trying to recite prayers, but most importantly attending to her passage through purgatory from the moment of death through her month mind. The form of the mourning mattered more than poor intercessors' ability to recite or interest in saying prayers. Dame Percivale asked her executor, within those three days after her death, to distribute 20 marks to poor householders within her parish. In return, these poor householders said Our Lady Psalter daily from that day until the month mind. She allowed sick, selected householders to say those prayers within their own homes, providing them with 'two meles of hote goode and holsom be it fisshe or flesshe as the season requireth and good bread and good thre halpeny ale' and 8d each. An additional daily service and meal from burial until month mind took place. She left 1d in money and a meal to twenty poor householders in 'my said place and after such refrecion had ev[er]y of them to retourne to the place of my buriall and there devoutly say v pater nosters v aves and a credo orells the psalme of deprofunde such of them as can say it'.[171]

In their lifetimes, as well as in their final testaments, people seeking outlets for their charity pursued individuals who outwardly manifested disability, a potent sign of 'deservingness' before the Poor Law reified such distinctions. Lee Palmer Wandell sees a transformation of representations of the poor through the sixteenth century, their physical weakness being imbued with a 'gesture' or posture of begging, but London churchwardens and testators sought physical manifestations of

---

[170] See also PRO, PROB 11/22, f. 39L. Brigden, 'Religion and Social Obligation', p. 86; on debt limits imposed by testators: Nicholas Terpstra, 'Confraternal Prison Charity and Political Consolidation in Sixteenth-Century Bologna', *The Journal of Modern History*, 66, 2 (June 1994), pp. 223–4.

[171] PRO, PROB 11/17, f. 219L.

need in the sick, lame and elderly.[172] In his perambulation through the
history of Portsoken Ward, Stow described the 'small cottages' in which
'poor bed-rid people' lived before that land, owned by the Holy Trinity
priory, was confiscated in the Reformation. 'In my youth, I remember,
devout people, as well men as women of this city, were accustomed
oftentimes, especially on Fridays, weekly to walk that way purposely
there to bestow their charitable alms'. Testified Stow: 'every poor man
or woman lying in their bed within their window, which was towards
the street, open so low that every man might see them, a clean linen
cloth lying in their window, and a pair of beads, to show that there lay a
bed-rid body, unable but to pray only'.[173] He evoked an image of
disabled supplicants, willing to pray for charitable men and women,
marking their presence and worthiness in linen and beads.

Retired and infirm priests also received charity for praying for souls.
Poor priests encapsulated intercessory power and immediacy to Christ
and his mercy in their ideal poverty. The fraternity of St Charity and St
John the Evangelist formed the 'Priests of Pappey', poor impotent priests.
'The brethren of this house becoming lame, or otherwise into great
poverty', explained Stow in his history of London, 'were here relieved,
as to have chambers, with certain allowance of bread, drink, and coals,
and one old man and his wife to see them served and keep the house
clean'. The Priests of Papey elicited, however, few and meagre gifts,
never more than £2 for the house.[174]

Poor children occasionally figured in burial rituals because they recalled a stage of innocence and closeness to Christ.[175] As with other

---

[172] Wandel argues that the representation of beggars became 'more complex' in the
sixteenth century, not just physical infirmity, but 'a gesture, a demeanor, a condition':
Lee Palmer Wandel, *Always Among Us: Images of the Poor in Zwingli's Zurich* (Cambridge, 1990), p. 100. Cf. accounts of vagrants laming their own children to 'counterfeit'
suffering: William C. Carroll, *Fat King, Lean Beggar: Representations of Poverty in the
Age of Shakespeare* (Ithaca and London, 1996), pp. 49–51.

[173] Morley, p. 151. Also related in Archer, 'Nostalgia', p. 21.

[174] Thoms, p. 55. See also *Chantry Certificate*, pp. 50–51. Early seventeenth-century
churchwardens in Allhallows London Wall inventoried books in the parish: a 'great'
Bible, two service books, a book of homilies, Erasmus's *Paraphrases*, and the book of the
'Disputacon of the Surples', but also 'two oulde books yt sometyme belonged unto the
Pappey'; GL, MS 5090/2, f. 155. In the *Chantry Certificate*, an inventory of the goods of
the brotherhood appeared with the summary of the property of Allhallows London Wall,
p. 37.

[175] The 'delightful innocence' of children extolled by medieval preachers: Hanawalt,
Growing Up, p. 41; cf. stress on literature of youthful sins: Ilana Krausman Ben-Amos,
Adolescence and Youth in Early Modern England (New Haven and London, 1994), pp.
11–14. Griffiths argues for nuanced consideration of children's 'malleability' and lack of
discretion, but also for the balance between original sin and innocence: Paul Griffiths,

categories of the deserving poor, innocent children wearing surplices or gowns with lights in hand and orderly processing displayed the testators' charity. Testators did not always identify the social status or institutional affiliation of these children before the Reformation. Charitable schools educating poor children to participate in the music and pageantry of the city existed in the early sixteenth century. Stow described Paul's School, built 'in place of an old ruined house, built in most ample manner, and largely endowed, in the year 1512, by John Colet, Doctor of Divinity, Dean of Paul's, for one hundred and fifty-three men's children'.[176] Many parishes regularly used children in their choirs, paying conducts to teach children to sing.[177]

The widow Maude Gowsell, in 1523, asked that 15 children carry 15 tapers to her burial in the cloister of St Mary's when the hearse formed. Hearses took many forms, some more elaborate than others, but in general provided a canopy over the body, normally coffined, and offered a convenient place for torches placed about the body. Parishioners and strangers could hire hearse cloths from parishes, as can be seen by the hearse cloth in the inventory of St Stephen Walbrook in 1558.[178] The tapers Gowsell endowed burned to the honour of God, Mary and the saints. Mindful of her own social status and its public importance even after her death, she requested that her body return to earth 'w[i]t[h] all suche dewyn sarwys as belongeth for me to have'.[179] In 1528, Jasper Shukburgh, who worshipped saints and wanted a pulpit, forwent torches at his burial. He still planned a dramatic burial, with 60 children of about 12 years in age bearing tapers about the hearse, standing by the church wall in their white surplices, and following the corpse into the churchyard. In return, each child received 3d.[180] Further, each child from Cornhill ward who came to the churchyard on St Hilary Day would receive figs, raisins and other fruits.[181] In 1531, William Bareham asked for ten children to carry ten one-pound tapers to his burial.[182]

Youth and Authority: Formative Experiences in England, 1560–1640 (Oxford, 1996), pp. 54, 58.

[176] Schools were founded in 1393 in St Paul's, St Martin le Grand, St Mary le Bow, St Dunstan's in the West, and St Anthony's. Schools were founded in 1394 in St Andrew in Oldbourne, Allhallows the Great, St Peter Cornhill, and in the hospital of St Thomas Acons: Morley, p. 100; Thoms, p. 28.

[177] Teaching singing children in St Mary Woolnoth: *Chantry Certificate*, p. 26, n. 3.

[178] GL, MS 3103, f. 32.

[179] GL, MS 9171/10, f. 47.

[180] GL, MS 9171/10, f. 116v.

[181] GL, MS 9171/10, f. 117.

[182] GL, MS 9171/11, f. 9.

Other vaguely defined groups may also have been poor recipients charged with pious duties. Ambiguous contexts suggest that many widows, goodwives and goodmen, not described as poor, or called friend, servant or relative, may have been poor. Goodwives and goodmen were likely aged as well.[183] A widow might simply have been a widow's good friend, but she might also have been a well-known, needy woman within a parish. More than half of gifts directed to goodwives, goodmen and widows before 1538 were in money. Gowns, directly related to burial processions, and other articles of clothing made the next significant category of bequests, with some rings that went to social peers. The used clothing bequeathed by testators might have been tokens of affection to friends or charitable bequests to needy, older men and women who could not outfit themselves. Rings emphasized friendship and lasting remembrance after the funeral services.

Some servants may have been downright poor, but many at least occupied social strata below their employers'. Employing kin and 'cousin' presented another way to provide aid to poor relatives or help a relative immigrate to London. Whatever their background, testators sought to help their servants marry or to survive until they found their next position. Money gifts for wages and dowries were the most bequests to servants and apprentices (69 per cent, or 195), with gowns far behind (14 per cent, or 41) before 1538. Testators supported former servants and apprentices with money and handed out a few gifts for gowns.

Outfitting burial processions comprised only one funeral expenditure. Food, however, often accounted for half the sum spent on funerals, 'the most expensive single item in a funeral account'.[184] Expenditure on food at funerals guaranteed spiritual refreshment (in remembrance and prayers) to the dead alongside literal refreshment to the living. Clare Gittings argues that funerals attended more to the needs of the living than the dead, but this interpretation does not place enough importance on the expectation of pious repayment of the meal by the living before the abolition of the doctrine of purgatory. Overseers of the Poor after the Reformation paid for food and drink at paupers' funerals in recognition of the benefit of bringing people together for remembrance, even if no longer for prayers.[185] Provision of meals and doles recalled hospi-

---

[183] Descriptions of age are notoriously imprecise, as are the various titles used to delineate stages of the life-cycle: Schen, 'Strategies of Poor Aged Women and Widows in Sixteenth-Century London' in Lynn Botelho and Pat Thane (eds), *Women and Ageing in British Society since 1500* (Harlow, 2001), pp. 15–16.

[184] Gittings, 'Urban Funerals', p. 176. Leaving food on graves to be eaten later by family, priest and the poor: Flynn, *Sacred Charity*, p. 67.

[185] Gittings, 'Urban Funerals', p. 176.

tality of the church and the aristocracy, a late medieval tradition prevalent in the countryside. The model of hospitality, primarily aristocratic, encompassed strangers, friends, travellers and the poor. The celebrated hospitality of the medieval period nevertheless saw some lords or ladies of the manor separating him- or herself from the poor by appointing an almoner to give charity at the gate.[186] Aspects of this idealized, face-to-face charity survived in doles in London before the Reformation. Even the first act punishing vagabonds and beggars in 1531 made exception for the doles connected to burials and obits.[187]

Attitudes and laws infringing on traditional practices undermined doles and Catholic mendicancy, but buttressed the importance of charity. To many reformers doles represented indiscriminate Catholic charity that, some feared, encouraged bands of beggars and vagabonds to progress noisily from funeral dole to funeral dole, across parish bounds. Vagabonds, but also 'ravenous wolves', bishops, abbots, priests and monks, and the 'counterfeit-holy' abused almsgiving, so that honest bede men were left miserable while the idle poor wreaked havoc in the country.[188] To combat 'abuse' of doles, the 1536 act for the 'Punishment of Sturdy Vagabonds and Beggars' tried to replace them with gifts to the poor box, the 'chest to comfortyn of the pov[er]tye' that was to replace the once customary bequests to the high altar for forgotten tithes.[189] The poor box allowed churchwardens and vestrymen to mete out charity to the deserving poor. As the numbers of doles declined, however, the new collection elicited little testamentary support. It may have drawn primarily lifetime giving, however, in response to the 1536 Injunctions instructing priests to urge parishioners to give to the poor, rather than to traditional devotions. Clergy were to instruct parishioners and pilgrims so 'that they do rather apply themselves to the keeping of God's commandments and fulfilling of His works of charity' than to 'superstitious' practices. Further, they were to tell them 'that it shall profit more their soul's health, if they do bestow that on the poor and needy, which they would have bestowed upon the said images or relics'.[190]

Discrimination between the deserving and undeserving, orderly and disorderly poor in late medieval and early sixteenth-century England

---

[186] Heal, *Hospitality*, p. 33.

[187] An Act concerning punishment of beggars and vagabonds, 22 Hen. VIII c.12; Paul Slack, *The English Poor Law, 1531–1782* (Cambridge, 1995).

[188] 'The Beggars' Petition against Popery', presented to Henry VIII, 1538: Baron John Somers, *A Collection of Scarce and Valuable Tracts* (London, 1809), pp. 41–8.

[189] 28 Hen. VIII c. 6.

[190] *VAI*, II, p. 6.

laid the foundations for later reformers' actions.[191] 'People were able to accommodate conflicting evaluations in their minds'; Rubin asserts, 'they might give charity in church, yet scoff at a beggar in the streets'.[192] As early as 1503, William Capell, draper and mayor of London, 'caused a cage in every ward to be set for punishing of vagabonds'.[193] Before 1525, testators identified the deserving poor by restricting gifts to those with need, good reputation, and modest debts for prisoners awaiting redemption. The clerk Petyr Drayton left £6 13s 4d to the poor, 'willinge that por householders and most impotent persones shalbe principally releved by it'.[194] Most testators allowed, even encouraged the executor's discretion in giving to the miserable, blind, impotent, sick, and so on. William Game left the residue of his estate to 'pour persones lame blind bedered impotent por maidens mariages to be maried in the church of St Mighell aforsaid' and to prisoners. He charged his executors 'to doo other like charitie and almesse dedes where as most nede or necessitie shalbe for the comforte and consolacion of my soule and all Christian soules and as they wolde be doon for in caase like'.[195]

The slow movement away from the face-to-face charity of funeral doles that began in the 1530s suggests that city inhabitants were still defining the deserving and undeserving poor. Charity, Heal has argued, was shifting from 'mutual amity' within a community to donations to others, 'readily articulated in monetary terms'.[196] The monetary nature of relief does not fully explain the transition, however, since bequests of money, food and clothing continued through the sixteenth century. Even with the collection of rates within parishes, churchwardens provided bread, cheese, meat and drink from parish funds and bequests left to their discretion.[197] In fact, some testators and parishes may have preferred gifts in kind, to prevent the 'disorderly' from spending their cash alms in taverns.

Although churchwardens eventually distributed funds collected through the poor box, before 1538 all bequests left to another's discretion rested on the conscience of the executor. Some testators, however,

---

[191] Archer, *Pursuit*, p. 203; Slack, *Poverty and Policy*. Historians generally agree upon a transformation in attitudes to the poor and relief from the late medieval through the Tudor–Stuart period.

[192] The relative prosperity and mobility of workers and the poor in the medieval period, during a time of labour shortage, contributed to contemporaries' distrust of the poor : Rubin, *Charity and Community*, p. 98.

[193] Stow, *A Survay of London*, p. 194.

[194] PRO, PROB 11/19, f. 65L.

[195] PRO, PROB 11/21, f. 317L.

[196] Heal, *Hospitality*, pp. 15–16.

[197] See Chapter 3.

feared that their executors and overseers would neglect their duties to the detriment of the souls of testators and others. Testators used reminders of conscience, friendship and holy censure to cajole executors. Alice Hamarsley, widow of a citizen and clothworker, left the residue of her goods to her executor to distribute to the 'poore and needy in Cornehill warde truylie and uprightlie, bytwixte god and his conscience'.[198] All executors would find themselves in need of an executor or two who would reciprocate the favour of seeing a will performed carefully. To bypass the problem of unreliable ones, Stow urged *inter vivos* giving. He wrote:

> I wish men to make their own hands their executors, and their eyes their overseers, not forgetting the old proverb: – for
> 'Women be forgetfull, children be unkind,
> Executors be covetous, and take what they find,
> If any body aske where the dead's goods became,
> They answere. So God me help, and holy done, he died a poore man'.[199]

His concern about women's memory of their first husbands' wishes was reflected in an Italian traveller's commentary of c. 1500. A scheming widow

> usually bestows herself in marriage upon one of those apprentices living in the house who is most pleasing to her, and who was probably not *displeasing* to her in the lifetime of her husband; and in his power she places all her own fortune, as well as that of her children, who are sent away as apprentices into other houses.[200]

The visitor believed that the custom of London granted widows too much control over the property of children, a 'corrupt practice' that cheated sons and allowed widows to remarry without bringing 'any discredit to a woman'. The 'ancient and laudable custom of London' urged male testators to divide their goods into three: one part to wives, one among the children, and the last to selves for charity and the performance of wills.[201] A later defence of the custom emphasized the wife's vulnerability to her husband's cheating in a city in which so much property was in moveables rather than land. In case the philosophical and biblical references to the strengths of women and marriage could

---

[198] GL, MS 9171/11, f. 198.

[199] Thoms, p. 44.

[200] *A Relation of the Island of England, c.1500*, Camden Society, Vol. 37 (London, 1847), pp. 26–7. Criticism of the Italian visitor's impression of English families: Hanawalt, *Growing Up*, pp. 146–7.

[201] Reference to the custom: PRO, PROB 11/24, fols 49R–50L. Also see Thomson, 'Piety and Charity', p. 181.

not convince husbands to preserve the custom, the author added the caveat that no man should be superstitiously attached to his worldly, temporal, transitory goods.[202]

Some testamentary evidence suggests that mothers and wives behaved quite differently than Stow or the commentator warned, and that dying husbands entrusted their widows with 'rule' over property and children. Through 1538, 66.67 per cent (88) of male testators named their wives executrices. These widows sustained business activity and oversaw their children's inheritances, secular responsibilities endued with injunctions to fulfil the pious and non-pious bequests of testators' wills. The citizen and organ maker William Wake, in 1517, left his wife half of his goods and tools, including an organ case for her to sell with the advice of his overseer, to pay his debts and provide for his soul's health.[203] In 1527, Joane Croughton, who had remarried, made an extraordinary testament, naming her husband executor. She required him to sell her house and lands in Derbyshire to the greatest advantage of her son Robert Waite, and to the wealth of her soul. She asked to be buried by her first husband.[204] Elisabeth Warley, widow of a goldsmith, left a great balance and weights to her son-in-law Robert Spicer. She asked her representatives and executors to collect the debt still owed her by members of the staple at Westminster.[205] Johan Devereux, for one, did grant her deceased husband's gown to her apprentice, along with some diaper linens and a year of his apprenticeship, rather common bequests to a servant or apprentice.[206]

While this database identifies children as a 'non-pious' target of testamentary bequests, the category is not a secular one. Settling one's estate and seeing to children's inheritance and upbringing were important Christian duties. Testators provided for their children and secured remembrance of themselves through bequests. The need to outline inheritances explains the greater number of non-pious over pious bequests.[207] Before 1538, money, household goods, leases or land, plate, clothing, goods in shops and residues of estates comprised 64 per cent (181) of gifts to children. Gifts directly related to remembrance or prayers, like gowns, rings, beads, jewellery, spoons, masers, goblets,

---

[202] A Breefe Discourse, declaring and approuing the necessarie and inviolable maintenance of the laudable Customes of London, printed by Henrie Midleton for Rafe Newberie (London, 1584) STC 16747, reprinted New York, 1973, pp. 25–6, 38–9.

[203] GL, MS 9171/9, f. 51.

[204] PRO, PROB 11/22, f. 138L. Married women needed their husbands' permission to write a will.

[205] PRO, PROB 11/24, f. 38R.

[206] GL, MS 9171/10, f. 262v.

[207] 2213 non-pious bequests to 1887 pious bequests.

comprised 24 per cent (47). In this period, testators infrequently left books to sons and daughters, as Viscountess Lisle did in leaving books and other goods to her son to be shared with his three 'noble' sisters. If he died, she asked that the twelve books be divided between her daughters Elizabeth Gray and Anne Willoughby.[208] The scrivener John Pyne left the books in his study to the care of his executor, to be given to his sons 'from tyme to tyme as they be disposede and willing to lerne and can occupie them'.[209] In 1536, the mercer Thomas Compton left a primer of gold and silver to his master's daughter.[210] The 'social breadth' of primers, their 'range and variety', and more widespread printing, would suggest that at least some of the untitled books in wills were primers.[211]

Testators remembered extended, adopted, or honorary family members in their last wills, although social status predetermined on what grounds children were adopted or accepted as godchildren. Dame Percivale named the male children 'which I have brought upp of alms', 'Bonefortune' and 'Penyfather', proclaiming their humble status and her charity. She had also raised two maid children, to whom she gave no surnames, but to whom she left ten marks at their age of twenty-one, as she had done for the boys.[212] Women's maternal roles and their presence at lyings-in seem to have broadened their interest in remembering godchildren.[213] A godparent was also known as 'God Sibling' or 'Gossip', though by the seventeenth century women who attended childbirth were called 'gossips'.[214] Perhaps in the early sixteenth century women acted as godparents more frequently than men, since female testators supported sixteen goddaughters and thirteen godsons, while male testators remembered only four goddaughters, but eighteen godsons. These female 'God Siblings' may have attended these children's births. Perhaps fathers' and husbands' focus on inheritance, especially through primogeniture, made them less inclined to spread their gifts across the sexes or to remember godchildren. Only a few gifts went to aunts and uncles, although testators might not have identified them as such. Compared to the case from Terling, these relatives drew less attention in the city, perhaps because the city had

---

[208] PRO, PROB 11/12, f. 73R.

[209] PRO, PROB 11/24, f. 49R.

[210] PRO, PROB 11/25, f. 269R.

[211] Duffy, *Stripping*, p. 211. Primers afforded the 'lay devotee some approximation to the order and tranquillity of monastic piety': ibid., p. 210.

[212] PRO, PROB 11/17, f. 220L.

[213] Hanawalt, *Growing Up*, pp. 45–51; Mendelson and Crawford, *Women*, pp. 153–4.

[214] Mack, *Visionary Women*, p. 29, note 36.

weakened extended family ties.[215] More gifts, largely in money, went to nieces and nephews, however. Sisters and brothers, including those called 'in-laws', received money (56 per cent, or 71), gowns (17 per cent, or 28), and other miscellaneous gifts (39 per cent, or 63), before 1538.

Gifts to kin included poor kin. Poor kin survived discrimination in charity since they were known at least by name, connected to the testator's life, and presumably worthy of aid. In addition to poor kin, however, testators considered kinfolk and 'cousins' in their wills. 'Cousins' represented a range of people close to the testator: friends, cousins and family. Before 1538, out of gifts to those identified as kin or cousin, but not labelled 'poor', more than half took the form of money. The next two leading categories of gifts to these individuals were gowns and rings. Even if not explicitly outlined in wills, gowns normally carried an obligation to attend a burial, or participate in processions. Others identified as friends and neighbours received money (39 per cent, or 127), gowns (31 per cent, or 99), rings (15 per cent, or 50), and other gifts (15 per cent, or 48) before 1538. While participants in a different stage of a burial procession, these bequests to friends and extended family resemble the ones that reached the poor to usher the testator's body from church to grave and onward through purgatory.

Donations to parishes and to the relief of the poor exemplified the connection between piety and charity in early sixteenth-century London. These gifts bridged the social differences within parochial boundaries, but purposefully did not overcome them. Parishioners and testators distinguished between the deserving and undeserving poor when selecting individuals or groups for charitable help. Their discrimination, and even self-interest in gift-giving, did not diminish the pious significance of charity.

Conclusion

The priest Roger Tonneshende's will of 1538 sets the stage for understanding the vast institutional changes brought by the Reformation in the late 1530s and after. Tonneshende opened his will with an invocation to God and Jesus, highlighting Christ's passion and bloodshed, hoping to be the 'p[ar]taker of the unspeakable Joyes of the everlasting inheritaunce prepared for me'. Despite his confidence in salvation through

---

[215] Keith Wrightson and David Levine, *Poverty and Piety in an English Village: Terling, 1525–1700* (New York, 1979), p. 92.

Jesus, he still hoped to be the 'p[ar]taker of the charitable prayers of all the saints', an old-style appeal to intercession allowed within the Henrician church. Tonneshende acted as an agent of the Reformation, helping to dismantle some of the institutions of the pre-Reformation church, but he profited little from the suppression of religious houses. He found himself in debt to the king's officials, having been paid only a penny for his work in the suppression. His will pleaded with them to show some consideration for his efforts and his debts at his death.

The gifts left in his testament echo his interest in new religious ideas. The priest left books to friends, colleagues and parish churches outside London in 1538. To his nephew, he left £20 towards his learning and all his Latin humanities books. Further, to a fellow of Queen's College, Cambridge, he left his new course of 'St Austen [Augustine] in Basel print' and a 'new course' of Saint John, Chrysostom. Significantly, he left an English Bible with a chain to three parishes so that the people could hear and read the same 'reverently' and thereby increase in the 'fear and love of God' in Protestant fashion.[216] This bequest contrasts with the priest Molinars, who left books only to his fellow priests, not to any particular parish. Protestantism may have strengthened the identification of priests or ministers with their congregations. Tonneshende followed the 'new ways', being guided by faith and the scriptures, but the course and the agents of Protestant reform in London left him behind.

The largely homogeneous form and ingredients of testaments in this period illustrates the unity of purpose and practice before the broadest changes of the Reformation. Wills before 1538 integrated pious plans for masses and prayers with bequests for the poor and for the repair of bridges and highways. A few wills revealed the gradual infiltration of the new ways and ideas of Protestantism that, when accepted, led to changes in contemporaries' approaches to charity. Below the level of parochial experience, testamentary evidence supports Christopher Haigh's claims that parish religious life changed little with the first wave of reform under Henry VIII. Wills indicate that religious reform wrought few changes in the *mentalités* of London inhabitants in these parishes. Reformers urged relief to the poor in place of money left for the veneration of images, but testators continued to express their piety mainly through traditional services and burials and the saints, ornaments and fraternities of the parish.

---

[216] PRO, PROB 11/27, fols 170L–170R. Preamble: 170L; rest: 170R.

CHAPTER THREE

The old and the new ways: wills and charity, 1539–1580

Charity and alms to the poor in pre-Reformation England fulfilled Catholic injunctions to perform good works, for the forgiveness of sins. Even after the beginning of the Protestant Reformation, however, official pronouncements coerced and cajoled relief of the poor, still seen as a pious Christian imperative. The years 1539 to 1580 ushered in a pattern of pious giving that stressed charitable bequests to the poor, although testators gave the greatest weight to gifts for friends, family, servants and associates, all connected by non-pious ties. Charity remained a significant component of piety, but testators began to emphasize their worldly or secular connections.

Reformers attacked not only the notion of 'good works', but also the doctrine of purgatory. These theological changes, coupled with the demise of pre-Reformation religious institutions, forced testators to alter final pious and non-pious bequests. The mediation of perpetual masses and the iconography of saints were removed after 1547, preventing testators from endowing chantries or cycles of traditional religious services to speed their souls through purgatory. The 1547 Royal Articles of Edward VI, however, protected testamentary bequests to the poor and differentiated (at least ideally) between property left to the poor and that left to 'superstitious' uses. One article asked whether any executors did not distribute the goods of the dead properly, 'especially such goods as were given and bequeathed and appointed to be distributed among the poor people, repairing of highways, finding of poor scholars, or marriage of poor maids'.[1]

The Reformation led Londoners and others in England to try to allow some flexibility in their final bequests, reflecting the wariness of testators regarding present and future religious doctrine. Although Scarisbrick has argued that the Reformation caught contemporaries unawares, testators' conditional phrases, like 'if the laws will allow it', demonstrated consciousness of the time's uncertainty.[2] Some testators tried to stipulate that money or goods reach family or charitable ends instead if

---

[1] *VAI*, II, p. 112.

[2] Scarisbrick, *Reformation and the English People*, p. 17; Brown, *Popular Piety*, pp. 234–5.

practices were outlawed, but religious and legal change prevented executors from shifting resources after their initial disbursement. The insecurity of reform, besides affecting will-making, muddled the relationship of the poor and the rest of society. The overall trend, in burials and celebrations in London, suggests a separation of rich and poor within parish, craft and the city – another facet of what historians have considered a watershed in English culture.[3]

Change in mid-sixteenth-century London appeared not only in religion, but also in the economic and demographic structure of the city. In 1552, inflation hit a high point in a city that by 1550 had begun its demographic explosion. Rising population added to anxiety about poverty and order, whether crime, prostitution and the threat of fire had quantitatively increased or inhabitants only feared they had. The instability of mid-century England, with rapid turnovers in the monarchy and ongoing religious transformations, created sixteenth-century Londoners' *mentalités*.

A few prominent citizens left their mark on their parishes, notably Sir Martin Bowes and Philip Gunter, and help us to peer into the religious uncertainty that marked mid-century. Bowes, goldsmith, knight, alderman, governor of hospital and Lord Mayor (1545–46), was a civic and parochial leader in St Mary Woolnoth who balanced Catholic and Protestant devotion, in tune with prevailing doctrines. Gunter, of St Michael Cornhill, did likewise in his long life. The skinner Thomas Hunt and Anne, his widow, show enthusiasm for puritanism, a growing sentiment in Elizabethan London, and for the charitable and pious contributions that tended to distinguish wealthy donors.[4]

---

[3] 'For urban communities in particular, the middle and later years of the sixteenth century represented a more abrupt break with the past than any period since the era of the Black Death or before the age of industrialization': Phythian-Adams, 'Ceremony and the Citizen', p. 57. Peter Burke describes the 'profound differences in world view' between the elite and the 'lower classes' by 1800, although popular culture showed 'resilience' against the reforms attempted by, first, the clergy and, later, the laity: *Popular Culture in Early Modern Europe* (New York, 1978), pp. 242, 270.

[4] For information on Bowes: 'Appendix B' in Carol Kazmierczak Manzione, *Christ's Hospital of London, 1552–1598: 'A Passing Deed of Pity'* (Selinsgrove, PA and London, 1995), p. 164. Hickman calls him a man of 'highly conservative religious opinions', 'From Catholic to Protestant', p. 128. See Ann Hughes on revisionist criticism of oppositional Puritanism: 'Introduction' to 'Anglo-American Puritanisms', *JBS*, 39, 1 (Jan. 2000), pp. 2–3.

Reform, restoration and survivals

A cluster of measures prior to 1539 constituted the last significant religious reforms under Henry VIII. The Second Royal Injunctions of 1538 under Henry VIII outlined religious changes beyond the reform of 1536. The 1538 Injunctions called for a Bible in English, not one in English and Latin, although an act of 1543 prohibited Bible reading by women, apprentices, servants and others of low degree to prevent their misunderstanding of it.[5] The Injunctions also struck down the practice of endowing and burning candles before images and other lights in the church, except in the rood loft, before the sacrament of the altar, and around the sepulchre at Easter. Images, instructed the document, spurred remembrance, but did not signify objects of pilgrimage or worship.[6] Although the doctrinal distinction recast the official purpose of images and lights, popular piety may have preserved older meanings and ends. Rules about images and lights coincided with the suppression of religious houses in 1538. At this point, Haigh argues, Henry 'stopped the Reformation dead', retreating from both Lutherans and Lutheranism.[7] In the first year of Edward's reign, parishioners in St Botolph's gathered 3s 3d for the light 'callyd the beme lyght', the only remaining of a row of lights once in front of the image of Christ on the rood screen.[8]

Edward VI's reign, however, brought the Reformation back to life, and wrought deep changes in parochial religious life. Interrogatories asked the fate of bequests for lamps, tapers and candles. Parochial lay organizations and Catholic clerics and hermits fell with the abolition of purgatory. Some chantries were confiscated in 1546, but the 1547 Chantries Act seized endowments for masses and outlawed religious services, particularly those relating to prayers for souls in purgatory.[9] Although religious houses had fallen in the late 1530s, the cells of anchors remained scattered about London. The anchoress Katherine Man gave up her cell attached to Blackfriars in the 1548 confiscation of religious property, for a 20s pension.[10] St Botolph's paid 'Sir Gregory', apparently one of the parish priests, wages and a 'benevolence' as late as 1550–51, and granted a stipend to the former clerk

---

[5] Apparently not followed: William Page, ed., *VCH: London* (Folkestone and London, 1974), p. 285.

[6] *VAI*, II, pp. 34–43, esp. p. 38.

[7] Haigh, *English Reformations*, p. 152. Wabuda argues for Henry's conservatism in the early 1540s: 'Bishops and the Provision of Homilies', p. 564.

[8] GL, MS 1454, Roll 54. Duffy, 'The parish, piety, and patronage', p. 136.

[9] Edward's Royal Injunctions (1547): *VAI*, II, pp. 114–30, 112; Kreider, *English Chantries*.

[10] *VCH: London*, p. 588.

Leonard. These wages would once have been tied to those prayers and masses, but now reflected the last payments to unconverted priests and clerks. The following year a widow rented the former priest's chamber, completing the dislocation of Catholic clergy from parishes and churchwardens' attempts to put parochial property to new money-generating uses.[11] Despite the official eschewal of purgatory and the displacement of people who provided prayers for souls, however, a testator might still solicit them. Fowk Pygott in 1552 expected his wife to bestow the residue of his estate for the 'glorie of god and the helth and profytt of my soule'.[12]

Edward's actions affected not only the staffing of churches, but also their ornamentation. Images were to come down 'so that there remain no memory of the same in walls, glass windows, or elsewhere', according to Edward's Injunctions, but under Henry worship of images ('idolatry') had only been curtailed.[13] The severity of these changes regarding traditional iconography caught some Londoners by surprise. Even in 1546 a London citizen and merchant tailor had left a canopy to cover the sacrament and a cross worth 26s 8d to a Nottingham parish, as well as copes and masses for souls for one year, not anticipating the removal of images and the prohibition of prayers for souls.[14] Parishes, not just individuals, reacted to these injunctions with varying speed. Iconoclasm in St Mary Woolnoth predated the last observations of obits and other services. Workers removed the irons before the high altar, took down the image of St George, installed 'newe glas at thende of the churche where Saint Mighell stode waying soules', and whited the church in 1546–47. More images in stained glass and plate came down or were sold when services ceased. The church brought down the rood in 1547–48, and spent 6d on a 'barell to put in the glas' to keep the church tidy during the renovations.[15]

Dismantling images followed in other parishes in London, gradually altering the interiors of churches by removing saints and inserting the Word. The end to purgatory and the intercessory power of the saints remade (or 'stripped') churches and slowly reformed inward piety by outward conformity.[16] A mason removed the stones on which holy images once stood and a workman received 16d for 'takynge downe

---

[11] GL, MS 1454, Roll 57 and preceding, Roll 58.

[12] PRO, PROB 11/35, fols 88L–88R. On purgatory: 'A Draft for Visitation Articles' (1549), VAI, II, p. 194 and p. 194, footnote 4.

[13] VAI, II, p. 126.

[14] PRO, PROB 11/31, f. 164R.

[15] GL, MS 1002/1A, fols 44–44v, 45v–46, 47v–48.

[16] Taken from Duffy, Stripping.

mary & John in the Rood loft' in St Michael Cornhill in 1547–48. The painter Mr Hether earned £15 there for painting scriptures about the church and 5s for putting the 'table', probably the Ten Commandments, above the poor man's box. 'Weytyng' the church cost £3 10s and costs related to painting the rood, perhaps with scriptures, amounted to 33s 4d.[17] The parish made these immediate alterations, but removals continued over a few years. The inventory of ornaments sold in the accounts of 1549–50 included mainly vestments and altar cloths to the total of £48 8s 4d. A mason paid 6s for the stone cross and tomb of 'Mr' Sutton that same year.[18]

Edward claimed property given to endow the 'fabric' or services of late medieval Catholicism. The King confiscated some plate and property related to 'superstitious' uses or the saints, particularly the goods adorning shrines and other ornaments, pictures and paintings. In providing a perpetual salary for an assistant to the choir in St Botolph's, however, he may have reimbursed the parish for confiscated goods.[19] These claims precipitated disputes between crown and parishes later in the century, but, in the meantime, caused parishes to convert chantry property into funds for the poor and for buildings that generated revenue. Parishes also sold the images and plate to purchase or build chambers and tenements, transforming iconography into real estate that sustained the church and its responsibilities. St Michael's, for instance, sold 322¼ ounces of plate to the goldsmith Thomas Mustian for £80 5s 3d and purchased ten chambers in the churchyard on 17 August 1548 with the proceeds. Noteworthy pieces included 'one ymage of o[u]r lady & an angell all gylt' of 66 ounces, a gilt pix, and a gilt 'crosse w[i]t[h] Mari & John' weighing 110 ounces. The following year the parish paid for taking down six more altars, some of which were likely related to the parish's vibrant guild life prior to reform.[20] St Botolph's suffered from its usual disorderly accounting and sought to trace the sale of curtains, hangings, altars and altar stones in 1551–52, finding resolution in June 1552.[21]

The conversion and confiscation of property in St Michael Cornhill demonstrated how the cityscape, as well as the interiors of churches,

---

[17] Statues of Mary and John stood on either side of the crucifix on the rood: Duffy, 'Parish, piety, and patronage', p. 133. GL, MS 4071/1, fols 27, 28–29. Bonner on later commands to undo scripture painting: *VAI*, II, p. 354 and p. 354, footnote 2.

[18] GL, MS 4071/1, fols 33, 34. The churchwardens probably should have said 'Dr [William] Sutton', the late medieval parson of St Stephen's who had been implicated in a plot against King Henry VII, but forgiven: Fabyan, *The Great Chronicle*, p. 256.

[19] GL, MS 1454, Roll 56 (1549–50) and successive years. The wage for two years was £10 10s and later £7.

[20] GL, MS 4071/1, fols 29v, 32.

[21] GL, MS 1454, Roll 58.

could be degraded after the Reformation. John Stow may have nostalgically recalled the ancient monuments of parishes, but he also bitingly criticized mismanagement of parochial resources and ruin of aesthetically pleasing spaces. His godparents, grandfather and parents had been buried in the church, helping to explain his chagrin at its altered appearance by the late sixteenth century. He regretted the parish church's efforts to alleviate their financial losses by building in the churchyard and against the walls.[22] He said of St Michael's,

> This hath been a fair and beautiful church, but of late years, since the surrender of their lands to Edward VI, greatly blemished by the building of lower tenements on the north side thereof towards the high street, in place of a green churchyard, whereby the church is darkened, and other ways annoyed

He also noted that the parish foolishly released property donated by Lady Lisle for an obit, but with rents from the messuage also intended for the use of the poor and for church repairs. 'The parishioners since gave it up as chantry land, and wronged themselves'. The churchwardens and parochial leaders, inconceivably to Stow, neglected to pursue a bequest dating to 1548 that similarly paid for repairs to the church and relief of the poor. ' ... But the parish never had the gift, nor heard thereof by the space of forty years after, such was the conscience of G. Barne and other executors to conceal it to themselves; and such is the negligence of the parishioners, that being informed thereof, make no claim thereunto'.[23]

Removal of 'superstitious' church goods and ornaments continued into the 1550s as parishioners reluctantly fulfilled reform or, more simply, staggered the costs of compliance. In St Michael's receipts and payments increased into the hundreds of pounds as the parish sold goods and paid for renovations and labour about the church.[24] Churchwardens brought in less than £20 in receipts in 1547–48, but more than £305 in 1550–51. In those years they spent, respectively, roughly £27 and about £299. In the accounts of 1550–51, the churchwardens of St Michael's paid two men 'for takyng downe of ye glasse in ye wyndos' and in the next accounts took down the rood loft itself, even though

---

[22] Although plainer interiors may have meant lower costs for church maintenance, other categories of spending increased for parishes, especially in the area of poor relief: Gibbs, 'New duties for the parish community in Tudor London', in *The Parish*, pp. 168–69, and graph, p. 164.

[23] Morley, p. 204–6.

[24] GL, MS 4071/1, fols 27, 27v, 37v, 39. Caroline Litzenberger, 'St Michael's, Gloucester, 1540–1580: the cost of conformity in sixteenth-century England' in *The Parish*, p. 235.

Christ, Mary and John had already been removed. In 1552–53 the churchwardens sold, for 12s, a couple of old vestments and altar cloths that seem to have belonged to the brotherhood of St Michael in the parish.[25]

In the absence of images and familiar services, testators' gifts to parish church repairs and 'werks' declined greatly after 1548, arguably causing a 'crisis in parochial religion'.[26] Plainer services and the suppression of plays and guilds described in the last chapter may have fostered neglect of the church fabric by removing popular festivals and causing parishioners to hesitate before bequeathing ornaments to the church. Between 1500 and 1548, churches received 92 bequests from 55 testators (23.71 per cent of all testators) for repairs, but after 1548 they received only 12 from eight testators (1.77 per cent). Even before 1548, parishes had inventively financed necessary repairs, suggesting that some of the sell-off of Catholic goods may have recycled older plate, eventually replaced with new plate.

Perhaps parishioners were less shocked by the initial sales than later historians and may have perpetuated the memory of parochial benefactors. Mid-century leaders might have personally known their Catholic forerunners. The churchwardens of St Mary Woolnoth sold their old plate for £64 6s 8d to Thomas Bowes in 1543–44, carefully noting the donors and the weight of each piece. In a vestry in December 1544, his father, the alderman Sir Martin Bowes, and other vestrymen directed the proceeds toward the repair of the church's timbers, leading, mortar and steeple. When the box had been replenished, Sir Martin Bowes and others were to buy like plate 'with remembraunce wherby the donours of the saide plate nowe solde may be had in contynuall prayer and remembrance like as theire intent was at the gyving of the same plate so nowe solde'.[27] Guardians of the church fabric saw the objects themselves as less important than donors' intentions to keep their parishes in good repair and well furnished.

The implements of services, the books of the church, and language changed under Edward, alongside these alterations of the church setting. The Church employed full English services beginning in 1548 and by 1549 the Book of Common Prayer supplanted the Latin services of earlier reform. Other devotional books in English followed. St Michael

---

[25] GL, MS 4071/1, fols 38v, 41, 41v.

[26] A crisis in parish finances and a 'collapse of allegiance' to Edwardian churches: Haigh, *English Reformations*, pp. 181–2; need for repairs, with sale of parish goods outdated by the Reformation to pay for them: Duffy, *Stripping*, p. 486; Whiting, *Blind Devotion*, pp. 94–5.

[27] GL, MS 1002/1A, fols 21v, 30v. Jones, 'Living the Reformations', pp. 273–4.

purchased eight Psalters in English in 1548 for 6s 8d. The churchwardens by 1548 purchased new songbooks and Erasmus's *Paraphrases* with a chain to hold it and paid the schoolmaster of Paul's to translate the mass and the Benedictus into English. As a further sign of the parish's conformity with new religious decrees, they released the singing man and conduct Robert Morecocke, who acted as a chantry priest in 1547, paying him a half year's wages and granting him an additional gift from the vestry.[28] Further reforms showed the intent to impose new services, depose old forms of worship, and prevent people from continuing their old piety in the newly cleared churches. High altars became communion tables that 'may more move and turn the simple from the old superstitious opinions', an idea supported by bishops' circulated notes for sermons in 1550 and in Ridley's Injunctions.[29] Pastors, who could marry, replaced priests and preachers became a way to spread reform. The 1552 Act of Uniformity introduced a new Book of Common Prayer that reformulated baptism, communion (no longer mass) and burial services, introducing the black rubric. The black rubric explained that communicants did not kneel as if the service were mass or to recall transubstantiation. This additional text, however, demonstrated the difficulty of setting old forms to new functions.[30]

Will preambles voiced new beliefs and echoed traditional ways in what Duffy has called the 'limits of the possible and the approved' as individuals coped with the radical changes in religious statutes.[31] The wills of Edward's short reign span the available pious range, from saints to God and Christ to more obviously Protestant statements of belief in salvation by faith. Most testaments from 1549–52 invoked God and made some reference to Christ, and some to Christ's Passion.[32] Men who dedicated their testaments in this way did not distribute their pious bequests any differently from men who did not, suggesting no relation between the

---

[28] GL, MS 4071/1, fols 27, 28–9, 29v. On the *Paraphrases* in churches: *VAI*, II, p. 117. For additional information on Morecocke: Hugh Baillie, 'Some biographical notes on English church musicians', p. 46.

[29] Haigh, *English Reformations*, p. 177; *VAI*, II, pp. 242–3.

[30] David Cressy and Lori Ferrell (eds), *Religion and Society in Early Modern England: A Sourcebook* (London and New York, 1996), pp. 47–8.

[31] Twenty-one bequests made for sermons 1549–52 and no bequests for lectures. ' ... Shifts in the preambles of these wills reflect not a deep-seated change of heart by the testators, but rather shifts in the limits of the possible and the approved': Duffy, *Stripping*, p. 523. On changes in preambles: Litzenberger, *The English Reformation and the Laity*, pp. 41, 56, 75–8, 118–20, 153.

[32] Twelve (33.33 per cent) referred to Christ's Passion (two or 40 per cent by women and ten or 32.26 per cent by men), 16 (44.44 per cent) to God or Maker (three or 60 per cent by women and 13 or 41.94 per cent by men), three (8.33 per cent) to God and Christ (all by men). Four (11.11 per cent) others referred to the saints (all by men).

preamble and the bequests (actions) of testators.[33] One man bequeathed his soul to God, 'desyring the blessed Virgyn Mary and all tholy company of heaven to praye for me that my Soule may be accepted in the sight of my Savior Ihn Christ', bringing his faith in Christ together with his faith in the saints.[34] In 1552 William Rysse of St Michael's, who trusted in Jesus Christ's Passion for the remission of his sins, left his soul to God 'desyring the chastyn congregation of the churche militant to pray with me and for me'.[35] His will proceeded in common fashion to leave small bequests to a number of familiar recipients: prisons, the poor of the parish, a spital, craft, and friends and kin. In addition, he asked for six preachers to say six sermons in the parish church, a show of Protestant faith alongside his appeal to the church militant.

In the familiar narrative of the Reformation, Mary Tudor's restoration of Catholicism reversed Edward's radical reform. She reinstated Catholic services, vestments and the 'fabric' necessary for traditional observances, during her reign from 1553–58 although she did not revive other key popular elements of traditional religion.[36] Parishes and individuals conformed to the new theological rules and redid churches' interiors once again. Just as St Michael Cornhill had taken certain immediate steps under Edward, so the parish did under Mary to renovate the church in Catholic fashion. The churchwardens paid for putting the high altar back into the church and removing the 'Newe' Protestant pews that had been built with their backs to the space where it stood. They also paid Thomas Howe to fix the organs, 'the small paire beinge broken in the takinge downe', and paid for altar cloths.[37] Mary restored the Catholic mass and once again forbade the marrying of priests, but she did not reintroduce the cult of saints or the notion of purgatory, although these popular aspects of pre-Reformation lay piety were potentially lucrative for restoring ornaments and church fabric.[38] A few Londoners writing wills under

---

[33] Number of women's wills too small to make similar comparison, since most were written with that dedication.

[34] PRO, PROB 11/33, f. 250L.

[35] GL, MS 9171/13, f. 1v.

[36] C. John Sommerville, *The Secularization of Early Modern England: From Religious Culture to Religious Faith* (Oxford, 1992), p. 68. Mary's focus on relationship with Parliament and on finances: Jennifer Loach, *Parliament and the Crown in the Reign of Mary Tudor* (Oxford, 1986); R.H. Pogson, 'Revival and reform in Mary Tudor's Church: a question of money', *Journal of Ecclesiastical History*, 25, 3 (July 1974), pp. 249–65. Music in her realm: Daniel B. Page, 'Uniform and Catholic: Church Music in the Reign of Mary Tudor (1553–1558)', unpublished Ph.D. dissertation, Brandeis University, 1996.

[37] GL, MS 4071/1, fols 43v, 43v–44.

[38] Ronald Hutton, 'The Local Impact of the Reformations' in Christopher Haigh (ed.),

Mary anticipated or hoped for the restoration of purgatory, an essential element of medieval religion, judging by their bequests for prayers. In 1558, George Owin provided a young cow to the parishioners of a rural church so that they would always pray for him.[39] Besides parochial prayers, testators hoped for the prayers of friends and neighbours. In 1558, Elisabeth Owen provided 5s for bread and drink among her neighbours to pray for her soul.[40]

In 1554 Bishop Edmund Bonner reminded London inhabitants of the 'old and laudable custom' of remembering parish churches and St Paul's in last wills, suggesting that ecclesiastical leaders hoped to recoup lost benefactions for the repair and renovation of churches and cathedrals.[41] Bonner legitimated these bequests by describing them as 'old and laudable', like other valued customs and traditions in the city and unlike the newfangled reforms, especially of the previous reign. Lifetime gifts trickled into parishes, as in St Botolph's in the mid-1550s when parishioners gave gold, goblets, 'corporas' cases, vestments and other ornaments. Gifts that arrived late in Mary's reign suggested that some parishioners tried to judge the restoration's stability before bequeathing towels, altar cloths and coverings for sacraments, like that given by Lady Peters in 1557–58.[42] Customary bequests to the church's high altar for 'forgotten tithes' had been prohibited, and just four bequests for them reappeared under Mary. St Michael, a wealthy parish, turned to a prominent parishioner for a loan to complete the work of restoration. They borrowed £25 from Philip Gunter the year after they remade stained glass windows, the 'Roode marye and Jhon', and the representation of St Michael.[43]

A detailed inventory of church goods from St Stephen Walbrook, made shortly after Mary's death, showed the supply of new or the survival of 'old' goods, ornaments and books in a parish church during the restoration. The careful document of 13 December 1558 enumerated vestments, canopies, altar clothes, hearse clothes and other fabrics. The parish still owned two copes of blue velvet with gold, since even with the Prayer Book of 1549 parishes could use copes for a part of the communion service or could keep them to cover communion tables.

The Reformation Revised (Cambridge, 1987), p. 131. Queen Mary's Articles (1554): *VAI*, II, pp. 322–9.

[39] PRO, PROB 11/42B, f. 88R.

[40] GL, MS 9051/2, f. 244v.

[41] *VAI*, II, p. 342.

[42] GL, MS 1454, Rolls 61–62 (1555–57). 'Corporas' refers to the corporal or fine cloth under the consecrated elements in mass: *Fraternity Register*, p. 79. GL, MS 1454, Roll 63.

[43] GL, MS 4071/1, fols 50–50v, 51v.

Many other vestments listed in the inventory were incomplete, signs that the parish had altered them to comply with Edwardian reform. Despite alteration, embroidered fabrics with images of the Trinity and saints, like the hearse cloth bearing an image of Sts George and Ursula, survived to the end of Mary's reign. Master Doctor Clement's name recurs frequently in the inventory, for lending and giving objects, from a canopy for over the sacrament to a pewter basin bearing an image of the crucifix. Clement may have styled himself the caretaker of these Catholic goods under Edward and returned them to the parish under Mary. The ornaments demonstrate the saints and devotions important to the parish before the Reformation: the name of Jesus, the Five Wounds, the Trinity, Christ, Mary, and John, Sts Stephen, Jerome, George and Ursula. Although Queen Mary had not revived pre-Reformation fraternities, the churchwardens inventoried the fabric according to location, such as the chapels dedicated to St Katherine and to Our Lady. Goods 'in the church' included a 'fayre rode Lofte', a fair crucifix 'of vj foote longe & Mary & John', and five bells and a 'Saynte Bell' in the steeple.[44]

Mary did not restore popular lay fraternities or the cult of saints so central to pre-Reformation lay piety, but she did revive other popular spectacles that stretched back in people's memories. Churchwardens in St Mary Woolnoth, after listing the costs of the knell and peal for Henry VIII at his death, had noted their last payments for Palm Sunday, Easter and Corpus Christi celebrations.[45] The priests and clerks of St Michael's enjoyed a drinking in the vestry on 'holly Thursday wytt sonday & corpos crysts daye', as long as the celebrations lasted during Edward's rule. Shortly after Mary's coronation, St Michael's reinstated the observations and celebrations around the sepulchre for Palm Sunday, Good Friday and Easter by paying for palms, construction of the sepulchre and lights for the watching. The parish also observed Whitsun and Corpus Christi once again.[46] Chroniclers depicted the rebirth of processions under Mary, those on St Katherine's Day, St Andrew's Day, Whitsun and Sundays being held in Latin with priests and civic leaders, 'after the old custome'.[47] These sacred observances returned the traditional practice of bringing together choirs,

---

[44] GL, MS 3103, fols 31v–34. The bells had either not been removed as ordered in 1549, or had been quickly rehung when Mary became queen. 1549 order: Whiting, *Blind Devotion*, p. 39; Duffy, *Stripping*, pp. 492–3.

[45] GL, MS 1002/1A, f. 44.

[46] GL, MS 4071/1, fols 27, 28–9, 46v, 47, 49v–50.

[47] Robert Fabyan, *The New Chronicle of England and France*, Henry Ellis (ed.), (London, 1811), pp. 712–14.

curates and bishops with the mayor and aldermen of the city, and with certain craft members. Processions included the poor, the school at Paul's, and the children of Christ's Hospital, incorporating the Reformation foundation that filled a former friary in the restoration of traditional celebration.[48]

Preambles to Christ could offer testators flexibility in accommodating religious change. Invocations to Christ's Passion unsurprisingly survived under Mary, since Catholics and Protestants emphasized the role of Christ in salvation through the sixteenth century.[49] Bonner's Injunctions for London (1555) stressed in particular Christ, the Cross, and Christ's Passion and Blood in commanding parsons, vicars and curates to instruct parishioners as to the 'true meaning' of ceremonies 'used of old time in this Church of England'.[50] Half of the men's and women's wills dedicated the testators' souls to the Passion and these wills resulted most frequently in pious observations. While trusting to the passion of Jesus Christ for his salvation Henry Swarland also trusted his soul to Mary and the Holy Company of Saints to act as 'intercessors for me to god'.[51]

In deciphering the meaning of parochial and testamentary compliance with new religious edicts, historians have put forth divergent explanations, from the political docility of the English to a widespread desire for social stability.[52] The leaders of parishes, not to mention crafts, may have ensured social stability through their actions, or shown their apathy by their limited reactions, but some groups may instead have tolerated, even anticipated heterogeneous opinions held by friends and neighbours.[53] Haigh assuredly writes that 'Church-

---

[48] John Gough Nichols (ed.), *The Diary of Henry Machyn, citizen and Merchant-Taylor of London. From AD 1550 to AD 1563*, Camden Society 42 (London, 1848), p. 87.

[49] On preambles stressing Christ's Passion and the power of the saints, Duffy writes that 'they represent an important aspect of Marian orthodoxy, the base-line of a Catholicism which was anxious to spell out that teaching which had dominated the Church's deathbed ministry throughout the later Middle Ages, and thereby to neutralize the claims of the reformers to a monopoly of faithfulness to a Christocentric gospel': *Stripping*, p. 519. Litzenberger, *English Reformation and the Laity*, p. 93.

[50] *VAI*, II, pp. 361–2.

[51] Two women and 15 men out of just 34 wills, hence impressionistic. Ninety-one per cent (32) and 61 per cent (49) of pious observations, respectively, in the wills of women and men calling on Christ. For example, GL, MS 9171/13, f. 84v.

[52] 'Tudor Englishman's sense of obligation to established authorities': Whiting, *Blind Devotion*, p. 172; cf. degree to which 'stability and continuity ... were clearly priorities': Litzenberger, 'St Michael's', p. 249.

[53] Ward, *Metropolitan Communities*, p. 99; McClendon, 'Discipline and punish?', pp. 117–18.

wardens' accounts tell us only what churchwardens spent, not what they thought, and certainly not what the rest of the parishioners thought', but hints of trouble seem discernible in these fiscal records. St Michael's churchwardens' accounts of 1555–56 include circling monsters biting each other's tails in the capital and in those of 1556–57, a stern-faced character greets the auditor on the first page.[54] The official document obscured any conflict or negotiation that parishioners worked out in their pews or in the church's meetings, but patronage of contradictory aims suggests wide variety in thought about the course of reform and reaction.

Although parochial records demonstrate compliance with reformation and restoration, a closer examination of accounts reveals the diversity of experience and attitude within the city, as seen in the patronage of two prominent citizens. Philip Gunter eventually ascribed to puritan teachings and encouraged them in his family and household, whereas Martin Bowes seemed to follow a moderate course that concentrated on preserving his family name in the parish church and in the city at large. In 1553–54, a cloth with the Ten Commandments and the scripture was hung in the belfry at the 'Requeste of Mr [Philip] Gunnter and others' at the same time as the sepulchre's frame was constructed.[55] Gunter may have hoped to preserve the scriptures and commandments that replaced Catholic icons in Henrician and Edwardian reform. That the deprived reformer John Pulleyne held Protestant services in Marian Cornhill and John Philpott was rector from 1562–67 demonstrates that the parish (and ward) had a strong identification with reform.[56] On the other hand, Sir Martin Bowes, 'of his benevolence and goode will' toward his parish, paid for the 'Roode and Mary and John and the crosse to be gilded and paynted', in August 1556. At Easter 1557, 'of his further benevolence' he 'did gyve a faire clothe for the Sacrament to be used in this churche which clothe is of clothe of golde and hathe ffower faire gilt buttones to the same'.[57] Coupled with the elaborate funeral he planned for his wife, Bowes's benefactions illustrate his self-serving efforts to imprint his name in the church's memory and his attachment to traditional piety, perhaps because it allowed for extravagant patronage.

---

[54] Haigh, *English Reformations*, p. 17; GL, MS 4071/1, fols 48v, 51.

[55] GL, MS 4071/1, f. 44v.

[56] Pulleyne eventually fled to Geneva in 1557; Philpott was suspended as lecturer in St Antholin's for preaching against wearing of vestments in 1566: Francis J. Bremer, 'William Winthrop and Religious Reform in London 1529–1582', *London Journal* 24, 2 (1999), pp. 3–4, 6.

[57] GL, MS 1002/1A, f. 1.

Not all parishioners acquiesced to religious change. One female resident in St Michael's habitually broke windows, whether that amounted to iconoclastic resistance or some form of mental illness is not clear from the accounts. Former chantry priests and conducts, including the curate Sir Olyver, the fraternity priest Sir William Leeke, and the conduct Robert Morecocke, occupied chambers owned by the parish in 1551–52.[58] Sir Olyver may have married, as a Mistress Olyver paid the rent through Mary's reign when he is no longer listed. He may have been a married cleric who fled Marian London, but she remained in the parish. In the accounts of 1554–55, 'Olyvers wyffs' door was fitted with padlocks, 2 staples, and a 'hapse' 'to kepe her from breakinge of the glasse wyndowes'. In the same accounts the churchwardens paid a plumber for twelve pounds of solder to mend the south side of the church, perhaps including destroyed windows. In 1559–60, the churchwardens paid a glasier for glass and mending windows and cryptically noted: 'Paide for A windowe in the curatts chamber to Mris olyver', 20s.[59]

Elizabeth restarted official, Protestant reform upon Mary's death, though with a difference from the courses followed by her father and brother.[60] Whether Elizabeth returned to Protestant reform for reasons of efficacy or personal theology, she reasserted the monarchy's supremacy over the Church and reinstated Protestant services. She relied on the Edwardian injunctions and prayer book, but avoided some religious controversy by omitting the black rubric. The Elizabethan Settlement of 1559 allowed priests to perform communion in Catholic vestments, leaving ambiguity in the performance of services.[61] The multiplicity of ideas regarding key doctrines and the wrestling between learned Lutherans and Calvinists in Elizabeth's reign call into question the *via media* theory of Anglicanism.[62]

Parishioners, however, especially those with social and civic positions to maintain, showed willingness to react flexibly to religious change and to differences in lay opinion. For some, a middle way through the doctrinal debates of the period entailed using pious charity to cement individual social standing and to maintain peace within the parish. Bowes and Gunter, who had served in parochial offices

---

[58] GL, MS 4071/1, f. 40v.

[59] GL, MS 4071/1, fols 47v, 62. 'Hapse' is a hasp, a fastener or lock.

[60] The Royal Articles of Queen Elizabeth (1559): *VAI*, III, pp. 1–29.

[61] For full discussion: Haigh, *English Reformations*, pp. 238 ff.

[62] Dismantling of *via media*: Tyacke, 'Anglican Attitudes: Some Recent Writings on English Religious History, from the Reformation to the Civil War', *JBS* 35 (April 1996), esp. pp. 139, 142–5, 167.

through the years of radical reform and restoration, adapted to the 'new' ways in Elizabeth's reign. After Mary's rule ended, Bowes continued to direct the church's expenditures, partly through his own example. In his lifetime, he made a yearly gift of 26s, for 6d in bread each Sunday to the poor, a gift that would not have been out of place in the late medieval parish.[63] In that same year (1560–61) he ordered the parish to give part of the sale of timber to the governors of Bethlehem and Bridewell.[64] In fact, this prominent citizen served as governor of Christ's in 1559–60 and of Bridewell in 1564–66. Bowes's outright support for the Catholic restoration and his leadership of post-Reformation foundations allowed him to navigate between reform and tradition – and to maintain his prominence as a civic leader and charitable model throughout his life. By the time of his death, Gunter had endowed a number of sermons and had encouraged the single woman who was a servant in his household to make a similarly Protestant or even puritan testament. William Winthrop served in various ward and parochial offices while also acting as a 'broker' for reform within and outside London, within the parish and in stranger churches.[65]

St Michael's responded to renewal of reform by putting up the pulpit and bringing down Catholic ornaments in 1558–59, buying 'Genevan' books the next year as well as a new chain for Erasmus's *Paraphrases*, and finally selling canopies, vestments, altar cloths and other necessaries for Catholic services.[66] The 'crisis' over repairs and church fabric continued: by 1559, the churchwardens of St Mary's held a vestry to obtain consent to sell plate, vestments and ornaments for 'urgent' repairs of leading and other parts of the church. Images that survived Edward's reign or had been restored under Mary were burned under Elizabeth and rood lofts destroyed.[67] St Stephen's rebuilt chapels, altars and rood loft in the accounting year ending 1556, only to pull down the rood in the year ending 1560.[68]

Although iconoclasm proceeded slowly and unevenly through parishes in post-Settlement England, it contributed to the success of the Reformation by the end of the 1570s by severing the visual connection

---

[63] GL, MS 1002/1A, f. 98.

[64] GL, MS 1002/1A, fols 98–98v.

[65] Bremer calls Winthrop a 'broker' in his careful analysis of the man's circle and activities on behalf of reform: 'William Winthrop', p.11.

[66] GL, MS 4071/1, fols 57–58v, 61v, 62, 67.

[67] GL, MS 1002/1A, f. 93v; Duffy, *Stripping*, pp. 568–9.

[68] GL, MS 593/2, fols 35v–36, 44v. 1560 marked year Grindal was 'allowed' to enforce destruction of rood lofts: Haigh, *English Reformations*, p. 244.

between parishioners and saints and sacred objects.[69] Breaking up lay people's graves and monuments also erased calls for prayers or images of saints, besides undoing the memory of charitable acts. In a parish church, Stow noted the 'defaced tombs, and print of plates torn up and carried away', suggesting that the tracings of monuments and engravings lasted after the images or words had been mangled. Uneven survival of ornaments and representations, if just for a few years after Elizabeth's ascension, caused anxiety over the strength of reformed ideas in Elizabethan England. Duffy argues that the old ways persisted despite the 'victory' of Protestantism, and the survival of pre-Reformation monuments and graves in the 'fair church' of St Stephen's suggests that old monuments, some with images and requests for prayers, outlived iconoclasm.[70] Aston's historical detective work on the painting, *Edward VI and the Pope: An Allegory of the Reformation*, unveils reformers' deep fears about lingering Catholic iconography and doctrine in Elizabethan England. The painting had been dated to Edward's accession and interpreted as a pictorial legitimization of his rule. Aston repositions the painting in, at least, the late 1560s and suggests that it may have been a barbed reminder to Elizabeth to continue her father's and brother's iconoclastic reform, to finish the English Reformation.[71]

The defacement of pre-Reformation monuments and the replacement of pre-Reformation uses and buildings led Stow to his criticism of social elites and their materialism in late sixteenth-century London. He remarked on the grandiose homes, more frequently than graves, built by wealthy London citizens standing in the post-Reformation city. Individuals began directing their wealth towards their own houses, families and friends, without the range of pre-Reformation benefactions once available in London. Stow's mention of crass post-Reformation uses for previously sacred spaces only added to the quiet criticism of parishioners who overlooked ancient charity and neglected current almsgiving in the growing city. For instance, he described the despoliation in the Augustinian Friars, remade as the Dutch Church, by the Marquis of Winchester, who 'sold the monuments of noblemen there buried in great number, the paving stone and whatsoever, which cost many thousands, for one hundred pounds, and in place thereof made fair stabling for horses'.[72]

---

[69] Duffy, *Stripping*, pp. 588–9; on the success of Protestantism by the 1580s: Haigh, *Reformation Revised*, p. 214.

[70] Morley, pp. 230–31.

[71] Margaret Aston, *The King's Bedpost: Reformation and Iconography in a Tudor Group Portrait* (Cambridge, 1993), pp. 131, 215; NPG 4165.

[72] Morley, pp. 189, 210.

Some Protestant iconography slowly replaced the holes left in the parish fabric by destruction of Catholic objects. In some of the parish churches of London, John Foxe's Book of Martyrs provided potent Protestant iconography in its woodcuts, as in St Michael's when they purchased the Book for 42s 6d and either Erasmus's *Paraphrases* or 'Mr Calvins institivtions yf the paraphrases cannot be had' in January 1572.[73] The parish had paid 5s for Erasmus's work and 20d for a chain to hold it in 1547–48, and 8d for another chain in 1559–60. The repeated purchase of the book shows the loss or theft of tracts required and repudiated through these years of religious uncertainty.

Protracted disputes over 'concealed' property arose under Elizabeth, as representatives of the crown sought to recover property quietly retained under parochial administration. Officials pursued property given to endow masses and prayers for souls that should have been turned over to commissioners in 1547, but was kept to fund poor relief and other parochial expenses. Robert Tittler argues that the Crown showed greater 'vigour' in this period than in the earlier periods of dissolution and confiscation.[74] In the first year of Elizabeth's reign the churchwardens of St Botolph's hastened to study royal records about the dissolution of the chantries, discovering that they owed £13 14s in arrearages.[75] Perhaps the churchwardens hoped to pre-empt any penetrating review of old records by outsiders that might have revealed other concealed property. In the 1560s, St Stephen's churchwardens hired counsel when they were called before the concealment commissioners in 1563 and when a man brought a seemingly specious claim to property that once supported an obit, in the same year. With Thomas Becon, their parson during Edward's reign and a Marian exile, they defended the parish from a claim by William Younge for property left to the parish by Sir John Cotes, for his obit kept by the Salters. The churchwardens paid for copies of depositions and replies throughout the suit, which referenced the conferral of property for the obit as well as alleged that a woman had given the property to the

---

[73] GL, MS 4072/1, Part 1, f. 15v. Record of purchase in CWA (GL, MS 4071/1, f. 99v) with 8s paid for Calvin's work. (GL, MS 4071/1, fols 29, 62.) On directing the book to a 'national' rather than an elite audience and the use of captions with the woodcuts in the 1570 edition: Susan Felch, 'Shaping the reader in the *Acts and Monuments*' in David Loades (ed.), *John Foxe and the English Reformation* (Aldershot, 1997), pp. 58, 64; on power of the woodcuts in Foxe's book: Margaret Aston and Elizabeth Ingram, 'The Iconography of the *Acts and Monuments*' in ibid., pp. 66–142.

[74] Tittler, *The Reformation and the Towns*, pp. 70–72; Kümin, *Shaping*, pp. 210–12; 'new enthusiasm' for uncovering concealment: C.J. Kitching, 'The Quest for Concealed Lands in the Reign of Elizabeth I', *TRHS*, 5th series, **24** (1974), p. 66.

[75] GL, MS 1454, Roll 65.

claimant in the last year of Edward's reign, suggesting that the claimant hinged his suit on ownership after the confiscation of chantry lands.[76] If Younge had hoped to capitalize on the renewed attempts to gain concealed property, or on the confusion surrounding property traceable to the Edwardian era, he underestimated the parish's willingness to combat such claims through litigation. Efforts to conceal property once granted for 'superstitious' uses hinged on parochial financial needs and the 'calculated errors of a determined parish', not on resistance to Protestant innovations.[77]

Although renewed iconoclasm cleared interiors once again and the Settlement re-established Protestant services in English, pockets of recusancy or Catholic sympathy survived in London. Former priests and monks survived, not to mention parishioners who had lived through vast changes. The one-time priest Sir William Leeke remained in St Michael's until his death and burial in 1566, events noted in the churchwardens' accounts.[78] Based on his books and his nostalgia for pre-Reformation architecture, monuments, and ways, John Stow, one of a family of parishioners in St Michael's, fell under suspicion of Catholicism. John Stow's widowed mother, Elizabeth, made a will in 1568 that left her soul to the Trinity and 'into the felloweshippe of the holy Company of heaven' and her body to the cloister of St Michael Cornhill, suggesting that the son may not have been the only family member still hesitant about reform.[79] Even in the late 1570s the parish needed to buy 72 new panes of glass for the church windows, suggesting images survived in stained glass.

---

[76] GL, MS 593/2, fols 48v–50v; GL, Add. MSS 284, one sheet, unfol. The Guildhall Library has misdated ('1540?') the series of undated complaints by William Younge and rejoinders by Thomas Becon, Roger Warfylde, Frances Kyglton and Thomas Bullocks over property and claimed in a suit, as referenced in CWA, 1563/4. GL, Add. MSS 280, 281, 284; *Chantry Certificate*, p. 81. Thomas Becon, D.D. (1512–67): *DNB*. Usual ending of concealment cases in litigation: Kitching, 'Quest', pp. 76–7.

[77] Kitching, 'Quest', p. 64.

[78] GL, MS 4071/1, f. 80v; *Chantry Certificate*, p. 7. Burial of William Leeke, 'a preeste': GL, MS 4061, unfol. (Buried 27 September 1566.)

[79] On Stow's library and the theory that John Stow's mother was a Protestant: Janet Wilson, 'A Catalogue of the "unlawful" books found in John Stow's study on 21 February 1568/9', *Journal of Recusant History*, 20 (1990–91), pp. 1–30, p. 2 especially. Thanks to Dr Daniel B. Page for this reference. Bremer also states that Mrs Stow was a Protestant as he relates the dispute between the brothers Thomas and John, springing from books in John's library and from Thomas leapfrogging the elder John in the mother's will: Bremer, 'William Winthrop', p. 7. On recusancy: Haigh, *English Reformations*, pp. 255ff; Marie B. Rowlands, 'Recusant Women 1560–1640' in Mary Prior (ed.), *Women in English Society*, pp. 149–80; Michael Questier, *Conversion, Politics and Religion in England, 1580–1625* (Cambridge, 1996), pp. 126–67. GL, MS 9171/15, f. 310v.

The invocations of wills continued the trend stressing Christocentric doctrine, apparent since Edward. Among women just less than half of the wills between 1558 and 1580 bequeathed souls to Christ's Passion or his bloodshed (48.48 per cent, or 16) and more than a third to God as Maker and Redeemer (36.36 per cent, or 12). Men bequeathed souls to Christ's Passion most often (58 per cent, or 79) and to God and Maker (20 per cent, or 27). Wills with invocations to Christ's Passion generated the greatest numbers of pious bequests, suggesting that a firm statement of faith correlated with confident charitable activity.[80] Invocations to the Trinity in the 1530s may have been a Protestant-leaning alternative to those to saints, but by the 1560s the Trinity had stronger associations with the 'old ways'. Interrogatories from 1560 called on churchwardens to ensure that images, pictures and paintings of the Blessed Trinity, among others, had been removed from churches.[81] Elizabeth Stow's 1568 invocation to the Trinity may have communicated more traditional religious views, suggesting change over time that undercut the 'ambiguity' of the invocation.[82] In keeping with earlier examples, few men or women had clergy at their will making, reducing the influence of ministers.

Wills expressing strong religious beliefs after 1558 imitated preambles, scriptures, sermons and other works. Imitation couched belief in familiar statements of faith that instructed hearers of the testaments in the same.[83] The distinctive preambles of this period reflect a spirit of evangelism or the conflict in divergent religious views. Protestant and Catholic Reformation wills adhered to Christocentric doctrine, though testators' references to election plant them firmly in the Protestant camp. Preambles offered some unambiguous statements of faith, especially of puritan belief, that imitated familiar texts. Concentration on original sin, an evangelical focus, rarely surfaced. The author and printer John Awdelay, however, noted Adam and Eve, his 'firste parents', and remembered the sins of his infancy, youth and latter age in his evangelical testament. He thanked God for making him a 'lyvelie' creature in his own image, although He could have made him 'some vile vermyn or uggly beast'. Awdelay regretted human sin – the cause of the 'most

---

[80] Among women, 270 bequests, or 71.43 per cent; among men, 222 or 57.96 per cent. Comparison of charitable giving by female testators who dedicated their testaments to Christ's Passion and those with other preambles shows a significant difference (z-score 18.47), as does the same comparison with male testators (6.32).

[81] *VAI*, III, p. 90.

[82] Cf. broad 'ambiguous' category for preambles, including references to Holy Trinity, Litzenberger, *English Reformation and the Laity*, pp. 172–3.

[83] Craig and Litzenberger, 'Wills as religious propaganda', p. 423; Flynn, *Sacred Charity*, p. 70.

grevous and bitter death of this my sweete lord and savior', Jesus Christ.[84]

In 1580, Edward Gadisdon celebrated Protestant gospel light freeing him from Catholic darkness, a battle against sin and ignorance incidentally waged by Catholic Reformation followers against Protestants. Gadisdon, making his will while sick and weak, thanked God for creating him and guiding him 'owte of the black darknes of error and ignoraunce (under whiche I was holden in my firste age) and call[ing] me into the cleare lighte of his moste holye worde'. Gadisdon relied on faith and salvation through Jesus Christ, trusting to be counted among the elect. He asked for burial in the 'comely and symple mann[er] as amongeste the Professors of the ghospell is used and allowed'. He left his best black cloak to his father 'not for the respecte of the valewe but in remembraunce of my Duetye'. With evangelical purpose he gave his brother a Geneva Bible to 'exercise himselfe in the worde of god and lawe of the Lorde' and another brother received a Testament.[85] Gadisdon endowed no sermons, leaving only personal books and admonitions to his family.

In another evangelical preamble the grocer Simon Smythe described his earthly body, but trusted in its renewal through the power of God. He called himself an 'unprofitable servaunte of god', contrasting the spiritual poverty of his soul and his worldly wealth, as pre-Reformation Catholics had. He enjoined his wife to pay all his debts, but in turn forgave what others owed him – or at least to a sum he could afford. 'And as soone as that is done I trust that my Saviour wilbe well pleased with her and me unto whose mercy I have in assured hope to have pardonne of all my synnes and wickednes and to have a place w[i]t[h] his electe nomber amen'. He affirmed the certainty of death and the uncertainty of its hour, returning to God the 'spirit which he of his fatherlie goodnes gave unto me when he fasshioned this my body in my mother's wombe'. He anticipated his soul's residence with the angels and blessed saints and looked forward to giving up his vile body for an incorruptible one at the Judgement.[86] 'According to the Scriptures', testators awaited the resurrection of body and soul at the Day of

---

[84] PRO, PROB 11/57, f. 269L. Awdelay (or Awdeley) flourished 1557–77, was a freeman of the Company of Stationers in 1559, and published ballads, news sheets and religious tracts: DNB.

[85] PRO, PROB 11/62, fols 232R–233L. His sentiment about conversion must have been common among dying Protestants of this generation, even if not many remarked on their earlier conversions: see Jones, 'Living the Reformations', p. 276. The Catholic Reformation, in its 'campaign for the conquest of souls', also fought against ignorance and sin: Pullan, 'Catholics and the Poor', p. 29. On the monetary value of bibles: Tessa Watt, *Cheap Print and Popular Piety, 1550–1640* (Cambridge, 1991), pp. 260–61.

[86] PRO, PROB 11/47, f. 223R, 224L.

Judgement, explained Anthony Warfeelde, brother to Roger Warfyld, party to the concealed property case in St Stephen's.[87]

The ease with which some Catholic symbols gained a place within the Protestant framework may have diverted popular doctrinal debate from the violence prevalent on the Continent. Testators employed or subverted the holy numbers of Catholic devotion to fit the new ways of Protestant London. John Maior in 1551 made provision for a modest burial in the churchyard of St Michael's, but also requested three sermons, one at his burial, in imitation of or in contrast to masses multiplied by a holy number.[88] Elizabeth Stevyns played on the pre-Reformation reliance on the weighty number 'five' of the popular late medieval devotion to the Five Wounds by asking for five sermons. She wanted the preacher Mr Maydewell or another learned man to preach a sermon at her burial and four on the following Sundays.[89] Reformers thought themselves capable of using popish property to godly and less 'superstitious' ends and they might also have desired to exhibit their 'true' piety. On the other hand, some testators with less deliberate motives may have confused the two sets of doctrine.

Vestiges of late medieval Catholic practices continued even in Reformation England, and of reformed religion under Mary. 'Survivals', the practices and beliefs persisting in conscious or unconscious adaptations and revisions, appeared in testaments and in parochial records.[90] St Michael's removed the rood and the great beam that once held it as they celebrated Elizabeth's coronation, but still paid for holly and ivy, traditional holiday decorations later decried by puritans. Elizabeth also restored an old ceremony, the Rogation procession, though without crosses, banners or priests wearing vestments.[91] Some revisionist histo-

---

[87] PRO, PROB 11/57, f. 9L.

[88] GL, MS 9171/12, f. 80. On suspicion of survival of 'popish trentals' in cycles of funeral sermons: Brown, *Popular Piety*, p. 246.

[89] PRO, PROB 11/34, f. 47L. She was a good friend of Sir Martin Bowes, leaving him a ring with her initials. Bowes also melded religious beliefs.

[90] Rudolph Binion, *After Christianity: Christian Survivals in Post-Christian Culture* (Durango, CO, 1986); Thomas, *Religion and the Decline of Magic*, p. 74; persistence of holy numbers: ibid., pp.178–9, 185. McClendon has pointed out that 'survivals' do not equal traditional practices or beliefs, but modify them: 'A Moveable Feast: Saint George's Day Celebrations and Religious Change in Early Modern England', *JBS*, 38, 1 (Jan. 1999), p. 15.

[91] GL, MS 4071/1, fols 57–58v; *VAI*, III, pp. 15, 309. Holly and ivy: Keith Thomas, *Man and the Natural World: Changing Attitudes in England, 1500–1800* (Oxford, 1983), pp. 75, 78. Hutton, *Merry England*, pp. 105, 123–4; Thomas, *Religion and the Decline of Magic*, pp. 62–5; David Cressy, *Bonfires and Bells: National Memory and the Protestant Calendar in Elizabethan and Stuart England* (Berkeley and Los Angeles, CA, 1989), pp. 23–4, 42. See Chapter 4 for more on Rogation and perambulation.

rians have turned the 'watershed' argument of traditional historiography on its head, arguing that a 'Reformation' that is not a watershed amounts to 'some Reformations'. Instead, we should understand that the piece-meal reform outlined by Scarisbrick describes more than official doctrine, but also the practices and beliefs of people adapting to new ways.[92] London inhabitants occupied church buildings that predated the Reformation, without ornaments and whitewashed, a short-lived pale cover and utilized former religious buildings for other purposes. St Botolph's profited from renting Trinity Hall for plays and marriages beginning in the 1560s, without removing the hall's 'sup[e]rstitous pictures in the glasse window' until the early seventeenth century.[93] Some clergy deliberately undermined Protestant services, mimicking Catholic ritual and chant and leading Bishop Ridley to forbid the 'counterfeit [of] the popish mass'.[94]

Legislation continued, reversed and restarted Protestant reform in the mid-sixteenth century, leading to changes in the services, ornaments and buildings housing worship. These changes did not necessarily remake piety, or at least did not obliterate 'old' or 'new' ways, but changes in the foundations in London showed the reach of change.

Foundations old and new

Alice Briggs's will, written in 1555, illustrates the melding of Catholic and Reformation pious and charitable aims expressed in some contemporary testaments. She made traditional pre-Reformation bequests, to prisons and for highway construction, but also supported the new foundations of Bethlehem, Christ's, and St Bartholomew's. She funded scholars' exhibitions, an act that could produce priests in Catholic England, but would produce puritan preachers in late sixteenth-century England. The gift of her own gold ring to her Reverend Father in God, Edmund Bonner, Lord Bishop of London, shows that she counted on him as an intimate advisor. The Marian restoration had brought Bonner's reinstatement and his pledge to be a personal, spiritual friend to those seeking absolution for the preceding Protestant schism. Bonner vowed

---

[92] Cf. 'revolution': Dickens, *The English Reformation*, pp. 102, 294 and Scarisbrick, *Reformation and the English People*, p. 17; 'the accidents of everyday politics and the consequences of power struggles' and 'Some Reformations', closing line of book: Haigh, *English Reformations*, pp. 13, 295.

[93] GL, MS 1454, Roll 67 showed rent of 44s 2d. The Vestry of 18 January 1606 called for replacing the stained with white glass, GL, MS 1453/1, f. 3.

[94] Related by Haigh, *English Reformations*, p. 176. See also *VAI*, II, p. 241.

help, if the parish priest or the bishop's representatives could not reassure those returning to the Catholic Church.[95] Briggs's token remembered a closer bond than even Bonner's formulaic promise of help for repentant schismatics proffered.

Reformers, in the litany of anti-clericalism heard throughout Europe, criticized monks, friars, nuns and parochial clergy for using endowments and gifts to live luxuriously rather than to aid the poor, sick and pilgrims.[96] Monasteries and nunneries had not garnered many bequests from early sixteenth-century testators, but they had been significant sources of relief for the sick and the poor. Stow's description of 'some small cottages, of two storeys high, and little garden-plots backward, for poor bed-rid people, for in that street dwelt none other, built by some prior of the Holy Trinity, to whom that ground belonged', pointed out the 'old' practice of supporting the elderly and infirm poor. These cottages offered a cautionary tale about declining charity in the city's new map of commercial activity.[97] The houses founded by a prior became the site of new retail businesses and herb and root gardens to supply markets. Stow showed that 'the poor bed-rid people were worn out' from the later reign of Henry VIII and into the reign of Edward VI, when a gun foundry and gardens became part of the neighbourhood. The 'homely cottages' were replaced by houses that 'rather want room than rent'. Edwardian confiscation stretched beyond religious houses to the lay organizations at the heart of parochial life, although records may not reveal the extent of formal charity offered by them. Parish fraternities and guilds relieved the parish poor, especially the elderly poor. Ben McRee has found little evidence of almsgiving in surviving parochial fraternity records, although their regulations demanded charity. The Chantry returns, however, illustrate guild or fraternity support of the bedridden and aged poor.[98]

Protestant critics petitioned for religious houses to become hospitals. After all, religious institutions had been originally founded by 'auncyent

---

[95] PRO, PROB 11/38, f. 185R. Brigden, *London and the Reformation*, p. 575; Foxe, Vol. 1, 1794 edn, p. 493.

[96] 'Ritual complaints': Lucien Febvre, 'The Origins of the French Reformation: A Badly-Put Question?' in Peter Burke (ed.), *A New Kind of History* (London, 1973), p. 55; Haigh, *English Reformations*, p. 41.

[97] Morley, p. 151; Steven Mullaney, *The Place of the Stage: License, Play, and Power in Renaissance England* (Ann Arbor, MI, 1997), orig. 1988, esp. pp. 15–20.

[98] Kreider argues that the chantry commissioners were not charged to record the charitable activities of institutions, despite allegations of misuse of donations, and those who recorded outlays only did so out of 'personal concerns': *English Chantries*, p. 174. McRee, 'Charity and gild solidarity', pp. 195–225; cf. Barron, 'The parish fraternities of medieval London', p. 27; Schen, 'Strategies of Aged and Poor Women', pp. 18–19.

fathers' for the relief of the poor, not for the ease of priests and monks, 'carnally lyvyng as they of late have doon'.[99] The citizens and Lord Mayor of London agitated for the foundation of hospitals and other institutions to succour the poor in place of, and with the physical accoutrements of, monasteries and nunneries in a post-dissolution petition. Despite civic enthusiasm for new foundations using goods for their 'intended' purpose of helping the poor, testators slowly adopted these institutions between 1549 and 1552. Perhaps they waited for the dust to settle or left the wealthy men who acted as governors to support the new foundations financially.

Social and religious critics provided diverse arguments in favour of rededicating institutions to the poor, from the benefits of relieving poverty to propagandizing for Protestantism. For 'Roderick Mors' and Simon Fish, using confiscated religious property in the care of the poor and sick differentiated reformed from Catholic piety. Henry Brinkelow, the former Grey Friar writing under the pseudonym Roderick or Roderigo Mors, likened the Catholic monks and priests to a 'sort of belly goddys, and idle stout strong lords', a 'sort of dronken bussardys'. The theme of others growing fat on the food and property of the poor, and even of buzzards feeding on the poor themselves, runs through the *Complaint* and other Protestant works about clerical corruption and greed. Brinkelow pleaded with Henry VIII to share the wealth of the Catholic Church and its institutions with the people of England, especially the poor, as the Germans had already done. He knew that the 'godly' in Parliament had ideas, but he wanted nonetheless to offer his advice. He urged the monarch to use bishops' lands 'to Gods glory to the comme[n]welth & to ye help of the poore', especially poor maidens and householders and the blind, sick and lame. As Brinkelow saw it, the distribution of former religious property among poorer cities and towns would ease subsidies on the poor and middling sort. He envisioned towns entering bonds in unison with the king, for the use of the church's temporal goods, paying back £3 on each £100 borrowed so that the sum would increase, rather than decay. As further protection of economic viability, he asked that cloth production be confined to cities and the great towns.

Brinkelow articulated the 'right' of the poor to relief through the city and warned against further misuse of the buildings and lands by post-Reformation guardians. The windfall of confiscated property but-

---

[99] Appendix 1, ('Petition of the Mayor, Aldermen, and Commonality of the City of London to King Henry the Eighth', 1538), London, Court of Common Council, Committee in Relation to the Royal Hospitals, *Memoranda, References, and documents relating to the royal hospitals of the city of London* (London, 1836), p. 2.

tressed this sense of a right to relief, but shrinking resources eventually weakened the same. Brinkelow hoped to see almshouses built for poor men 'such as be not able to labor, syck, sore, blynd, and lame' who would 'have poore whole women to mynystre vnto them'. His gendered concept of nurses – and his notion of employing the poor to care for other poor – reflected his social context and widespread parochial practice. With this plan to care for poor men through the labour of poor women Brinkelow's tone turned strident. 'And for Chrystes sake ye rulers, loke vpon your hospytals, whether the poor haue their right there or no. I heare that the masters of your hospytals be so fatt that the pore be kept leane and bare inough: the crye of the peple is heard vnto the Lord, though ye wyll not heare'. In his vision of a better and reformed society, physicians and surgeons would care for the poor without taking money from them. Schools would educate the children of poor men and others in Hebrew, Greek and Latin, the languages of Biblical exegesis.

Petitioners and critics argued that poverty and poor people had deleterious effects on social order. The need to maintain good order propped up the right of the poor to relief. Brinkelow warned English rulers to remember first, the commonwealth and the poor and second, to contemplate their own political health. He believed that bishops caused mischief as surely as the oceans held water.[100] A few years later when he lamented London's attachment to superstition and idolatry, he again singled out the lack of adequate provision for the poor as the 'thinge aboue all other infidelityes, [that] shall be our dampnacion'.[101] Foxe recorded the words of a Marian martyr, the lawyer and gentleman of London, Bartlet Greene, on the subject of charity and confiscated church goods. Greene wrote to Elizabeth Clarke of the great sums once spent on copes, vestments and ornaments in the church, further complaining of how such goods could have been sold to relieve the poor, but had not been.[102]

The first petition by the mayor, aldermen and commonalty of London depicted the miserable people in the street who offended 'clean'

---

[100] Henry Brinkelow, *The Complaint of Roderick Mors and The Lamentacyon of a Christen against the cytye of London*, Early English Text Society, J. Meadows Cowper (ed.), (London, 1874), [1542?], pp. 51–3. The *DNB* dates the text's first publication (tentatively) as 1545. *OED* on the definition of buzzard as a worthless, stupid or ignorant person, with example drawn from a 1545 sermon by Latimer likening bishops to 'bussardes'.

[101] Brinkelow, *The Lamentacion of a Christen Agaynst the Cytie of London*, Early English Text Society, Extra Series, No. 22 [1545], p. 80.

[102] John Foxe, *The Second Volume of the Ecclesiasticall Historie, Containing the Acts and Monuments of Martyrs* (London, 1610), p. 1685.

persons. The petitioners did not simply denigrate the poor, but appealed to Henry's mercy for the 'relyef of Crystes very images, creatyd to hys owne symlytude'. Christ's images were the poor, sick and blind in St Mary's Spittle, St Bartholomew's and St Thomas's Hospitals and the Abbey at Tower Hill. Likening the poor to Christ reiterated medieval conceptions of the poor that had survived reform. The petitioners also appealed to Henry's royal position and piety by calling him the defender of the poor, reminding him that the poor would remember his wealth, health and prosperity in 'contynuall prayer' if he saw to their aid.[103]

A second petition by London's citizens promised to use the vacant houses to exalt Christ's doctrine, alleging that the 'Anti-Christ', the Bishop of Rome, had founded the Grey Friars. The petitioners aimed to ease the burden of the poor on parishes, a burden that they suspected had increased with the dissolution of the monasteries and friaries and the city's population growth. Henry responded to these petitions by establishing St Bartholomew's Hospital and St Thomas's Hospital in Southwark for the poor and sick and Bethlehem, or 'Bedlam', for the insane.

Edward VI continued the royal endowment of hospitals and institutions, relieving poverty and restoring pageantry through the foundation of Christ's Hospital for fatherless children in the former Grey Friars. The institution admitted 400 poor children in November 1552 and, at Christmas, the orphans helped to fill the void in public ritual left by Edward's reforms. The children made a godly civic procession that contrasted with the uneven parochial observance of Corpus Christi and feast days like the Assumption and the Nativity of Our Lady.

> On Christmas day in the afternone, when my Lord Mayor and Aldermen rode to Pawles, all the children of Christes Hospitall stoode in aray, from St. Lawrence Lane, in Cheape, toward Pawles, all in one liuery of gownes of russet cotton and red caps, both men children and the maydens, [the latter with] kircheifes on theyr heades, all the masters of the hospitall beginninge first, next them the phisicion and iiii surgeons, with bandes about theyr neckes of white and grene satten, and betweene euery xx children, one woman keeper, which children were in number xvii[xx] [340].

Bringing the children and their keepers out on Christmas day 'to be sene of the citte' became a tradition in London. In addition, the Monday after Easter in 1553 before Edward's death, the children processed through the city to hear the sermon at St Mary's Spital, a spectacle called a 'godly sight' by Wriothesley.[104] Edward had 'put downe alle

---

103 *Memoranda, References, and documents*, p. 2.
104 Wriothesley, *A Chronicle of England*, Vol. II, pp. 80, 82.

goyng abrode of processyons, and the sensyng of Powlles at Wytsontyde, and the Skynners' processyon on Corpus Christi day, with alle others, and had none other but the Yngliche procession in their churches', upending the traditional sacred calendar of pre-Reformation London. Some parishes kept the holy days and others did not, 'soche was the devysyon'.[105] New godly spectacles might replace the older processions and festivals.

New charitable institutions and new moral campaigns showed the range of organizations and actions in Edwardian London meant to mould the behaviour of the poor. Edward granted Bridewell as a work-house for the idle poor, using his lands of the dissolved Savoy in 1553 as part of a larger plan for moral reform and good order. A 1553 covenant between Edward and the mayor, commonalty and citizens of London called for the examination of suspicious places, such as taverns, alehouses, gaming and dicing houses, dancing schools and cockpits, the suspected haunts of the able-bodied poor. The citizens' petition for Bridewell in 1552 described three types of poor: 'the succourless poor child, the sick and impotent, the sturdy vagabond, or idle person', the last of whom would be the future inmates.[106] City and monarch joined in the effort to locate vagabonds and other masterless people and ultimately bring them to correction, perhaps at the 'post of reforma-tion', a pillar erected in the Cheap for moral correction at the end of Edward's reign.[107] In 1543, the Lord Mayor had undertaken a cam-paign to duck prostitutes in the Thames, a punishment that would continue into the seventeenth century.[108]

Without pre-Reformation institutions, the state, the parish and the family joined in relieving the poor, mixing formal and informal relief, in what became the model in early modern England. Edward's Letters Patent of 1553 called for the instruction of children in honest callings, for the good of the commonwealth.[109] Parishes also endeavoured to

---

[105] John Gough Nichols (ed.), *Chronicle of the Grey Friars of London*, Camden Society, vol. 53 (London, 1852), pp. 56, 59.

[106] *Memoranda, references, and documents*, p. 63; 'The Citizens of London to the Privy Council on Their Suit to the King for Bridewell, 1552' in *TED*, Vol. 2, pp. 307–8. Bishop Ridley made an odd statement that Bridewell would do for lodging Christ, but he must have been thinking of the Christ-like, impotent poor not the idle targeted by the citizens' petition: 'Bishop Ridley to Cecil on the Same Subject, 1552' in ibid., p. 312.

[107] *Chronicle of the Grey Friars*, p. 78.

[108] McIntosh, *Controlling Misbehavior*, pp. 115–16; Crawford, *Women and Religion*, pp. 42–3; campaign against prostitution: Archer, *Pursuit*, pp. 249–54. Cucking stools were also used to punish scolds and women violating market rules: CLRO, Rep. 27, f. 68; Rep. 34, f. 10.

[109] *Memoranda, references, documents*, p. 65.

apprentice children in honest occupations, formal agreements slowly replacing early sixteenth-century informal arrangements for setting abandoned or orphaned children to work.[110] Parents, householders and masters bore responsibility for educating their literal and metaphorical children in piety and for keeping them from lewdness and idleness. Thus two aspects of bawdry in particular seemed most threatening to contemporaries: procurement for apprentices and employment of one's own children or servants as prostitutes. Henry Machyn described a 'man baude sett up one the pelore for bryngyng unto men prentes harlots, the whyche they gayff hym and them serten of ther masturs goodes and wastyd' in April 1556. A woman and her child landed in pillory, the mother for bawdry and her own child who had been 'browth to hordome'.[111]

Assessed rates and pleas for donations, to support hospitals occupying pre-Reformation buildings, showed a tentative move toward involuntary, lifetime gifts. The City of London had already agreed to maintain the hospitals in exchange for the initial royal grant of the pre-Reformation monastic foundations. In 1548, the Common Council assessed the city for 500 marks per year, and the companies for the same, to pay for St Bartholomew's Hospital. Parochial collectors for the poor supported the hospitals later in the century, though parishes might use compulsory rates to funnel money for the care of parish charges. St Michael, for instance, supported Mother Palmer in Bethlehem, in 1577–78, with money collected for Christ's.[112] St Stephen's churchwardens in 1573 paid Mistress Warfelie for keeping a child until that child gained admittance to 'the hospitall', Christ's. Similarly, they paid for caring for a woman in childbed and nursing her infant until sent there.[113] A memorandum from St Mary's showed that the collectors for the poor turned their collections over to Christ's Hospital, as well as to pensioners within the parish.[114]

Sir Richard Dobbes, Lord Mayor, asked parishioners throughout London in 1552 to give to hospitals. From testaments, however, only two gifts reached Christ's Hospital, five went to St Bartholomew's, one to another hospital, and one to a lazar house, a pre-Reformation institution.

Testators gave only modest support to hospitals under Mary, although Bonner enjoined curates to remind testators of the poor and

---

[110] See GL, Add. MSS 217 (dated 1587) and group from the early seventeenth century: GL, MS 1506/1–5. Further discussion in Chapter 5.

[111] Nichols, *The Diary of Henry Machyn*, pp. 104, 112.

[112] GL, MS 4071/1, f. 111.

[113] GL, MS 593/2, f. 62.

[114] For example: GL, MS 1002/1A, fols 106v–107.

'especially to solicit for the maintenance of the hospitals of the city of London'.[115] The absence of testamentary enthusiasm persisted through 1580. Testators may have relied upon parochial rates to fund institutions, the trend suggested in 1548. Testators left less than 2 per cent (1.57 per cent, or 12) of their pious bequests to the lame, impotent poor in St Bartholomew's and St Thomas's Hospitals. Gifts to Christ's Hospital rose slowly between 1558 and 1580 to 2 per cent (2.22 per cent, or 17) of all pious bequests, ranging in value from 5s to £100, compared to 1 per cent (1.17 per cent, or 5) of all pious bequests before 1558.[116] Distant hospitals, like the hospital and lazar house in Waterford, Ireland supported by one female testator, also garnered bequests.

Like under Edward, the children of Christ's Hospital offered a ready pool of deserving and orderly poor for privately endowed burial processions as well as corporately funded civic events in Elizabethan London. They did not participate in burial processions, from this sample, during Mary's reign. In 1578, Elizabeth Rice, who had supported the Irish hospital, desired the children to 'accompany my bodye to the buryall from my howse as theie are accustomed to doe to their benefactors'. She distributed a dole to the poor at her burial and another later, by her executor's discretion.[117] Henry Machyn described a sumptuous funeral procession drawing on the parish poor, the craft members, and Christ's Hospital for mourners in 1561.

> The sam day was bered in Cornyll mastores Hunt wedow, and the chylderyn of the hospetall and the masters wher at her berehyng with ther gren stayffes, and the xxx chylderyn syngyng the Paternoster in Englys, and a xl pore women in gownes; and after the clarkes syngyng, and after the corse, and then mornars, and after the craftes of the worshepfull compene of the Skynners; and ther dyd pryche the byshope of Durram master Pylkyngtun; after to the Skynners halle to dener.[118]

Ann Hunt gave £100 to Christ's without outlining their funerary role. The dinner described by Machyn capped the funeral experience, linking

---

[115] Christ's two gifts ranged from £2 to more than £3, St Bartholomew's five gifts ranged from less than £1 to £5, £10 to the 'hospital', and one non-monetary gift to lazar house. VAI, II, p. 368. Bequests to hospitals under Mary: three to Christ's, two to St Bartholomew's and two to Bethlehem.

[116] For example, GL, MS 9051/3, f. 22v. Significant difference: z-score of −2.44.

[117] GL, MS 9051/4, fols 151–151v. Christ's began earning income through burial money and children hired as singers and mourners after 1570, but the annual amounts were small, usually £50–£130: Manzione, Christ's Hospital, p. 86.

[118] Nichols, The Diary of Henry Machyn, p. 255. See Ann Hunt's will, PRO, PROB 11/44, fols 201R–203R. Christ's instructed children in singing, training that had once been prevalent in the parishes of London.

the dead and the living in a last meal and encouraging remembrance after the burial.

Bequests to prisons, traditional targets of Catholic acts of mercy to the imprisoned and the captive, survived Protestant innovations. Prisons provided a familiar focus for giving in the absence of traditional targets, but they also struck a chord with Protestants who identified with worldly suffering. Gifts focused on refreshment, alms and the relief of debts, totalling 35 bequests (11.15 per cent of all pious bequests). Citizens oversaw the function of prisons, like in 1550, when the keeper of the Bread Street Counter landed in Newgate wearing 'wydowes almes', or leg irons, for cruelty to prisoners. As during Edward's reign, gifts to prisons in and about London continued with 12 bequests (10.43 per cent).[119] Gifts to prisons fell slightly between 1558 and 1580 to 58 bequests (7.58 per cent). Roughly half of the gifts to prisons granted relief of debts, with other gifts mainly for general alms. Outside of bequests to prisons, testators forgave all or part of 71 debts, sometimes in return for the debtor's charity to the poor or care for a specific person. One warned his executors 'not to procure the undoinge of any my debters', especially those not in his new account book.[120] Testators rarely outlined loan or work schemes (two bequests) or supported scholars or poor maidens (15 bequests).

London inhabitants slowly adopted Reformation foundations in their testaments, but paid their assessments and, at least in higher social groups, made lifetime benefactions to new foundations and schemes rather than follow an older model of testamentary charity. Testamentary bequests for burials, however, showed continuity with older patterns of charity, even while exhibiting elements of reformed piety.

Death, burial and commemoration

Alice Briggs, in the mid-1550s, returned to pre-Reformation practices to help her reach salvation by hiring an honest priest to sing for Christian souls for two years. Her bequest for mourning gowns was a type, however, that survived reform. Between 1538 and 1548 traditional burial and commemoration services continued in the parishes of London with testators still disposing of goods for the health of their souls.[121]

---

[119] Wriothesley, *A Chronicle of England*, Vol. II, pp. 42–3. Ranging from less than 2s to £2, with a median of 10s.

[120] PRO, PROB 11/53, f. 121R.

[121] GL, MS 9171/11, f. 209v. A widow's will of 1547 in which she left all her goods to two women to pay her debts, burial costs and see to her soul. Leaving goods to other women has been called 'personalism': Erickson, *Women and Property*, p. 228. We should

Doctrinal change, the abolition of purgatory and the cult of saints, altered parochial observances for the dead, but did not lessen the significance of funereal observances. The churchwardens of St Stephen's in their 1558 inventory described a hearse cloth of gold with a black velvet border and silk fringe 'brodered [embroidered] w[i]th Image of St George and Sainct Vrsula and a Case for it' that would not survive the Elizabethan period.[122] St Mary Woolnoth held the usual obits for Dame Brice and Mr Amadas and fulfilled the obligations of the chantry of 'Noketts Foundation' until the abolition of purgatory. By 1547–48, the churchwardens accounted for half-year expenditures for obits, adapting to statutes mid-way through the fiscal year.[123] St Michael Cornhill, in 1547–48, also celebrated obits and maintained the rood light and other lamps or lights about the church.[124]

Burials and funerals still consumed testators' attention in last wills in Reformation London, despite recent change and older ambivalence about 'pomp and vainglory'.[125] In 1549, Edward Myldemay limited burial costs to 40s and instead left a generous gift of £6 13s 4d to the parish poor, from whom he could not request prayers. He may have attempted to distinguish his burial from a pre-Reformation one by planning a gift to the poor that outstripped the pomp of his funeral. His last testament provided for repairs in St Botolph's, too, a type of bequest that declined in Edward's reign.[126] Wriothesley's account of the funeral procession of the Lord Mayor's wife applauded him for similarly limiting mourning. The Lord Mayor provided only 12 score (240) gowns for two poor men and two poor women in each parish and for 40 inmates of St Bartholomew's, and 'noe blacke to none of th' aldermen, but onely to his officers and the cheife mourners', a 'godly act' praised by Wriothesley.[127]

---

remember, however, that these personal and moveable goods encompass a widow's fortune for her own bequeathing after her deceased husband had settled the bulk of the property. For example of inventory of costs relating to death and burial, see inventory attached to will of Katheryn Bracye: Ida Darlington (ed.), *London Consistory Court Wills, 1492–1547*, London Record Society 3 (London, 1967), p. 153.

[122] Requested by Sir Rowland Hill: GL, MS 3103, f. 32. He was a knight, sheriff (1541) and Lord Mayor (1549): John Strype, *A Survey of the cities of London and Westminster ... By John Stow* (2 vols, London, 1720), Vol. 2, Book 5, pp. 131, 132.

[123] GL, MS 1002/1A, fols 2v, 4v, 8, 19, 33v, 37v, 42, and throughout. For Thomas Nocket's chantry and Dame Elizabeth Brice's obit see *Chantry Certificate*, p.26; Stow, 1890, p. 212. GL, MS 1002/1A, fols 45v–47v.

[124] GL, MS 4071/1, f. 27.

[125] Rubin describes funerary and chantry extravagance in the late fifteenth century in *Charity and Community*, p. 297.

[126] PRO, PROB 11/32, f. 214L.

[127] Lord Mayor Anthony Jude, or Judd: Wriothesley, *A Chronicle of England*, Vol. II, p. 44; 1550. See also Strype, *A Survey*, Vol. 2, Book 5, p. 132.

Services related to burial reflected the uncertainty of practice and 'custom' in the midst of religious change in mid-century London. While wills before the Reformation often referred directly to services for the dead, from dirige to Requiem, after 1548 wills began to leave more to 'custom', a word that allowed the testator room for 'equivocation'.[128] Elizabeth Stevyns requested eight clerks to bring her body to the earth 'singing suche godly psalmes before me as is accustomed for the deade', trusting her executors to know her meaning and, incidentally, the current statutes.[129] Lettys Lane also depended upon her executor's discretion to stage an appropriate burial service. She asked to be brought to the city's gate 'and from thens to be carryed to the foresaid p[ar]ishe of Saynt Stevyns with suche prests and clerks as shalbe thought meete' in a procession of 24 poor men and women and her servants in black coats.[130]

In contrast to the godly sights and requests of Edwardian testators, the funeral procession of Lady Bowes in 1553 exemplified the enthusiasm of some in London for the restoration of Catholic services and sumptuous spectacles soon after Edward's burial in August. Henry Machyn described the lengthy herald's funeral procession for the wife of prominent citizen Sir Martin Bowes, benefactor of St Mary's rood and London's hospitals.[131] For the October burial, Bowes outfitted 100 men and women, and hung the house, street, and church with 'blake clothe, and with ther armes a-pon the blake'. Machyn described four great tapers, four great gilded candlesticks and two great white branches, the traditional lights of a Catholic burial. The Company of Clerks and the priests followed the hundred mourners, and 'then came the corpse with iiij penons of arms'. The extravagance of the funeral became apparent in the 'cheyffe mornars': 'my lord mare and the sword beyrer, and ser Hare Hubbellthorne and ser Rowland Hyll knyghtes, and mornars many, and ij knyght(s) more, and dyvers gentyllmen, and after the craft of Goldsmyth(s)'. A dirige followed and 'the marow after a goodly masse song in Laten, and a sermon, and when all was done they whent to dener' at Bowes's house.

---

[128] Jonathan Wright, 'The World's Worst Worm: Conscience and Conformity during the English Reformation', *SCJ*, 30, 1 (1999), pp. 113–33; Olga Valbuena, 'To "Venture in the Rebels' Fight": History and Equivocation in Macbeth', *Renaissance Papers*, (1994), p. 108; Wabuda, 'Equivocation and Recantation During the English Reformation: The "Subtle Shadows" of Dr Edward Crome', *Journal of Ecclesiastical History*, 44, 2 (April 1993), pp. 224–42.

[129] PRO, PROB 11/34, f. 47L.

[130] PRO, PROB 11/35, f. 79L.

[131] *Diary of Henry Machyn*, pp. 46–7. Parenthetical additions made by the modern editor.

Elaborate funerals after 1558 continued to unite rich and poor in processions that emphasized yet temporarily transcended the social order in the final moments of an individual's presence above the ground. Even without prayers for souls, the participation of the poor in mourning continued an older practice of the wealthy asking for spiritual help from the poor. The provision of gowns, however, worn by the poor long after the funeral had ended, still marked the vast differences in social status between rich and poor. Thomas Muschampe's extended preamble in 1578 looked forward to the reunion of his body and soul at the day of judgement and his rise with Abraham, Isaac and Jacob, in imitation of Edward's 1547 Injunctions. He inverted the usual testamentary order by beginning with the forgiveness of debts and a series of bequests to the poor. Only further down in his will did he ask his 'old friend', the painter-stainer Robert Greenwood, to make three dozen escutcheons bearing his and his late wife's arms.[132] This subtle inversion reinforced the difference of his attitude toward burial, although he still promoted his lineage through it.

The preferred Protestant and Catholic processions differed not in their apparel, but in their length and services. Muschampe planned a funeral procession that shared elements with Lady Bowes's, yet differed by forgoing excessive mourners in favour of a smaller group of poor men and women and selected family, servants and associates. He granted to 31 apprentices, servants, friends and family and to 24 poor people black garments, gowns to men and cassocks to women. Social rank and sex determined the type and cost of garment. Muschampe stated outright that anyone given black cloth was to wear it at his burial.

The influence of the Reformation on testators' burial plans comes through in their bequests for mourning gowns and other tokens over this period. From 1538 to 1548 more than half of the gifts to friends and family were in money (43.18 per cent or 19) or gowns (13.64 per cent or six). In the same period testators concentrated bequests to children on providing portions (69 per cent or 54) while other gifts went to forms of remembrance (23 per cent or 17). Bequests for gowns could be helpfully unspecific, perhaps even allowing recipients to add 'to pray for my soul' without including that forbidden catch-phrase in a testament. Bequests of gowns to kin and acquaintances between 1548 and 1552 comprised 17.4 per cent (107) of such items, second only to money gifts. Pious gifts followed this pattern, with money first (73.58 per cent, 220) and gowns second (20.74 per cent, 62). Some testators asked or required neighbours, parsons, clerks, craft and the poor to

---

[132] *VAI*, II, p. 130; PRO, PROB 11/60, fols 181R–186L.

participate in mourning, explicitly or implicitly, through such bequests.[133] The serving man Nicholas Marks, in common with some wealthy people from the early sixteenth century, demanded burial 'w[i]th funerall expens honeste and not sumptuouse'.[134] During the Catholic restoration bequests for gowns declined, an indication of religious uncertainty about burial services and ambivalence about public display. Among gifts to friends, family and associates, gowns (8.2 per cent, or 31) fell behind money (36.24 per cent, or 137) and rings (12.43 per cent, or 47) as ways to express affection and secure remembrance.

The evolution of non-pious bequests to friends, family and servants in the mid-sixteenth century echoes overall change in burial and commemoration. Wills probated between 1549 and 1580 left consistent bequests of money and gowns, more than 39 (1226) and 10 (323) per cent respectively of all non-pious bequests (3089). In wills probated between 1549 and 1552 rings (13.98 per cent, 86) closely followed money (36.1 per cent, 222) and gowns (17.4 per cent, 107) out of all pious bequests (615). By 1558, rings became a favoured gift (12.4 per cent or 47) to show affection and garner remembrance, compared to gowns (8.2 per cent, 31) or money (36.2 per cent or 137) out of all gifts (374). By 1580, slightly more than 41 per cent (867) of bequests were in money and slightly more than 8 per cent (185) in gowns. John Dodd outfitted a mourning party by leaving eight gowns to the poor, including one man he named, and gowns to friends and family.[135] In a document mainly concerned with providing rings, some with death's heads, and black robes and cloaks, John Pickeringe asked his wife and two friends to nominate twelve poor people for a black gown each, without calling it a funeral procession.[136] Slightly more than 11 per cent (234) of bequests were rings, mostly directed to friends.

Mary's omission to restore the cult of saints and prayers for souls contributed to a trend toward remembrance of the person, whereas before the Reformation pious remembrance of the soul ranked first in memorializing the dead. Private tokens, like rings and articles of the testator's clothing, may have spurred private remembrance of the person, as opposed to the person's soul. Thomas Muschampe produced a long list of friends and family to receive rings, most bearing his arms for a 'poore Remembraunce of me, and of my good will'. He left £10 for

---

[133] The number of observations reaches 74. As stated previously, however, observations do not count the number of individuals asking for such attendance, only the numbers of gifts linked to such attendance.

[134] GL, MS 9051/2, f. 150v.

[135] PRO, PROB 11/60, f. 296R.

[136] PRO, PROB 11/62, f. 263L.

dinner among the company and a like bequest for all mourners.[137] One testator left a gold ring to a friend as a 'remembraunce of old fryndshipp that hath bene betwene hym and me'.[138]

Rings and other tokens reflected the deceased person and sometimes his or her occupation. Fraunces Benyson asked his executors, his wife and brother, to engrave rings for nine friends with death's heads and letters, probably monograms, as they saw fit.[139] The gift of rings promoted lineage or the individual, but for goldsmiths like Muschampe it also served as a final and lasting reflection of their craft. Similarly, women could leave tokens that reflected the work of their lifetime. A widow left handkerchiefs edged or worked in black to men and women as a remembrance of her and a mourning symbol.[140] A freeman of London expected his wife to dispose of the residue of his estate as she thought best 'and to geve unto my fryndes and kinsfoulke, as she shall thinck meet for a Remembraunce of me'.[141] The couple may have discussed possibilities before the husband's death, or he may have trusted her to choose suitable tokens from other parishioners' examples.

Small private tokens may have supplanted parochial monuments and the more intimate gifts formerly left to parishes, such as altar clothes. Rings continued an older symbolism of death, with death's heads and engraved phrases expressing the brevity of life and the flesh, and commended the donor to the remembrance of the living. A goldsmith designed a ring for thirteen friends and family saying, 'All fleshe is grase', an evocative declaration for the living.[142] In 1544, George Crowche, part of a Protestant circle in St Michael's including his former servant Thomas Hunt and his wife Ann, gave numerous 'deadesman hedde' rings and one with a motto around the head: 'Truste in Christes bloode and none other'. Crowche lived by this creed, having opened his testament with an affirmation of justification by faith and not salvation through his own works.[143] The iconoclasm of later stages of reform, under Edward and Elizabeth, may have elevated small tokens over large funeral monuments.

While testators gave plate and remembrances to craft guilds and rings with initials or with religious sayings or symbols to friends and families, bequests for parochial monuments rarely figured in testaments. After

---

137 PRO, PROB 11/60, fols 181R–186L.
138 PRO, PROB 11/42B, f. 208R.
139 PRO, PROB 11/53, f. 121L.
140 GL, MS 9051/3, f. 268.
141 GL, MS 9051/3, f. 141.
142 PRO, PROB 11/55, f. 196R.
143 PRO, PROB 11/30, fols 121L–123L, rings on 122L, 122R.

the removal of images from churches and former religious houses in the late 1540s, testators and their spiritual and secular advisors may have hesitated to redecorate parishes with monuments vulnerable to religious change. Thomas Stevyns in 1549, however, called for a 'rememberaunce of my deceas' by a stone on his grave or a pillar. His widow went further in describing the content of her engraved memorial: 'Pray for the soule of Elizabeth Stevyns late wyfe of Thomas Stevyns Goldsmyth'.[144] Despite her lasting call for prayers, she trusted her soul to Jesus Christ, the 'only mediator and advocate' between God and humankind.

Other postmortem ties to the parish also loosened after 1558, due to the twin pressures of London's population growth and the resumed Reformation, perhaps weakening the allegiance that might have precipitated testamentary bequests to the church fabric. Between the expectation of eventual bodily resurrection and the reality of overcrowded burial sites within London, testators simply bequeathed their bodies to the earth from whence it came rather than to specific places within their parish church or churchyard.[145] More than half of the testators from 1559–80 (55.62 per cent, or 94) left their grave locations unspecified or to their executors' discretion rather than requested burial in a named place (44.38 per cent, or 75).[146] A cook 'in love and charity' with the world requested a Christian burial 'according to the Lawes of this realme' in 1563, but otherwise left details unspecified.[147]

Those testators who specified burial location developed a distinctly Reformation-style burial in contrast to the pre-Reformation model. The widow Katerine Mathewe outlined her plans in 1571: the presence of her coffined body within the church to the knell and peals of the bells, as 'accustomed', and finally a funeral sermon. The Episcopal instructions of 1560 permitted one short peal before and one after the burial, a description repeated by Bishop Sandys.[148] After the burial, Mathewe desired a drinking among her neighbours. She left £4 9s 2d in ready money and gold rings to sell for the £7 celebration.[149] In 1578, John Wetherhill wished to be buried in the cloister by his child and brother without 'mourninge ringinge of bells or any like vayne ceremonies',

[144] PRO, PROB 11/33, f. 52L; PRO, PROB 11/34, f. 47L.

[145] Harding explains that population growth meant that parish churches could not accommodate all parishioners: '"And one more may be laid there": the Location of Burials in Early Modern London', *The London Journal*, 14, 2 (1989), p. 113.

[146] Z-score between two proportions of 1559–80, showing significant difference: 2.94.

[147] GL, MS 9051/3, f. 30Av.

[148] Clare Gittings studies the development of coffining, especially in the seventeenth century: *Death, Burial and the Individual in Early Modern England* (London and Sydney, 1984), p. 114. *VAI*, III, pp. 62, 309.

[149] GL, MS 9171/16, f. 82v.

only the one knell lasting for one hour according to the current custom.[150]

Sermons represented another aspect of the emerging Reformation funeral package, though some testators added sermons to traditional services, like John Bodnam did in St Stephen's in 1541 when he asked a person learned in divinity to preach the word of God at the mass of Requiem.[151] Sermons extended a pre-Reformation tradition, but Protestant preaching aimed to turn parishioners away from 'superstition' and towards the new ways. The Second Royal Injunctions of 1538 and those of 1547 mandated at least a quarterly sermon 'wherein ye shall purely and sincerely declare the very Gospel of Christ, and in the same exhort your hearers to the works of charity, mercy, and faith' and not to pilgrimages or money, tapers, or candles for relics or images.[152]

Reformation sermons reflected a personal involvement in the edification of a congregation and, for women especially, offered an opportunity to influence the religious views of fellow parishioners. A burial 'sermon preached by some devout lerned man to the lawde and prayse of god and to the edifying of the congregacon that shalbe there p[re]sent' cost the skinner Thomas Hunt 10s.[153] The Skinners had once supported the Corpus Christi procession in London and perhaps Hunt wanted to fund a godly community gathering in his will, written in 1557, but probated in 1559 during Elizabeth's reign. His widow, Anne Hunt, went further in her 1560 will by leaving £6 for a dozen sermons and £5 each to the preachers Mr [Richard] Alvey and Mr [Miles] Coverdale, as well as £100 for poor scholars studying divinity at Cambridge and Oxford.[154] She patronized specific men, unlike her husband's general call for 'some' learned man, and showed her allegiance to some of the formative puritan lecturers in London. The widow Hunt's bequest to prominent preachers and puritans, especially Coverdale who had been key to the dissemination of Protestantism and resistance to vestments, also reinforces the impression of the diversity of religious belief in St Michael's since at least the 1540s. The parish sold off many of its remaining Catholic ornaments and goods in the year 1561–62, after some of its parishioners had already adapted to the new Elizabethan Reformation.[155]

---

[150] PRO, PROB 11/60, f. 210L.

[151] PRO, PROB 11/28, f. 288R.

[152] VAI, II, p. 37. See p. 39 on the need for licences for preaching. VAI, II, p. 115.

[153] PRO, PROB 11/42B, f. 107R.

[154] PRO, PROB 11/44, f. 202L. See DNB entries on Richard Alvey and Miles Coverdale. Both of these men had returned from their Marian exiles by 1560. On Skinners' Corpus Christi procession: Morley, p. 232.

[155] GL, MS 4071/1, f. 67.

Sermons evangelized, instructing listeners in Protestant theology to the 'glory of god and to the Augmentacon of his churche'.[156] The number of gifts towards sermons increased greatly with the return of Reformation under Elizabeth, reaching 72 (9.41 per cent of all pious bequests), compared to 21 (6.69 per cent) in 1548–52, and six (5.22 per cent) during the Catholic restoration.[157] Even in the last quarter of the sixteenth century, bequests for sermons played on central external aspects of Catholic devotion. In 1579, Dorathie Tatton asked for thirty sermons in the year following her death, harking back to the trental of masses of the pre-Reformation church.[158] The 'unprofitable servaunte of god' Raynolde Nott claimed to have done two men wrong and berated his own 'sinfull boddie' in 1563. He left 40s for four learned preachers to give sermons in St Stephen Walbrook and a further 40s to Thomas Becon, vice dean of Canterbury and former parish parson, for four sermons in Stoughton in Kent.[159] In 1575, the doctor of phisick Symon Ludford, also of St Stephen's, hoped that Master Nowell Dean of Paul's 'maie be hadd' to give a burial sermon 'to the edefieng of gods churche' for 20s, or else another 'sober and Learned preacher' for 10s.[160]

Testators who could call on such well-known individuals added to their own social and pious prestige among their fellow parishioners. Between 1550 and 1580, nine women and 22 men requested burial sermons, or cycles of sermons. Women made some of the largest bequests to hire preachers: cycles of 12 and 30 sermons. Testators sometimes asked for the parish parson, but other times requested notable preachers in London, like the Dean of Paul's, Thomas Becon, Coverdale or Robert Crowley. Churchwardens' accounts sometimes noted the benefactor of commemorative sermons to memorialize the men and women whose gifts glorified God and edified the congregation. No testators left provision for lectures, readings and lectures held separately from services in parish churches that were important elements of parochial worship and instruction. Payments for lectures in parish accounts, however, shows that these events fell to parochial responsibility, not voluntary or testamentary endowments. St Botolph's churchwardens first mention a 'reader' only in the accounts of 1569–

---

[156] PRO, PROB 11/48, f. 151L.

[157] The periods ending in 1552 and in 1558 show no significant difference in the endowment of sermons (z-score of 1.21), but between 1558 and 1580 a significant difference is apparent (z-score of 5.59).

[158] PRO, PROB 11/62, f. 111R.

[159] PRO, PROB 11/46, f. 140R.

[160] PRO, PROB 11/57, f. 291R.

70. In 1570–71, St Mary's paid for a year's worth of sermons by three men.[161]

Commemoration and mourning also occurred in trade or craft guilds' participation in the burial processions and funeral dinners of deceased members. During Henry's last decade testators clothed company fellows with gowns (37 per cent or seven) and rings (16 per cent or three). Testators connected the dinners or 'drinkings' they donated for members to the craft's attendance at burial, often layering professional bonds with friendship through the common gifts of dinners, gowns, rings and money.[162] After 1558, gifts to companies focused on dinners or recreations and mourning, with a few for remembrances.[163] The recreations favoured by testators transformed the burial observance of companies from one based on masses and prayers to one based on commemoration without formal pious observances related to purgatory. Testators made their names and their lineage more permanent by furnishing plate and craft dinners without asking for prayers in return. John Mathewe, a cook, left plate to his Company and 6s 8d for a drinking after bringing him to the church. Further, he left his ring to a friend and fellow cook to wear for life then pass on to another cook with the same charge.[164] Similarly, the waxchandler Thomas Scampion left 10s to his Company for a 'memorye' of him.[165] Some followed bequests for dinners with gifts to the poor of the guild.[166]

Besides dinners for mourners and friends, testators supplied spice buns, cake or bread to the poor, neighbours and company on the day of burial to mark community ties. Falling under the phrase 'manner and custom', this practice possibly escaped other wills. Robert Cutlard, in 1578, distinguished his celebration from boisterous recreations or drinkings by provisioning 20s for a breakfast for 'my bretheren in Christe that are in London with whome I most kepte company in my Liffe time/ that they maye in christe reioyce together and be thanckfull unto god for my deliv[er]aunce oute of this vale of miserye'.[167] Nicolas

---

[161] Paul Seaver, *The Puritan Lectureships: The Politics of Religious Dissent, 1560–1662* (Stanford, CA, 1970), pp. 83–4; on duties of Readers: *VAI*, III, pp. 67–8. GL MS 1454, Roll 72; GL, MS 1002/1A, f. 159v.

[162] Testators left one gift to a dinner and four for drinkings, with two other gifts connected to burials and five left unspecified, but likely with funereal purposes. While few, these bequests outnumber those to hospitals. Also see Ward, *Metropolitan Communities*, pp. 100, 111.

[163] Eleven bequests for dinners or recreations (one-third), seven for burial duties (one-quarter), and three (one-tenth) to remembrances.

[164] GL, MS 9171/12, fols 142–142v.

[165] GL, MS 9171/12, f. 67.

[166] For example, see PRO, PROB 11/41, f. 49L, a gift of coals and fuel.

[167] PRO, PROB 11/60, f. 261L.

Marshe, skinner, outlined a drinking with spice bread and wine at his own home and a spice cake and bun for each to take home, by the Company's ancient custom.[168] Muschampe exhorted his executors as well 'to prepaire good and holsome spycebreade, accordinge to the auncient use of the Cytie of London against my buriall daie' and to distribute it among his neighbours and the members of the Goldsmiths' as a remembrance.[169] Elys Bodley, parson of St Stephen's, asked his executors to go out with his friends and kinsfolk to give three spice cakes and three buns to each household in St Stephen's and St Botolph's Billingsgate parishes in 1547.[170] Bodley, a native of Kent, may have been honouring a country tradition by demanding this face-to-face distribution by the husband and wife who were executors and kin to Bodley.

Post-Reformation burials showed continuity with the traditional significance of death and commemoration in pre-Reformation parishes, although many Protestants championed simpler and smaller burials and services. The poor still played important roles in funeral commemoration, but attitudes towards them and about charity hardened through the sixteenth century.

Poverty and charity

The Seven Works of Mercy inextricably linked piety and charity in pre-Reformation England. Protestant reform reaffirmed the nexus between charity and piety by equating the goods of the Church with those of the poor, although reform altered some forms of almsgiving.[171] Edwardian Injunctions, besides the religious changes outlined previously, also moulded parishioners' pious and charitable actions. The Injunctions required church attendance, sober and charitable behaviour, and visits to the poor and the sick on holy days.[172] Parishes often erected a pew for the collectors for the poor at the church door, to encourage parishioners to pay their rates promptly and willingly.[173]

Testators responded to the cultural imperative to remember the poor: bequests to the poor rose between 1548 and 1580, as seen in Table 3.1. The monetary values of gifts to the poor and to non-pious ends di-

---

[168] PRO, PROB 11/41, f. 174L.
[169] PRO, PROB 11/60, f. 184R.
[170] PRO, PROB 11/32, f. 36L.
[171] VAI, II, p. 10.
[172] VAI, II, pp. 10, 125; Thomson, 'Piety and charity', p. 182.
[173] For example, GL, MS 1454, Roll 72 (1569–70).

Table 3.1   Percentage of gifts to poor, out of all pious gifts[174]

Year	To poor (%)	To poor (N)	Other pious (N)
1548	36.95	109	186
1552	67.52	212	102
1558	52.17	60	55
1580	67.19	514	251

Table 3.2   Values of non-pious and pious gifts (to nearest £)

Year	1548	1552	1558	1580
Non-pious	1077 (63.1%)	968 (56.1%)	1426 (89.1%)	10872 (82.5%)
Pious (all)	416 (24.4%)	534 (30.9%)	117 (7.3%)	1363 (10.3%)
To poor	214 (12.5%)	224 (13%)	57 (3.6%)	942 (7.1%)

verged, however, with quantifiable testamentary wealth directed to friends and families, as shown in Table 3.2.

Although modern analysis of testaments shows that charity increased through the mid-sixteenth century, the nostalgic John Stow lamented the state of voluntary giving and hospitality after the Reformation. The donors of alms in 'old times' 'gave great relief to the poor'.

> I myself, in that declining time of charity, have oft seen at the Lord Cromwell's gate in London more than two hundred persons served twice every day with bread, meat, and drink sufficient; for he observed that ancient and charitable custom, as all prelates, noblemen, or men of honour and worship, his predecessors, had done before him ...

Stow appealed to tradition, summarizing Venerable Bede's history of prelates 'having peradventure but wooden churches' who nonetheless gave generously to the poor. Their wooden churches contrasted with the edifices of sixteenth-century London, even if the interiors of the post-Reformation churches may have been poorly outfitted. Prelates had 'on their board at their meals one alms' dish, into the which was carved some good portion of meat out of every other dish brought to

---

[174] The given year shows the end date of a cluster of years. Significant differences between these years ending: 1548 and 1552 (16.09), 1552 and 1558 (3.19), and 1558 and 1580 (–9.51). The cash figures have been corrected for inflation but, even uncorrected, the figures show the disparity between the known value of gifts to family and friends and those to pious ends.

their table ... '. One poor prelate divided his silver dish 'among the poor, therewith to shift as they could, till God should send them better store'.[175] Stow avoided a direct comparison between Catholic and Protestant charity, but emphasized instead the perceived stinginess of his fellow Londoners after the Reformation.

Stow also described how late sixteenth-century Londoners forgot their predecessors' charity, not to mention neglected to follow their charitable example. He mentioned the destruction of the tomb belonging to the former mayor Robert Drope and his wife Lady Jane (Johane) Lisle, even though their 'liberality to that church and parish' of St Michael had paid for church renovations, construction of a conduit in the ward, charity to the poor and pious bequests for obits. The church filled their vault with the body of a deceased alderman instead in 1596. Although St Michael's suffered 'annoyances' from their crowded burial spaces, Stow's commentary suggests that at least some inhabitants hoped that luminaries would not be uprooted to make room for later burials. Perhaps since the Viscountess had died childless she did not have close family to pressure the parish to preserve her place in the church. The Elizabethan Proclamation against the destruction of church monuments by 'sundry people, partly ignorant, partly malicious, or covetous' attempted to preserve the good memory of individual benefactors and their families by prohibiting spoliation of monuments that did not 'nourish any kind of superstition'.[176]

Whereas Stow's descriptions of new businesses and homes contrasted the liberality of Catholic England with display in Protestant times, Foxe elided the Catholic example to recall the primitive church instead. In the primitive church of the Old Testament, the root of true Protestant piety, 'Widowes had the charge, and gathering for the poor men and strangers'. Bartlet Greene asked Elizabeth Clarke to note the condition of those in the almshouses and prisons of London, where some Protestants suffered under Mary. 'Alas that Christ so hungereth, and no man will feed him: is so sore opprest with thirst, and no man will give him to drinke: destitute of all lodging, and not relieued: naked, and not clothed: sicke, and not visited: imprisoned, and not seene'.[177] Through the martyrology, Foxe urged readers to perform charity, especially as it furthered the Protestant cause and succoured persecuted reformers.

---

[175] Thoms, p. 34.

[176] Morley, pp. 205–6. 'Prohibiting Destruction of Church Monuments' [Windsor, 19 September 1560, 2 Elizabeth I], TRP, Vol. II, p. 146.

[177] Foxe, The Second Volume, p. 1685. On collection of charity for congregations in Marian London: Usher, '"In a Time of Persecution": New light on the secret Protestant congregation in Marian London' in David Loades (ed.), John Foxe and the English Reformation (Aldershot, 1997), p. 245.

The parish poor box attempted to bring bequests and donations in line with reformed religious doctrine, supporting the needy rather than 'superstition'. William Lytchefylde's gift to the chest in 1548/49 indicated that it stood at the high altar's end of St Botolph's church, having dislocated tithes in the space of the church as it was intended to do in testaments.[178] No testamentary gifts to the poor box preceded 1548, however, and only six gifts (1.91 per cent of pious gifts) followed during Edward's time, although the Injunctions of 1547 urged clergy present at deathbeds to persuade testators to make donations to it over 'blind devotions'.[179] In 1550, William Buckney left £1 to the poor box and William Rysse gave £1 to it for the relief of the poor, in God's honour. Some articles ordered ministers to 'exhort' communicants to give to the box each Sunday, perhaps as they passed by the box on the way into the church, stressing lifetime gifts.[180]

Although the Edwardian command that urged gifts to the poor box came at the cost of traditional tithes to the high altar, the box survived under Mary. In wills, it still drew only a couple of gifts and never replaced the pre-Reformation customary bequest to the high altar for forgotten tithes. St Mary's churchwardens itemized 21s 5d given to the poor at Christmas from the 'church box', however.[181] Parishioners apparently filled the poor box with voluntary giving and fines rather than through wills, perhaps recognizing or resenting the connection to Edwardian reforms. Elizabeth's first articles and injunctions questioned parishes as to whether or not the boxes had even been constructed.[182]

The few examples from wills indicate the common use of poor boxes and the reliance on churchwardens' discretion in emptying them. Thomas Hunt finished his execution of a friend's will, leaving funds to poor boxes and adding more than £3 'for the releif and comfourth of the poor people in a byting wethin the said parryshe according as shalbe thought good' by the churchwardens and masters of the parish. Hunt hoped that the stock would purchase coals to be sold to the poor at times of inflation.[183] Creating a stock to subsidize the purchase of coals despite price fluctuations presaged later programmes to manipulate

---

[178] PRO, PROB 11/32, f. 266L.

[179] Individual gifts ranged from just over a shilling to more than £3. See Duffy, *Stripping*, p. 505; *VAI*, II, p. 127.

[180] GL, MS 9171/12, f. 50v; GL MS 9171/13, f. 1v. See Ridley's Articles for London, *VAI*, II, p. 240. *VAI*, II, p. 193 and footnote 4. Contrary to Lytchefylde's will, Cox described old boxes 'near the chief entrance' to churches: *The English Parish Church* (London, 1914), p. 312.

[181] Only five bequests to the poor box after 1558. GL, MS 1002/1A, f. 63.

[182] *VAI*, III, pp. 3, 16–17.

[183] PRO, PROB 11/42B, f. 109R. A few gifts provided coals to the poor.

markets or safeguard against future economic crises. Henry Swarland, upholder, made separate bequests to the high altar and the post-Reformation poor box in 1555 and even asked for burial by the poor box.[184] He made no requests for prayers from the poor, but his grave, near the high altar judging by the location of the box in other parishes, assured remembrance by poor and wealthy parishioners. An Elizabethan bequest of 2s 6d to the poor box passed directly to the curate and churchwardens 'for the more discreete bestowing of the same', reflecting the customs surrounding the distribution of funds from the box.[185]

Ecclesiastics inquired after inhabitants' actions and implied that the parish depended materially on collected rates and morally on charity. Ridley's Articles for London Diocese (1550) reiterated the desire to see testaments fulfilled, as did Bonner's Articles for London Diocese (1554) and Elizabeth's Royal Articles (1559). Sandys's Articles reiterated familiar concern for the performance of wills. They further asked: 'Whether there be any person or persons within your parish of ability, that obstinately or frowardly [sic] refuse to give reasonably towards the help and relief of the poor, or do wilfully discourage others from so charitable a deed, and what be their names'.[186] The next article inquired about the hospitals of the city, supported by obligatory donations and through hoped-for contributions. Homilies to be read in the churches, from 1562, also stressed the importance of alms and questioned the extent of charity. Giving alms and showing mercy to the needy glorified God and exhibited a Christian vocation, being one of the 'manifold duties' required by God. Yet, 'such is the slothful sluggishness of our dull nature to that which is good and godly, that we are almost in nothing more negligent and less careful than we are therein'. Although in practice testators and parishes aided the poor after the Reformation, the homily's chastisement of 'merciless misers' with their 'stony hearts' stoked

---

[184] Pearl downplays the significance of municipal efforts: 'Puritans and Poor Relief: The London Workhouse, 1649–1660' in Donald Pennington and Keith Thomas (eds), *Puritans and Revolutionaries: Essays in Seventeenth Century History Presented to Christopher Hill* (Oxford, 1978), pp. 228, 229; but elsewhere she emphasizes the importance of those efforts, as well as ones to keep a supply of grain for times of shortage: 'Social Policy in Early Modern London', in Hugh Lloyd-Jones, Valerie Pearl and Blair Worden (eds), *History and Imagination: Essays in Honour of H.R. Trevor-Roper* (London, 1981), pp. 119–20. On later sixteenth-century efforts: Slack, *From Reformation to Improvement*, pp. 54, 63–5. GL, MS 9171/13, f. 84v.

[185] GL, MS 9051/4, f. 221v. 'Discreet' meant judgment in speech or action or prudence and circumspection. Another testator left money to the poor box, to be distributed as other money had been: PRO, PROB 11/46, f. 283L.

[186] *VAI*, II, pp. 240, 353; *VAI*, III, p. 6. Repeated in [Edwin] Sandys' Articles for London Diocese (1571): *VAI*, III, p. 311.

the urgency of helping the needy after the dissolution of religious houses and fraternities.[187]

Testamentary charity often brought rich and poor into contact, particularly around death. Economic change widened the gap between social groups, however. The rituals associated with death and burial, through reform and restoration, facilitated charity, but religious reform may have made transcending the divide between rich and poor more difficult.[188] Dinners for neighbours and craft seemed to separate the abject poor from testators' social equals. On the other hand, the 'custom' of distributing spice breads at funerals temporarily eased social distinctions. The widow Jane Spencer asked for spice bread at her burial, handed out 'as well amonge the poore as the Riche', within the parish of St Michael's.[189] Spice bread and doles nourished the poor in return for their presence at funerals or for their participation in mourning processions, though the reciprocal power of praying for wealthy dead souls had evaporated. Between 1553 and 1558, one-third of pious gifts to the poor were in gowns or cloth, thus continuing the pattern of distinguishing the poor through their conspicuous mourning apparel.[190] The 1555 Poor Law carried sartorial distinction further by requiring licensed beggars to wear badges when begging in the streets. Between 1559 and 1580, testators left 229 gowns to the poor to wear in connection with burial and services, 44.55 per cent of all pious bequests made to the poor.

'Indiscriminate' doles at burials had once been the responsibility of religious houses and wealthy individuals dispensing hospitality. Burial doles had been officially condemned in 1536, and only three gifts of money or bread were specifically identified as doles, 1549–52, ranging in value from £2 to £6 13s 4d. Wriothesley claimed that at Henry VIII's burial '21 thousand and more' poor men, women and children had collected alms from noon until six in the evening. Restrictions of civic pageants, such as the city watches from 1539 until 1548, resulted in a 'great losse to poore men' by blocking another avenue for indiscrimi-

---

[187] 'An Homily of Alms-Deeds, and Mercifulness towards the Poor and Needy', *Sermons, or Homilies, Appointed to Be Read in Churches in the Time of Queen Elizabeth, of Famous Memory*, Book II, (New York, 1815), Early American Imprints, no. 34346, pp. 322–35.

[188] Patrick Collinson argues that religious change made 'it more difficult for those distances to be bridged and for tensions to be expressed, contained and surmounted by ceremonies and rituals': *The Birthpangs of Protestant England: Religious and Cultural Change in the Sixteenth and Seventeenth Centuries* (New York, 1988), p. 31.

[189] PRO, PROB 11/35, f. 127L; GL, MS 9171/13, f. 2.

[190] Twenty gifts, out of 60 noted to the poor, or 20 per cent out of all pious bequests in this period.

nate relief.[191] Without detailing his wishes, in 1563 Peter Flawter left 50s for burial and a dole to the poor, according to his executor's discretion.[192] William Edwards disposed 6s 8d among living kinfolk, with the stipulation that the money reach the poor if none be found alive.[193]

Despite prohibition of doles at burials, sixteenth-century Londoners found other ways to relieve the poor by mimicking pre-Reformation gifts to poor parishioners and householders. Sir Martin Bowes, knight and alderman, left 26s to distribute 6d in bread to six poor householders each Sunday in 1560–61, and reiterated the bequest in his will. Since he paid for his daughter's laystall in the cloister of St Mary Woolnoth that same year, he may have been establishing an anniversary for her through charity. The parish sold its remaining implements and ornaments of Catholic worship in 1563–64 and later, suggesting some confusion about reform, or resistance to it, within the parish.[194] In the early 1570s, St Michael's recorded the distribution of 52s in bread as provided through the will of Robert Dunkins.[195] Commemorative bequests endowed by the Percivales before the Reformation survived religious change to provide money and coals to the poor. Bowes imitated notable parishioners by endowing his own gifts for bread and coals to the poor.[196] A baker sent dozens of loaves of bread to the poor in all towns where he had once lived.[197] Similarly, the maidservant and single woman Elizabeth Christopher earmarked 15s for her burial and for the poor, all at the discretion of her aunt, her executrix.[198]

Since the form of those gifts resembled earlier ones, some testators took pains to differentiate the purpose of gifts to the poor from the traditional solicitation of prayers for Christian souls. Robert Waynam in 1552 asked his son to exercise discretion in spending the residue of his estate 'to the glory of god and the relief and comforte of the poor membres of Christe', likening the poor to Christ in late medieval fashion, but not making a plea for prayers. The scrivener John Maior in 1551 excused his neighbour of half of a debt on condition that the

---

[191] Wriothesley, *A Chronicle of England*, Vol. I, pp. 100, 181. As Slack points out, the act of 1536 outlawing 'indiscriminate almsgiving' was not renewed, but the ideas behind it survived in the thinking about poverty in sixteenth-century legislation: *The English Poor Law*, pp. 9–10.

[192] GL, MS 9171/15, f. 188.

[193] PRO, PROB 11/28, f. 110L.

[194] GL, MS 1002/1A, fols 98, 109v, 118 (1563–64), 187v (1576–77).

[195] GL, MS 4071/1, f. 98.

[196] GL, MS 1002/1A, fols 98, 104.

[197] PRO, PROB 11/29, f. 206L.

[198] GL, MS 9051/3, f. 41.

neighbour paid the other half. He bequeathed the repayment of 20s to the poor, 'not to thintente to pray for but to be thankefull unto God and to praye for the kynge'. Maior aided the poor, but in this case directed their concern towards the king, as the 1547 Injunctions duplicated earlier allowances to pray for the monarch.[199] Maior's bequest for three sermons would help the poor and his fellow parishioners to understand the difference in intent as well as the different objective of their prayers. The absence of requests for prayers may not have hindered an executor or a mourner from praying privately, of course.

Prayers for the monarch and the prominence of royal and elite arms replaced the prayers for souls and images of saints and holy figures that had once filled parish churches. The architecture and services of the church reinforced the political and social order, as did charity. St Mary's churchwardens recorded, 'Item paied the xvijth of November 1565 to a smyth for mending & setting up one of the banners of armes in the quyre' 4d.[200] Arms had hung in churches before the Reformation, but the images were balanced by other pious iconography. Parishes stored weapons, as seen in St Michael's 12d payment to John Hawley for powder to 'scowre the harquebrushes in the Churche' in the 'Armor lofte'. The same year churchwardens rang bells and paid for a prayer of thanksgiving to celebrate the 'overthrowe geven to the Turke' at Lepanto and Queen Elizabeth's coronation anniversary.[201]

In addition to forgoing outright requests for prayers for souls in wills, testators and parliamentary and civic leaders distinguished their relief of the poor from the pre-Reformation, indiscriminate model of charity. What had been medieval ambivalence about indiscriminate charity became official policy against it. England began to impose obligatory contributions to the poor that also regulated recipients. While the governments of other European countries also controlled and centralized relief, only England paid for a system by taxation. The act 'Touching the Punishment of Vagabonds and other Idle Persons' (1550) repealed provision for the enslavement of vagabonds (1547), but restated their punishment by whipping. Poor children were to be put to work and the impotent poor relieved, in part by allowing their begging by license. In

---

[199] GL, MS 9171/12, fols 80v, 81v. VAI, II, p. 136.

[200] GL, MS 1002/1A, f. 124. On pre-Reformation churches with arms: Graves, 'Social space', p. 312.

[201] GL, MS 4071/1, fols 98, 111. (accounts of 1571–72) See STC 16508, 16508.3, 16508.9, 16509, 16510 from Kisby, 'Books'; prayer also included in STC 24716, *Newes from Vienna the .5. day of August .1566. of the strong towne and castell of Jula in Hungary*, London: John Awdelay, 1566. See 'Compendious Chronology of Joyful Occasions, 1558–1702': Cressy, *Bonfires and Bells*, pp. 90–92; Queen's coronation as replacement for lost holy days and festivities: ibid., pp. 50–66.

1552 the act 'For the Provision and Relief of the Poor' confirmed earlier acts and stipulated that parishes choose collectors of alms, register the impotent poor collecting aid and forbid begging.[202]

Innovative approaches to relieving poverty survived the religious fluctuations of the mid-century. Mary did not turn back statutes regarding the poor and poverty when she restored Catholicism, although Protestant polemic suspected Catholics of indiscriminate charity. Bonner re-emphasized the Seven Works of Mercy, however, when he required parsons, vicars and curates to instruct parishioners in the articles of the Catholic faith. The Elizabethan Homilies explained 'good deeds', measured by ends and intents, in relation to 'faith', which assured that the works were not 'dead, vain, and fruitless' as in the 'feigned' religion of Catholics.[203] Under Elizabeth the act 'For the Punishment of Vagabonds and for Relief of the Poor and Impotent' (1572) repealed earlier statutes, reiterated the whipping of vagabonds, added 'branding' by burning ears, and continued the practice of registering and aiding the impotent poor. A 1576 act required constables to search alleys for inmates. Collectors for the poor accounted for the collection and distribution of rates in parishes.[204]

Mid-century marked a period of higher inflation that some testators knew reduced some of their neighbours to poverty. Nevertheless, the stationer John Awdelay [Audelie] in 1575 thanked God for his relative material success, using it emblematically to stress the importance of charity and the indignity of poverty. Having written *The Fraternitye of Vacabondes* and the twenty-five orders of knaves, he had purportedly studied the types of vagabonds, rogues, swindlers and their female partners who populated the ranks of the idle poor.[205] Awdelay acknowl-

---

[202] Paul Slack, *The English Poor Law*, pp. 13–14; *From Reformation to Imrovement*, p. 21. Nuremberg's restrictions to local poor, based on need and moral tests: Steven Ozment, *Magdalena and Balthasar: An Intimate Portrait of Life in Sixteenth-Century Europe Revealed in the Letters of a Nuremberg Husband and Wife* (New Haven and London, 1989), orig. publ. 1986, p. 158; the 'coalition [of Catholics and Protestants] for welfare reform in the 1530's' in Lyon: Davis, 'Poor Relief, Humanism, and Heresy' in *Society and Culture in Early Modern France* (Stanford, CA, 1987), p. 35. 1 Edw. VI c. 3 and 3&4 Edw. VI c. 16. C.S.L. Davies, 'Slavery and Protector Somerset: the Vagrancy Act of 1547', *Economic History Review*, 2nd series, **19** (1966), pp. 533–49. 5 & 6 Edw. VI c. 2.

[203] *VAI*, II, p. 338. 'A Sermon: Of Good Works annexed unto Faith', *Sermons, or Homilies*, Book I, pp. 38–46. In another sermon, good works showed obedience to God, testified to justification, and 'stirred up' others to glorify God: 'An Homily of Good Works, *Sermons, or Homilies*, Book II, pp. 232–3.

[204] GL, MS 4071/1, f. 107.

[205] John Awdelay, *The fraternitye of uacabondes* (London, 1575, 2nd ed.), STC 994. Watt stresses his Protestant preamble and printing of godly ballads: *Cheap Print*, pp. 50–51, 274–5, 286.

edged the Lord's pleasure in blessing him with goods, 'though in aboundance not so great', that enabled him to bestow charity on others rather than claim it. He thanked God for

> mercie shewed towardes me farre greater than to manie of my bretheren in gevinge me a contented minde and blessinge my small labours that in all my distressed p[o]verties sickenes and griefs he hath allwaies provided for me and myne to serve our necessities rather makinge us able to be helpefull to others than burdenous to manie.

His will, however, exhibited little evidence of his ability to be helpful to others outside the residue left to his wife's discretion to honour God. He and his wife may have discussed appropriate charity before his death, or he may have left decisions to his wife. The omission of detailed charitable bequests perhaps signified that he had distributed aid primarily in his lifetime, nearly impossible to measure, rather than through his last will.

Awdelay sounded a familiar note on the importance of work, acknowledged by Brinkelow's schemes to regulate cloth production and the economy to ensure work in towns and cities. Awdelay enjoined his children to be 'good members' of the Commonwealth by following their 'vocation' from God and not 'to be Drones or burdenous to this our countrie and comonwelth'. His thanks to God and warning to his children stressed the benefit of work, the importance of relief, and the pious rewards for leading a salutary life.[206] 'An Homily Against Idleness' reminded listeners that idleness was a 'grievous sin' and, drawing on St Paul, that 'if there were any such among them that would not labour, the same should not eat, nor have any living at other men's hands'. Catholic leaders similarly emphasized labour in their approaches to poor relief.[207]

Parishes and testators tried to set the needy and worthy poor on work, in line with statutes and church orthodoxy. Churchwardens employed ageing or aged poor men and women in menial tasks to supplement other forms of relief, since only 'by reason of age, debility

---

[206] PRO, PROB 11/57, fols 269L–269R. The homily against idleness acknowledged the danger to the commonwealth, not to mention the idle person, from the 'Mother' of all evils: *Sermons, or Homilies*, Book II, pp. 441–2. The 'civic benefit' of work was not limited to the ideology of Protestant England, despite Weber's arguments: Max Weber, *The Protestant Ethic and the Spirit of Capitalism* (New York, 1958), pp. 35–40. In seventeenth-century France and Italy, policy alternated between 'back-breaking labour and an endless round of sacred readings and devotional activity': Pullan, 'Catholics and the Poor', p. 33.

[207] 'An Homily Against Idleness': *Sermons, or Homilies*, Book II, pp. 439, 440. Jütte, *Poverty and Deviance*, p. 198.

of body, or want of health', did a person escape the admonition to labour. St Stephen's, for example, paid poor men to keep the church door and blow the bellows for the church organ for the year, as they had earlier been paid for bearing torches in Catholic services.[208] Thomas Hunt provided a stock of £100 to the governors of Bridewell, St Thomas's and Christ's Hospital to set the poor to work in drapery of wool cloth, with oversight by the company. Testators left a handful of bequests to the worthy poor among the young, especially poor scholars and poor maidens. Only two gifts for work schemes or loan programmes surfaced between 1549 and 1552, one a gift from Hunt. He intended his stock to provide loans to young free men of the Skinners, 'thought worthye' by master and wardens at the end of apprenticeship and their years as journeymen, to establish them in their trade.[209]

Parish churches and churchwardens also helped needy parishioners bridge troubled times by taking goods in pawn. In 1568, St Botolph's bought a strong box with six locks to hold the stock for the parish and the aid of parishioners, especially the poorer ones. The parish agreed that the curate, deputy, elder churchwarden, two gentlemen and one nominated 'anncyent freman' would each hold one key to the strong chest containing the church's stock. Only with the consent of all six men would the elder churchwarden distribute the stock.

> And further yt is agreed that if anye of the sayd pishioners shall hereafter have occasyon to employe the said Stocke or anye p[ar]te therof for his or theire necessarie use and rather beinge a poore man beinge thought mete to have the same by the consent of the said sixe p[er]sons, then the sayd p[er]son or p[er]sons so desieringe the same, layinge into the sayd cheste sufficient pawne therfore maye have yt for suche tyem as also shalbe thought good so as always the Stocke be redye yerelie at the accompte to be answeryd[210]

This example, and the few notes of goods held in pawn in wills, illustrates the range of remedies available in times of temporary or conjunctural poverty. Some widows similarly contributed to the loans available in sixteenth-century London, helping people meet shortfalls or find the capital for their trades. One woman used the bill of debt for £22 from one man to pay her debt to another, as she settled her accounts.[211]

---

[208] 'An Homily Against Idleness', *Sermons, or Homilies*, Book II, p. 439. For example, GL, MS 593/2, fols 26v, 37v, 39v.

[209] PRO, PROB 11/42B, fols 108L, 111L. Six bequests, from £5–£40.

[210] GL, MS 1454, Roll 71. The 'elder' churchwarden referred to the man in his second year of office-holding. In St Botolph's, two churchwardens served overlapping two-year terms.

[211] PRO, PROB11/61, f. 137R. In rural areas, widows made a 'fertile source of free-floating capital': Erickson, *Women and Property*, p. 194; mid-seventeenth-century example

Statutes added legislative weight to parochial and individual practices that categorized the 'deserving' and 'undeserving' poor. The tag 'deserving' adhered to those poor whose behaviour and lifecycle circumstances met the fluctuating moral and demographic demands of the parish. Churchwardens, through their discretion, acted as gatekeepers of the parish requirements for charity. Widows, for instance, often were the 'bulk of the "respectable" poor', as in St Michael's accounting of £23 11s 3d received for the poor in 1570. The year's recipients were 'mothers' and 'goodwives', not all of whom were widowed, and two 'goodmen'. Only at Christmas, Easter and All Hallows did churchwardens make general payments to the 'poore of ye p[a]risshe' of roughly £3. The parish spent only £14 6s 4d through the year.[212]

Contemporaries recognized the potential economic and social problems for less wealthy widows, but tightly stretched parish resources meant that even widows had to show and preserve their deserving status. Remarriage improved widows' economic well-being, but poor widows remarried with difficulty and therefore depended on parochial benevolence.[213] Sermons drew on St Paul's warning to Timothy 'to eschew and refuse idle widows, *which go about from house to house, because they are not only idle, but prattlers also, and busy-bodies, speaking things which are not comely*'.[214] The criticism of widows encapsulated in Paul's exhortation castigated widows not merely for idleness, but for loose speech as they went around their neighbourhood, a gendered conception of the dangers inherent in women's disorderly speech.[215] One church-

---

in rural area: Robert Tittler, 'Money-lending in the West Midlands: the activities of Joyce Jefferies, 1638–49', *Historical Research*, 67, 164 (Oct. 1994), pp. 249–63.

[212] Erickson, *Women and Property*, p. 203. GL, MS 4071/1, fols 96v–97.

[213] Vivien Brodsky, 'Widows in Late Elizabethan London: Remarriage, Economic Opportunity and Family Orientations' in Lloyd Bonfield, Richard M. Smith and Keith Wrightson (eds), *The World We Have Gained: Histories of Population and Social Structure* (Oxford, 1986), pp. 123, 143, 147; widows as 'objects of pity' or the 'bulk of the "respectable" poor': Erickson, *Women and Property*, pp. 227, 203. See also Barbara J. Todd, 'The remarrying widow: a stereotype reconsidered' in Mary Prior (ed.), *Women in English Society 1500–1800* (London and New York, 1985), pp.74–9; B.A. Holderness, 'Widows in pre-industrial society: an essay upon their economic functions' in Richard M. Smith (ed.), *Land, Kinship and Life-Cycle* (Cambridge, 1984), p. 431. Many widows' dependence on a 'helpmeet': Erickson, *Women and Property*, p. 197.

[214] 'An Homily Against Idleness', *Sermons, or Homilies*, Book II, p. 440.

[215] Wriothesley even recounts the execution of a scold in 1550: *A Chronicle of England*, Vol. II, p. 36. David Underdown, 'The Taming of the Scold: the Enforcement of Patriarchal Authority in Early Modern England' in Anthony Fletcher and John Stevenson (eds), *Order and Disorder in Early Modern England* (Cambridge, 1985), pp. 120–21; Amussen, 'Gender, Family and the Social Order' in ibid., pp. 207–8; Elizabeth Foyster, 'A Laughing Matter? Marital Discord and Gender Control in Seventeenth-Century England', *Rural History* 4, 1 (1993), pp. 11–16; Gowing, *Domestic Dangers*, p. 62.

warden recorded: 'given to wydowe pteriche [Partridge?] at her goinge out of this parishe in the p[re]sence of Mr p[ar]son and my fellowe churchwarden 20s.'. Churchwardens assessed widows for clerk's wages and parsonage expenses and included them in the list of parishioners in arrears, a list likely read aloud at the year-end audit. Parishes might try to collect arrears when a widow remarried; William Olyver refused payment of his wife's 10s debt for rent to the parish in the mid-1550s.[216]

The resident poor, those who had long resided in or served a parish, also figured as the deserving poor, though their behaviour did not pass without scrutiny. Long residence meant that churchwardens knew the character and habits of the older poor. Not all of the elderly ended their lives poor, their social status having a bearing on the difficulties of ageing. The organ maker John Howe not only inhabited St Stephen's and built and fixed its organs, but he and his father had both served as churchwardens. He seems to have lived into old age, as did his wife. Each of them required assistance as they aged and the widowed Mrs Howe needed further help after his death. Reformation changes, and Howe's purchase of 133 pounds of organ pipes from St Stephen's in 1550, may have reduced the income of the Howes as they aged. The Ludfords' similarly long attachment to the parish pricked the consciences of their fellow parishioners for more than twenty years. After the couple's deaths, their daughter, for whom the parish had once redeemed her pawned clothing, had no success in doing the same.[217]

Alongside new statutes and attitudes regarding poverty, civic and parliamentary leaders began a campaign against idle and disorderly behaviour that also threatened forms of popular recreation. The idle poor engaged in play instead of labouring, embodying the 'undeserving' poor, contrasted with the deserving aged and impotent poor. Reformers in 1542 attempted to prohibit the frequenting of alehouses during Sunday services to curb blasphemy, swearing, gambling, and so on.[218] In 1550, the Lord Mayor and sheriffs broke up playing tables in bowling alleys and houses around Paul's Wharf and Aldgate and warned the 'divers simple persons and vagabondes ... that they should neuer more haunt such places'.[219] In the last year of Edward's reign the sheriffs

---

[216] GL, MS 1002/1A, f. 169; GL, MS 1454, Rolls 60–61, 68.

[217] GL, MS 593/2, fols 18, 60, 65, 75, 76–76v, 78v.

[218] Burke notes that reform of popular culture was 'not exactly new' in 1500: *Popular Culture*, p. 217; Spufford also argues against the newness or unfamiliarity of reform to the sixteenth-century English: 'Puritanism and Social Control?', p. 44 and throughout; Slack, *From Reformation to Improvement*, pp. 32–3; Hutton, *Merry England*, pp. 111–13. 'An Homily Against Idleness'; see also Mullaney, *The Place*, pp. 49–50. VAI, II, p. 86.

[219] Wriothesley, *A Chronicle of England*, Vol. II, p. 43.

whipped seven women 'for vacabondes that wold not labor, but play the unthryftes'. Further, the mayor 'dyd gret correccione unto powre pepulle', putting them in carts or setting them in pillory, 'both men and women'.[220] George Crowche gave £30 to the poor in his birthplace in 1544, 'provided that no idell man nor woman whiche will not labour and be hable, and may have labour to gett a penny and will not, shall yn anny wyse have anny parte of the foresaide almes'.[221]

Side streets and alleys integrated the poor in compact parish neighbourhoods, accounting for 'much "evell rule"' according to the Common Council in 1551.[222] That closeness precipitated legislation against overcrowding: restrictions on inmates and lodgers, some of them strangers and foreigners, to prevent plague, fire and crime. Official regulation and personal charity complemented one another by maintaining a degree of order and helping the poor clustered in alleys. In a small inner-city parish like St Michael's, alleys and tenements prevented the insulation of wealthier individuals from their poorer neighbours. In 1554–55, the parish spent £5 9s 4d on certain named poor in Harp Alley and St Nicholas Lane, with £5 in one lump sum to the poor in the street side, alleys and churchyard in the parish.[223] Ann Hunt bequeathed £10 to the poor dwelling in the street side of the parish, £3 to the poor dwelling in alleys of the parish, and 10s to the poor near Leathersellers Hall, 'dwelling by my garden'.[224] Similarly, Hugh Tedar left 2s to the poor folks of Stidmer Alley.[225]

Reform of behaviour and popular culture continued through Mary's reign. In her first year, the mayor and sheriffs of London dug up popular bowling alleys around the city in 1553.[226] Social disorder wrought by vagabonds and 'unthrifties' worried the Catholic leadership as it had the Protestants. In addition, rebellious people threatened the Catholic restoration politically and religiously. For example, one man

---

[220] Nichols, *Chronicle of the Grey Friars*, pp. 73, 77.

[221] PRO, PROB 11/30, f. 122L.

[222] Quoted in Archer, *Pursuit*, p. 242. On focus on problems associated with poverty: pp. 242–5.

[223] This contrasts with nineteenth-century London where the 'social distance between rich and poor expressed itself in an ever sharper geographical segregation of the city'. Poor districts, unlike in the less-differentiated early modern city, were a *'terra incognita'* except to 'intrepid missionaries and explorers' writing for a fearful, yet voyeuristic middle-class audience: Gareth Stedman Jones, *Outcast London: A Study in the Relationship between Classes in Victorian Society* (Oxford, 1971), pp. 13–14. GL, MS 4071/1, f. 48.

[224] PRO, PROB 11/44, f. 202R.

[225] GL, MS 9171/15, f. 273.

[226] Wriothesley, *A Chronicle of England*, Vol. II, p. 105.

preached at Paul's Cross at the queen's bidding, but 'was pullyd owte of the pulpyt by vacabonddes, and one threw hys dagger at hym'.[227] Chroniclers may have preferred to blame outsiders or marginalized members of society rather than respectable or at least resident Londoners for resistance to the restoration of Catholicism. Contemporaries conflated vagabondage with social and political disorder, and even rebellion, well into the seventeenth century. Whippings took place at the 'reformation post', where punishment of the body was believed to lead to a change in morality or behaviour.[228]

Youth, with their potential for unruliness, troubled authorities like the disorderly poor did. Loans and scholarships for young men and dowries and employment for young women could help to keep them able-bodied workers. Ecclesiastical and royal authorities therefore attempted to shape the behaviour and morality of youths.[229] Young intellectuals formed a core of reforming Protestants, showing their affinity for intellectual or religious rebellion. Apprentices represented instability, especially in periods of economic crisis.[230] Visitation articles and injunctions through the sixteenth century emphasized instructing young people in true doctrine. In 1571–72, the churchwardens of St Botolph's Aldersgate noted the sex-segregated galleries within the church for maidservants and apprentices. St Michael's vestry called for seats to be made in the quire for poor folks and servants in 1576. Later, the vestry allowed for maidservants' places near the 'womans pues' along with similar places in the quire.[231]

Public control of the behaviour of the young, poor and masterless men and women filtered into private concerns with children's futures and characters. Testators worried over their children's likelihood of making a living in economically difficult times and even of overcoming their weaknesses. In her 1559 will, Blanche Crofton provided her son Thomas with an annuity of £20 for three years while he studied the common law. She promised him £200 cash, two standing cups, assorted silver, brass and pewter, and leases to tithes in the North only if his

---

[227] Nichols, *Chronicle of the Grey Friars*, p. 83.

[228] Nichols, *Diary of Henry Machyn*, p. 164; pillar erected in Cheap for correction described in *Chronicle of the Grey Friars*, p. 78. Beier, *Masterless Men*, p. 6; the confusion of vagabondage and disorderliness continued into the seventeenth century as contemporaries used the label 'vagabond' to discredit radical religious prophets: Mack, *Visionary Women*, p. 110.

[229] Griffiths, *Youth*, pp. 6, 202–3, 221–2; Ben-Amos, *Adolescence*, pp. 200–201, 238–9.

[230] Brigden, 'Youth and the English Reformation', *PaP*, **95** (May 1982), pp. 37–67; Archer, *Pursuit*, pp. 1–9.

[231] GL, MS 4072/1, Part 1, fols 20v, 28. St Botolph's paid for the 'yonge mennes gallerie' and the 'maydens gallerie' in1571–72: GL, MS 1454, Roll 74.

learning coalesced into a living. As might be expected from a woman asking five different preachers to make sermons, she also wished him to lead a 'godlie and decent lief'. She warned him against troubling her executors lest he lose the entire bequest.[232]

Restrictions on testamentary bequests to the poor echoed civic concerns over behaviour and order and about the administration of gifts. Women tended to impose moral restrictions on bequests directed to the poor and others while men did not before 1553. Before 1538, all bequests left to another's discretion rested on the conscience of the executor and from then until 1548, only 15 per cent depended upon parish officials rather than executors. Women entrusted executors with 2.38 per cent (four) of their gifts; men likewise entrusted 11.45 per cent (15) of their gifts to them. Women left none to the charge of parish officials and men left 5.34 per cent (seven) of their bequests to the oversight of officials. Women, however, restricted their gifts to those of 'good name and fame' (70.83 per cent or 119), while men did not (0). Men for the most part placed no restrictions upon their gifts (77.86 per cent, or 102). Jane Spencer provided 60 gowns for 46 poor men and women 'of honest name fame and conversancy' to be 'appoynted' in St Michael Cornhill and for 14 men and women she named in her will.[233] Between 1558 and 1580, a quarter (24.45 per cent, or 89) of women's and slightly more than a quarter (27.08 per cent, or 88) of men's bequests relied on the executor's discretion, a less formal mode of regulation than depending on churchwardens. Before 1580 those men who relied on executors were in most cases relying on their wives.[234]

The gender difference in imposing charitable restrictions suggests that women practised more discriminating charity, sooner than men did. Women's household roles – including overseeing servants, going to market through London's streets, engaging in money-making tasks – may have hardened their views of the deserving and undeserving poor. Cultural attitudes about the poor, rather than fewer resources, may have slowly revised English charity and poor relief. Beyond their everyday experiences, women may also have adopted new religious ideas that influenced their testamentary restrictions. The link between piety and charity held through the sixteenth century, and women's greater discrimination may reveal an earlier, more enthusiastic embrace of reformed piety. Reformed theology reified distinctions between deserving and

---

[232] PRO, PROB 11/43, f. 35L.

[233] PRO, PROB 11/35, f. 127R.

[234] The percentage of husbands naming wives as executrices in wills was more than 65 per cent, but less than 75 per cent through 1580. After that date the figure drops.

undeserving that had surfaced even in late medieval England.[235] Perhaps in life men had been able to communicate their wishes or demonstrate their intentions, as well as command respect for choices, as women had not. But that men named their wives as executrices also suggests that they handed over discretionary power, anticipating women's discrimination.

Trusting to the discretion of executors or churchwardens may have continued an older practice of face-to-face charity. The handful of gifts (six) to poor householders often depended on the discretion of executors or parish officials who recognized the deserving of the parish. Edward Myldemay bequeathed £10 to the poor of St Botolph's in 1549, asking that the churchwardens or the alderman's deputy pay 4d to each poor household within the parish.[236] His executor, his brother from Danbury, Essex, would be less likely to know deserving householders than would other parishioners. In turn, Myldemay expected his executor to distribute £2 to the poor householders of Chelmsford, apparently his birthplace. One testator charged the curate with the distribution, 'in his presens', of 10s to the poor of the parish in 1563.[237] The curate's presence could insure the residence of the poor in the parish, their neediness, and the intimacy of charity.

The men and women of mid-century London sought a balance between commands to give to the poor and prohibitions against indiscriminate charity. The connection between charity and piety was not broken by the Reformation or changes in the growing city, but it had to adapt to new social and religious circumstances.

Conclusion

Charity remained essential to piety in the century's middle years, through Edward's radical reforms, Mary's restoration of Catholicism and Elizabeth's settlement, even as involuntary giving grew. Bequests show that contemporaries sought out individuals and institutions familiar to them, from prisons to the parish poor, but not the newer hospitals or unknown poor across the city. Without purgatory to necessitate prayers for souls, however, the poor lost an important spiritual function in the parish. This loss coincided with greater public scrutiny of the behaviour and morality of the poor and an apparent increase in the numbers of

---

[235] Rubin, *Charity and Community*, pp. 291–2, 297; Brown, *Popular Piety*, p. 185; Thomson, 'Piety and Charity', pp. 182–3.
[236] PRO, PROB 11/32, f. 214L.
[237] GL, MS 9171/15, f. 161v.

poor within London. The uniformity of pre-Reformation bequests and patterns had been broken, destabilizing not only the shared goals of pre-Reformation testators, but also of the pre-Reformation city. Survivals, or the shells of Catholic piety within Protestant structures, allowed some parishes and testators to sustain an older culture in diluted form, or to exploit differences to showcase puritan piety. Efforts at social control and creative solutions to alleviate poverty marked the last period of our study.

CHAPTER FOUR

Piety and the Reformation parish, 1580–1620

London enjoyed peace in the later sixteenth century, without Catholics and Protestants rioting, even massacring one another in the streets, as happened in some continental cities. Debate over the severity of social and religious tensions has characterized recent historiography on London.[1] The city's demographic growth, economic development that widened the gulf between rich and poor, and religious heterogeneity could have destabilized the city. Remnants of older piety, revivals of traditional parochial life, and new parish activities eased London parishioners into the Reformation. Charity and new solutions for poverty also calmed the city, a discussion that will be taken up in the next chapter. Parishes continued to renovate their church interiors and reform their services and lectures. Individual parishioners also expressed reformed piety in their funeral practices and in their last wills and testaments. Parallel to the pre-Reformation link between the 'fabric' of the church and the cloth of community life, parishioners in post-Reformation London brought together their support for the structure and decoration of their parishes with that for their family and associates.

Parishes and parochial bonds remained central to London life, even after extensive religious change. In civic politics and administration, parochial leaders continued to shape and fulfil directives from the city and national governments. Aldermen depended upon wardmotes and vestries for the collection of rates and the interaction with members of parishes, wards and companies. Select vestries in place in some parishes by the 1590s were 'not necessarily unrepresentative'; hence vestries served as the 'cockpit' of local government.[2] Complementary social control and responsiveness by city elites marked civic rule.

---

[1] See debate between Ian Archer and Steven Rappaport on the extent of social mobility and stability in the city: cf. *Pursuit*, p. 50 and *Worlds*, pp. 379–80. Recent work by Ward on craft guilds has suggested that craft members tried to avoid sectarian tensions: *Metropolitan Communities*, pp. 110–13; McClendon emphasizes the tendency among Norwich civic elites to avoid religious disputes and violence through toleration of heterodoxy: 'Discipline and punish?', pp. 99–118.

[2] Archer, *Pursuit*, p. 69.

Culture in cities and towns in the early modern period centred around religious and civic rituals, including burials, perambulations and festivals. The loss of religious guilds had meant the end to some pageantry in cities and towns; the decline in ritual has been linked to social stratification and urban decay or distress. In large part, the end of ceremonials began in the early sixteenth century as many local economies contracted and could no longer support the expense of large festivals.[3] Renovation of the parish fabric and reform of popular piety illustrate the change in London life in the late sixteenth and early seventeenth centuries. The evidence from London wills and churchwardens' accounts suggests a similar emphasis on the distinction and distance between the privileged and the poor. Testators asked craft members and individuals they knew, who were connected through a social or economic network, to attend funerals and weddings. Fewer occasions across boundaries of rank and parish or neighbourhood illustrated, and reinforced, the hierarchy of social groups. In the earlier period, ceremony, personal and civic, had blurred social distinctions and allowed at least the temporary redefinition of social boundaries.[4]

Reworking the fabric

Parochial expenses included general maintenance needs, like repairing damaged or worn steeples, and special requirements of the new services and design of a Protestant church. The 'crisis' in church fabric precipitated by the early stages of the Reformation continued in the late sixteenth and early seventeenth centuries. That only a few gifts intended for the church's ornaments and building surfaced after 1581, reinforces the impression of impoverished churches struggling to maintain buildings, renovate interiors with Protestant furniture, and fulfil devotional obligations.[5] The value of pious money gifts did not decline greatly, but

---

[3] With the loss of religious guilds, towns lost their 'cultural dominance': Phythian-Adams, 'Urban Decay in Late Medieval England' in Philip Abrams and E.A. Wrigley (eds), *Towns and Societies: Essays in Economic History and Historical Sociology* (Cambridge, 1978), p. 184. Further, he notes that Coventry had become 'distinctly more stratified than theretofore' with the loss of city-wide pageantry: *Desolation of a City*, p. 274; Clark and Slack (eds), *Crisis and Order*. Corpus Christi in Coventry is one of the better-known examples of city pageantry: Phythian-Adams, 'Urban Decay', p. 177.

[4] The actions of Catholic Reformation Italian confraternities show a similar tendency to reinforce, rather than transcend, social hierarchy and topography: Black, *Italian Confraternities*; Ronald F.E. Weissman, *Ritual Brotherhood in Renaissance Florence* (New York, 1981).

[5] See also Archer, *Pursuit*, pp. 170–73; Kümin, *The Shaping*, pp. 214–15.

they did not keep pace with the growth in the value of non-pious gifts to friends, families and business associates.[6] These gifts before the Reformation had fostered the worship of holy figures, centred communal piety in the church, and helped to fund everyday operations and repairs of the parish. The loss of shrines and altars to the saints, Jesus and the Virgin Mary emptied the interiors of churches, destroying some expressions of lay piety. Although interiors and ceremonies were 'sterilized', new Protestant services required communion tables and books, among them the Book of Common Prayer, psalter, English Bible in the largest volume, homilies and Erasmus's Paraphrases. Bishop Sandys's Articles for London Diocese (1571) outlined the books and furniture, including a pulpit, 'necessary and requisite for Common Prayer and administration of the Sacraments', a list reiterated and enforced through the successive decades.[7]

The sheer cost of rebuilding and outfitting churches, let alone any lingering animosity to reform, meant that some parishes slowly adapted to Protestant doctrine. Episcopal agents sometimes prompted parishes to purchase the books and goods necessary for the new services. Only with the threat of 'an excommunicac[i]o[n]' did St Michael's churchwardens purchase Erasmus's Paraphrases in 1586–87, for 13s. St Michael's also suffered a puritan preacher to give a 'seditious' sermon, showing that their lack of printed requisites did not signal resistance to Protestant ideas. In the 1590s they paid for a new desk for the 'paraphrases', bought a new Bible, and mended their Book of Common Prayer.[8] In 1610, the Bishop ordered St Mary's churchwardens to purchase Bishop Jewel's works, for 23s.[9] St Michael's churchwarden paid 25s 9d for a 'boke of Bishopp Jewell & a lock & a key to fasten it', and made a separate payment for a 'new deske' for it.[10]

Conformity to reform occurred over years, not in one set of purchases and renovations. Old images bled through layers of whitewash, necessitating frequent payments to paint over medieval Catholic wall

---

[6] The value of non-pious gifts rose from more than £16 000 between 1580 and 1601 to more than £26 000 before 1620, while pious gifts totalled just more than £4200 by 1601, but only just over £3100 by 1620.

[7] Book of Common Prayer, New Kalendar, Psalter, English Bible in the largest volume, two books of homilies, a table on a frame for Communion, silver Communion cup and cover, pulpit, Paraphrases of Erasmus, the Ten Commandments, and a strong chest or box for alms for the poor: VAI, III, pp. 303–4. 'Sterilized services of the Book of Common Prayer': Haigh, *English Reformations*, p. 288; Gibbs, 'New duties', p. 168; Kisby, 'Books in London Parish Churches, c. 1400–c. 1603'.

[8] GL, MS 4071/1, fols 126v, 136. Related in Seaver, *Puritan Lectureships*, p. 216.

[9] GL, MS 1002/1B, f. 389.

[10] GL, MS 4071/2, f. 12v.

paintings and images on church and vestry walls.[11] In 1588, St Michael's vestry ordered the repainting of the defaced Ten Commandments and 'other godlye sentences' on the church wall. Traditional images still hung in old windows, especially those in less accessible parts of churches. Costs for new glass to remodel windows, like for 'amendinge the Vestrie windowe' in St Michael, suggests that 'superstitious' images might have remained outside the nave, not easily visible to the congregation.[12] St Botolph's vestry agreed to remove 'all the sup[e]rstitous pictures in the glasse window at Trinitye Hall' in January 1606 [1607], replacing them with white glass at the parish charge. Trinity Hall had been the home of the parish's fraternities, but became a regular meeting place for the ward mote inquests and other gatherings.[13] St Mary Woolnoth may have taken the least expensive approach to cleansing windows of surviving Catholic images: they simply whited two windows by the vestry door in 1601–02, during the Bishop's visitation.[14]

Structural, outdoor repairs became urgent, for reasons not having to do entirely with the Reformation 'crisis' in the church fabric. After the late medieval boom in church building, deferred repairs followed in the early modern period. Archer speculates on the meaning of the renovations in the decades prior to Archbishop Laud's arrival, and on whether ceremonialism and nostalgic pride might fuel the work. Simply poor repair and the passage of time, however, necessitated some action, though parishioners might avail themselves of an opportunity to fund certain images or words about the church that satisfied their own piety within religious guidelines. In 1619, St Michael's churchwardens paid Goodman Smith 5s 10d for 'mending one Jousts howse in Harpe Alley broken w[i]th a stone that fell from the Steeple'. The church's steeple dated from 1421, when parishioners had laid the first stone of the 'new' foundation, and was crumbling by the early seventeenth century.[15] Even in 1607, the wind had twice blown down the steeple's vane and paint had peeled from its cross.[16] In St Mary's, a bell clapper and stone fell from the steeple, damaging nearby buildings.[17]

---

[11] For example, the costs of plastering and whiting the church and vestry in St Mary: GL, MS 1002/1B, f. 366.

[12] GL, MS 4072/1, f. 42; GL, MS 4071/2, f. 33. The churchwardens may have meant 'deteriorated' writing on walls.

[13] GL, MS 1453/1, f. 3.

[14] GL, MS 1002/1B, f. 330v.

[15] Archer, 'Nostalgia', pp. 33–4. GL, MS 4071/2, f. 50. The end of the first volume of churchwardens' accounts includes a drawing of the church's old steeple: GL, MS 4071/1, f. 196; similitude in GL, MS 90/2–7, f. 37.

[16] GL, MS 4071/1, fols 185, 186, 189.

[17] GL, MS 1002/1B, fols 389v, 420v.

Like their churches, the revenue-generating tenements and other property bequeathed by parishioners also needed repairs and renovations, even protection. Further investment in repairs made these properties, some of them the remnants of pre-Reformation endowments for masses and prayers, even more valuable to parishes. By 1588–89, the churchwardens of St Botolph Aldersgate had repeatedly warned that the church's buildings and tenements in Black Horse Alley needed immediate repair.[18] Churchwardens fought suits over concealed property late in the century, waging these costly legal cases to prevent loss of revenue for the fabric and relief of the poor. St Michael had built in the churchyard in the 1550s, but in the 1590s faced a suit over whether the rents had once served only superstitious uses. The parish successfully argued that the income from the churchyard properly belonged to the poor. St Michael's churchwardens viewed the repairs to the parish's houses in Bishopsgate Street and, in 1600, repaired houses in the churchyard where poor widows and others lived, since they were ready to fall.[19]

A combination of voluntary and involuntary contributions funded parochial rebuilding campaigns. Loans and assessments generated the capital, functioning as an obligatory contribution exchanged for authority over the allocation of church space. An elite parishioner risked, at the least, shame for not participating in the church's beautification and, at worst, exposure if he or she held opposing religious beliefs. In 1620, St Michael's churchwardens collected £130 from nine men, including Mr Slany, the Alderman's Deputy, and other men who sat in the church's most expensive pews, according to the 1603 assessment. A marginal note, added later, remarked that this sum was repaid only in 1624. Out of this loan, the churchwardens repaired the steeple and the church, but also spent 21s 2d for repairing the stone pulpit in the churchyard, £40 for painting the church, £9 for glazing windows, and £39 for 'whitinge and playsteringe the Church'.[20]

Eighty-three men and women contributed £73 7s 10d for repairs in early seventeenth-century St Mary Woolnoth, combining obligation and voluntarism in funding church works. The donors included many parishioners, not simply office-holders, and seem to have represented a significant percentage of householders. Five women and a number of strangers, who would not have served as churchwarden or other parochial official, contributed to the campaign. Many of the other men's names ring familiar, for their service, minister or churchwardens and auditors, or for their earlier gifts to the parish. The amounts gathered

---

[18] GL, MS 1454, Roll 91.
[19] GL, MS 4071/1, fols 136v, 189v; GL, MS 4072/1, Part 1, f. 82.
[20] GL, MS 4071/2, fols 52v, 53v.

varied greatly, showing that not just wealthy parishioners could, and did, contribute to the church works. Two women left only 6d, the smallest gifts received. Thirty-five men and women (42 per cent) gave 5s or less, a modest gift. Sixty-five (78 per cent) contributed £1 or less. Six prominent male citizens and parishioners showed their patronage in large gifts, of £6–£40, for repairing and glazing the windows and for painting about the church. By 1608–09, however, the churchwardens referred to the 'assessment' (£43 10s 3d) of certain parishioners, 69 men and two women, for finishing the repairs. In 1610, they paid for setting up three escutcheons in windows, possibly to recognize prominent donors who paid for the new windows.[21]

Parishioners also sustained the church fabric and services through their fees for baptisms, churchings, marriages, burials, and the use of funerary goods, although these mandatory contributions did not make up for the loss of voluntary bequests to the church fabric. The amounts collected changed little between the early and late sixteenth century, despite inflation. In the miscellaneous papers bound into the church-wardens' accounts of St Michael Cornhill, figures from 1521, 1569 and 1589 show that funeral fees decreased slightly between 1521 and 1569, perhaps because the peal no longer called people to the dirige and mass. Parishioners paid for the ringing of bells, with fees ranked by the size of the bell, the length of ringing time, and whether or not the knell rang at night or during the day. The bells retained their old names: 'Rus', the largest bell, named for its donor, William Rus; 'Michael' and 'Mary', named for the patron saint of the church and the Virgin Mary. The 'Rus' bell had been replaced prior to 1588, but in November the church-wardens met with Mr Mott and other labourers to weigh the great bell which had been used 'in steade of Rus & not lyked of'. The parish made an agreement with the founder to cast a new Rus bell, and to have a musician 'sounde the bell', satisfying parishioners who missed the sound of the old bell.[22] Although the churchwardens neglected to record

---

[21] GL, MS 1002/1B, fols 369–370v, 377v–378, 388v. The parish had about sixty to one hundred tithable houses by 1638, although the population had undoubtedly expanded by that later date: Liu, *Puritan London*, p. 27.

[22] The large bell, 'Rus', cost 8s for six hours, the next or 'Michael' for six hours with three peals cost 7s and the 'Mary' cost 6s along with three peals. The latter cost 16d for a one-hour knell. Lesser bells were also available for hire: GL, MS 4071/1, fols 192v–193, 198, 198v. Stow explains that John and Isabel Whitwell bought the sixth bell with the alderman William Rus, in 1430: Morley, p. 205. Obit for William Rus: GL, MS 4071/2, f. 199; *Chantry Certificate*, p. 6. On the recasting: GL, MS 4071/1, fols 130–130v. William Overall claimed that the parish enjoyed a reputation from 'early time' for the fine peal of bells: William H. Overall (ed.), *The Accounts of the Parish of St Michael, Cornhill, in the City of London, from 1456 to 1608* (London, 1871), p. xxvi.

the critics and their complaints, lay people preserved a facet of old parochial life, the familiar sound of their church's prized bell.

Parishioners paid for the use of communal objects and space, like the bells, but also notably for the part of the church's ground used for a grave. In 1589, burial in the upper side aisles or chapels in the choir or chancel cost 15s, while burial in the church body cost 10s and in the cloister 3s 4d in St Michael. Strangers paid double for the privilege of burial in the church ground. Parishioners were loaned the parochial 'buriall clothes' for free, but strangers paid 8d for the best cloth and 4d for the 'worst'. Although parishioners enjoyed use of the burial clothes, hanging additional 'blacks' about the church brought extra charges. In St Michael's in 1616–17, the parish collected 20s 'for the blacks hanged about the bodye of our Church at the ffunerall of the said M[aste]r Vernon', a prominent parishioner and benefactor.[23] St Mary's buried their donor Henry Butler in the vault under the north chancel and collected £3 3s 4d for the grave and the 'composition for blackes about the body of the church'.[24]

Churchwardens even collected fees when favourite donors and prominent parishioners were laid to rest outside the parish. Funerals and burials generated revenue for and brought respect to parishes, but also reinforced communal bonds. St Mary's churchwardens, in 1601–02, received 13s 4d for Dame Mary Ramsey's 'laistall', although she was buried in Christ's Hospital, and collected 3s 4d for ringing the bell for her. The parish also garnered 20s for the blacks which 'should have byn set upp in our church as if the funerall had bin there kept'.[25] Dame Ramsey's polite and humble request for burial in Christ's showed that the hospital and the parish expected her burial in her parish. She begged the governors to remember her charitable bequests to them, and to other worthy causes, recalling the earlier practice of prominent inhabitants and patrons to ask for burial in the Grey Friars, the home of Christ's Hospital. Her 10s stipend to the keeper of her monument, 'which is allreadie prepared for the interringe of my bodie', signalled her confidence in the appropriation of Hospital space for her commemoration, despite the humble supplication in her testament.[26]

---

[23] GL, MS 4071/1, f. 192v; GL, MS 4071/2, f. 32v. His benefactions to church included silver pots (worth £24–£25), loaves of bread distributed to poor at Sunday morning prayers for a year, a yearly sermon on 'the day of his Funerall', and money 'for rubbing a monument' for him and Alderman Houghton: GL, MS 4083, fols 89–89v, 98v.

[24] GL, MS 1002/1B, f. 419.

[25] GL, MS 1002/1B, f. 330. See Chapter 5 for full discussion of Ramsey's benefactions to the poor and to Christ's.

[26] PRO, PROB 11/98, fols 191L–192R.

Despite assessments and collections, testamentary bequests benefiting parishes did not evaporate, especially if they sustained aspects of popular piety. The draper Stephen Barker left £4 to St Mary Woolnoth to purchase a black burying cloth in 1603.[27] In 1619, the goldsmith Simon Sedgwick left a black cloth to the same parish, to be laid over the coffin when taking corpses to their graves. He had also asked to be buried decently, perhaps giving a gift to ensure the same for other parishioners.[28] In 1603, the citizen and goldsmith John Kirbie left a 'turquoise [Turkish] carpet' for the vestry table, as a token of his good will, since the parish had paid 24s for a carpet for the communion table in 1586/87. His generosity to the parish denoted his social rank or wealth, as like gifts had traditionally done, but the stipulation of the gift's placement in the vestry demonstrated the shift in parochial focus, more expressly linking piety and service, without becoming secular. In the early sixteenth century, a benefactor would have outfitted an altar, supplied a priest's vestment, or left other implements of worship, for the honour of the saints, remembrance of souls or maintenance of the mass. Kirbie's gift went to the vestry, the group exercising discretion in the relief of the parish poor. His service as churchwarden in 1601–02 provided another impetus for leaving a gift to the vestry: he had also served the parish, even working with some of the vestry.[29] The carpet seems to have been one of the luxury 'appurtenances' in the testator's households, of which he also mentioned a looking glass and a 'best picture'. Because Kirbie lumped his possessions into large bequests, the value of his estate is indicated only by the hints of the rare decorative objects within it.

Responsibility for repairing and maintaining the church building and interior conferred some control of the space on lay people, or at least the lay leaders of parishes. Churchwardens appeared to exercise discretion over renovations, but parishioners sometimes pointedly reminded them to preserve the parish's fiscal health. In the poorer parish of St Botolph's, the vestry limited the churchwardens in 1619 to a yearly budget of 40s for ornaments and repairs. Once churchwardens passed that threshold, they had to seek vestry approval and, when finished, produce a careful accounting of all expenditures for repairs. If the churchwardens ignored the vestry's commandment, the statement and oversight of the 'better

---

[27] PRO, PROB 11/102, f. 217L.

[28] PRO, PROB 11/135, f. 28L.

[29] GL, MS 9171/20, f. 30v. By 1608–09, the churchwardens had to pay 3s for mending the 'turkey carpet' given by Kirbie: GL, MS 1002/1B, f. 374. Similarly, a carpet used for St Michael's communion table: GL, MS 4071/1, f. 126v. Service as churchwarden: GL, MS 1002/1B, f. 329.

part' of the parish, they would be personally responsible for paying any difference. Bishops' articles, however, stressed churchwardens' duty to keep churches, chancels and churchyards clean and in good repair, irrespective of parishioners' oversight. Pressures on churchwardens to fulfil ecclesiastical orders and to satisfy their parishioners may have contributed to the apparent drop in enthusiasm for occupying the office.[30]

Renovations of church interiors, paid by parishioners' fees and voluntary contributions, utilized the Word to decorate churches and to edify congregations, exemplifying Protestant architecture and design in late Elizabethan London. Colour returned to the 'stripped' church interiors, but instead of saints, parishioners saw more obvious reminders of royal authority, of wealthy donors and of Bible-centred worship. Mr Massey, painter and churchwarden in St Stephen's, painted Psalms and arms in the chancel, the Ten Commandments, and twelve angels with the arms of the Grocers, and made and gilded the Queen's arms inside the church in 1600.[31] In 1607–08, St Mary's churchwardens paid the Walton men about £13 to paint the church door, five windows, church pots, a partition in the church, the gallery, the pulpits, 'the three tombes', and 'all the pillars of the church in oyle Cullors as the now they be and for cullowring of the iron bares in the church windowes'. They also painted the Ten Commandments and, in the two east ends, the credo and the Lord's Prayer. The parish also erected the king's arms and an image of Jehovah in the chancel window.[32]

Alongside the Word of God, the arms of the monarch, crafts and prominent parishioners were painted about parish churches (indeed, Figure 4.1 illustrates the inclusion of national and civic imagery used within them around this time). Arms of patrons and royalty had been present in late medieval churches, but those secular representations had been buffered by the presence of images and shrines to Jesus, Mary and the saints. On the outside of St Stephen's on the street side, Massey and his workmen affixed the Queen's and Grocers' arms, and 'mayny other armes about the same, w[i]th the other things aboute it and the Angeles overheade houldinge of armes'.[33] Massey's exterior work mimicked the style of his interior painting, to show the parish's support of the Queen and its relationship with the Grocers. St Mary's must have made last minute changes in their design, since the parish paid 12d to the painter 'that wold have painted the kings armes in our church'.[34] Parishioners

---

[30] GL, MS 1453/1, f. 10v; VAI, III, pp. 310–11.

[31] GL, MS 593/3 (unfol.) (1600).

[32] GL, MS 1002/1B, fols 366–367v.

[33] GL, MS 593/3 (unfol.) (1600).

[34] GL, MS 1002/1B, f. 355.

4.1   Image of a dragon. Guildhall Library MS 4835 (Holy Trinity the Less), Vol. 1 (1582–1662), f. 19 (1593–94). With permission of the Guildhall Library, Corporation of London.

recognized the political ramifications of the monarch's arms, as in the case of a parish restoring the arms of Charles I and adding those of Charles II in 1660, after the preceding 'warre, troubles, sorrowes, changes of affaires, settings up and pullings down of governors and revolutions of government'.[35]

---

[35] GL, MS 90/2–7, f. 51; Carole Levin, *Heart and Stomach of a King: Elizabeth I and the Politics of Sex and Power* (Philadelphia, PA, 1994), p. 17; heraldry in medieval churches: Graves, 'Social space', p. 312.

Construction of pews and pulpits within churches made at least outward conformity with the Protestant doctrine painted on walls easier to enforce. Pews faced the pulpit, the focus of the Protestant church and its services and sermons. In February 1589, the churchwardens in St Michael paid a joiner for a wainscot door for the 'lowe readinge pulpett' and for locks and keys to that door and for 'dyuers pewes' in the church. This work, and other repairs to glass and wainscoting in the church, occurred in time for the Archdeacon's visitation to the parish. In 1610–11, the churchwardens focused on the pulpit: £4 6s to a painter for 'paintinge & gildinge the pulpitt head', 6d for a ring for the pulpit's door, 8s 4d to a joiner for work on the pulpit and the clerk's pew, 17d for boards and nails for pulpit head, 9s 9d for fabric, and 20s 4d for silk fringe.[36] Parishioners also adorned the preacher who spoke from that pulpit. St Mary's bought a yard of fabric and crimson taffeta for their minister's hood, worn during the church service, since he was a doctor of divinity.[37] The parishioners were probably as anxious as the minister to show his credentials through his attire. In the early 1590s, St Michael's paid a man for mats and workmanship relating to the communion table, another important feature of the new church interiors. In the same year, the churchwardens put up wainscoting in the vestry.[38]

The arrangement of pews allowed parishioners to focus on and listen carefully to the preacher or lecturer – and made their attendance at services easier to trace.[39] In 1610, the parish vestry ordered the churchwardens to permit ancient parishioners to sit in the chancel pews to hear sermons better. They justified their order to churchwardens and parson by reminding them that the parishioners had paid for repairs to the chancel. They decreed that the parson would pay for future repairs if aged and ageing parishioners could not sit in those choice seats, a sign of the bargaining over the church's space and access to it. In 1612–13, the churchwardens recorded charges relating to making four new pews in the body of the church and altering others.[40]

Special arrangements, like those for the elderly and hard-of-hearing, mitigated the inequities created by pew rental. Parishioners rented pew space, an example of fees like those for graves allowing the appropriation of shared church space. Pews, and the sex-segregated seating within them, were not new to England's Reformation churches, but discussion

---

[36] GL, MS 4071/1, f. 130v; GL, MS 4071/2, f. 12.

[37] GL, MS 1002/1B, f. 351v.

[38] GL, MS 4071/1, fols 136v, 137. For frame and footstep relating to communion table in 1615/16: see GL, MS 1002/1B, f. 420.

[39] VAI, III, p. 307.

[40] GL, MS 4072/1, fols 103–103v. GL, MS 4071/2, fols 19v, 53.

of assessments and seating plans became a more prominent part of parochial records.[41] Pew assignments highlighted social ranking, but parishioners and church leaders focused on the pious imperative to hear God's message, through sermon and lecture. In 1603, St Michael's vestry recorded the assessment of pews, showing that the most prominent men, like the Alderman's Deputy, Mr Anthony Soda, paid 10d, the next tier 8d, and so on, down to 4d.[42] Even a man later fined for selling alcohol during sermon time, Mr Callys, paid 5d for his seat. Men and women sat separately, but no women were recorded separately in the assessment. Women did figure in disputes over seating brought to the vestry, indicating women's recognition of the social status demonstrated in pew arrangements.[43]

Pews oriented the congregation to the preacher, but the ordered pew seating also provided ways for the morally upright, or even 'godly', within the parish to take steps to prevent immorality and sexual license among single women and men. Maids may have deeply resented cultural assumptions that they attended church to flirt with young single men, as noted by the maids who challenged a (lost) pamphlet alleging their vanity and moral laxity. The 'maids' replied,

> 'And where he alleageth that we doe mispend our time in the Church in gazing and looking about us, and that our coming thither is not to pray: surely he himself was not very well occupied in the Church, and prayed but litle (as it seemeth) when he stood gazing & loking about him at us, to marke what we didde'.[44]

Poor and single women, however, created anxiety about the social order, perhaps especially in religious settings. Protestant books altered services

---

[41] Margaret Aston, 'Segregation in church' in W.J. Sheils and D. Wood (eds), *Women in the Church* (Oxford and Cambridge, MA, 1990), pp. 237–94; Underdown, *Revel, Riot and Rebellion: Popular Politics and Culture in England 1603–1660* (Oxford, 1985), pp. 29–33; Haigh, *English Reformations*, p. 33; Schofield, 'Archaeological evidence', p. 50; Richard Gough, *The History of Myddle*, David Hey (ed.), (Harmondsworth, 1981), pp. 80–83.

[42] GL, MS 4072/1, f. 102v.

[43] For example, GL, MS 594/1, fols 64, 88. On pew rates as new fund-raising: Hutton, *Merry England*, p. 119; cf. French on medieval fund-raising: 'Fund-raising in late medieval Somerset', pp. 118–19.

[44] *A letter sent by the Maydens of London, to the vertuous Matrones & Mistresses of the same, in the defense of their lawfull libertie. Answering the Mery Metting by us Rose, Iane, Rachell, Sara, Philumias, and Dorothie*, Henry Binneman for Thomas Hacket, London, 1567, STC 16754.5, sig. Biiij–Biiijv; Ann Rosalind Jones, 'Maidservants of London: Sisterhoods of Kinship and Labor' in Susan Frye and Karen Robertson (eds), *Maids and Mistresses, Cousins and Queens: Women's Alliances in Early Modern England* (Oxford and New York, 1999), pp. 21–32, esp. p. 28; Crawford, *Women and Religion*, pp. 48–9.

to correct women's behaviour, in the event that prescriptions failed. Articles and injunctions forbid churching a single woman without her 'due penance' before giving birth, 'to the satisfaction of the congregation', or that she 'at her coming to give thanks do openly acknowledge her fault before the congregation at the appointment of the minister'.[45] St Mary Woolnoth constructed a 'maydes loft' in the church, reifying the gender and social distinctions drawn in the Reformation church's floor plan.[46] Beginning in 1583, they paid 'Mistress Peirson' 20s yearly for 'governing' the maids while they attended services. In 1593–94, her blindness necessitated hiring another woman to help her, for 6s 8d. St Botolph's churchwardens paid a man to 'rule' the apprentices 'and others' sitting near the belfry, probably all male servants or poorer men.[47]

Testators and parishes, having constructed pulpits and pews by which to facilitate sermons, helped to widen and sustain the pool of preachers available for sermons and lectures, by providing exhibitions to poor scholars. The pious testator John Stockeley, a wealthy citizen and merchant tailor, granted £40 to the master and wardens of his craft, rather than his parish, to maintain four poor scholars in divinity, 'to come forth to the publique good of gods holie service'.[48] Some parishes paid for their study of divinity, a form of parochial evangelical leadership. Piety, especially of scholars at Oxford and Cambridge receiving exhibitions, helped to determine the choice of recipients, though residence or a strong connection to the parish counted as well. In 1591–92, St Stephen's granted five scholars 'exhibitions' of 40s for their studies, a benevolence that continued for years to those and other scholars.[49] St Michael's provided £5 to the son of Goodman Ames, a scholar at Cambridge, 'to helpe him to be a Bachellor of Arts (yf itt please god)', even though the parish usually concentrated on pensions for the aged, sick, and orphaned or abandoned poor.[50]

Sermons and lectures became a focal point of parochial worship, supplying religious edification for the hearers in the pews, not to mention the socializing suspected by the godly.[51] Parochial assessments

---

[45] *VAI*, III, p. 308.

[46] GL, MS 1002/1A, f. 307; for servants, see GL, MS 4072/1, Part 1, f. 25v.

[47] The parish later made a partition in the maids' seat: GL, MS 1454, Rolls 86, 95, 96. Griffiths, *Youth*, pp. 194–5.

[48] PRO, PROB 11/123, f. 54R.

[49] GL, MS 593/2, f. 83.

[50] GL, MS 4071/2, f. 21.

[51] St Botolph Aldersgate had a lecture by 1564, St Mary Woolnoth by 1580, St Michael Cornhill 1575, St Stephen Walbrook by 1583: Seaver, *The Puritan Lectureships*, pp. 123, 124, 304, 148. Seaver calls St Stephen a 'relatively poor parish', but more properly, it is a small parish with a number of wealthy parishioners.

supported lectureships, not testamentary bequests. The vestry in St Michael's, in 1588, called for the churchwardens to gather the collection for the lecture, held Fridays and Sundays. By 1590, the vestry decreed that the parson and churchwardens should go house to house through the parish to draw on the 'good will' and 'benevolence' of the parishioners – reminding, even intimidating them to pay their assessments for the lecture.[52] Protestant sermons and preachers continued a medieval tradition, but used the survival of an older pious form to maintain the momentum of Protestant religion in Elizabethan London.

Testators' bequests for sermons embroidered on the life of the parish in several ways: edifying the congregation, honouring God, and perpetuating the memory of donors within the parish. The suspicion of maidens' motives in church attendance hint at the social bonds reinforced through pious activities, even through sermons or lectures.[53] Sir Thomas Ramsey, knight and alderman, requested a good and godly preacher to preach 20 sermons, over two years, in his parish. The sermon cycle, repeating and extending like an anniversary of his death and burial, mimicked and subverted the Catholic repetition of masses.[54] In 1608, William Pitchforde endowed a monthly Sabbath sermon in the parish of his birth and christening, outside London, for three years. By contrast, he funded 12 sermons for St Stephen Walbrook and St Mary Colchurch, for days those churches lacked them, suggesting the prevalence of them in London parishes. The endowments of sermons by individuals offset the comparatively light Elizabethan mandate for four sermons each year and a homily on other Sundays.[55] Pitchforde's evangelical bequest bolstered the worship of two city parishes and strengthened the foundation of devotion in his birth parish. Brian Calverley, by contrast, funded four sermons for remembrance of him in one year, in addition to his burial sermon.[56]

Bequests for perpetual sermons established pious remembrances of the wealthy patron, as well as celebrated God's Word, to unite the altruistic and the self-promoting aspects of benevolence. One endowment by an exceptional citizen, Sir Martin Bowes, became a significant

---

[52] GL, MS 4072/1, Part 1, fols 43v, 50. Seaver dates the founding of St Michael's lectureship in 1575: *Puritan Lectureships*, p. 124; for examples of their lecturers, see pp. 142, 197.

[53] Jones, 'Maidservants of London', p. 28.

[54] PRO, PROB 11/75, f. 308L. On survivals: McClendon, 'A Moveable Feast', p.15; Binion, *After Christianity*; Thomas, *Religion and the Decline of Magic*, p. 74.

[55] PRO, PROB 11/113, fols 147R–148L. Cox believed that less preaching occurred during Elizabeth's reign than at other times, but he may not have considered the number of endowed lectures and sermons in some parishes, perhaps especially urban ones: *Pulpits, Lecterns, and Organs in English Churches* (London, 1915), p. 84.

[56] PRO, PROB 11/71, f. 158R.

event in his parish for decades to follow. Bowes's bequest for a yearly sermon became a central anniversary in his parish, with fragrant grasses and flowers strewn about and frankincense burned to cover malodorous smells that lingered in the church. He had left his mark on St Mary's and London throughout his lifetime, giving a new rood loft under Mary and serving as Lord Mayor and governor of Reformation hospitals. On 'his day', the clerk tolled a bell to call the Goldsmiths and the parishioners to hear the sermon, endowing his 'Protestant' bequest with 'Catholic' overtones of a pealing bell.[57] Bowes required that the Goldsmiths attend in his former parish home – and the churchwardens collected fees when the craft neglected to appear. In November 1603, for instance, the company's warden and renter gave 5s 4d to 15 poor men and women for the craft's absence.[58]

Other bequests keyed sermons to dates that survived the reduction in the traditional Catholic calendar, and linked testators to these days. Anne Gunter, widow of Philip, prominent parishioner in St Michael, made a perpetual endowment of two sermons yearly, stipulating that they follow 18 January and Trinity Sunday.[59] William Bailie bequeathed his tenements in Jelly Alley near the Drapers' Hall to the parson and churchwardens of St Michael Cornhill, to pay perpetually for a sermon by 'some godlye learned preacher', on the Sunday following Low Sunday.[60] The wealthy James Robinson referred to the 'visitation' in his testament, the suddenness of plague forcing him to leave large sums of money to friends, family and craft, with little detail or commentary. He did, however, detail his desire for four sermons yearly in his parish, to be held on St James, All Saints, Philip and Jacob's Days, and Candlemas, acknowledging the popularity of remaining holy days for drawing people to hear sermons or showing his own enthusiasm for attending sermons on those traditional dates.[61] Philip and 'Jacob' must be Saints Philip and James the Apostle, celebrated on 1 May, and Candlemas the sanctioned Purification of the Virgin, 2 February.

The number of endowments for perpetual or cyclical sermons decreased, however, and instead testators more frequently asked for a

---

[57] GL, MS 1002/1A, f. 241; GL, MS 1002/1B, f. 420v. For more on Bowes's 'highly conservative religious opinions', see Hickman, 'From Catholic to Protestant', pp. 128–9.

[58] GL, MS 1002/1A, f. 347. Ward, *Metropolitan Communities*, pp. 110–11.

[59] PRO, PROB 11/68, f. 131R. In addition to a sermon by a godly preacher at her burial, f. 131L.

[60] PRO, PROB 11/108, f. 112L. The gift also provided coals or wood worth £5 for the poor: GL, MS 4083, f. 87v.

[61] GL, MS 9171/19, f. 449v. Cressy, *Bonfires and Bells*, pp. 3, 6–7. In regards to preaching sermons on holy days to attract more hearers: Judith Maltby, *Prayer Book and People in Elizabethan and Early Stuart England* (Cambridge, 1998), p. 39.

godly and learned preacher at their burials.[62] The decline in these types of bequests may indicate the Reformation's momentum in London by 1580. Official requirement of licences may have dampened lay enthusiasm for setting up multiple sermons, especially if godly men could not easily preach. Archbishops and their delegates combated heterodoxy by controlling parochial preaching, ordering preachers to carry licences and making licences harder to obtain after the mid-1560s.[63] In the 1580s, St Michael's paid a fee to 'avoid' an excommunication for 'sufferi[n]g a preacher to preache in o[u]r Churche beinge unlycenced'. At the end of the decade, the churchwardens paid 2d for a brief from the Bishop of London 'forbiddinge that enye man shoulde preache w[i]t[h] oute his Lawfull Lycence'. In 1609/10, they paid 16d for two books of 'banes & the names of minysters', perhaps a directory of the licensed preachers.[64]

Testamentary bequests for sermons began to decline around 1600, however, particularly among women, who had been early proponents of such endowments. Women's adoption of new testamentary patterns suggests that they continued to be enthusiastic leaders in reforming piety. Greater religious certainty in the late sixteenth century, at least in London, may have obviated the need for urgent testamentary bequests. After 1597, no female testators in these parishes established cycles of sermons or even asked for ones at their burials. Their lack of bequests coincided with puritan criticism of burial sermons, affordable only for the rich.[65] Just as women adopted newer charitable restrictions more enthusiastically than did men in the middle years of the century, they continued to support 'new ways'. Contemporaries remarked on female audiences at lectures and sermons, where they likely heard the criticism of burial sermons and planned their testaments accordingly. One commentator complained that Stephen Egerton's listeners were mostly women, and vain women at that.[66] Even when women heeded the ideas preached by divines, however, curbing their bequests for sermons, they faced gendered criticism of female 'vanity', similar to the superficiality angrily denied by the 'maidens' of London.

Financial support for new parochial activities and uncertainty over the appropriateness of certain endowments coincided with reformers'

---

[62] For example of requesting a godly and learned preacher, see PRO, PROB 11/71, f. 312L.

[63] On licensing: Seaver, *Puritan Lectureships*, pp. 204–5.

[64] GL, MS 4071/1, fols 126v, 134; GL, MS 4071/2, f. 10.

[65] Thomas, *Religion and the Decline of Magic*, p. 604.

[66] Seaver, *Puritan Lectureships*, p. 64. On women's eventual predominance among sermon attendees: Patricia Crawford, *Women and Religion*, pp. 77–8.

attempts to prohibit popular celebrations and 'sport' that seemed 'superstitious' or occasioned heavy drinking. 'Hot' puritan preachers and moderate contemporaries alike sought the divine causes of plague and natural disasters, some finding them in lay conduct. Although Charles I triggered the most intense disputes over sport, in the midst of growing agitation about ceremonialism and Archbishop Laud, Elizabeth's reign offered unclear signs about the future of some popular festivities. Thomas Becon, one-time minister in St Stephen's, attacked 'merry-making', perhaps because more holy days were listed in 1560 than in 1552 under Edward. Some of the new national holidays replaced saints' days and traditional festivals, especially by superimposing them upon the former sacred calendar, although reinventions 'did not necessarily reflect the persistence of traditional piety'.[67] Although new celebrations layered the old days, drinking and customary parochial fund-raising elicited the wrath of reformers, suggesting that the new could not simply disguise the traditional.[68]

Testators and parishioners, however, found ways to institute new, or re-invent traditional occasions that suggest popular yearning for communal fun and ceremony. St Mary Woolnoth had saved the charitable bequests of pre-Reformation donors, like the Percivales, and still sporadically marked the distributions to the parish poor as Sir John's '(obijt)' day. Obit stood for the anniversary of his death, simply enough, but its parenthetical citation reminded the parish of the old service behind the 'ancient' gift. Similarly, the parish strewed herbs and straw about the church for the excitement surrounding Sir Martin Bowes's endowed sermon – alternately called his sermon day and Saint Martin's Day, although that saint's day was not included in official church calendars.[69] Obits and saints' days had been removed or reduced in the Elizabethan church, and although fewer parishioners remained to recall

---

[67] Hutton, *Merry England*, pp. 111–52, esp. 123–4, 128; Underdown, *Revel, Riot, and Rebellion*, pp. 82–90. November 17 as Elizabeth's accession and St Hugh of Lincoln's day, so that 'the national dynastic observance was conveniently grafted on to a regional custom, and the ringing could simultaneously satisfy conservative religious instincts and honour the Protestant queen': Cressy, *Bonfires and Bells*, p. 51, also pp. 53, 55, 59; cf. McClendon, 'A Moveable Feast', p. 26.

[68] On the loss of popular festivities: Phythian-Adams, 'Ceremony and the Citizen', pp. 57–85; although church ales were not a London phenomenon: see Judith Bennett, 'Conviviality and Charity in Medieval and Early Modern England', *PaP*, **134** (Feb. 1992), pp. 19–41. On forms of popular fund-raising, especially Hocktide celebrations: Katherine French, '"To Free Them from Binding": Women in the Late Medieval English Parish', *Journal of Interdisciplinary History*, **27**, 3 (Winter 1997), pp. 387–412.

[69] GL, MS 1002/1B, fols 355, 359v, 389, 395v, 418v. David Cressy, *Bonfires and Bells*, pp. 6–7.

the pre-Reformation or Marian church, vestiges of saints' presence remained in the parochial calendar.[70] Saints also survived in images about churches, both before and after renovations, as when a haberdasher in St Stephen's paid for a window showing the stoning of the patron saint of the church. The same man supported John Downham, puritan lecturer, but anxiety about less thoroughly reformed parishioners misconstruing the images must have worried the hottest among them. Indeed, the queen herself may have helped to sate a popular hunger for the traditional female saints and the Virgin Mary.[71] Reminders of the old monuments and practices survived through Anthony Munday's edition of Stow's *A Survey of London*, dedicated to the Lord Mayor, purchased by city parishes and aldermen. Parochial readiness to purchase the book, and to give Munday a monetary gift, reinforces the argument that Stow's book expressed burgeoning defence of 'sport'.[72]

The adoption of anniversaries of national and religious victories – against popish plots and rebels – reinforces the impression of Protestant success, in part through reform's willingness to offer new anniversaries and objects of devotion. Celebrations, solemn moments or anniversaries observed by parishes revolved around recent national triumphs or the articulation of new national worries in local and parochial contexts in the late sixteenth and early seventeenth centuries. Charity, a consideration of the following chapter, and public observances were mandated, and freely given or expressed, by parishioners in support of the military and royal aims of the government. Parishes prayed in thanksgiving for Christian victories over the Ottoman Empire and for the death of Süleyman the Magnificent in a siege in Hungary in 1566.[73] Parishes and celebrations also marked triumphs over domestic enemies and dangers. St Botolph's, at the order of the Lord Mayor, rang bells to celebrate the 'apprehension of the Traytors' in 1586. These individuals had been involved in the Babington Plot, supporting Mary Queen of Scots, the restoration of Catholicism and the removal of Elizabeth I.[74] In addition, in the early seventeenth century parishes yearly commemorated the nation's safe delivery from Gowrie's conspiracy and Guy Fawkes's infa-

---

[70] Maltby, *Prayer Book and People*, pp. 38–9.

[71] Henry Andrewes's bequests related in Archer, 'Nostalgia', p. 34. Levin, *The Heart and Stomach of a King*, pp.18–19.

[72] See GL, MS 1002/1B, f. 431v; CLRO, Rep. 33, f. 239v. In 1617, the Court of Aldermen presented Munday with £60 for his 'encouragem[en]t' after he presented a copy to each alderman. On Stow's book as a defence of 'sport' at the end of Elizabeth's reign: Hutton, *Merry England*, pp. 136–7.

[73] *Newes from Vienna*, printed by Awdelay.

[74] GL, MS 1454, Roll 89. Rosemary O'Day, *The Longman Companion to the Tudor Age* (London and New York, 1995), pp. 27, 171; Cressy, *Bonfires and Bells*, pp. 90–92.

mous Gunpowder Plot.[75] Parish churches celebrated coronation days by strewing herbs, lighting candles and ringing bells. St Mary's paid for ringers at the prince's 'installment' in 1610. Parishes celebrated royal anniversaries and liberation from danger: 'crownation day' and a 'night of Joyfullness' for the Princess Palatine's safe delivery of a son. Parishes paid for ringers, and often for their bread and beer. Parishioners also prayed especially for deliverance from bad weather.[76]

London developed local festivals and celebrations in addition to participating in these national moments of thanksgiving or holiday. The Lord Mayor's Show and procession became increasingly significant through the later sixteenth century while traditional gatherings, like the Midsummer Watch and religious processions, declined or disappeared. As Archer has argued, the procession emphasized elite power and elite responsibility to the poor, highlighting the dependence of the poor and resulting in less social integration. Peter Burke, by contrast, has argued that the display linked learned and popular traditions and contributed to the development of popular political consciousness.[77]

Parishes also re-established prominent features from the traditional sacred calendar, like Ascension Day and perambulation during Rogationtide. Visitation articles and injunctions regulated the perambulation, limiting what was said, worn or carried, all to prevent 'popish ceremonies'.[78] The ceremony retained religious elements, but took on greater 'secular' importance, in the obligation and necessity to view church lands and tenements. Poor parishioners and women

---

[75] For example, see GL, MS 4071/2, f. 19. On 5 August 1600, the brothers Alexander (Master of Ruthven) and John (3rd Earl of Gowrie) Ruthven attempted to collect James VI's debts to them, or attempted to kill him. The brothers were killed and declared guilty of treason: DNB. In the Gunpowder Plot, Guy Fawkes famously plotted to blow up Parliament. On Gunpowder Plot commemorations: Cressy, *Bonfires and Bells*, pp. 141–55. On books and various prayers of thanksgiving: see Kisby, 'Books in London Parish Churches'.

[76] GL, MS 1002/1B, fols 367, 388v, 407v; GL, MS 4071/1, f. 128. On coronation day: Cressy, *Bonfires and Bells*, pp. 50–66. Many of the dates are listed in Cressy, *Bonfires and Bells*, pp. 90–92.

[77] Archer, 'Nostalgia', pp. 23–5. Lawrence Manley sees a 'heightened emphasis on acquisition, mobility, wealth and status, and a deepening symbiosis between London and the centralized, bureaucratic state' in the Mayor's inauguration: 'Of Sites and Rites', in David L. Smith, Richard Strier, and David Bevington (eds), *The Theatrical City: Culture, Theatre and Politics in London, 1576–1649* (Cambridge, 1995), p. 48. Burke, 'Popular Culture in Seventeenth-Century London' in Barry Reay (ed.), *Popular Culture in Seventeenth-Century England* (London and Sydney, 1985), p. 43.

[78] *VAI*, III, pp. 15, 309. See Thomas, *Religion and the Decline of Magic*, pp. 62–5; Cressy, *Bonfires and Bells*, pp. 23–4; Hutton, *Merry England*, pp. 142–3, and on revival in Restoration, p. 247; Maltby, *Prayer Book and People*, p. 39.

had little part in these continuations of old parish practice, but instead children and 'substantial men' acted for the parish. In 1609–10, the churchwardens paid 6d to six boys, 'at our goinge about the boundes of the p[ar]ishe on Assencon daye'. They contributed 10s to a dinner at a nearby tavern for other participants in the ceremony marking the parish's limits. To finalize their efforts, the churchwardens paid 2s 'for the brasse plates sett upp in the boundes of our p[ar]ish'. In the accounts of 1610–11, the churchwardens paid 15s 1d for a dinner when 'we wente about the bounds of the p[ar]ish w[i]th Mr Chauntrell & divers of the p[ar]ishenors' and 8d to 'divers boys' of the parish who went along. The minister, churchwardens and 'certeyne other' parishioners spent 24s at the Golden Fleece tavern, after a later perambulation.[79] St Mary's churchwardens bought silk points for children on Ascension Day at the perambulation. On another occasion, they gave apples and cakes to children during rogation week to visit the boundaries.[80]

Although revivals and new secular festivals in the city helped to make up for lost celebrations, testamentary bequests echoed the Protestant doctrine and worship displayed and implemented in parishes in London. Gifts to parishes within and outside the city seemed intended to help those churches lacking the fundamental books and goods needed for proper worship. William Houghton, citizen and stacioner, left a 'new Testament of the lardgest size and last translation', as well as service book and psalms, to poorer St Botolph Aldersgate, in 1620. The lack of a Bible, not to mention service book and psalms, violated injunctions and made proper instruction of the congregation impossible. As Kümin has shown, St Botolph's depended on income from dead parishioners' bequests and fees. The parish's difficulty in collecting assessed fees in Elizabeth's reign suggests that poverty and apathy among part-time residents of the parish, or those who only kept stables there, made the outfitting of services and the church particularly troublesome.[81] Houghton, like other testators, gave presents reflecting his occupation and indicating his pious views. In addition to his parochial bequests, Houghton provided his brother Edward, a preacher in 'Gayton in Northampton', with the 'booke of Martires in two volumes'. John Foxe's text constituted an essential resource for and legitimation of preachers and served as a new kind of Protestant iconography for the instruction of congregants in the history of mar-

---

[79] GL, MS 4071/2, fols 9v, 12, 18.

[80] 'Points' are needlepoint or lace. GL, MS 1002/1B, fols 319v, 332; see also 4071/2, f. 18.

[81] Kümin, The Shaping, p. 114; GL, MS 1454, Rolls 68–73, for example.

tyrdom and persecution under Catholicism.[82] The new-style, Old Testament name of Houghton's young kinsman, 'Moses', suggests a family network of puritanism.[83]

Houghton's gifts also illustrate Londoners' concern with parishes in smaller towns and in the countryside, especially those to which they were tied through family heritage. For a wealthier donor, gifts to birth parishes or old family homes reiterated social status and evangelized in smaller towns, bringing together social and pious motives. In 1608, William Pitchforde, a citizen and grocer, endowed sermons in London, but gave £10 to 'Light Brockhurst co. Salop', where he had been born and christened, to purchase a service book and Bible and to mend pews.[84] Mending pews eased the minister's task of assembling his flock for instruction in Protestantism and the Gospel, for which he would use the appropriate service books. William Brockbancke, besides giving the poor of Witcham 40s, left £5 to the parson and churchwardens there to purchase a Communion cup.[85]

Donors making large gifts imprinted their individual and familial identities on parishes and churches, legitimating the prominence of their arms or pew seats within the church. This pattern of patronage continued medieval practice, although the style and substance of post-Reformation gifts had changed alongside doctrine. John Vernon bequeathed two silver pots to hold wine on the communion table, valued at £24–£25, bearing his arms and the statement, 'The guift of John Vernon Merchaunt of the Staple of England giuen to the Parishioners of the Parish Church of St Michaell in Cornhill London'. He allowed that 'when they are old and not seemely to stand upon the Communion Table' the parishioners could have new ones made, with the same decoration.[86] One of St Mary's six most generous donors, Henry Butler, citizen, draper and parishioner, gave £40 for 'new making' of the west window. The churchwardens listed a number of charges in January 1606 for those alterations, requiring 245 feet of glass, and of the two lower south windows. A painter coloured iron bars in the windows, and he or another craftsman placed arms in the west window, probably Butler's arms. In that same

[82] Aston and Ingram, 'The Iconography', pp. 66–142, esp. pp. 67, 80; on elevation of preaching in the books: Felch, 'Shaping the Reader', p. 53.

[83] GL, MS 9051/6, f. 43v. Gaydon in Warwick? Tyacke's study of puritan naming points to Old Testament names and puritan baptismal names: 'Popular puritan mentality in late Elizabethan England' in Peter Clark, Alan G.R. Smith, Nicholas Tyacke (eds), *The English Commonwealth, 1547–1640: Essays in Politics and Society* (New York, 1979), pp. 77–92, esp. pp. 78, 82–3.

[84] PRO, PROB 11/113, f. 147L. Brockhurst, in Shropshire.

[85] PRO, PROB 11/129, f. 45R; *VAI*, III, p. 303.

[86] GL, MS 4083, fols 89–89v.

year, the joiner made two new pews, '(in one of w[hi]ch Mrs Butler is to be set)'.[87] His gift beautified the church and made his wife's pew an important construction project. St Michael's honoured 'Mrs Garnett', who gave a 'pulpett cloth' made 'fitt' by Master Ampleford, by having her name embroidered on it for all to see. Churchwardens paid for hassocks and mats for the same pulpit.[88]

Although the famed and wealthy had long patronized churches, building and outfitting them, the wealth accumulating among London merchants and traders led to greater promotion of the self in the gifts granted to parish churches. The advertisement of these donations unsettled the balance between selfish and selfless charity. The parochial and institutional practice of displaying exemplary acts and celebrating noteworthy donors helped to transform the impulse for private charitable giving through the later sixteenth century. Tablets or monuments hung or erected for all to see bore donors' names, also recited in year-end financial audits. Public recognition encouraged those of a similar background to contribute to the poor, illustrating membership in the ranks for whom largesse was possible and even obligatory. Haigh describes the 'more-or-less voluntary payments of the living' to lights and collections before the Reformation, but even those gifts balanced altruistic and selfish motives for giving. Mauss argues for the survival of the 'atmosphere of the gift, where obligation and liberty intermingle' long into capitalist, modern societies.[89]

St Botolph's listed benefactors to the poor, for an example of good and charitable behaviour.[90] These lists or tables differed from bede rolls, or the obvious display embedded in funeral processions and masses in the pre-Reformation period, in that they made no pleas for repayment in prayers by those helped. In 1608, St Michael's made a 'Table of Remembrance' of 'charitable benevolences' of deceased parishioners, listed by the vestry, and 'suche others as shall here after according to their good examples bestowe any further charitable benevolence to the releif of the poore Inhabitants of this p[ar]ishe'.[91] Phillip Holeman of Broad Street gave 40s to the poor of St Botolph's in gratitude for 'one of the poore', sitting in a doorway near the corner house at Maidenhead

---

[87] GL, MS 1002/1B, fols 360–362v. See f. 371 for his payment of the second half of his gift.

[88] GL, MS 4071/2, f. 12v. Hassocks are firm cushions for kneeling.

[89] Haigh, *English Reformations*, p. 29; Mauss, *The Gift*, p. 65.

[90] The vestry book begins with Proverbs 19:17: 'He that hath mercy upon the Poore, rendeth unto the Lord. And the Lord will recompence him that w[hi]ch hee hath given'; GL, MS 1453/1, f. 1.

[91] GL, MS 4072/1, Part 1, f. 100v.

Alley and Aldersgate Street, who rescued him from 'beeinge murthered by treacherous p[er]sons'.[92]

Testators, remarking that their own largesse should prick others' consciences to act likewise, attested to the display power of gifts and memorials of them that hung in the parish church or craft halls. Auditors and vestrymen discussed the same theme in meetings. In 1614, 'the charitye and liberalitye of a gentlewoman who suppresseth her name' allowed the construction of five shops at the east end of St Botolph's church. Her £36 gift generated 10s for a sermon, 40s for forty poor people, and 40d for the clerk and sexton, all to be paid on her birthday, also the feast of St John the Baptist or Midsummer Day. William Court and Thomas Metcalfe contributed £10 to the same project, for the use of the poor. Her anonymity led one scribe to ascribe her actions to an anonymous gentleman, later corrected when the identity of Jane, the daughter of Roger and Jane 'Giankins', became known.[93] The draper Brian Calverley gave twenty marks to 'the amending and erection of the poore womens howsen in Beache Lane', with the expressed hope of encouraging others to do likewise. 'And I praye god to move the hartes of the Worshipfull of the companye of Drapers to suche charitye that the same maye be augmented'. Calverley called on his social and occupational allies to follow his charitable lead. In 1615, the widows in the almshouses in Beech Lane received a further £4.[94]

For more humble parishioners, traditional forms of labour, especially the devotional yet paid work of women, illustrated their care for the parish church fabric. Mrs Chauntrell, the spouse of the man paid for supplying and writing in the parish's parchment books, was paid 2s for embroidering in white satin the name of the woman who had donated the pulpit cloth. Women still cleaned the church and its ornaments, as when the churchwardens paid Mrs Collingham 11s for 'washing'. Her husband earned 2s 6d for mending the coffin cloth and cushions, while she earned money by washing the church linen.[95] Sara Mendelson and Patricia Crawford have rightly pointed out the 'invisibility' of women's paid work, when husbands were often paid for their wives' labour.[96] This case suggests, however, that men might perform some tasks typi-

---

[92] GL, MS 1453/1, f. 6.

[93] GL, MS 1453/1, fols 8, 4. [Two books were bound together, and the first was bound with the folios out of order.]

[94] PRO, PROB 11/71, f. 158R; 11/125, f. 330L. Testators may have resisted backing unknown individuals, or have preferred donating help within their own crafts in their lifetimes. An almshouse run by the Company allowed control and discrimination over the poor within it.

[95] GL, MS 4071/2, Part 1, fols 16, 16v, 18v.

[96] Mendelson and Crawford, *Women in Early Modern England*, p. 341.

cally labelled women's work, especially perhaps when the repairs were rough, as opposed to fine embroidery executed by the wife of a skilled scribe like Chauntrell. While the candles that had been such a part of pre-Reformation devotion no longer burned, the parish still paid 'the Chaundler Mrs Wilsonn' 36s 6d for eight dozen candles for the lectures.[97] St Mary's also purchased 44 pounds of candles from Katherine Vanderbeck, the widow of waxchandler 'Gosson' Vanderbeck, for the lecture.[98]

In contrast to the examples of shared responsibility for and investment in the parish fabric, churchwardens and sextons supervised lay access to the church, to prevent loss. Keys and locks guarded the public spaces and objects, including Bibles and service books, of the church, even though parishioners gained some control over the space of the church, and the objects within it, by their loans and fees.[99] Parishes protected collections, by placing an iron plate on the poor men's box, 'to keepe it from pyckinge'.[100] Even pieces of church buildings could disappear: a thief was caught trying to cut away the leads over St Mary's porch in 1609/10.[101] The expense of books, like the 'booke of Marters' stolen from St Michael's in the early seventeenth century, led the churchwardens to buy chains and locks to protect 'the bookes in ye Churche'.[102] St Mary's locked its copy of Stow's Survey.[103] In 1610–11, St Michael's churchwarden paid 12d for a new key to the parchment book of christenings and burials, perhaps to safeguard private information.[104] Besides information needed to prove marriages and baptisms, registers included notes of curious or fabulous events, although less frequently in the parchment copies compiled by James I's order. The scribe Chauntrell's careful Greek note identified a hermaphrodite born to William Baker, in St Michael Cornhill in 1609, in only one of the surviving registers from the period. The learned hand recorded the

---

[97] GL, MS 4071/2, f. 16; for title, see f. 19.

[98] GL, MS 1002/1B, f. 403; see f. 393v for her husband's burial. See also GL, MS 7635/1, unfol. Alternative spellings: 'Gozen' and 'Vanderbecke'. The 1593 return of strangers lists him as Gobert Van Derbecke, married to Katherine, and calls him a silk weaver: Irene Scouloudi, *Returns of Strangers in the Metropolis 1593, 1627, 1635, 1639: A Study of an Active Minority*, Quarto Series of the Huguenot Society of London, Vol. 57 (London, 1985), p. 213.

[99] GL, MS 4072/1, Part 1, f. 69v.

[100] GL, MSS 4072/1, Part 1, f. 69v; 4071/1, f. 126v.

[101] GL, MS 1002/1B, f. 381.

[102] GL, MSS 4071/1, f. 189v; fols 136, 137.

[103] GL, MS 1002/1B, f. 431v.

[104] GL, MS 4071/2, f. 12v. Before 1603, instructions called for weekly public readings of the registers: Will Coster, 'Popular religion and the parish register 1538–1603' in *The Parish*, p. 98.

unusual birth, but in a language not widely read in the parish and in a book likely kept locked in a box by 1609.[105]

Similar to the limits on access to space, parishioners imposed limits on churchwardens' use of parochial funds for convivial meals. Balancing maintenance of the church fabric with responsibility to all parishioners, including the poor, could force changes in longstanding parochial practices. Repasts for churchwardens, ministers, vestrymen and prominent parishioners who conducted church business fed a more select group on the whole parish's charge, unlike during the perambulation. When St Michael's renter churchwarden and the minister held a 'meetinge for alteringe the pewes in the Chauncell', they spent 5s at the 'Mermaid', a favourite site for meals. The churchwardens and other parishioners met there again to distribute money to the poor, spending 5s on food and drink and even 6d for a 'Singer at the Mermaid'. Testamentary bequests to the parish poor typically included a small sum for the churchwardens' and sextons' 'pains' in distributing them. Another dinner, costing 13s 4d, entertained the parson, churchwardens and 'divers' parishioners when the repairs to the houses in Bishopsgate were made.[106] Churchwardens in St Mary's spent 2d on candles for 'Accompt night', to light the church for those coming to hear and participate in the audit of their accounts, but made no mention of a dinner.[107]

Trouble arose in St Michael's, however, over the more expensive dinner held at the audit of the churchwardens' accounts, when the parson, the Deputy and others spent 40s 8d at the Mermaid and the churchwardens submitted an additional 26s 8d for the same. Parishioners must have complained about the use of community funds: a later marginal note stated that 'No allowaunce to be herafter made for an awdite dinner'.[108] The audit represented parishes' serious fiscal accounting of their funds, increasingly stretched by parochial, civic and even national needs. Although church- or help-ales had not been part of London's charitable and convivial ventures, or at least surviving records omitted them, parishioners in the city objected to a handful of leaders eating and drinking what had been bequeathed or assessed for the poor and

---

[105] The child was born in October and buried in December: GL, MS 4062, f. 45v; not in GL, MS 4061, unfol. I owe special thanks to Dr James Powell for the translation and to Dr Jeffrey Lerner for discussion of the same. The scribe wrote: 'androgynos', meaning 'man woman', as used by Plato, *Symposium* 189e. For payment to Chauntrell for entering names in parish registers, see GL, MS 4071/2, f. 10v. Coster, 'Popular religion and the parish register', pp. 94–111, esp. pp. 97–9.

[106] GL, MS 4071/2, fols 10, 12.

[107] GL, MS 1002/1B, f. 344.

[108] GL, MS 4071/2, f. 10v. In fact, the cost of the Ascension Day decreased: GL, MS 4071/2, f. 49v.

the church.[109] Even post-Reformation parishioners tried to sustain their funds, chastising parochial leaders for mismanaging them instead of helping the whole parish.

London's continued growth necessitated new projects overseen by parishioners, the elite and middling members often filling parochial and civic roles. The parish, parishioners and city shared a responsibility to complete public works. St Botolph's tried to free itself from costs relating to 'the pumpe' because it was 'no p[ar]te of the churche', in the late 1580s. In 1591/92, however, the churchwardens spent £8 8s 10d to mend it, pledging that church rents and goods would not be used in this way again, although they also supplied 66s 8d for it in 1593/94.[110] Testators also left bequests for these kinds of projects. In 1604, John Conyers left £100 to his son's oversight for the proposed conduit in Aldersgate Street with lead pipes to bring water to it, over seven years.[111] A smaller work provided light for Sherborne Lane, toward St Swithins Lane and Lombard Street, by hanging a lantern and candle in the evening at the end of the church by the parsonage door.[112]

Parishes devised new funds to maintain the church fabric, while also utilizing traditional fees and values to force or encourage parishioners to contribute to the same. Parishioners and testators recognized the prestige in endowing renovations, separating the older calls for prayers from their efforts to sustain and recast worship in the altered, Protestant church. Just as before the Reformation, the 'fabric' of church and community reflected and bolstered piety in the parish. The pattern, however, showed the influence of royal and wealthy patronage and charity.

Reformed piety

Reforming popular piety mirrored the remodelling of church interiors and exteriors that emphasized Protestant texts, the preacher's pulpit and pews for orderly listening and worship. Concern over the moral

---

[109] Bennett, 'Conviviality and Charity', p. 34.

[110] GL, MS 1454, Rolls 89, 90, 93, 95. This may be the pump shown in Treswell's survey of property once belonging to the Fraternity of the Holy Trinity: Schofield (ed.), *The London Surveys of Ralph Treswell*, London Topographical Society, No. 135, (London, 1987), figure 4 (p. 36). Long tradition of public and private collaboration on these projects: Thomson, 'Piety and charity', p. 188.

[111] PRO, PROB 11/105, f.19L. Thomas Hayes built the conduit in 1610, which burned in the Great Fire and was not rebuilt: Schofield (ed.), *The London Surveys*, p. 35 and figure 4 (p. 36).

[112] PRO, PROB 11/122, f. 60R.

character of congregations, including poor members, produced extreme descriptions of society and its godliness, or lack thereof. Edification, and the controversial charitable actions sometimes legitimated by this religious charge, lent some preachers and ministers a reputation for creating strife among neighbours through their fiery sermons and commandments regarding alms.[113] Protestant or puritan preachers, especially in the early seventeenth century, saw their efforts as a mission to educate parishioners in the ways of 'true' religion. Efforts began with young children and youths, with success in conversion. Even foundlings enjoyed community support at their baptism, with churchwardens paying 'Gossips' to attend, as expected when any child was received into Christianity. Parishes also participated in the catechizing movement, instructing youth in the Book of Common Prayer's statement of faith and in the Ten Commandments, Articles of Belief and Lord's Prayer, in special periods set aside before services. In 1604, St Botolph's paid the sexton for 'his paynes in warninge the young p[e]rsons to come to catechisinge & to keepe the churchyard cleane from annoyaunce of children'.[114] Suffer the little children – and young apprentices and servants – to come to church, but in an orderly fashion for worship.

Outward commandments and formalized parochial instruction of the young demonstrate expectations regarding popular piety, but uncovering the 'felt' pious experience of parishioners 'in the pews' – or in the places they lived and worked – remains a vexing problem for historians.[115] Testamentary preambles provide one hint of the extent of testators' adoption of the new language and theology of Protestantism. Although preambles require caution when used as an indicator of individualized piety, they do reflect a general cultural mood or model of piety. Imitative preambles parroted devotions, just as mimicry in medieval

---

[113] See the following chapter for discussion of charity, as well as Schen, 'Constructing the Poor in Early Seventeenth Century London', *Albion*, 32, 3 (Fall 2000), pp. 450–63. Hill calls puritanism 'bourgeois' and notes 'common people's hostility' to doctrine of original sin when seen as basis of poverty: 'William Perkins and the Poor', pp. 233, 236–7. Cf. the 'missionary intent', compassion of protestant preachers in regards to common people and problem of poverty: Duffy, 'The Godly and the Multitude in Stuart England', *Seventeenth Century*, 1, 1 (1986), pp. 33–5. On divisiveness of Puritan lectureships: Sommerville, *Secularization*, p. 67.

[114] GL, MSS 4071/2, f. 48v; 1453/1, f. 2v. Griffiths, *Youth*, pp. 179, 186. See Duffy on the catechizing movement and chapbooks educating children, the illiterate and the poor: 'The Godly and the Multitude', pp. 35, 49; *VAI*, III, p. 305.

[115] Although 'the core of a study of English Reformations must be a political story', Haigh argues that most people were just 'conformists': *English Reformations*, pp. 21, 290; Litzenberger wants to see 'how official policies played in the pews', but must rely heavily on episcopal decrees and returns despite analysis of broad pious categories in wills: *The English Reformation and the Laity*, p. 2.

Catholicism demonstrated the active embrace, not passive acceptance of popular pious trends.[116] Christocentric preambles emphasized Protestant theology about salvation and, sometimes, election. Some testators referred to the 'fruition of the pr[e]sence of the dyetie with the election in the kingdome of heaven'; that is, their hope to be a member of the elect.[117] Ministerial influence could act on testators' minds, in their churches and on their deathbeds. Thomas Papworth's deathbed will reflected the bedside presence of Mr Buckminster, curate of St Mary Woolnoth – or the pastor attended because Papworth asked to see him during his last moments. Papworth left his soul to God, 'trustinge onely thorow the death and blood sheddinge of Jesus Christ to be an inheritour of the kingdome of heaven and his body to the earth to be buryed at the discretion of his ov[er]seer'.[118]

Out of the 123 wills produced between 1581 and 1601, 50.41 per cent (62) contained preambles dedicated to Jesus Christ, commemorated as the sole redeemer or the passionate sufferer on the cross. Another 35.77 per cent (34) of testaments contained invocations to God as Maker and Redeemer or to God and Jesus Christ. Only 12.20 per cent (15) lacked any sort of preamble. Out of the 105 wills from 1602 to 1620, 45.71 per cent (48) spoke to Jesus Christ. Roughly 35 per cent (37) invoked God or God and Jesus, but 18 per cent (19) had no preamble. Some testators may have hidden their piety in plain preambles, especially if they remained Catholic.[119]

In addition to the preamble, testators' requirements for burial sites and restrictions on the style of mourning also reveal popular piety. Although financial support for new or revived celebrations and services marked the later Tudor and early Stuart church, and less for other pieces of the parish fabric, a subtle change in burial and grave locations suggests the depth of social, demographic and religious shifts through the course of reform. Papworth's testamentary concern about his salvation, but apparent disregard for his interment, marked an emerging Protestant ethos about graves and burials. Between 1580 and 1601, 47 per cent (58) of testators asked for burial within their own parishes, but an equal number left the place to executors' discretion or simply unspecified. After 1601, 25 per cent (26) did so, but most testators (75 per cent, or 78) depended on others' discretion or said nothing about their preferred burial sites. As to grave locations, whether testators asked for burial in their own parishes or not,

---

[116] Craig and Litzenberger, 'Wills as religious propaganda', pp. 415–16; Flynn, *Sacred Charity*, p. 70.

[117] PRO, PROB 11/90, f. 264R; PRO, PROB 11/81, f. 355R.

[118] GL, MS 9171/17, f. 5.

[119] Duffy, *Stripping*, pp. 505–14.

77 per cent (85) before 1601 and 87 per cent (91) before 1620 left them unspecified or asked executors to choose. The minority still asked for burial by family, by pew door, or in the churchyard.[120] In contrast, before the Reformation and even prior to 1580, testators had carefully described their grave locations, planning to rest near family or in areas of the church identified with their individual or familial identity.

Testamentary attention to the place of burial and the exact location of the grave had declined in importance for post-Reformation Londoners, a significant cultural shift reflecting a few developments in the city and in Protestant thought. Demographic and religious factors weakened outward loyalty to burial within the parish or in a named place. The testators who left their burial to the oversight of executors were likely interred in their own parishes, but they no longer expended so much energy planning the location of their graves. Overcrowded late sixteenth and early seventeenth-century churchyards and churches, requiring sextons to register new graves to lessen 'anoyances that maye happen in openinge the ground', in part explained why testators expended less space in their wills on last resting-places. The iconoclasm of the Reformation had also cleared elaborate monuments and perhaps weakened testamentary attention to the location and style of graves. Harding argues that evidence of pre-Reformation destruction and sale of monuments suggest that neither religious change nor sixteenth-century demographic pressure created a 'casual attitude' to memorials after the Reformation, but less attention to graves combined with more bequests of rings and tokens for remembrance suggest testators invested in different forms of commemoration.[121]

Perhaps as a change in will-making practices, Londoners depended on pre-death discussions, more than their wills, to convey burial plans, disguising attitudes to the afterlife and to religious services. Testators may have relied on their lifetime discussions with spouses, family members and executors rather than testamentary edicts. Even a change in will-making, however, could reflect newer pious practices that testators may have wished to avoid. If testators obscured their piety in preambles for fear of persecution, they could also diffuse criticism or attention by omitting attitudes about graves and funeral services.[122] Testators, how-

---

[120] See GL, MS 9051/5, f. 65. 38 before 1601, 14 to 1620.

[121] GL, MS 4072/1, Part 1, f. 104v. See Harding, '"And one more may be laid there"', p. 113; Harding, 'Burial of the plague dead in early modern London' in J.A.I. Champion (ed.), *Epidemic Disease in London* (London: Centre for Metropolitan History Working Papers Series, No.1, 1993), pp. 53–64, on-line at *http://www.ihrinfo.ac.uk/cmh/ epiharding.html* and 'Burial Choice and Burial Location', p. 129.

[122] Harding believes that this development 'reflects a change in the nature of willmaking

ever, had long used formulaic phrases and restated prior arrangements for charity, burial or inheritance in their wills, perhaps especially when warning and cajoling friends and family to see final instructions fulfilled.

Aspects of Protestant doctrine also weakened testamentary stress on the location of graves. The Protestant and Catholic Reformations' eschewal of worldly concern for the flesh contributed to new attitudes towards burial. Post-Reformation remembrance of piety or friendship, especially through rings and other tokens worn by friends and family, lessened the importance of the body's resting place, traditionally a means to the commemoration of the soul. Bodies waiting for the Day of Judgment increasingly did so embalmed, and in coffins, though some modestly avoided the penetration of their deceased loved ones' bodies.[123] The slow evolution of a proto-funeral industry, coupled with crowded burial sites graded by cost, helped to create greater social distinctions among the dead.[124] In planning for his herald's funeral, George Kevall requested a funeral 'performed according to my habillitie, with all reverence', with escutcheons hanging over his body and from the pulpit. He wanted the four beadles of Bridewell to wear black gowns and carry his body to the church, probably in a coffin that parishes provided for bringing bodies to their graves.[125]

Puritan disgust with the body, bereft of the personality that left the physical body at death, altered attitudes toward the corpse. A carpenter who described himself as aged, sick and weak, reminded hearers of his will that 'our worldly and Transitorye Cogitacons and thoughtes doe soone perishe and come as noughte'.[126] He made his will in readiness of death, but emphasized the end of thought rather than the decomposition of the body. Perhaps the understanding that death shut down the mind explained the stress on portable tokens of remembrance like rings, that spurred contemplation and memory of the dead individual and his or her affection for or bonds with the living.

---

and executorship rather than an absolute decline in concern for the location of burial': 'Burial choice and burial location', p. 122; Duffy, *Stripping*, pp. 504–5.

[123] Gittings argues that this trend originated in 'unease at the prospect of physical decomposition': *Death, Burial and the Individual*, p. 13; cf. apparent casualness in regards to autopsies in Lutheran Germany: Ozment, *Magdalena and Balthasar*, p. 101.

[124] On development of heralds' funerals with embalming: Gittings, 'Urban Funerals', pp. 179ff; that charging for burials 'begins to set out a hierarchy of location', even before the Reformation: Harding, 'Burial Choice and Burial Location', pp. 130–31.

[125] PRO, PROB 11/98, fols 132L–132R.

[126] Gittings, *Death, Burial and the Individual*, p. 47; Thomas, *Religion*, p. 605; Beaver, *Parish Communities and Religious Conflict*, pp. 96–110. PRO, PROB 11/81, f. 114L.

New pious attitudes toward selfish display and funeral extravagance also surfaced in the shorter funeral processions escorting testators' bodies to their graves, a sign of ongoing reform in the city. Even in their reduced form, however, funerals and burial needs helped to embroider on and repair the fabric of post-Reformation churches, sustaining an older activity that had long been central to the cultural and financial vitality of parishes. The immediate funeral procession and service persisted, although the living no longer prayed (openly) to help the dead reach salvation after the Reformation. Between 1581 and 1601, 49.8 per cent (497) of all pious gifts took the form of gowns, followed by 47.8 per cent (477) in money. Between 1601 and 1620, the percentage of gowns decreased to 37.43 per cent (277) and money gifts rose to 55.27 per cent (409). Declining bequests for gowns, shortening processions, may reflect the attitude expressed by one of London's ruling class in 1588: 'there shall be no blacks or such like vain pomp or ceremony used, that in mine own opinion do rather agree with popery and paganism than with the rule of the gospel of God'.[127] Nearly 97 per cent (641) of pious bequests connected to burials and funeral processions, between 1581 and 1601, paid poor men and women for their attendance.[128] From 1602–20, more than 96 per cent (329) of such bequests went to poor men.

Although women comprised 16.2 per cent of testators to 1620, not far from the 18.7 per cent they comprised to 1601, their bequests for processions declined. The decline in the number of processions endowed by women coincided with a decrease in the number of cycle or burial sermons bequeathed by women in their last wills. Like their earlier lead in adopting restrictive charitable clauses that could be identified with the new ways of Protestantism, women may have heeded their male preachers who, from their authoritative positions in pulpits, denigrated the self-promotion of the wealthy, whether through burial sermons or funeral processions. Because men and women hired their own sex for burial processions, when women showed little interest in funding burial processions, poor men dominated hired mourners. Social changes in London, the greater emphasis on craft life without other mixed or single-gender lay organizations like religious guilds, may have lessened women's opportunities for public commemoration or involvement.

Hiring the poor as principle mourners created a more seemly procession than outfitting great numbers of friends, associates and extended

---

[127] Quoted in Hickman, 'From Catholic to Protestant', p. 124.

[128] Forty per cent (265) of these bequests went to poor women and 50.1 per cent (332) to poor men, with 6.6 per cent going to the 'poor', not specified by sex. See also David Cressy, *Birth, Marriage and Death: Ritual, Religion and the Life-Cycle in Tudor and Stuart England* (Oxford, 1997), pp. 396–455.

family. Earlier testators may have assumed that the same corporate entities would supply their mourners, but deliberate naming of body-bearers and attendants allowed testators to exercise discretion in 'hiring' the poor, since mourning still functioned as employment for needy parishioners in Reformation parishes. Testators asking for burial in 'honeste and comelie' fashion, as their Christian right, invited family, poor parishioners and parish officials to participate in mourning processions. Some named certain poor mourners, or asked executors to draw them from craft or parish. In 1583, John Spencer asked for 20 poor men to follow his body, along with his wife, children, brother and servants, but stipulated 'noe other morners at all'.[129] Migration to the city strained kin ties, but Spencer's mandate went beyond accepting relatives' absence to excluding them from a mourning party. Providing brown-blue, not black gowns, Richard Hadley hired 30 poor men to accompany his body along with the clerk and sexton, the latter officials 'to have eche of the one [gown] somwhat better then the reste'.[130]

Although requesting poor mourners above others highlighted testators' selfless actions, inviting inmates of Christ's Hospital nonetheless added to the spectacle and promotion of lineage and self when testators planned their funerals. The citizen and goldsmith Frauncis Shute provided £3 to the poor children at Christ's, on condition that the children sing psalms at his burial. The inmates augmented the musical component of his last moments above ground, but did not replace mourners, especially those of his social rank. The gesture demonstrated his charitable nature, as did his recent election to the board of governors of Bridewell. Although he seems to have died before serving, he wished to immortalize his connection to Bridewell in his testamentary declaration.[131] Shute also left 15d to each of his Company's almsmen, to the total of £1. He gave the far greater sum of £9, however, for a dinner for those of the livery who attended his burial. He left his brother, sister, good friend and male gossip each gold hoop rings reading, 'Remember to dye'.[132]

Testators hoped for long-term remembrance among friends, neighbours and family, above short-term mourning. Gifts to friends and family took on greater significance in remembrance and expressions of piety. A gentleman left rings or bracelets to family members and friends for a 'poore remembraunce of our acquainetunce'.[133] To family and

---

[129] PRO, PROB 11/66, f. 193L.

[130] PRO, PROB 11/92, f. 95L.

[131] He is not listed as a governor of the royal hospitals: Manzione, Appendix B, *Christ's Hospital*, pp. 158–97.

[132] PRO, PROB 11/111, fols 336R–337L.

[133] PRO, PROB 11/98, f. 58L.

acquaintances, robes made up just less than ten per cent of non-pious gifts before 1601 (9.82 per cent or 170), falling to less than six per cent by 1620 (5.63 per cent or 84). The popularity of rings (15.24 per cent or 264 and 18.58 per cent or 277 in the same periods) outweighed that of gowns, another example of smaller burial processions and groups of mourners.[134] These testators seemed more concerned with perpetuating remembrance among their friends and family than bringing them into burial processions. Bequests for mourning gowns continued, however, to reach poor men and women. Rings, engraved with death's heads or seals, and wedding rings recalled the testator and the transitory nature of human life. The symbolic tokens reminded the recipient of the giver and of his or her own eventual demise, pious phrases about death and remembrance making clear that no one escaped their mortality. Personal clothing and apparel figured in small numbers as well in these later wills.

Tokens of affection or remembrance concentrated on the ephemeral flesh and the brevity of earthly compared to eternal life after death. Testators made death's heads popular emblems on rings, stressing the impermanence of bodies, despite a hope for affectionate remembrance after death. Posies and symbols on other rings referred to heaven and everlasting life. One testator asked that the phrase 'He lyves in blysse that gaue me this' adorn his rings. Dame Ramsey requested the saying 'Remember thy end to lyve forever'.[135] Some left rings that had belonged to ancestors or inscribed them with their own initials or names, no longer asking for the prayers of their survivors, but hoping for kind remembrance. John Strahan, who left a series of bequests for sermons, hospitals, stranger churches, relief in a few parishes and ministers, also gave the widow of Cornelius Spirinck his own gold ring with the 'pelican pulling out her harte'.[136]

As others had done with holy numbers, Strahan played on a traditional Catholic symbol to ensure the widow's remembrance of him through the gift of the pelican ring. Medieval Catholics mistakenly believed that pelicans wounded their breasts to feed their young, just as Christ had shed his blood and sacrificed himself for the redemption of sinners.[137] The importance of the symbol within the pre-Reformation

---

[134] Money before 1601 constituted 46.77 per cent or 810 bequests and 47.55 per cent or 709 between 1601 and 1620.

[135] PRO, PROB 11/75, f. 177R; 11/98, f. 193R.

[136] PRO, PROB 11/105, fols 282L–282R, f. 283L. Katherine 'Spirink' was a native of Brussels, he of Antwerp, but they had lived in London, where he worked as a notary, for 24 years. They were also identified as members of the Italian Church: Scouloudi, *Returns of Strangers*, p. 208.

[137] Rubin, *Corpus Christi*, pp. 310–12. Corporas cloth with pelican part of Nocket's Chantry in St Mary Woolnoth: GL, MS 1005/1, f. 15.

mass and in relation to the *Pater Noster* made the ring, on the face of it, a strange choice for the Protestant testator. Protestants and Catholics, however, found the image a potent one for pious contemplation since it reiterated the central importance of Christ's Passion in theology, for salvation and redemption from sin. To a Protestant, the pelican represented the sacrifice on the cross and its redemptive value, rather than the presence of Christ's flesh in the mass.

The rings or tokens of remembrance left by testators perpetuated the memory of the dead, without giving survivors a way to 'help' them in their experience in the afterlife. Without purgatory to exert demands on the living, the dead became less immediate to them. Reformation theology had filtered into testaments, notably that referring to the ephemeral character of life, with the promise of the resurrection of the body at the Day of Judgment. The Catholic notion of purgatory had linked the living and dead in expectations of prayers and cycles of masses and anniversaries. The soul imprisoned in purgatory required the help of the living, resembling the poor shackled in prisons or debilitated by ill health. Survivors' distress over death may have originated in the shortened grieving period, since masses extended over days, months and even years had been discontinued.[138]

When testators chose to limit their mourning processions, perhaps giving small rings in lieu of gowns, they often inserted conditions in case family or executors disobeyed their pious demands. Involuntary contributions to charity and Reformation hospitals supplanted older threats of divine retaliation for poorly executed bequests, suggesting a turn toward financial, not purely spiritual, arm-twisting. Some testators ordered donations to Christ's Hospital if restrictions on processions were not followed or fulfilled, as when Frauncys Barnarde, citizen and cook, forbade his wife to wear mourning apparel, or to force others to wear it. If she refused, he demanded she pay a penalty of £20 to the hospital. Irrespective of this conditional bequest, he gave 20s to Christ's for the children to accompany his body to burial and £3 for a 'potacion' for those of the company of Cooks who also escorted his body.[139] The children of the Hospital sang, as well as processed, providing the 'pitiful' sight noted by earlier chroniclers and perhaps providing an orderly group of young and deserving poor to mix with family and friends. Eight testators depended on the children of Christ's Hospital, who embodied the neediest, worthiest poor.

---

[138] Gittings links twentieth-century denial of mourning with puritan attitudes toward death: 'Urban Funerals', pp. 172–3; *Death, Burial and the Individual*, p. 122.

[139] PRO, PROB 11/83, f. 217L.

Although many testators cut back on conspicuous display of wealth in their funeral arrangements, some continued to draw on the ties of family and clientage in outfitting mourners and providing dinners or recreations. Burials in the sixteenth and early seventeenth centuries still affirmed publicly the status of testators and their survivors. For example, one testator provided gowns to servants, stepchildren, cousins, friends, preachers and the poor, to mourn his passing.[140] Individuals provided bread or drink to the poor and separate dinners or recreations for friends, distinguishing further between relief of socially segregated individuals and gratitude or affection among neighbours and intimates. Social segregation facilitated the distribution of charity and the collection of deference, persisting into eighteenth-century England. This fostered, and reflected, the gradual decay of vertical community ties, like the potlatch studied by anthropologists. The practice demanded vast outlays of wealth, even bankrupting societies by the disposal of goods, to assert a position above a neighbouring community. In the sixteenth and seventeenth centuries, the practice of focusing more narrowly on what constituted 'community' further restricted the flow of money and goods to the lower orders.[141]

Contemporaries, however, recognized the significance of funerals and even funeral pomp to parochial life and the ritualized sharing of food and camaraderie, highlighting the dissonance between a parish's social needs and austere, reformed practices. Trends in funeral practice limited display, but parishes counted on prominent parishioners' funeral services to contribute to the religious life and social prestige of the church. Dame Ramsey's service, with family and associates of the civic leader's widow in attendance, not to mention the monument erected at her grave, would have brought honour and attention to the parish church. The churchwardens collected fees and registered her benefactions in a separate book, but did not share in the solemn significance of her funeral and burial.[142] Although Dame Ramsey could not assume an

---

[140] PRO, PROB 11/90, fols 192L–192R. By contrast, Stone argues, 'The decay of the gigantic and fantastically expensive funeral ritual attended by literally hundreds of kindred, cousins, retainers, domestic servants and poor was another symbol of the same shedding by the social elite of outer layers of familial and extra-familial client ties, and a slow withdrawal to a more private domestic experience': *Family, Sex, and Marriage*, p. 95.

[141] Heal, *Hospitality*; E.P. Thompson, 'The Moral Economy of the Crowd in the Eighteenth Century', *PaP*, 50 (1971), pp. 76–136; Archer, *Pursuit*, p. 60. On bankrupting societies: Mauss, *The Gift*, p. 83. Community as 'social organisation … characterised by social interactions': Archer, *Pursuit*, p. 58; for debate on 'community' see special issue Kowaleski (ed.), 'Village, Guild, and Gentry'.

[142] GL, MS 1002/1B, fols 331, 332.

administrative role like her husband did in Christ's Hospital, she left rich gifts that gave her prominence among the other benefactors and rulers of the hospital. Her will demonstrated that testamentary giving supplemented *inter vivos* support for the home for fatherless children, a model likely followed by other testators as well. She left a tenement to the Mayor and City of London to maintain Bridewell and Christ's and St Thomas's Hospitals. She also left £2000 for her executors and the Treasurer and Governors of Christ's to buy tenements with rents worth £100 yearly, to maintain preachers in the hospital and in poor parishes in the city and to help 12 poor scholars in Oxford and Cambridge. She referred to lifetime donations, including a fee simple in Essex for a writing school in the Hospital, a grammar school in Essex, and aid for ten poor widows, yearly. Ramsey's careful preparation of her burial site in the institution, and her rhetorical humility in requesting it, gave the wealthy donor an extraordinary legacy reflecting her charity that could have enriched her parish church as well.

Burial sermons also demonstrate reformed piety, becoming another element in mourning and in burying a Protestant body. Sermons like this filled a gap between the pious desire for smaller processions and the community's tradition of joining together for a communal event. Between 1580 and 1620, the percentage of testators requesting at least a (single) burial sermon rose to 12.05 per cent (27), compared to the period 1559–80, when 8.22 per cent (24) did. Male and female testators acknowledged edifying the congregation and honouring God, but not commemorating themselves, when they asked for a preacher 'of the worde of god' to preach a burial sermon, or the increasingly less common cycle of sermons.[143] Choosing well-known, better-educated preachers reinforced the social status enjoyed by the testator during life, and electing one's parson to provide the funeral sermon reaffirmed bonds between some parishioners and their ministers or lecturers, especially when they shared religious views. William Massey, the painter-stainer who put the Commandments on the walls of St Stephen's, gave 40s to his minister, Dr Merriall, 'as a token of my love unto him soe as he preach at my buriall'.[144] Merriall's guidance in the parish exemplified godly concern with religious conversion of non-Christians and with the instruction of his own congregation. Richard Hadley gave the lecturer 'Mr Alsoppe' 40s to preach at his burial, a provision that appeared in the codicil, witnessed by the parson, Mr Buckminster, of St Mary Woolnoth.[145]

---

[143] For example, see Jane Ludford's will: PRO, PROB 11/90, f. 172R.

[144] GL, MS 9051/6, f. 39v. For other examples, see PRO, PROB 11/71, f. 158R; 11/78, f. 14R; 11/90, f. 192R; 11/105, f. 282L; 11/111, f. 336R; GL, MS 9051/5, f. 24v.

[145] Evidence that Alsoppe is lecturer: PRO, PROB 11/98, f. 192R; Hadley's will: PRO,

Wealthy London inhabitants and citizens endowed sermons in the parishes of their birth, for myriad possible reasons. They may have wished, selfishly, to prove that they had prospered since leaving their smaller towns for the big city and, piously, to remind others of their certain deaths and to evangelize where fewer sermons might have been endowed. Henry Smith asked that 'stranger preachers', perhaps French or Dutch Calvinists, give four to six sermons yearly in Stoke Prior, where he had been born. Christopher Gaylor made a more humble bequest for a single sermon by Mr Wallis, vicar of Dartford in Kent. He also left a gift to the poor there, making it likely he had been born there, or still had family in the town. Raphe Lownes, a citizen and girdler, left extensive charitable bequests to hospitals and prisons in London in 1619, but he also left a series of gifts and tokens to ministers and scholars outside London, and to the poor in the same places.[146]

Some of the parsons and lecturers named by testators were well-known puritan figures. Brian Calverley asked Robert Crowley, a nonconformist preacher since the 1560s and of great fame in the city, to give the sermon at his burial in 1587. In his preamble from 1606, John Strahan honoured Christ, who died to free him from everlasting death and damnation, and asked to be buried in St Michael Cornhill to await resurrection. He requested a funeral sermon by Mr Haywarde of St Mary Woolchurch, but also left a series of gifts that revealed puritan leanings. He left bequests to the poor of a few parishes, and to the poor of the French and Dutch congregations, the latter a rare bequest in the parishes in this study. For a token of remembrance, he left a gold ring bearing his arms to Doctor Soame, the Master of Peterhouse, Cambridge, and a puritan. He left 40s for a ring, as a token of remembrance, to Master Doctor [John] Dix, minister of St Bartholomew Exchange, a man identified as an Anglican lecturer by Seaver.[147] He left similar rings to three other ministers, of his own and nearby parishes.[148] William Wickes, a haberdasher in St Michael Cornhill, gave £3 to the preacher (and Presbyterian) Giles Wigginton and £5 to the 'godly poore' in the plague year of 1593. He granted his soul to God and Christ in his preamble, 'in the assuraunce of a lively faithe that I am one of the number whiche he hathe elected to be saved'. He asked to be buried in

---

PROB 11/92, f. 95R. He added the codicil six months after the first part was formalized and one month before the document was probated.

[146] PRO, PROB 11/108, f. 267R; 11/114, f. 86R; 11/133, fols 314L–315L.

[147] On Crowley, who died on 18 June 1588, close to seventy years old (*DNB*): Seaver, *Puritan Lectureships*, pp. 205, 30, 123. On Soame: ibid., p. 184; on Dix: ibid., p. 194.

[148] PRO, PROB 11/105, fols 282L–283R.

the 'new churchyard' until Christ's coming and the Day of Judgment brought his resurrection.[149]

These testators, like prominent citizens before them, could balance their bequests among radical, moderate, and conservative aims and targets. Pious gifts helped to accentuate religious differences, but non-pious ones smoothed these distinctions and reinforced the social and political networks in the city. David Hickman argues that London aldermen adopted 'an essentially Protestant understanding of customary devotional practice', while McClendon finds 'tolerance of religious heterogeneity' in Edwardian and Elizabethan Norwich.[150] The testamentary gifts of Gunter and Bowes and of prominent citizens like Strahan suggest that London's inhabitants settled into their religious beliefs, not merely choosing between Protestant and Catholic, but between strands of Protestantism. Strahan's gifts, for instance, of rings and jewels to aldermen, the king's physician and other servants of the court, and many merchants and neighbours suggest that he tempered his puritanism with useful gifts to elites in London and members of the court.[151]

Bequests to one's parish minister could seem a conservative choice in comparison with those to puritan preachers and lecturers, as when Anne Atkinson left death's head rings to her parson, Thomas Buckminster of St Mary Woolnoth, and his wife, Alice.[152] A number of men left gifts to St Stephen's pastor Roger Fenton, but one of those men also left a slew of gifts to puritan divines.[153] A 'poore unworthy servant' of God, John Stockeley, citizen and merchant tailor, asked that the 'Bretheren' and Christian friends accompany his body to burial. Besides his £5 'token' to Fenton and £10 for a 'token of my love' to his old pastor, Hayward of Woolchurch, he left money to 'ministers of gods most holy

---

[149] PRO, PROB 11/81, fols 355R–356L. Seaver, *Puritan Lectureships*, p. 158. Wickes must have meant the New Churchyard, a newer cemetery at Bethlem, consecrated in 1569 after the devastating plague year of 1563. He died in another severe plague year, but the first recorded plague death was in June 1593, after his death, which is not recorded in the register. His will was written in February 1593 and probated in May 1593. (GL, MS 4061, unfol.) See Harding, 'Burial choice and burial location'.

[150] Hickman, 'From Catholic to Protestant', p. 133; McClendon, 'Religious toleration and the Reformation: Norwich magistrates in the sixteenth century' in Nicholas Tyacke (ed.), *England's Long Reformation* (London and Bristol, PA, 1998), pp. 103, 105–6.

[151] Litzenberger describes a 'third phase' in studying religion, not in forming local studies or building a 'false dichotomy' between Protestants and Catholics, but emphasizing 'a wide range of religious beliefs' instead: *The English Reformation and the Laity*, pp. 2–3. PRO, PROB 11/105, fols 282L–283R.

[152] PRO, PROB 11/69, f. 33R.

[153] See PRO, PROB 11/108, fols 355R–356L; 11/113, fols 267L–268R; 11/123, fols 396R–398L; 11/123, fols 53L–55L.

word', all labelled servants of the Lord and Jesus Christ. He left £5 to 'Harison of Lyton' and £3 each to Egerton, Travis Wooten, ffoorth, Watson, Denyson and 'Hewes of Kingston'.[154] Female testators in this sample did not leave similar gifts to identifiably puritan preachers. The single woman Isabel Anderson, either a servant or apprentice in the cloth trade, supported three ministers of the word of God, none of whom was identified as puritan by Seaver.[155]

The testament of Henry Smith, citizen and draper, illustrates the methodological limitations of studying preambles in isolation from the rest of the testament, especially if trying to ascertain religious identity. A plain preamble could usher in other bequests exhibiting more radical religious ideas. Smith bequeathed money to a small list of preachers in 1606, some of whom were puritan lecturers who had been removed from their positions, yet his plain preamble dedicated his soul simply to God and Jesus Christ. He asked that his body be buried and 'decently accompanyed to the grave w[i]th my lovinge frendes w[i]thoute any mournenge apparrell'. Smith might have attended the lectures and sermons of the four preachers he remembered. He identified 'Mr Randall' as the minister of St Andrew's, meaning John Randall who served there from 1600–22 and whose sermons were published posthumously, 1622–40. He also left £5 to 'Mr Egerton', saying that he used to preach at Blackfriars. His gift helped support Stephen Egerton, the nonconformist lecturer who had been removed from his position at St Anne Blackfriars in 1604 and not restored until 1607. The draper gave the same amount to 'Mr Smithe', apparently another suspended lecturer, explaining that he used to preach at 'St Nicholas Soper [?] Lane'.[156] George Busbye, a citizen and clothworker making six small bequests, left a will with a simple preamble, but 12d each to a minister and to a 'preacher now in troble' in 1600.[157]

The religious books left to friends, family and associates similarly reflected reformed piety and testators' earnest hope that recipients would heed the texts' contents. Besides works relating to medicine and law, testators left Bibles to family, including a 'little' Bible that could be carried on travels. The merchant tailor Edward Gaddisdon, of St Botolph,

---

[154] PRO, PROB 11/123, fols 53L–55L.

[155] GL, MS 9051/6, f. 11v.

[156] PRO, PROB 11/108, fols 266L–268L. On Randall: Seaver, *Puritan Lectureships*, p. 199; see STC 20669, 20672, 20675, 20681, 20682, 20683. On Stephen Egerton: ibid., pp. 223, 225. It is not clear which Smith this is. Similarly, I cannot identify the fourth minister, 'Dr Medus'. The testator seems to have confused this parish with St Pancras Soper Lane.

[157] GL, MS 9171/19, fols 206v–207.

must have anxiously considered his brothers' piety as he made his last will. To his brother John he left a Geneva Bible, so that 'he shoulde exercise himselfe in the worde of god and lawe of the Lorde'. He left his own Testament to his brother William, another gift that encouraged the sibling's full reform.[158] Women occasionally left books that similarly revealed their piety and devotional circles. To her friend Mrs Tipper, Elizabeth Younge left a handkerchief and a prayer book, 'w[hi]ch shee was wont to reade on in my howse'. She left handkerchiefs and rings, more personal gifts, to other female friends. This widow also granted 20s to male and female friends 'to make merry'.[159]

Women and men with property desired to avoid strife after their deaths, precipitated by the careless neglect to finalize last wishes, as if to deny, irresponsibly, death's inevitability. Testators made their wills so as not to create family quarrels and suits and left tangible tokens of affection and directives urging family peace. With equanimity, Dorothy Kemp alleged the strength of her mind despite her sickness and extreme age, explaining that 'my glasse of life is almost runn out. And being desirous to settle that little contencon after my decease doe make and ordayne this my last will and Testament'.[160] Elizabeth Younge's will was probated within four days of its writing, but it was a complicated one. It fulfilled the property distributions requested by her husband in his May testament, showing the care that went into a document that was seemingly written close to death, but had been discussed, even drafted before then.[161] Her will was written the day after her husband's will was probated, suggesting that she tied up loose ends before her own death: the execution of her husband's will and the writing of her own. The extent, and the agony, of death in the 1603 plague reminded some Londoners of the verity behind their formulaic statements about death's certainty and its uncertain hour. Agnes Holgate communicated her will 'about eleven of the clock in the forenoone of the same daie, and after the buriall of ffrauncis my daughter the same daie', 24 August.[162] The will reached probate the last day of the month, showing how quickly the plague moved through her household, possibly under quarantine. She left her soul to God and trusted the merits of Christ to save her during the visitation.

---

[158] Law and medical books, respectively: PRO, PROB 11/74, f. 5R; PRO, PROB 11/101, f. 243R. Bibles: PRO, PROB 11/62, fols 232R–233L; GL, MS 9051/5, f. 293v; PRO, PROB 11/114, f. 51R. 'Little' Bible: PRO, PROB 11/133, f. 314R.

[159] GL, MS 9051/5, f. 48v.

[160] GL, MS 9051/6, f. 11.

[161] GL, MS 9051/5, f. 48v.

[162] GL, MS 9051/5, f. 300.

Protestantism shaped the family and household, especially through the reformation and governance of the behaviour of children, siblings and servants achieved in last wills. Wills concentrated on 'non-pious' recipients, including offspring and servants. Warnings regarding inappropriate, even ungodly actions and attitudes tempered the affectionate sentiments behind gifts to family. Conduct books and popular pious and moral literature emphasized the importance of good order within families and households. Testators hoped for the 'godly' and virtuous upbringing, and living, of their daughters and sons. A trumpeter, dying of the plague in the home of a parishioner, left all his goods to that man to raise his son in virtue and to keep him in school.[163] Parents fretted over their children's futures, as during the 1603 plague year when one father defined the inheritance due to his children in case his wife died before being able to make her own will. Parents beseeched executors and wards to teach and oversee children. A widow left her two daughters to guardians 'where they maye be vertuouslye and skilfully broughte upp and taughte howe to gett theire living honestly in time to come'. One man worried about two of his sons' habits, warning that if they proved to be bad husbands, engaging in gaming or drinking, their parts would be void and go to his other, 'good' son. He demanded that the worrisome sons and their mother 'shalbe loving and peaceable togethere, and that e[a]ch shalbe aiding and assisting to other, and especially that my sonnes shalbe loving & obedient to their Mother, and not to see her wanting for any thing to theire powers'.[164]

Exhortations to model, 'godly' behaviour became more prevalent, focusing squarely on the family as an important stone in the edifice of an orderly reformed society.[165] Wills' semi-public nature permitted the restatement of prodigal children's misdeeds to a wider audience, one often granted supervisory roles to see children bend to a deceased parent's will. The circle of family and friends who knew the contents of wills recognized, in a parent's testamentary forgiveness, good

---

[163] Portion of catechism in Cressy and Ferrell (eds), *Religion and Society*, pp. 73–8. Excerpt of William Gouge, *Of Domesticall Duties* (1622) in Mary Abbott, *Life Cycles in England, 1560–1720: Cradle to Grave* (London and New York, 1996), pp. 180–89. Becon's catechism as early (1559) example of conduct literature, with more published in seventeenth century: Crawford, *Women and Religion*, p. 39. 'Godly' as well as virtuously: GL, MS 9171/17, f. 132v; schooling: GL, MS 9171/19, fols 351v–352.

[164] GL, MS 9051/5, f. 324v; PRO, PROB 11/69, f. 33L; GL, MS 9051/6, f. 39v.

[165] Note 'many signs that private godliness and public morality were labelled as feminine concerns, especially towards the end of the seventeenth century': Mendelson and Crawford, *Women in Early Modern England*, pp. 225–31, esp. pp. 226, 229. Family as metaphor for state, and therefore not 'private': Amussen, *An Ordered Society*, pp. 1–2.

parenting and love, even for wayward children. One man complained of his two 'undutifull' sons. 'Yet because the worlde shall take "notice" that I do forgive them and that I am mynded to provide for their future mayntennce (yf they wilbe ruled)', he made provision for their inheritance. Implicitly, however, he left a condition for executors to disinherit the sons later if they tried to sell their annuities.[166] Fathers tried cajoling, one leaving a silver spoon to a son 'soe that he behaved himselfe a dutiefull and obedyent child toward his mother, and not stubborne and disobedient unto her as heretofore he had byn to him'.[167] Entreaties to avoid or leave off quarrelling, made before an audience at the recitation of a will's contents, might have carried greater weight among family members and neighbours than testators' more personal deathbed pleas.

Bequests to kin or extended family within and far from London also urged pious reflection and even conformity. London weakened some attachments with extended family, but did not break the ties of lineage. John Brookebancke sent 33s 4d to people with the surnames of Brookebanck, Dixon and Robinson in the parish of his birth, Windermere. He asked that they meet in the parish for dinner, 'orderlie gyving god thanckes before they goe to the same'.[168] His request that they thank God belied the fact that they would thank him as well, at least for the length of the meal. Highlighting the three surnames, Brookebancke hinted that he no longer knew his distant kin, who in turn would likely have some surprise at the largesse of a distant, wealthy relative from London. Kin who moved to London, however, often worked as servants in relatives' households. In this way, they seemed much like other deserving poor or servants and apprentices needing preferment. One testator helped a poor kinsman in Bedlam in 1595.[169] Jeffrey Rusham, a married gentleman, stated, 'I have divers of my sisters children and others of my kindred that have some want whiche in conscience I thinck I am bounde to have consideration of', especially as he had no children of his own to inherit his lands, tenements and property.[170]

Servants comprised another element of household, and sometimes of extended family, whose confessional identity figured in testaments. One woman, Dame Van Lichetervilde, asked her children not to 'suffer her [her 'old' servant Jacqueline] to have anye povertie, asmuche as unto them shalbe possible for she hath done me good service and hath not

[166] PRO, PROB 11/125, f. 330R–331L.
[167] GL, MS 9051/6, f. 43.
[168] PRO, PROB 11/78, f. 151L.
[169] GL, MS 9051/5, f. 44v.
[170] PRO, PROB 11/74, f. 5L.

forsaken me in all my afflictions'.[171] She also left Jacqueline a bed, bedding and clothing. The servant Jacqueline needed attention, having come to London as a religious refugee with her mistress, also leaving her family behind in Catholicism. The same testator preferred that her children grow up in poverty rather than return to papacy in the Low Countries and supported other refugees like herself in London's stranger churches. Money rewards after 1580, as before, were the most common gifts to servants. Testators bequeathed money (71.69 per cent, or 119) for dowries and last wages from 1581–1601. In the period between 1601 and 1620, fewer bequests (little more than 65 per cent, or 81) were in money. In the two periods, testators also gave servants gowns (7.23 per cent, or 21, about 19 per cent or 24) to be part of a household mourning party. Testators looked after the future of servants and ensured funerary remembrance by them.

Testators' bequests to crafts, friends and family joined traditional piety with reformed religious notions and demonstrated the layered allegiances of London's inhabitants. Testators hoped to be memorialized through their bequests, a final connection between the living and the dead. In 1592, a cook entrusted the wardens of his company with the yearly sum of 4s, for thirty years, to maintain his portrait within the hall.[172] Perhaps after the term of the bequest his colleagues and apprentices would have died as well, negating the self-aggrandizing memorial, or he may have hoped the company would maintain it thereafter. Modest gifts marked friendship, but only remotely linked the living and the dead. Death or everlasting life with Jesus Christ severed the connection once fostered by the prohibited doctrine of purgatory.

Dinners and recreations after 1580 brought together members of the same company or social grouping, rather than people from across the parish or city, for a remembrance of the deceased. Division of hospitality intended for friends, neighbours, kin and the poor reinforced social groupings during an occasion that had once emphasized common religious and social ties, even if temporarily. Testators left provisions for dinners among the Company, sometimes specifying that such events occur among the livery or yeomanry. William Massey, painter-stainer, provided a dinner and recreation on the day of his burial to the livery of the company, in 1616.[173] Eating and drinking, even if restricted within social strata in the later sixteenth and early seventeenth centuries, continued a medieval tradition that arguably helped the living more than the dead. A widow provided a drinking for the master and wardens of

---

[171] GL, MS 9051/5, f. 13v.
[172] PRO, PROB 11/83, f. 217R.
[173] GL, MS 9051/6, f. 39v.

the Freemasons and a fund to 'make merry' among a group of her neighbours, female and male, in 1596. Through such occasions, whether for neighbours or company members, individuals accrued 'honour and influence', further dividing levels of society.[174]

Conclusion

Recasting traditional parochial events, formulating new communal pious and social occasions, and changing burial and funeral practices illustrate the extent of the reformation of piety in London's parishes. Church and civic leaders concentrated on outfitting and repairing churches, while preachers and some influential parishioners focused on remaking the pious attitudes and practices of those in the pews. Bequests to networks of family and friends also articulated reformed piety, showing how Protestantism, or even godliness, could be encouraged and stipulated in households and neighbourhoods.

Parishioners continued to support their church fabric, sometimes through traditional testamentary bequests of the books and objects necessary for worship or for popular pious needs, like burials. More often, however, inhabitants paid their fees for their appropriation of church space, pews in their lifetimes or graves after death, contributed to voluntary collections, and paid involuntary assessments. Labour, like the traditional devotional tasks of cleaning churches, shrines and images of saints, continued in these Reformation churches, but increasingly wages minimized the pious dimensions of work. Parishes hired men and women to oversee the furniture of Protestant services, but also hired them in lieu of or to supplement relief. The furniture, decoration and floor plan of churches reflected Protestant services and doctrines.

Obliquely, the preambles and testamentary provisions surrounding funeral practices and grave locations exemplify the dissemination of reformed piety. Preambles deliberately echoed the most puritan doctrines and discreetly voiced mainstream theology. The special gifts, tokens and other provisions in wills, however, go beyond preambles in showing how testators adapted to new pious expectations. In particular, burial sermons and aid to non-conformist preachers showed a network of ordinary people who heard the edifying words of godly lecturers and adopted new pious attitudes. The decline in women's endowments of burial sermons exemplified their responsiveness to emerg-

---

[174] GL, MS 9051/5, fols 48–48v. 'Honour and influence': Jeremy Boulton, *Neighbourhood and Society*, p. 138.

ing religious notions. Many Londoners shunned large funeral processions and spectacular burials in favour of sermons and tokens of
remembrance to be worn and passed on by friends and family. The cycle
of sermons endowed by some testators gave a pulpit for established and
puritan preachers, not to mention perpetuated the memory of prominent, deceased men and women.

Developments in charity and in relief of the poor also showed how
the Protestant Reformation had become established in late sixteenth-
century London. The Word that surrounded parishioners in wall paintings
and reached them from the pulpit influenced how they gave charity in
wills and through less formal means, and how they perceived the worthy poor.

CHAPTER FIVE

Charity and social control, 1580–1620

The sixteenth and early seventeenth centuries marked a transition between ideals of medieval face-to-face alms and eighteenth-century 'benevolence' in the history of English charity. Through the 1500s, testators, parishes, London's government and Parliament gradually established a system of involuntary rates to provide poor relief. Beginning in the later sixteenth century, but culminating in the eighteenth century, charity accentuated social difference and furthered worldly or civic goals.[1] The English Reformation did not end voluntary gifts to the poor, as contemporaries feared that it would, but it redirected charity and altered charitable motives. Pre-Reformation emphasis on prayers for the dead had made the poor indispensable to the eternal life of donors, creating a mutually beneficial community, though not one peopled by peers. Post-Reformation Londoners sensed the danger to giving, and charitable feeling, when religious change denigrated the recipient and devalued the exchange itself. Testators by 1580 eschewed helping the unknown poor, instead utilizing occupational, social or parochial ties to identify the worthy poor, or to thank friends and family with final tokens of respect and affection.

Parochial and testamentary relief, even before the articulation of the Poor Law in 1598 and 1601, reflected awareness of poverty and uneasiness with the un-Christ-like poor.[2] Just as testators sought out the worthy poor, so parishes discriminated among and regulated charitable recipients in London, refining the distinction drawn between the deserving and the undeserving poor. Demographic, religious and economic changes and pressures necessitated centralizing relief in the hands of various political authorities – hence the similarities across Protestant

---

[1] On the eighteenth-century 'philanthropy of benevolence' (humanitarian, self-serving and sentimental): David Owen, *English Philanthropy: 1660–1960* (Cambridge, MA, 1964), p. 14. Slack distinguishes between being 'in charity' and 'beneficence', one an ideal of a harmonious community and the other charity based on specific goals and directed to chosen groups: *Poverty and Policy*, p. 22. Transition to 'public good' because of political overtones of 'common weal' after 1603: Slack, *From Reformation to Improvement*, pp. 75–6.

[2] 39 Eliz. c.3 and 43 Eliz. c.2.

and Catholic Europe, but suggesting differences in individual contexts. Comparative studies, beginning with Brian Pullan's article, stress continuity between Protestant and Catholic approaches to charity in the later sixteenth and seventeenth centuries: Europeans limited or banned begging, exercised secular control over relief, and centralized control of charitable institutions. Significantly, the punitive and regulatory aspects of relief and the poor in the sixteenth century became a 'European phenomenon'. Catholics and Protestants nurtured and healed body and soul, but the repudiation of prayers for souls in Reformation England erased the analogy drawn between Christ and the poor in pre-Reformation England and in Catholic Europe.[3]

Increased charitable giving could seem contradictory to the spirit of late-century Protestantism and society, although the poor absorbed pious bequests once directed to religious houses, chantries and fraternities, especially after the mid-century's uncertainty. While the vision of Christ's 'very images' had spurred Catholic charity, the Reformation view of the poor altered the purposes of and incentives for charitable giving. Pre-Reformation giving in England was predicated on serving Lazarus and on securing prayers for souls. While Reformation donors still ascribed to helping others with the material goods 'lent' to them by God, they could no longer publicly request prayers. Hence they might hope to reform recipients' behaviour, to make them godly, in their own images.[4] The tension between selfish and selfless motives increased in the new religious climate, complicated by other developments. London's spectacular growth through 1620 also widened the gulf between rich and poor, even as urban crowding and its consequences heightened awareness of poverty.

Centralizing relief

Developing legislation reflected parochial and testamentary practice that had evolved through the sixteenth century. The 1598 poor law statute, coming at the end of an economically difficult decade for Lon-

---

[3] Quote from Slack, *Poverty and Policy*, pp. 9–10. Catholics established houses of charity in a spirit of 'extended monasticism', but placed more emphasis on salvation than behavioural conformity: Pullan, 'Catholics and the Poor', pp. 30, 32. 'Poverty has ceased to be a holy state and has become presumptive evidence of wickedness', writes Hill in describing the traditional view of Puritans and the poor: 'William Perkins and the Poor', p. 218.

[4] On reform of behaviour in general: Robert von Friedeburg, 'Reformation of Manners and the Social Composition of Offenders in an East Anglian Cloth Village: Earls Colne, Essex, 1531–1642', *JBS*, **29**, 4 (October 1990), pp. 347–85.

doners, echoed earlier provisions for setting the poor to work and to apprenticeships, repeated the prohibition of begging, and punished rogues, vagabonds and sturdy beggars, whipping and returning them to their birthplace. Ultimately, 'dangerous and incorrigible rogues' went to jail. Although sentiment ran against feared masterless men and women, some Londoners worried that outlawing begging would cause a decline in charity, even to the worthy poor. The face-to-face interaction between recipients and donors of the medieval period, even if expressed through a representative almoner, could spur contemporaries to generosity, whether out of guilt or the intimacy of giving directly to an individual. After 1580, however, begging in the streets and at doorways may have precipitated unrecorded, lifetime, giving. Even parochial officers might hear a sad tale and make a one-time gift, like that of St Stephen's to the wife of a waterman, a trade known to contemporaries to be an especially poor one.[5]

Parish leaders – churchwardens, vestry men, 'ancient' parishioners – oversaw the distribution of involuntary rates collected within parochial bounds and of voluntary, testamentary bequests left to their care and discretion. Relief consumed more of a parish's resources, and more of churchwardens' time. Although churchwardens traditionally distributed outdoor relief on behalf of the parish, their role increased as testators more often asked them to oversee particular bequests. Thus parishes helped to centralize relief of the deserving poor, in part because testators chose ministers, churchwardens and overseers of the poor to identify them, before the finalization of the Poor Law.[6] Testamentary gifts left to parochial discretion reached a recognized group of needy recipients within the parish, often a list of women and men named in churchwardens' accounts and vestry minutes, year after year. After 1580, accounts and minutes showed greater care in accounting for all funds spent by the parish, an indication of the strain on funds exerted by poverty and of the general expansion of record-keeping. Although accounts and minutes had always been formal records, the scribes and selected leaders seemed reluctant to incur the disapproval of auditors. The care taken in documentation, even in defensively justifying outlays, also

---

[5] On statute: Slack, 'Appendix: Statutes Relating to the Poor', *English Poor Law*. 39 Eliz. c. 3. Archer stresses that 'communitarian sentiments' lost ground to the 'extraction of deference in return for patronage, in particular through the exercise of poor relief': *Pursuit of Stability*, pp. 92–3. GL, MS 593/2, f. 93; on Southwark watermen in St Saviour's parish: Boulton, *Neighbourhood and Society*, p. 97.

[6] Gibbs, 'New duties', p. 174. This serves as another example of how the parish was of 'primary importance' to Londoners' identity: Archer, *Pursuit of Stability*, p. 83. Few privately organized charities in London by 1650: Andrew, *Philanthropy and Police: London Charity in the Eighteenth Century* (Princeton, 1989), p. 3.

5.1   Picture of a man (John Kettlewood?). Guildhall Library MS 1002/1A (St
Mary Woolnoth), first page for the year 1563–64, f. 116. With permission
of the Guildhall Library, Corporation of London.

hinted at discord over responses to individuals soliciting aid from a
particular parish.

Testators might trust parish officials to judge the worthiness of potential recipients and, incidentally, limit their friends' and family's
interaction with the potentially disorderly poor. Men who served as
churchwardens and exercised influence in parishes, like Sir Martin Bowes,

also shaped civic policies regarding the poor and guided the institutions housing and correcting them. Figure 5.1 hints at the importance seen in the role of churchwarden in the self-portrait of John Kettlewood (probably added after the account was written). Simple relief, through parochial and civic mediators, replaced more complex patterns of expectation, help and gratitude, perhaps contributing to patterns of deference noted in the eighteenth century.[7] Collectors for the poor gathered rates to support poorer parishes, for example in St Stephen's, St Dionis Barkchurch, and St Olave Hart Street for the benefit of St Sepulchre's. Collectors also gathered for the use of hospitals and other institutions, using those contributions to pressure civic institutions to admit needy children and sick or impotent adults, otherwise chargeable to the parish. Collectors and Christ's Hospital arranged for portions to be withheld for relieving pensioners, like the collectors in St Mary Woolnoth who kept £4 16s 8d, out of the £30 8s collected in 1580.[8] Although the beneficiaries of these assessments may have been unknown to the rate-payers, the vestry men, churchwardens and governors who disbursed the funds discriminated among petitioners as individual testators would have done, justifying their payments in annual audits, before the 'most' or 'better part' of the parish.

The preceding chapter showed the increase in non-pious bequests to friends, family, servants and associates, in excess of the amounts left to the poor and to other recipients. As a proportion of all pious bequests, however, those to the poor peaked in the period 1580–1620, as shown in Table 5.1.

Table 5.1   Percentage of gifts to poor, out of all pious gifts

Year	To poor (%)	To poor (N)	Other pious (N)
1558–1580	67	514	251
1580–1601	83	885	171
1601–1620	75	597	194

As edicts and visitation injunctions had earlier urged, 'superstitious' endowments had been transformed into useful, even godly support for the worthy poor. Although the poor may not have comprised two-thirds of London's population, certain areas of the city, in particular

---

[7] Archer, *Pursuit of Stability*, pp. 92–3.

[8] CLRO, Rep. 32, fols 157–157v. GL, MS 1002/1A, f. 220v. On tension over portions allowed to remain for outdoor relief in parish: Archer, *Pursuit*, pp. 159–60.

large extramural parishes, witnessed a substantial increase in the numbers of poor.[9]

Bequests left to parishes depended upon the discretion and careful administration of churchwardens and prominent parishioners. Testators relied on executors, linked by family or professional ties, and churchwardens or parsons to enforce restrictions on pious bequests. From 1581–1601, 61 per cent (285) of restrictions laid on pious bequests depended upon executors, churchwardens or other parish officials, though most gifts (53.55 per cent of all pious bequests, or 535) went free of any stated restrictions. From 1601–20, 35 per cent (170) of restrictions depended on the same agents, though fewer bequests compared to the earlier period (35.14 per cent, or 260), reached targets without some restriction. Most non-pious bequests went without restrictions or understandably stipulated the age at or pattern of inheritance.[10]

Testators' reliance on parochial oversight and their dependence on restrictions illustrate that individuals had adopted the moral imperatives and religious apparatus of the post-Reformation parish. John Taylor expected St Botolph's to manage his £20 by collecting five per cent interest on it yearly. He was a grocer who left an estate worth £850 in his will of 1589, including the gift to pay for bread and coals for the poor. Taylor protected the bequest from a downturn in his accounts, telling his executors to reduce his children's portions to pay other legacies first, 'especially the twenty pounds to St Buttalles p[a]rishe without Aldersgate'.[11] In her will of early May 1595, Alice Daniell left 40s to the poor, to be distributed by her executors, Richard Griffin, St Botolph's minister and Ralph Treswell, map maker. Although her will was probated within six days, she had not waited until illness to make her first one: she revoked earlier ones, and asked to be buried between her two husbands.[12] Elizabeth Younge also left 40s to the same parish's poor, in care of the churchwardens, in June 1596.

These gifts to the poor of the parish had additional benefits: they gave donors a chance to reaffirm publicly their and their peers' social status. In 1591, John Mathew asked for 'discreete and substanciall

---

[9] See Chapter 4, fn. 6 for disparity in amounts directed to non-pious and pious ends. Rappaport argues that W.G. Hoskins overestimated the proportion of poor: *Worlds within Worlds*, p. 172; cf. Archer, *Pursuit*, pp. 150–54.

[10] Two hundred and sixty pious bequests without any restrictions. Non-pious bequests without restrictions: 81.04 per cent, or 1428 between 1589 and 1601; 84.47 per cent, or 1273 between 1602 and 1620.

[11] PRO, PROB 11/81, f. 135L. Taylor's will was not probated until 1593, emphasizing the careful planning in his testament.

[12] GL, MS 9051/5, f. 24v.

p[a]rishion[er]s' to distribute his bequest to the poor of St Michael's, drawing on the respectable parochial leaders, perhaps citizens like him-self.[13] Because he relied on the overseers for their pains in distributing his 20s bequest to the poor, Thomas Swanne left 20s for a 'merry meetinge' among them in 1598.[14] Undoubtedly, he might expect that in eating and drinking by his kindness, they would commemorate him and perform the task. In 1601, Dame Ramsey, widow of a knight who was an alderman and a former sheriff and mayor, left 40s to each of three London parishes, expecting the churchwardens to relieve

> the most neediest and poorest of their parish[io]ners by the discre-
> tion nomination and allowance of Twoo of the parish[io]ners ...
> being the most principall and cheifest parish[io]ners of reputac[i]on
> ... chosen and elected to that end by the said severall parish[io]ners
> at the vestries to stand directors of the said distribuc[i]on duringe
> the pleasures of the said severall parrishes

She implicitly requested that men of high status, approaching that enjoyed by her deceased husband, oversee her bequest.[15]

Reliance on male churchwardens and vestries – London may have had one elected female churchwarden – signalled a change in the role of women in distributing relief. Even the death of a churchwarden did not open the door for exceptional service by a woman. In 1617, Marian Bill turned over her late husband's account, 2 May 1617 to 12 September 1617, to the other churchwarden in St Michael Cornhill. Richard Bill had been the renter churchwarden until he died, 12 September. By 10 October the new renter churchwarden, Andrew Yeardley, was in office. St Michael Cornhill noted her actions in the same bold face they used for male churchwardens and although she may have acted in Richard's place, since the accounts do not indicate the length of his sickness, at his death she was officially displaced.[16]

Nascent ideology about the poor's culpability for their poverty helped to formulate gendered roles, for potential donors and their representa-tives. This ideology demonized the undeserving, reducing them to stereotypes, and cast suspicion on the deserving poor as well.[17] The behaviour of recipients could besmirch the character of donors, perhaps

---

[13] GL, MS 4071/1, f. 191v.

[14] GL, MS 9051/5, f. 121.

[15] PRO, PROB 11/98, f. 191L. Mullaney describes the 'ostentatious display' in funer-als: *The Place of the Stage*, p. 40.

[16] For case of Bills, see GL, MS 4071/2, f. 35v; Maryan (?) Gerens, St Andrew Hubbard, 1508/09: Kümin, *The Shaping*, p. 40; female churchwardens outside London: Mendelson and Crawford, *Women in Early Modern England*, pp. 50, 56–7.

[17] Slack, *Poverty and Policy*, pp. 25–6; transformation of the poor of Christ into the poor of the Devil: Pullan, 'Catholics and the Poor', p. 25.

especially women guarding their sexual reputations in contrast to single pregnant women. Although most men continued to name their wives executrices of their wills, entrusting them with significant legal and fiscal responsibilities, the slow transference of bequests to male parishioners and churchwardens distanced women from public charitable activity. Richard West, in 1599, depended on his wife, his executrix, to parcel out his £10 bequest to the poor in St Botolph's within six months, but with the consent of churchwardens and overseers of the poor.[18] He envisioned a role for her in handing out charity, in choosing the needy with the advice of parish leaders. Not all male testators, or their widows, desired to participate in such public almsgiving. The widow Mistress Dalby sent Master Crackplace, with the £3 2s gift to poor men and women from her late husband, to meet with the vestry in St Michael's in 1616, instead of attending herself.[19] Her absence may reflect emerging notions of appropriate gender roles in charity, lessening the public nature of her responsibility for seeing her husband's will done and minimizing her own contact with the sick, poor and aged of her parish. Not until the eighteenth century would English charitable institutions develop a public role for wealthier, respectable women, and then only with some difficulty.[20]

The problems surrounding the charitable dole bequeathed by Lady Mary Ramsey explains the hesitation to have respectable women in direct contact with the poor when mayhem could erupt. A few years after her death, Nicholas Bourman published 'An epitaph' for Ramsey with the explicit permission of her executors that first outlined and praised her generosity to the poor, impotent, aged, godly and abandoned. He lauded her daily service to God and the 'dutie done' by which she gained immortality. After the first poem to her accomplishments, however, Bourman added 'A sufficient defence and reasonable excuse concerning the mischaunce that hapned at Leaden Hall after the funeral of the worshipfull Lady Mary Ramsey so solemnized'. He described mishaps and 'misevents' at her funeral dole, where the executors intended to give it away 'well and iust'. 'Misrulie' folk 'that headlong runne, and will not be fore warnd' were to be blamed, not the executors or even Ramsey posthumously, for the harm that befell

---

[18] PRO, PROB 11/94, f. 274R.

[19] GL, MS 4072/1, Part 1, f. 110v.

[20] Dependence on male professionals to run eighteenth-century hospitals: Norberg, *Rich and Poor in Grenoble*, pp. 172–3. Women supported maternity causes, not those charities directed to foundlings or the treatment of venereal disease: Andrew, *Philanthropy and Police*, pp. 72, 87. See Chapter 6 for further discussion of women's role in charity.

them.[21] The 'Epitaph' reads as a posthumous celebration of her charity, but also as a justification for the dole and an attempt to set the responsibility for any trouble squarely on the poor, not on the executors or even the testator.

The ideas regarding poverty and charity that relegated women to silent roles behind churchwardens and other executors necessitated marking the deserving poor. Parishes adopted distinctive clothing to identify the 'poor' who were in receipt of alms, or those granted permission to beg. Badges marked the deserving poor, as illustrated by St Michael's purchase of 14 'Tynnes for the poore pencioners to weare on their brests'.[22] Churchwardens in St Botolph's and St Stephen's also provided badges for the poor in the seventeenth century. A 1620 vestry in St Botolph's resurrected the distinctive black clothing for the poor, so common through pre-Reformation mourning, by providing it free of charge to those in the parish living by alms.[23] The special ornaments and clothing worn by the poor made their destitution plain, and therefore justified solicitation of relief obvious to parishioners. Although testators' provision of mourning gowns before and after the Reformation intimated the wearer's status, badges were more powerful symbols of an impoverished social position. Symbols and eventually social control, inherent in relief, marginalized poorer women and men from respectable society.

Statutes to identify, control and punish beggars and vagabonds relied on parishes, a further indicator of the administrative unit's importance in devising and implementing national policy on poverty. Parochial construction of stocks and the careful record of payments for whipping only occurred with regularity, however, very late in the sixteenth century, after earlier laws providing for public punishment of vagabonds. St Mary Woolnoth recorded the construction of stocks only in the accounts of 1597/98.[24] The carpenter employed by the parish built them at the church door, for parishioners to see when they attended church services or for the poor to observe when they solicited aid. Churchwardens in St Mary's had paid a man for keeping the poor at the

---

[21] Nicholas Bourman, *An Epitaph upon the decease of the worshipfull Lady Mary Ramsey, late wife unto Sir Thomas Ramsey Knight, sometime Lord Maior and Alderman of the honorable Cittie of London. Whereunto is annexed certaine short epigrams, touching the mortalitie of man. Published by the consent of the executors*, (London: R. Read, 1602) STC 3415, sig. Bv. Archer explains that the beggars were crushed to death: *Pursuit*, p. 169.

[22] GL, MSS 4071/1, f. 166v; 4071/2, f. 18. Badges cost 14d.

[23] GL, MS 1454, Roll 101; GL, MS 593/2, f. 100v; GL, MS 1453/1, f. 13v.

[24] GL, MS 1002/1A, f. 308v. An Act for the punishment of rogues, vagabonds, and sturdy beggars (1598): 39 Eliz. c.4.

church door as early as 1542/43. The earliest recorded whipping of 'two rogues' at this site came in 1600/01. The following year, the parish paid for the making and painting of a staff to ward for beggars and vagrants, stepping up efforts to correct the idle poor. The accounts from 1604 again listed the purchase of a staff for the warder for 'vagabonds & other pore'.[25] St Stephen's laid out £1 4s 6d 'for a poste to stand against the church for correction of vagraunts p[er]sons accordinge to the lawe' in 1598/99. In succeeding years, the parish repainted the post, although parish sources do not reveal if weather or frequent use peeled the paint. Churchwardens, in 1604/05, paid a man to carry beggars from the church, whether merely out of the parish or to Bridewell the records do not tell.[26] St Michael's built its stocks in 1603/04. In 1599–1600, however, the churchwardens had paid 15s to Edward Crooke for a few tasks, including 'whippinge of wanderinge people according to the Statute', calling it 'punisshinge Vagabounds' a couple of years later.[27] Architectural remnants and art, not to mention law, show that whipping remained the usual punishment, but this scribe may have lumped putting the poor in stocks with corporal punishments.[28]

The widespread adoption of posts and stocks only with the final articulation of the Elizabethan Poor Law illustrated lingering ambivalence about the connection between charity and punishment in parishes. Stocks humiliated vagabonds and 'sturdy beggars', or others who defrauded their fellow inhabitants, and presented them for parishioners to scorn and from which to draw a moral lesson about the dangers of idleness and poverty. Contemporaries nonetheless may have read another lesson in the experience of the poor: the responsibility for charity in the midst of suffering. Wandel has argued that despite the silencing of the poor through prohibitions on begging, the voicing of their misery through sermons forcefully articulated charitable duties. Calls to contribute to common stores motivated donors by conscience and thoughts about grace, not 'self-interest'.[29] London parishes enforced not only the regulation of the poor, but oversaw the protection of consumers to prevent undue want. St Michael's churchwardens paid 23s for 'Scales beams & waightes for the ward to weight bread',

---

[25] GL, MSS 1002/1A, f. 19; 1002/1B, fols 325, 338, 351v.

[26] GL, MS 593/2, fols 96v, 107v.

[27] GL, MSS 4072/1, Part 1, f. 83; 4071/1, fols 164, 169, 174v.

[28] *A Harlot's Progress*, 4, engraving, 1731: David Bindman, *Hogarth* (London, 1981), p. 59; Plate 4 of Market Cross, Bungay, Suffolk, showing the shackles on the whipping post: Mary Abbott, *Life Cycles in England*, pp. 250–51.

[29] Wandel, pp. 154–6; Book of dearth orders, 1587: Slack, *From Reformation to Improvement*, pp. 54–5.

protecting parishioners and the ward from underweight, overvalued bread in 1613.[30]

Reluctance or ambivalence in following the letter of the most punitive aspects of the law, such as branding, suggests uneasiness with the conflation of vagabondage and poverty. Historians' easy restatement of the dichotomy between 'deserving' and 'undeserving' glosses over the contemporary ambivalence and indecision about the same categories, the blurring between those impoverished by idleness or vice and those reduced by ill fortune or sickness. Maimed soldiers, for instance, were at once riotous vagrants and deserving servants of the state. Movement, migration and simple vagrancy, fostered the demographic and economic growth of early modern towns and cities.[31] The peculiarity of London's case – rapid, substantial population growth through in-migration – heightened parochial and civic concern regarding masterless individuals. Single vagrants may have migrated in search of work, as some families did as well.[32] The problem of vagrancy worsened quantitatively and qualitatively between 1560 and 1640, because of population growth, landlessness and the spread of wage-labour. The 'netherworld of vagabonds poised to overthrow society' portrayed in rogue literature exaggerated the number of groups of idle, disorderly people, although the genre's 'verisimilitude' reflected contemporary fears.[33]

Geographical segregation of the poor in certain streets echoed their cultural and legal marginalization through punitive statutes. Suburbs became identifiably poor neighbourhoods in the seventeenth century, fomenting disorder and crime, and breeding disease. Alleys and lanes mixed into neighbourhoods with finer houses, but the city showed an overall pattern of wealth in the centre. Lodging travellers and migrants in tenements or alleys and running alehouses constituted part of the 'economy of makeshift', for those on the brink of poverty.[34] Alehouses,

---

[30] GL, MS 4071/2, f. 23v. Although an earlier example, Fabyan recounted a collier sitting in pillory in Cornhill because his sacks of coals were not 'Justly sysid'; *The Great Chronicle of London*, p. 296.

[31] 35 Eliz. c. 4: An Act for the necessary relief of soldiers and mariners. Replaced by 43 Eliz. c. 3. David Rollison, 'Exploding England: the dialectics of mobility and settlement in early modern England', *Social History*, 24, 1 (Jan. 1999), pp. 1–16.

[32] Migration 'appears as a slippery slope rather than a safety net for the poor': Beier, *Masterless Men*, p. 29; Joan R. Kent, 'Population Mobility and Alms: Poor Migrants in the Midlands during the Early Seventeenth Century', *Local Population Studies*, 27 (1981), pp. 35–51.

[33] Beier, *Masterless Men*, pp. 7, 14, 16.

[34] Jones, 'London', p. 126; alleys as 'bastions of crisis mortality': Archer, *Pursuit*, p. 13; worsening conditions in the suburbs in the later sixteenth century: Slack, *The Impact of Plague*, p. 165. On piecemeal incomes: Hufton, *The Poor of Eighteenth-Century France*, esp. pp. 69–127; Schen, 'Strategies of Poor Aged Women and Widows', pp. 17–25.

tippling houses and cheap lodging provided hospitality to vagrants and migrants after the dissolution of Church institutions that had helped travellers and poor migrants. Parishes, the city and Parliament attempted to curtail these practices, to control crime, disorder, moral turpitude and even fire.[35] The parish of St Botolph's prohibited any persons receiving poor relief 'yf they be found to intertaine inmates lodgers or keepe their children sonnes or daughters eyther married or marriageable w[i]thin their owne houses & dwellinge' after the benefit of three months' warning.[36] The Court of Aldermen enforced city and parliamentary legislation against the keeping of inmates and lodgers, the common tactic of the elderly people and those skirting the line between poverty and survival. In July 1607, the Aldermen ordered Robert Colwell, an inmate found in Walbrook ward with his 'wyfe children and famelye', to the Compter until he promised never to return to London as a lodger.[37] St Dunstan's in the East similarly restricted recipients of relief from taking in inmates and fined anyone, payable to the poor box, who placed the poor in alleys. Individuals within these pockets, however, could still gain relief, like Goodman Goffreye Barnarde and Goodman Hollowaye, supported by St Michael's in 1581–82.[38]

By the late sixteenth century, London's shrinking labour market less easily absorbed migrants, foundlings or orphans. Foundlings had rarely surfaced in the earliest churchwardens' accounts, possibly because these abandoned infants became almschildren, welcomed into wealthy households as servants and living examples of the householders' benevolence, but this practice changed late in the sixteenth century. In the 1590s, St Stephen's churchwardens more frequently paid wet nurses hired from outside the city to bring the parish's charges for christening, covering the costs of travel and baptism.[39] At least some of these foundlings were illegitimate, the years 1581–1640 marking an early high point of illegitimacy in the sixteenth and seventeenth centuries. Across this period, 3.80 per cent of all baptisms were illegitimate births, but only 1.60 per cent were illegitimate in 1661–1720.[40] The peak reflected an apparent

---

[35] Beier, *Masterless Men*, pp. 79–82; Peter Clark, 'The Alehouse and the Alternative Society' in Donald Pennington and Keith Thomas (eds), *Puritans and Revolutionaries: Essays in Seventeenth-Century History Presented to Christopher Hill* (Oxford, 1978), p. 48; Slack, *From Reformation to Improvement*, p. 55.

[36] GL, MS 1453/1, f. 3.

[37] CLRO, Rep. 28, f. 60; see also Rep. 25, f. 6v and Rep. 27, f. 84.

[38] On St Dunstan's: Archer, *Pursuit*, p. 184. GL, MS 4071/1, f. 119v.

[39] GL, MS 593/2 f. 126v.

[40] Illegitimacy rose again in the eighteenth century, with illegitimacy of 3.75 per cent of all births 1721–80 and 4.51 per cent 1781–1820: Peter Laslett, *Family Life and Illicit Love in Earlier Generations: Essays in Historical Sociology* (Cambridge, 1977), pp. 134–5.

increase in abandonment and a preoccupation with the problem in London. After all, children born in parishes collected relief there, as did Anne Boswell, a poor maid born in St Mary's, when she received 5s by the consent of the 'elders' of the parish.[41] Conforming to punitive laws and reacting to the costs of rising illegitimacy, parishes combated the problem of abandonment through work schemes and social control. St Botolph's churchwardens hoped to place responsibility for these children squarely in the hands of overseers, proclaiming in 1597/98: 'Theis charges for nursing of children and such lyke to be no more charged in the Churchwardens accompts but in the accompt of the surveyors according to the new Statute'.[42]

Although stocks, posts and implicit fears about wandering poor men and women suggest a great gulf between rich and poor, some traditional aspects of parochial life bridged that gap, at least temporarily. Lower ranking employees inhabited a social strata barely above that of the poor, leading vestries and hospitals to discipline surveyors and beadles for 'consorting with vagrants in alehouses'.[43] Public display involving the poor continued, but occurred in abbreviated spaces of time and place: in shorter services around death and civic celebrations for limited ends. The poor participated in burials, but the month's minds and obits that formerly multiplied charitable bequests were gone, as were the formal prayers for souls. Impoverished men and women of 'good name and fame' continued to play important roles in ushering deceased parishioners to burial, in processions and funerals. Although funeral practices encompassed less extravagant display, parishes still used processions and formal mourning as ways to relieve their deserving poor. The sexton of St Michael's drew fire for circumventing usual practice in not hiring the poor of the parish, over the poor of other parishes, for burials.[44]

Like the survival of mourning processions, the incidence of doles illustrates that contemporaries, even after 1580, persisted in some of the traditional practices that had once knitted together parishes. Despite earlier prohibitions against funeral doles, contemporaries found ways to distribute aid and link it to their final services, without requiring prayers for deceased souls or encouraging poor men and women to wander throughout the city collecting them. In 1601, George Kevall, writer of Court Letter and a herald, asked for a dole following his funeral 'when the bell toleth for me'.[45] John Spencer, the same man who

---

[41] GL, MS 1002/1B, f. 351v; Laslett, *Family Life*, p. 133.
[42] GL, MS 1454, Roll 98. 39 Eliz. c. 3.
[43] Told in Archer, *Pursuit*, p. 223.
[44] GL, MS 4072/1, Part 1, fols 89–89v.
[45] PRO, PROB 11/98, f. 132R.

had restricted mourners to the poor and his household, left 20s to the poor at his burial, and 'duringe my syckenes at the Bell towlinge'.[46] The dual bequest shows a rare testamentary example of a lifetime gift because the final version of his will was composed within sixteen days of its probate, and the funeral dole. Although Reformation England scorned 'good works', Spencer might have hoped that a gift made in sickness would speed his recovery or demonstrate his penitent spirit.

Some testators restricted their doles to the poor of their own parishes, continuing the trend toward centralizing relief within parochial bounds, perhaps to prevent 'mishaps' like those seen by Lady Ramsey's executors. In legislation and in private charity, residence and familiarity allowed judgment of worthiness. Thomas Dalbye left £5 in alms, to be paid the day of his funeral or within a 'convenient' time, asking that the poor in Harp Alley, in St Michael's where he dwelled, receive special consideration. Dalbye's consideration of tenants in a particular alley of his parish curtailed cross-city pilgrimages by the poor, especially in times of sickness and plague.[47] In 1603, James Marshe left 20s to the poor of the parish at the time of his death, to be distributed by his wife with the advice of the churchwardens and overseers of the parish.[48] William Houghton, avoiding an indiscriminate dole and ensuring recipients resided in the parish, gave poor parishioners 20s in bread, 'to be given them at theire houses'.[49] Houghton implicitly restricted his gift to poor householders, decent people who had fallen on hard times in 1620.

Gifts of bread, clothing and shelter for the parish poor also echoed traditional forms of charity. A bequest to St Michael's provided 52 loaves of bread for the year, an echo of wealthy parishioners' gifts for regular doles of bread, money or coals through the year, before the Reformation.[50] As John Percivale had once left gowns, labelled with Jesus' name, to poor mourners from whom he solicited prayers, so these Reformation testators after 1580 clothed the poor in sturdy, wearable coats. In 1606, the draper Henry Smith left coarse clothing to fifty poor men, 'againste wynter to keepe them warme'.[51] His gift was no more

---

[46] PRO, PROB 11/66, f. 193L.

[47] PRO, PROB 11/127, f. 466L. Slack argues that testators separated the poor and vagabonds, especially at funerals and burials, because of fear of disease and disorder and that this facilitated a trend towards the redrawing of social boundaries, 'respectable society being newly and more tightly defined': Slack, *Poverty and Policy*, p. 24; Archer, *Pursuit of Stability*, pp. 96–7.

[48] GL, MS 9171/19, f. 409v.

[49] GL, MS 9051/6, f. 43v. Houghton had also given the large copy of the testament and other service books to his parish, mentioned above.

[50] GL, MS 4071/1, f. 120.

[51] PRO, PROB 11/108, f. 267L.

altruistic or selfless than one procuring prayers: his occupational identity, centred on cloth and retail clothing sales, was linked to the apparel. William Bailey, in a will probated in 1606, left tenements near the Draper's Hall to the relief of the poor, under the supervision of the parson and churchwardens. In return for these tenements, he expected the parish to hold a yearly sermon on Sunday after Low Sunday by 'some godly learned preacher'. He left £5 to provide wood or coals to the poor as well.[52] His testament imposed no specific moral conditions on inmates, but his endowment of a sermon indicated his concern with the religious edification of all parishioners, wealthy and needy.

Testamentary bequests to prisons remained consistent despite the changes of the Reformation and the development of more punitive attitudes to the poor. Despite, or because of, the symbolic resemblance between prison and purgatory, the prison remained a potent charitable image.[53] Before 1548, testators drew parallels between the refreshment they provided to prisoners and the refreshment these prisoners' prayers would provide their souls in purgatory. Testators may have used this external resemblance to prove their mercy to prisoners and captives, not the sole province of Catholic acts of mercy. After the Reformation, testators may have continued to ponder their own destination after death. In a radical Protestant context, prisons may have mirrored the imprisonment of the unreformed, or the less than puritan, in lingering earthly darkness and ignorance. The value of monetary gifts to prisons increased between 1580 and 1601 to £582 compared to £132 between 1558 and 1580, but their proportion of pious bequests after 1580 decreased from 8.1 per cent (62) to 4.83 per cent (51) in 1580–1601 and further to 3.67 per cent (29) from 1601–20.[54] Prisons began to lose their potency as a metaphor for spiritual concerns after 1600, suggesting less concern about usury, an earlier motive for helping debtors in prison. As the pious metaphor of incarceration for small debts broke down, the way for the eventual conflation of prisons and workhouses, crime and poverty had been cleared.

Prisons represent familiar pious targets from the pre-Reformation period, but also may have alleviated lifetime and deathbed guilt related to the greater incidence of debts, loans, and entrepreneurial risk and

---

[52] PRO, PROB 11/108, f. 112L. GL, MS 4083, f. 87v. This would be the second Sunday after Easter.

[53] Religious metaphors remade in literature and philosophy under 'persistent pressure from the past': Rudolph Binion, *After Christianity*, p. 23.

[54] The difference between gifts to prisons in the years ending 1580 and those ending in 1601 is significant (z-score of 6.54), as is the difference between 1601 and 1620 (z-score 2.64). Guilt about usury as motive: Brigden, *London and the Reformation*, p. 50.

success. Consideration to friends or business associates may also have reflected the traditional practice of aiding the *poveri vergnosi*. Besides her gifts for sermons, her charity to the poor, and her bequests to the three prisons and two compters in London, Elizabeth Younge freed 'Runyan' in the Fleet from all the debt he owed her, probably through her inheritance of the residue of her husband's estate.[55] Her husband, a freemason and marbler, had died shortly before her after hurriedly making a will, leaving few bequests besides the residue of his estate to his wife. She probably had not lent Runyan money or goods directly, though some women did engage in lending. Dame Ramsey, in leaving 40s for poor prisoners, asked that her executors show compassion for worthy people and for those imprisoned for small amounts.[56] Debt limits set for the relief of prisoners, common in the early as well as the late sixteenth century, meshed with newer demarcations between the deserving and undeserving poor.

The acknowledgement of pawning and debt, stopgap measures against poverty, also reflected the growing credit economy in early modern England and burgeoning capitalist investment by citizens and inhabitants of London. More testators mentioned interest rates in the late period of this study. One testator returned the silver spoon pawned by a father to his son and in compassion gave an old suit to the impoverished father.[57] Another testator referred to interest collected from debtors. He enjoined his executors to 'take noe interest of any person whatsoever, for anie money, that shalbe owinge at the tyme of my decease'.[58] For others, last wills made loans into outright gifts. The fiscally prudent Henry Smith, however, told his executors to sell the £14 in pawned goods he held at his death, to complete his accounts.[59]

Even the timing of outdoor relief endured from pre-Reformation models. In St Michael Cornhill in 1580–81, churchwardens provided charity at Christmas, Easter and Michaelmas. While these dates remained in the fiscal and religious calendar of Reformation England, they had traditionally served as dates for charity in a Catholic sacred calendar and would certainly have been remembered as such by older parishioners.[60] In 1580, parishioners who remembered Mary's reign, even Henry's, remained. St Michael's had been the most enthusiastic

---

[55] GL, MS 9051/5, f. 48v. Husband's will: GL, MS 9051/5, fols 47–47v.

[56] PRO, PROB 11/98, f. 192R.

[57] GL, MS 9051/6, f. 43v.

[58] PRO, PROB 11/135, f. 293R.

[59] PRO, PROB 11/108, f. 266R.

[60] GL, MS 4071/1, f. 117v. Cressy, *Bonfires and Bells*, p. 6; Jones, 'Living the Reformations', pp. 273–5.

parish when it came to testamentary bequests for fraternities and the
Stow family parish, John Stow being suspected of being Catholic. In the
accounts of 1581–82, when Thomas Stow(e) was one of three churchwardens, the scribe noted the passing of an individual, from a bygone
religious era: 'for p[ar]son Smythe his grave sometyme a Monke at
tower hill'.[61] The churchwardens in St Mary Woolnoth maintained the
Percivales' bequests to the poor of the parish and ward, long after
religious change had negated other stipulations of their wills. The churchwardens named them – and their later pious imitator, Sir Martin Bowes
– and made certain days their 'property', anniversaries of their deaths,
remembrances of their charity. Even in 1612/13, they distributed 10s to
the poor on the 'obijt day' of Sir John. Churchwardens also used St
Martin's Day and Sir Martin's sermon day interchangeably.[62]

Efforts to centralize relief of the poor also enabled city leaders to
begin more organized responses to epidemic disease. Officials urged
flexible charity to alleviate the plague's misery and implemented new
health policies to combat the disease in late sixteenth-century London.
St Michael's, in 1582–83, purchased 'fyftye Redd wandes for the
p[ar]ishe' for 5d, for the 'visited' to use, as did St Botolph's. The
churchwardens hired a surveyor, Master Cannon, for 5s 4d to survey
poor visited houses in 1592–93, the plague-ridden poor being a special
concern for all parishes that feared the spread of disease in overcrowded
places or through casual migration. The following year, the churchwardens paid 4d 'for setting two red crosses' in the parish, presumably
to mark the visitation. They also made a series of small payments to
help households in Finch ('Fynke') and Birchin ('Burchen') Lanes, where
a number of children infected with the plague lived. The vestry, in
October 1593, abandoned their usual habit of distributing alms on
certain eves, spaced evenly throughout the year, in favour of more
frequent outlays in an extraordinary moment of need.[63]

Although St Michael's had taken steps to contain earlier rounds of
the plague, the severity of the epidemic in 1603 – and increasing familiarity with centralized treatment of the poor – led the parish to send the
'diverse poore' to a parochial pesthouse for their 'diate Phisick and

---

[61] Wilson, 'A catalogue of the "unlawful" books', pp. 1–30. GL, MS 4071/1, f. 118;
the Parish Register identified him as William Smythe, 'an olde preeste lyinge in ye house
of Roberte Salisburye' and claims in a marginal note that he was 100 years old '&
upwarde': GL, MS 4061, unfol. (6 Oct. 1582).

[62] Percivales: GL, MS 1002/1B, fols 317v, 399v. St Martin's, Sir Martin's: GL, MS
1002/1B, f. 355; cf. f. 395v.

[63] GL, MSS 4071/1, fols 120, 146v, 148, 149v; 4072/1, Part 1, f. 60. Also GL, MS
1454, Roll 93. See Slack, *The Impact of Plague*, esp. pp. 199–226.

kepinge' during their illness. In 1606/07, St Michael's churchwardens noted the 'making of fyve crosses uppon houses infected', and paid a man to ward the door of one infected house for 11 days.[64] During the plague year of 1603, Edward Cotton left £10 to the 'visited poore'.[65] The plague years clustered about 1580 may have impressed Londoners with its power and increased their concern as it hit strongly once again in 1603. Even in 1609, the churchwardens in St Mary's provided five 'white wands' for the use of the parish.[66]

Evidence of centralized relief, and private charity, marked the period after 1580. Although the distribution of aid showed the slow evolution of legislation and practice in London, the forms of aid showed continuity with the past. The schemes and work plans advocated in vestries and testaments, however, illustrate how parochial and civic leaders and testators helped to develop far-reaching changes in poor relief.

Schemes and work

The sixteenth century ushered in experimental solutions to poverty that departed from medieval almsgiving and moved towards mid-seventeenth-century workhouses established by the Corporation of the Poor. Institutionalized, centralized relief reflected nascent concern for the impact of charity on recipients, rather than the benefits of it for the donor. Early reformers explored employment as an additive or alternative to charity and, especially, indiscriminate relief, but did not envision property redistribution. Schemes to employ the poor and to alleviate poverty, or at least remove the poor, were the city's attempts to cope with demographic expansion and under- and unemployment. The city's efforts coincided with state aims, at least until the costs of those aims overburdened parishes: to maintain social order, to support the military and its veterans, and to further international goals for trade and empire. Poor relief in the seventeenth and eighteenth centuries clearly aimed to reform the poor and even to incorporate punishment in aid. The 'inclination to promote Publick Good' triumphed over 'love, kindness or natural affection' in the eighteenth century, but intimations of this shift surfaced in the sixteenth century, in London testators and parish officials' concentration on public order and neighbourliness.[67]

---

[64] GL, MS 4071/1, fols 172v, 185v.

[65] PRO, PROB 11/101, f. 343L.

[66] GL, MS 1002/1B, f. 381.

[67] 'Indiscriminate alms-giving by the rich man in his castle has yielded place to a careful search for the industrious or impotent poor conducted by bourgeois churchward-

Parishes and hospitals employed the poor, often in menial tasks, to supplement their relief and pensions. Potential solutions for poverty hinged on those who scraped by, through a blend of work and charity, becoming nurses for those who, due to age or impotence, could not manage alone. Older, even elderly, men and women worked for parishes in tasks that were often, though not exclusively, gendered.[68] Part-time work for women, often widows or goodwives, included nursing abandoned and orphaned children and pregnant women. In the late 1580s, St Michael's churchwardens gave two women 9s 10d for helping a poor woman 'broughte a bed in St Michaels Cloister of two children'. Another woman gave birth in the churchyard, perhaps assisted by some of the widows and goodwives who rented rooms there. Women also nursed children and the sick, like the Goodwife Reynolds paid 5s by St Michael's churchwardens for keeping a lame child for two months in 1597–98. The churchwardens also hired, for 3s, a poor woman in Harp Alley to nurse a child for two weeks.[69] Men also were paid for nursing children and the sick. Goodman Goldston and Goodman Wrenn nursed a child named John Allison, who became sick and died, for St Michael's.[70] The parish paid Goodman Hawley 3s and 3s 4d to care for two women, the second one 'in her sicknes', in 1584–85.[71] These payments to men, however, may have masked the labour of women in their households, given the vagueness of 'nursing', a category that could refer to wet-nursing. Single men and widowers could care for older, weaned children without female help.

When allocating some of the least desirable jobs in a parish, necessity and gender drove the decisions of churchwardens and vestries to hire women or men. St Stephen's hired two poor women from a neighbouring parish to visit the sick in 1582/83, for 6s 8d. Because churchwardens

---

ens': Hill, 'William Perkins and the Poor', p. 218; Pearl calls the Corporation a 'forerunner of the workhouse movement' of the late seventeenth century: 'Puritans and Poor Relief', p. 210. Andrew, *Philanthropy and Police*, pp. 3–5; on difficulty of determining donors' motives: Owen, *English Philanthropy*, p. 69. Cf. co-existence of 'flourishing corporate and voluntary sector and a powerful central authority and legal system': Slack, *From Reformation to Improvement*, p. 163.

[68] Brodsky, 'Widows in Late Elizabethan London', p. 124; Diane Willen, 'Women in the Public Sphere in Early Modern England: The Case of the Urban Working Poor', *SCJ* 19, 4 (1988), pp. 559–75; aged parish paupers became a 'more distinct group' than other poor in the late seventeenth century as their earning opportunities declined and formal relief replaced informal aid: Tim Wales, 'Poverty, Poor Relief and the Life-cycle: Some Evidence from Seventeenth-Century Norfolk' in Richard M. Smith (ed.), *Land, Kinship and Life-Cycle* (Cambridge, 1984), p. 387.

[69] GL, MS 4071/1, fols 125v, 132, 135.

[70] GL, MS 1454, Roll 98.

[71] GL, MS 4071/1, f. 124.

and vestries engaged their own poor first, resorting to outsiders suggests that finding people willing to enter plague-ridden homes was difficult. St Michael's sexton, Tittle, was paid to watch 'the sick of the plague' for 6d a day in June, July and August of 1603–04. The churchwardens might have coerced him into undertaking the dangerous task because of his frequent appearances before the vestry for drunkenness and other moral offences. The least savoury of this medically oriented work, 'searching', was gendered, in that women searched corpses to determine the cause of death. Searching could draw on female wisdom and authority in other contexts, but the statute establishing searchers to determine plague called for 'ancient' women. The order threatened them with the loss of pensions if they refused to serve and subjected them to corporal punishment if they lied or otherwise shirked their duties. St Stephen's paid two women 6s 8d to inspect the dead bodies in the parish.[72] Payments for red wands in other parishes signal the use of searchers, who carried these wands during their work.

Certain tasks fell to men, like keeping parishes clean, carrying away dead animals, cleaning out privies, and punishing vagrants. Rakers, scavengers and even sextons engaged in these activities. 'Markham', whose wife had been ill and ended up in St Thomas's Hospital, warded for 'Wand[e]ring beggers' for the vestry in St Michael's in 1601–02. Men meted out corporal punishment to vagrants. Other men 'watched' church doors, to keep the poor orderly. Wages did not rise significantly through the sixteenth century, making the payments for small jobs an important part of lesser parochial officers' incomes.[73]

Parochial employment may have kept these women and men barely out of abject poverty, but previous service by a spouse or family member and long-time residence in the parish also influenced determinations about worthiness for employment and relief. Churchwardens and vestrymen knew the character and need of these individuals, and by extension, their families. Katherine Markham was given 4s 4d in clothing before entering St Thomas's, and was later nursed by a goodwife in the parish, with 'divers drinckes'.[74] Sextons received pensions and char-

---

[72] GL, MSS 4071/1, f. 172v; 539/2, fols 71, 72. Richelle Munkhoff, 'Searchers of the dead: Authority, marginality, and the Interpretation of Plague in England, 1574–1665', *Gender and History*, 11, 1 (April 1999), pp. 1–29; cf. authority in searching body to determine sex: Kathleen M. Brown, '"Changed … into the Fashion of Man": The Politics of Sexual Difference in a Seventeenth-Century Anglo-American Settlement' in Catherine Clinton and Michele Gillespie (eds), *The Devil's Lane: Sex and Race in the Early South* (New York and London, 1997), pp. 43–4.

[73] GL, MS 4071/1, f. 169; wife's illness: f. 167. Gibbs, 'New duties', p. 166.

[74] GL, MS 4071/1, fols 167, 169v. 'Divers drinckes' must be medicinal potions or draughts: *OED*.

ity, in addition to their pay as general handy men around the church and churchyard. In St Mary Woolnoth, the 'poore' of the parish in receipt of a testator's charitable bequest included the clerk, sexton, 'scole mistris', some men and a number of widows.[75] Long-term female pensioners, paying reduced rent for housing or performing some task, often included widows or wives of parish officers and servants. In St Stephen Walbrook, the sexton's wife, a pensioner in her later widowhood, helped in the nursing of two foundlings. St Stephen's treated the three young children of the deceased sexton Richard Muddle as they did other orphaned or fatherless pauper children. Within one year of his death, by 1593/94, each of the children was mentioned for the last time, settled or dead. Joanna Muddle stayed for a year with John Stearne, probably in service, for which he was paid £2 12s. Emmanuel Muddle died in the same year, while the last son, Richard, was clothed and sent to the 'sodyares', or soldiers, by the appointment of the 'masters' of the parish.[76]

Parochial accounts illustrated the precarious social position of other temporary or occasional employees whose wages amounted to relief. In St Stephen's, for instance, a nurse's theft demonstrated her own desperation. The churchwardens hired Mary Russell in 1612 to nurse two foundlings. The following year she cared for two more orphans, Stephen John and Mary Stephens, named, as many foundlings were, to commemorate their parochial origins. The parish paid Russell 50s, and spent 24s 4d on clothing and blankets for the children. The following entry in the accounts, however, listed 12s 'for redeeminge the childrens clothes when Mary Russell their nurce had pawned them at a brokers'.[77] The parish farmed the children out to a couple in Hertfordshire, firing the former nurse and not hiring her again. When these children lived to adulthood they often changed their names, obscuring their origins and making them elusive to historians.

Although churchwardens tended to those who had been born in the parish, and whose close family had served the community, they also tried to co-ordinate relief with extended family, institutions or other parishes when possible. Parishes pressed the expectation that formal and informal charity, corporate and familial aid combined to help the elderly and infirm. Through the later sixteenth century, churchwardens and collectors for the poor tried to streamline the provision of relief,

---

[75] GL, MS 1002/1B, f. 423v.

[76] GL, MS 593/2, fols 85–88, 119.

[77] Waistcoats, shoes, coats worth 4s 4d, smocks, coarse clothes, bibs worth 3s 9d, aprons, doublets 6s 6d, to make the clothes 12d, shoes, petticoats, blankets, hose, coats, aprons, and porter to carry them 8s. 9d. GL, MS 593/2, f. 120v.

even for the deserving poor, with parishes and institutions sharing charitable costs. For six months in 1589, the churchwardens of St Mary Woolnoth reimbursed Goodwife Wood for boarding a child, Edward Humble, the orphaned son of the late Thomas Humble, parishioner and clerk through the 1580s. The parish paid for half his apparel, schooling and other 'petty charges'. In June, the churchwardens paid the treasurer of Christ's Hospital 30s to admit him into the institution.[78] The vestry in St Michael's pledged 40s for his entrance, since Thomas Humble had also served in that parish.[79]

If orphaned and abandoned children survived the nursing stage, then parishes oversaw their education, apprenticeship or admittance to Christ's. Amy Louise Erickson has not found a distinction between the costs of raising boys and girls, but more research with churchwardens' accounts may be necessary to compare survival rates and placements of boys and girls cared for by parishes. Studies of other early modern countries and cities have shown lower survival rates for girls than for boys.[80] St Michael's accounts recorded William Hammon's agreement with the vestrymen on 29 April 1593 to maintain and bring up the female foundling 'Orphan Mychaell', with his bond of £6 13s 4d, to 'for ever discharge the saide p[a]rish of her'. The parish also cared for Hannah Crakall, daughter of the deceased parishioner Miles Crakall, for years, paying for her education in 1609–10. Her father apparently died intestate, for the parish met with the Lord Mayor and Court of Aldermen to secure a portion of his goods to care for her.[81] Mary Walbrook, another of the tellingly named St Stephen Walbrook found-

---

[78] GL, MS 1002/1A, f. 260.

[79] GL, MS 4072/1, Part 1, f. 46v. The churchwardens' accounts requested more than 55s for the child, however: GL, MS 4071/1, f. 132v.

[80] GL, MS 593/2, f. 132v. For analysis of statutory foundations of apprenticing poor children and the circumstances: Pamela Sharpe, 'Poor children as apprentices in Colyton, 1598–1830', *Continuity and Change* 6, 2 (1991), pp. 253–70; on parochial placements: Ilana Krausman Ben-Amos, 'Women apprentices in the trades and crafts of early modern Bristol', *Continuity and Change* 6, 2 (1991), pp. 232–4. Erickson, *Women and Property*, p. 59. Valerie Fildes found that, in general, more boys than girls were abandoned in London, a fact that she explains by the sex ratio at birth and that she shows contrasts with other European cases: 'Maternal feelings re-assessed: child abandonment and neglect in London and Westminster, 1550–1800' in *Women as Mothers in Pre-Industrial England: Essays in Memory of Dorothy McLaren*, (London and New York, 1990), pp. 150–51. 'Delayed-action infanticide' of girls, partly because female babies left with wet-nurses longer than boys: Christiane Klapisch-Zuber, 'Childhood in Tuscany at the Beginning of the Fifteenth Century' in *Women, Family, and Ritual in Renaissance Italy* (Chicago, 1987), pp. 104–5. Also, shrinking opportunities in segregated occupations in Bristol: Ben-Amos, 'Women apprentices', pp. 233–7.

[81] GL, MSS 4071/1, f. 144v; 4071/2, f. 7v; 4072/1, Part 1, f. 103.

lings, lived to school age, unlike the others in a small group sent 'out to nurse' before 1618. Following the usual practice, St Stephen's paid for her nursing and clothing while she lived outside London, but they also paid 12d for her education.

Surviving records of service and 'adoption' arrangements illustrate the multiple sources of relief and suggest that some of these children were fatherless rather than orphaned. In 1604, St Botolph's vestry oversaw an agreement between one Keene and Henry Shawcrosse, in which Keene gave him 20s for apparel for Elizabeth, the daughter of the deceased John Shawcrosse. Keene married Elizabeth's mother, discharging the parish of all further costs for the (former) widow, while Henry promised not to ask the parish for money to care for Elizabeth. In May 1604, the Draper Thomas Gedney made an indenture with the same churchwardens, Richard Osmotherhaw and Richard Betts, for the daughter of Elizabeth Dormer, who had been married to John Dormer.[82] Like the other agreement, this one attempted to release the parish from any further obligation to care for the child. The churchwardens took the agreement one step further, however, by stipulating that the parishioners and 'all the hospitalls of the City of London' would be free of any charges stemming from the newly born child taken in by Gedney. Service could be a form of adoption, mimicking the experience of early sixteenth-century almschildren.[83] In 1610, St Botolph's allowed a cordwainer in a neighbouring parish to take a child as an apprentice, 'to make him his adopted child', freeing the parish of further charges.[84]

Mothers and relatives also entered contracts with churchwardens over young boys. St Michael's churchwardens, in 1591–92, gave 10s to Goodwife Grene, 'beinge sick to put her sonn forth to Learne to sowe', at the Deputy's appointment. Goodman Grene's burial followed this arrangement, suggesting that his illness and the family's poverty necessitated arrangements for the boy's training. A parent might resist putting children into service, however, as did Goodwife Squyer. The vestry in St Michael's ordered her in 1602 to place her child in service, threatening to send both of them to Bridewell and to rescind her pension if she refused. By 1606, she had satisfied the vestrymen, who gave her a gown by a deceased parishioner's bequest.[85]

Surviving indentures demonstrate how parochial officers transferred responsibility for orphans from themselves to another party. The twelve-

---

[82] GL, MSS 1453/1, f. 2v; 1506/1, unfol.

[83] Like modern 'fostering': Sharpe, 'Poor apprentices', p. 255.

[84] GL, MS 1453/1, f. 5. The child is described as the son of Edward Pulford, not 'deceased' or the 'late'.

[85] GL, MSS 4071/1, f. 141v; 4072/1, Part 1, fols 87, 97.

year indenture of Edward Stephens 'al[ia]s Johnes' to William Massey, painter-stainer, bears three names on the outside of the manuscript: Edmund Brockbanck, churchwarden, Frauncis Kydd, scrivener, and Johanne Newman.[86] Before the name of Newman was associated with the boy, the parish paid Thomas Harris, the sexton, to care for the aptly named child abandoned in St Stephen's in 1583. For four years, the parish paid for the child's clothing and boarding, and paid Harris £4 in wages and £3 9s 4d for a pension. Arthur Dannsye of 'Kyngston' took the child for a quarter year in 1586–87, before Massey kept him for 46 weeks. After this trial period, in which the parish mended and made more clothes for Stephens, Massey took the boy as an apprentice. The churchwardens recorded the 12d cost for his indenture and a fee of £2 12s for his apprenticeship. Edward Stephens's experience seems typical, in that parishes maintained children for years before apprenticing them as early as four years old.[87] St Stephen's continued to nurse and train children in subsequent years – being a wealthy parish, it could afford the costs, unlike a parish like St Botolph's.

Although parishes intended to save these students and apprentices from misery, some of the children rebuffed parochial aid and placement in labouring positions. In 1597/98, St Botolph's churchwardens paid for nursing a child and provided a new coat to her, but before the year had ended, they remarked that she had 'run away'. The parish transferred their benevolence to another child.[88] The child who ran away may have been old enough to take control of her own life and labour. The tribulations of surviving and finding work may have paled in contrast to the uncertainty of working conditions for pauper apprentices. Edward Stephens's few temporary arrangements illustrated the instability of their living situations as well. St Michael's churchwardens spent 14s on 'motley clothe' for Francis 'the Ideott' who had been brought from St Ethelborough to be placed with a knight who

---

[86] GL, Add. MSS 217, unfol. See GL, MS 4071/1, f. 124 for evidence of Kydd's occupation. Even influential parishioners did not escape the vagaries of fortune. Brockbanck would later depend on the good will of his brother William, who returned Edmund's money to him, but not his household goods. Those goods went to a cousin, to see that Edmund was buried properly. He also gave a servant £5 to drop all suits against Edmund, who had lost his money: see PRO, PROB 11/129, fols 45L, 46L (44v, 45v). William Brockbanck had been in trouble with the Grocers in 1579 over uninspected merchandise: Ward, *Metropolitan Communities*, p. 52.

[87] GL, MS 593/2, fols 74v (clothes), 76v, 77v (indenture), 78v (fee). Pauper apprenticeships, not limited to orphans or foundlings: E.G. Thomas, 'Pauper apprenticeship', *Local Historian*, **14**, 7 (1981), pp. 400–406. Apprenticeships were made any time between four and 20 years, though eight was common: Sharpe, 'Poor apprentices', p. 255.

[88] GL, MS 1454, Roll 98.

lived in Mile End Green.[89] Francis may not have been a child, but his mental or intellectual deficiencies left him powerless to oppose parochial plans to settle him in 'service' with a knight, dressed in outlandish cloth better to fulfil his 'occupation' of amusing others.

Undoubtedly, service did not always bode well for young men and women, even if parishes trusted that these contracts would result in decent work and even new families. The vestry in St Stephen's, in two meetings in 1594, took up the sad case of an orphaned child, lamed while in service with one man who was warned to use him better or else lose the child's labour.[90] The chronicler Henry Machyn expressed his outrage over the sad case of a young maidservant carded to near-death by her mistress. Carted through London, 'a woman with a bannor pentyd with (a) yong damsell and a woman, with a carde in the woman('s) hand cardyng her mayd nakyd pentyd, the whyche she left butt lytyll skyn of her'. These incidents reminded contemporaries of potential neglect or even brutality in domestic service and apprenticeship, although treatment of servants ranged from kind to cruel.[91]

The extent of early seventeenth century under- and unemployment, and the depth of poverty in the city, led to a new and radical attempt to remove the young and poor from London. In *A Good Speed to Virginia* (1609), Robert Gray used natural and classical examples to suggest colonization as a remedy for the 'calamities' of overpopulation. After all, 'Our land hath brought forth but it hath not milk sufficient in the breast thereof to nourish all those children which it hath brought forth.'[92] In the period 1618–22, London parishes joined the Virginia Company in trying to send poor children to the new colony. In 1622, the Court of Aldermen 'thought fitt' to send a second group of children 'that haue noe meanes of livinge' to Virginia, pledging £500 from the city.[93] St

---

[89] GL, MS 4071/1, f. 187. Although 'idiots' were among the deserving '"naturally disabled,"' Francis's placement suggests that parishes found them 'work' when they could. On poor lunatics and mentally disabled persons: Michael MacDonald, *Mystical Bedlam: Madness, Anxiety, and Healing in Seventeenth-Century England* (Cambridge, 1981), p. 6.

[90] GL, MS 594/1, f. 31.

[91] 'Carding' refers to combing wool for manufacture. Although this case dates from 1552, the episode represents one end in the range of treatment of servants in the early modern period: *The Diary of Henry Machyn*, p. 17; range of servants' experiences: Crawford and Mendelson, *Women in Early Modern England*, pp. 104–8; 'work' as employment and regulation of morality: Griffiths, *Youth*, pp. 355–6.

[92] In Joan Thirsk and J.P. Cooper (eds), *Seventeenth-Century Economic Documents*, (Oxford, 1972), pp. 757–8. Removal of idle to colonies: Beier, *Masterless Men*, p. 150.

[93] CLRO, Rep. 36, fols 196v, 236v. Robert Jütte, *Poverty and Deviance*, p. 168. The single study of this scheme puzzles over why London inhabitants did not support it: R.C. Johnson, 'The transportation of vagrant children from London to Virginia, 1618–1622'

Stephen's collected more than its share in the first years to send to the Chamber of London, as befitting a wealthy parish that often made payments disallowed in other parishes and was ordered by the Court of Aldermen to contribute to the care of the poor in St Sepulchre's. St Michael's churchwardens contributed 10s to satisfy the assessment, but never mentioned the scheme again. St Mary's either did not participate, or left the accounting to the collectors. Accounts in the city alternately referred to sending 'boies' and 'poore children' to Virginia, but St Botolph Bishopsgate gave 5s to Goodwife Norman 'to send her daughter to Virginea' in 1621–22.[94]

The country, as well as the investors in the Company, had a vested interest in the success of the colony in Virginia, but parishes did not support the effort as they supported other aspects of military and state interest. Many parishes were not enthusiastic about this experiment, judging by shortfalls and inconsistencies in accounts of collections. Parishioners and parochial leaders supported the state's military actions on the Continent, even relieving stranger refugees and 'vagrant' maimed soldiers, but they left the costs of overseas expansion to entrepreneurs. The arrival of enslaved Africans in Virginia before 1619 and the 'Massacre of 1622' in which 347 settlers died may also have sapped enthusiasm for sending white, albeit poor and marginalized, children to the colony.[95]

Testamentary charity also supported schemes for work, while bolstering the centralization of relief in parishes and institutions. Parochial collections and lifetime donations from inhabitants supported Christ's Hospital, but testators began to support the institution in significant ways late in the sixteenth century, after initial reluctance. Londoners may have responded to demographic pressure and the perceived increase in poverty and abandonment with donations, or Christ's may have finally absorbed the bequests that formerly benefited religious

---

in H.S. Reinmuth (ed.), *Early Stuart Studies: Essays in Honor of David Harris Willson* (Minneapolis, MN, 1970), pp. 137–51; esp. 149–50. See brief reference to 'ragged children' included in the 4000 emigrants to Virginia 1618–1621: Kenneth R. Andrews, *Trade, plunder and settlement: Maritime enterprise and the genesis of the British Empire, 1480–1630* (Cambridge, 1984), p. 323.

[94] GL, MS 593/2, f. 133v; payment to St Sepulchre's: CLRO, Rep. 32, fols 157–157v. GL, MSS 4071/2, f. 48; 2593/1, fols 252, 263; 4524/1, f.182.

[95] For example: GL, MSS 5026/1, f. 12; 4956/2, fols 283v, 293. Records show support from 21 parishes. William Thorndale, 'The Virginia Census of 1619', *Magazine of Virginia Genealogy*, 33 (1995), pp. 155–70; Betty White, *The Origins of American Slavery: Freedom and Bondage in the English Colonies* (New York, 1997), pp. 72–4; Anthony Salerno, 'The Social Background of Seventeenth-Century Emigration to America', *JBS*, **19**, 1 (Fall 1979), pp. 31–52.

institutions. Nevertheless, the Hospital could not alleviate the problems of abandoned and orphaned children. By the 1580s and 1590s, between 550 and 650 children swelled the walls of Christ's, making the admittance of more children difficult for parishes and individuals.[96] The problem only worsened. By 1641, contemporaries reported 926 children admitted to Christ's, with 103 set into apprenticeships, discharged or deceased.[97] In wills composed between 1580 and 1620, 21.4 per cent (48) of testators left gifts to the hospital, compared to 4.46 per cent (ten) who did for other hospitals. Of these donors to Christ's, five were women, representing 21.8 per cent of all female testators between 1580 and 1620 (39) and 43 were men, or 23.2 per cent of all male testators (185).[98] Although the actual numbers are small, the percentage of donors represented is significant, as are the bequeathed monies.

Socially prominent men buttressed their status by serving Christ's and other hospitals during their lifetimes. They and their female relations crafted their charitable, pious reputations through lifetime donations, testamentary bequests, and graves or monuments in the institutions. Sir Thomas Ramsey, who besides being a former mayor, was also a governor of Christ's from 1582 to 1587, split his goods in two. He left one half for his wife, and the other half to his will, of which he gave the first half to Christ's Hospital. He wrote his will in the middle of his service, although it did not reach probate till 1590, remembering his charge 'as ye will answer before God at the hour and time when you and we shall stand before him to render an account of our doings'.[99]

Provision for Christ's and even the lukewarm support for the Virginia venture showed willingness to try institutional solutions to alleviate childhood poverty. Benefactions also illustrated how civic, parochial and individual funds could be pooled to match the costs of various forms of relief. As the parish replicated state aims, especially in disciplining the undeserving poor and encouraging work in London and even abroad, so testators furnished similar funds for setting the poor to work. Testators slowly adopted loan or work schemes as suitable pious bequests, while sixteenth-century legislation set the poor to work in

---

[96] Archer, *Pursuit*, p. 157.

[97] *A Psalme of Thanksgiving – to be sung on Monday in Easter Holy-days at St Mary's Spital for founders and benefactors* (by children of Christ's Hospital) (London: R. Oulton, 1641) TT E.669.f.4 [5].

[98] Christ's absorbed most bequests to hospitals (85.29 per cent, or 29 in 1581–1601 and 68 per cent, or 17 in 1602–20). No significant difference (z-scores of 1.39 and .15) between the periods ending 1580 (29 gifts, 3.79 per cent), 1601 (34, 3.22 per cent), and 1620 (25, 3.16 per cent). Manzione found that most legacies were small and that of the large ones, 13.8 per cent were left by women: *Christ's Hospital*, p. 84.

[99] PRO, PROB 11/75, f. 307R. Quoted in Manzione, *Christ's Hospital*, p. 121.

early manufactures and punished idleness.[100] Between 1580 and 1601, only three testators left single bequests for loan or work schemes, or helped to pay for scholars' exhibitions or apprentices' training. All three testators were prominent individuals in the city, with the fortune to make the substantial endowment that such funds required. In 1584, Anne Gunter, widow of the long-lived parishioner and Skinner Philip Gunter, left £100 to help poor young beginners from her deceased husband's company.[101] Sir Thomas Ramsey left a stock of £200 to the Grocers, for the wardens to lend in sums of £50 to young retailers for two years at a time.[102]

Testators who established these labour or loan programmes targeted one example of poverty in London: migration to the city of young single people in search of work. The common stipulation limiting the length of aid illustrated that loans were temporary measures to help young adults enter a trade or set up a household. These bequests could reflect the testator's self-centred concern with social status and illustrate his or her selfless benevolence, akin to providing for burial processions and doles. Alexander Every, the third testator leaving such a gift, provided £100 for a loan scheme among the Clothworkers for the relief, use and better maintenance of poor young men of the company, 'of which sorte I knowe a greate manye at this daye', in 1588.[103] In return, Every hoped that 'in the bestowing and Letting thereof they will from time to time remember me and my good will unto the saide companye by whiche others maye be the more moved to lyke actions'. Every scattered nearly £700 in charitable bequests in country parishes and in London, also making substantial bequests to his servants.

The gradual adoption of loan schemes for poor apprentices suggests that by the early seventeenth century social mobility was difficult to achieve through guilds, if such mobility had ever marked guild life.[104] In the first two decades of the seventeenth century, six testators endowed 25 of these programmes. Londoners depended on masters of crafts or parish churchwardens to see their bequests fulfilled. In 1606, Henry Smith, a

---

[100] Jordan claims that testators slowly adopted apprenticeship funds, but 'were zealously concerned' with loans for apprentices and journeymen: *The Charities of London, 1480–1660*, p. 172.

[101] PRO, PROB 11/68, f. 131R. The scribe claimed that Gunnter was 92 at his death: Overall, *Accounts of the Churchwardens*, p. 198.

[102] PRO, PROB 11/75, f. 307R–308L.

[103] PRO, PROB 11/73, f. 269L.

[104] Rappaport argues that apprentices enjoyed social mobility through participation in companies: *Worlds within Worlds*, p. 172; Archer cautions against underestimating social tensions in city: *Pursuit of Stability*, pp. 8–9. See also Ward, *Metropolitan Communities*, pp. 73–4, 80.

citizen and draper, left 14 bequests for advancing family and poor boys, including £50 to both the Company of Merchant Adventurers and to the Drapers, to make loans to young men, all brothers in the companies.[105] In 1612, the citizen John Newman arranged for his craft, the Grocers, to use a stock of £1000 to generate a yearly stipend of £50 for his son. The son, Anthony, whether by his own initiative or through 'ill counsell', was not to trouble the executors or company, on pain of losing his annual income to his brother, John, the executor. At Anthony's decease, Newman expected the craft to repay £900, keeping £100 to loan money to young men of the company for two years at a time.[106] Newman kept his profligate or troublesome son on a short tether and repaid the company for being his trustees with loans for industrious young men. Perhaps Anthony was also to contemplate the value of work.

Work schemes, loans and dowry funds helped to ease the transition from youth to adulthood or, for migrants, from countryside or village to city. Some testators made provisions, though only 11, for dowries for poor maidens, to mitigate the economic difficulty of setting up a new household. The radical Gerrard Winstanley later suggested a state dowry fund, though he intended property restructuring, unlike wealthy Londoners imagined.[107] Between 1580 and 1620, testators left 62 monetary gifts to female servants and apprentices, and 116 to male servants and apprentices, to pay deserved wages and sometimes to offer help with marriage or settlement. Londoners' bequests for loans and work outside the city would perhaps slow the steady stream of migrants, potential 'vagrants', into the metropolis. Henry Smith left £20 to set ten poor boys to work in Edmonton, where he owned a house. He asked that the 'chiefs' of the parish set them to work with 'pynne makers' or in some other suitable trade.[108] Charles Glascock, citizen and grocer, left a £50 stock to provide work for poor parishioners in his birthplace in Essex, in 1612, outdoing his father's bequest for a £20 stock.[109] For those who had already arrived in London, Anthony Every made a donation to maintain selected poor young men in his parish, but limited the support to no more than three years.[110]

Testators also saw to education for the poor – at least for poor boys. Henry Smith, after setting up apprenticeships, paid for schooling poor boys in Edmonton, chosen by agreement of the churchwardens, overse-

---

[105] PRO, PROB 11/108, f. 267L.
[106] PRO, PROB 11/123, fols 396R, 297R.
[107] Gillis, *For Better, For Worse*, p. 101.
[108] PRO, PROB 11/108, f. 267L.
[109] PRO, PROB 11/122, f. 60L.
[110] PRO, PROB 11/73, fols 268L–268R.

ers and the schoolmaster. Although Smith also aided the poor in London parishes, he paid for no schooling within the city. Smith's business-like approach in his will, noting interest rates of eight per cent for the increase of money left to his executors for four-year terms, echoes his practical endowment of schooling and training in a trade to encourage self-sufficiency and to prevent poverty. In addition, he left £100 to buy land in Stoke Prior, his birthplace in Worcestershire, after four years. He expected the churchwardens there to purchase land with the advice of his brother, Stephen Smith, the vicar. He earmarked 40s of the yearly rent to pay Strangers for four to six sermons yearly. With the remaining rent, he wanted the 'poorer sorte' of boys educated, chosen by his brother, two or three of the 'chief' of the parish, and the churchwardens. To George Smith in Edmonton, likely a relative, he left £5, 'in hope he will not waste yt but encrease yt'.[111]

Employing the poor, teaching them trades and new habits of production in England's pre-industrial economy, and providing dowries and loans, eased the way for young men and women, but did not challenge the social and economic status quo. Parochial and testamentary efforts recall Max Weber's thesis on the Protestant ethic and its connection to capitalism.[112] Catholics and Protestants, however, both set the poor to work and sought new methods of relieving poverty, suggesting that the inhabitants of European cities and states became accustomed to an increasingly capitalist way of life. English parishes used employment to supplement, but not to replace outright relief. Adjusting to economic change came at a social cost, especially in the 1590s when Londoners perceived great economic distress and suspected greedy hawkers and middlemen of inflating prices. In 1598, Hugh Alley made a survey of the marketplaces within London and listed the names of the aldermen and deputies in charge of them. He wrote his 'Caveat' to plead with Londoners not to enrich themselves by the impoverishment of their 'poore Neighbours'. He blamed 'Haglers, Hawkers, Huxters, and Wanderers' for buying goods and reselling them at raised prices, especially in the few years preceding his survey, and creating 'great dearth and scarcety'. While invoking an ideal of neighbourliness, he bemoaned the 'great Decaye, or rather, the playne abbolishm[en]t, and exterminacon of good deedes, often done unto others ... in these, our soe daungerous and unhappie dayes'.[113]

---

[111] PRO, PROB 11/108, f. 267R; fols 266L–268L.

[112] Weber, *The Protestant Ethic*, pp. 27, 36–8, 44.

[113] Ian Archer, Caroline Barron, Vanessa Harding (eds), *Hugh Alley's Caveat: The Markets of London in 1598*, London Topographical Society, Publication No. 137 (London, 1988), pp. 43, 47.

Schemes and plans to employ and relieve the poor highlight the concern with order in the sixteenth century. Teaching habits of labour, even if the work completed was insignificant, and moving the poor to birth parishes or to a colony, placed masterless men, women and children under masters. Reformers of relief, however, did not stop with economic efforts, but combated the moral and social disorder they perceived in the lives of the poor.

Social control

Historians have long debated the connection between Protestantism, and its more radical offspring, and social control, although social regulation, like the discrimination between deserving and undeserving poor, was not new to the sixteenth century.[114] The special circumstances of Protestantism in England partly explain parochial regulation of morality and behaviour, but other influences precipitated that control, and even the inconsistencies in relief. Myriad factors – legislation, sporadic economic contractions as in the 1590s, population growth in the City and its suburbs, and reliance on parochial resources for relief – hardened distinctions between the deserving and undeserving poor in the late sixteenth and early seventeenth centuries. Nevertheless, testators, parishes and the local and national government continued relieving the destitute, even some who might otherwise have been deemed unworthy recipients. Anne Ramsey, for instance, a pregnant woman travelling to her brother in Sussex who carried a warrant from justices of the peace alleging that her husband was imprisoned for a £300 debt, gained 12d from the parish.[115] Perhaps he accumulated the debt from a loss at sea or in trade, considered legitimate reasons for asking for aid and for securing a letter that opened parochial coffers. Testators and parishes often distinguished, however, between those with trifling and those with large debts, when deciding worthy charitable recipients. Their misfortunate indebtedness qualified them, but the large debt necessitated a warrant to legitimate aid.

---

[114] McIntosh, *Controlling Misbehavior*, pp. 1–19; von Friedeburg, 'Reformation of Manners', pp. 347–85; Spufford, 'Puritanism and Social Control?'; Methodism's 'double service' as the religion of the industrial bourgeoisie and the proletariat, instilling 'work-discipline': Thompson, *The Making of the English Working Class* (New York, 1966), pp. 355–6; early Methodism as a vehicle for women's independence and organization: Deborah Valenze, *Prophetic Sons and Daughters: Female Preaching and Popular Religion in Industrial England* (Princeton, 1985), pp. 65–9.

[115] GL, MS 4071/2, f. 48. On strong connections between ideology and regulation in the sixteenth century, see McIntosh, *Controlling Misbehavior*, pp. 200–201.

Working out the parameters of individual charity, parochial relief and civic responsibility became more urgent as the city grew into the seventeenth century. Social and moral problems pressed parishes already burdened by financial responsibility for the deserving, leading parochial leaders to peer more closely at all of their parishioners, but especially at the poor. Confusion existed over the boundaries of parochial obligations and of city and/or private responsibility. When wealthy parishes cared for the sick, impotent and very young or very old, residing in or wandering into their bounds, they often tried to reduce their assessments for supporting outlying, poverty-stricken parishes elsewhere in London. Parishes also resisted assuming civic expenses. St Botolph's attempted to control expenses tied to municipally-oriented projects, like the maintenance of water pumps, as they wrestled with the strains of poor inmates and poor parishioners.[116]

Economic and demographic pressures alone do not explain parochial attention to the reform of behaviour. Moral strictures, similar to those imposed on the poor by churchwardens, vestry men and testators, also burdened parishioners not receiving charity. Of course, the parish could not reach as far into the lives of these parishioners as those falling on the poor rolls, without imposing a Genevan-style consistory in London. Churchwardens' accounts included fines for moral breaches and for special allowances to break religious rules, most of which went to the poor box. In 1598–99, Mistress Sallawaye, Robert Startforde and George Grave (twice) paid fines of 3s 4d for opening shops on holidays, while Master Crooke paid 6s 8d for a licence to eat flesh in Lent. Two men, including one 'Henry Callis' or 'Callice', paid fines of 20s for selling 'drinke under measure' in 1605–06, sums distributed to poor widows in the parish. The next year Callice paid 12d to the poor box, 'for pennaunce injoyned him for suffringe tiplinge in his house on the saboth day at service time'. In 1610–11, Master Emmyns and Master Martin paid greater fines for the same offence, 7s 4d. Churchwardens and pastors limited the diversions available to parishioners during services or sermon times. On 17 October 1617, the churchwardens collected 5s each, from 'twoe w[hi]ch were inebriated at the Fleece', a nearby tavern, with a similar fine for drunkenness the following year.[117] That these fines and fees reached the poverty-stricken demonstrated the survival of the link between the fabric of the parish community and charity, even after the Reformation.

---

[116] GL, MS 1454, Rolls 94, 95.

[117] Licences to eat flesh: GL, MSS 4071/2, fols 49v, 160 and 1002/1B, f. 383. Fines: GL, MSS 4071/1, fols 180, 180v, 184, 185; 4071/2, fols 11v, 36v, 40.

Oversight of behaviour, especially of single men and women and poor congregants, and efforts to restrict activities that competed with worship, like drinking at Callice's tippling house, exemplified parochial concern with the good behaviour, even godliness, of rich and poor inhabitants.[118] Expectations of, or exhortations to, godliness affected parishioners, as it did the supplicants of relief. Historians have focused on the predilection of puritan preachers to call their parishioners the 'vulgar rabble' and 'ignorant people', debating whether the labels should be taken at face value or understood as evangelistic rhetoric.[119] St Michael's may have been concerned about church attendance and, at the least, the appearance of conformity, when in 1587 the vestry decreed that any clerk or sexton leaving during a service or sermon would pay 3s 4d for the use of the poor – and the churchwardens would pay the same if they neglected to enforce the rule. The prescriptive warning hinted that the social group representing potential churchwardens hesitated to fine minor officers. The battle against parishioners' drunkenness netted the unfortunate sexton of St Michael's, Edward Tittle, who petitioned for reinstatement in 1603. The vestry admonished him to be of good behaviour, 'to leave going to taverns and alehouses', and incidentally to clean the church better, when it rehired him.[120] The vestry could not employ him while he set a poor example to other parishioners. Drunkenness, rather than drinking, incurred retribution, as St Stephen's paid 12d for the 'Nurce to drincke', along with meat, cheese and apparel for the foundlings in her care.[121]

Prominent individuals, churchwardens, civic officeholders or parsons influenced parochial decisions about the worthiness, even godliness, of supplicants to and employees of the parish. Charity edified a congregation, especially when exemplary sufferers were held up before the parishioners. Notation of certain expenditures deviated from the usually terse style as churchwardens hastened to prove recipients' worthiness and suffering to the congregation. Certificates, warrants and heartfelt narratives helped to open hearts and coffers. St Stephen Walbrook's churchwardens gave 7s 2d to 'divers other poore, ministers, captives and distressed p[er]sons uppon their severall certificates urged to be

---

[118] von Friedeburg's study demonstrates that those presented for petty offences 'were not disproportionately drawn from the village poor', but I would argue that in deciding the deservingness of charitable recipients churchwardens and parishioners did focus on the behaviour of the poor: 'Reformation of Manners', p. 378.

[119] Duffy, 'The Godly and the Multitude', p. 32; cf. Hill, 'William Perkins and the Poor', p. 233.

[120] GL, MS 4072/1, Part 1, fols 40, 89.

[121] GL, MS 593/2, f. 126v.

read in the Church at tymes'. Even testators supported poor ministers, like the citizen and draper George Busby, who gave Master Dorrell, 'a preacher now in troble' 12d in 1600, while he gave the same to Griffin, the minister at St Botolph.[122]

Parsons pressured churchwardens to relieve impoverished strangers, a group not easily considered more deserving than the local poor. St Stephen's parson, Doctor Merriall, commanded churchwardens to relieve those who lost tongues or ears to Turks or who cast aside family, friends, and fortune for the sake of their religious conversion – all exemplary Christian or, better yet, Protestant persons. The churchwardens, for example, gave 5s at Merriall's request to an Italian scholar, who 'hath forsaken his contrye and frends for the cause of Religion'. The parish had cared for foundlings and orphans, and supported individuals with testimonials or certificates alleging loss by fire or other casualties, but Merriall expanded the parish's charity. Churchwardens noted payments at his request to poor ministers, including one who had losses in Ireland. He preached in the parish in 1618–19, a godly way of 'singing for his supper'. Explanations of similar outlays emphasized Merriall's request or presence at the moment, legitimating the unusual gifts to strangers at the year-end audit. A lesson for parishioners also sprang from summary expulsions and denials. In contrast to these small bequests, the churchwardens gave 1s to a 'poore woeman to gett hir out of the p[ar]ish'.[123] Ministers, captives of Muslims and pirates, and refugees of wars against Catholics and the Ottomans, because of preoccupation with trade and the defence of Protestantism around the world, passed charitable tests, but a poor Englishwoman who might burden the parish with a young child failed the tests of good reputation and behaviour.

On the other hand, parishes sometimes resisted orders from parochial, civic and royal leaders, and instead preserved resources for the resident, known poor. Exigency and ideology caused this resistance. Not all supplicants, even those carrying letters, were godly, let alone Christian, but perhaps most offensively to certain churchwardens and auditors, they absorbed the charity that rightfully belonged to a parish's own poor and impotent residents. In St Michael Cornhill, in 1614–15, the renter churchwarden relieved poor strangers who carried letters, like the Persian 'Nycholas Argoro' who brought letters from the Lords

---

[122] GL, MSS 593/2, f. 129; 9171/19, f. 206v.

[123] GL, MS 593/2, fols 131–132v. Mr Merriall began as parson in 1616 when Dr Fenton was sick (f. 127), no longer served by 1627 (f. 154), and was granted a pension in 1629 (f. 157v). Many parishes in London dispensed relief similarly, but not without criticism and debate: Schen, 'Constructing the Poor', pp. 454–5.

of the Council, and other poor men with letters, even royal ones. In the final accounts, Argoro received 2s 6d, but the space at the right of the folio for the other two men is blank. In all three cases, the churchwardens decreed that 'the like is not to be allowed hereafter', such gifts 'beinge a verry evill presidente'. In the same year, the upper churchwarden resented the influence of the parson Doctor Ashbold and the Alderman's Deputy, giving money to a poor, sick 'Grecian', but asserting 'the like notwithstandinge not to be allowed hereafter'. By the year 1619–20, however, another hand produced the written accounts, and the parish allowed disbursements to those who suffered losses by disaster and war.[124] Perhaps a hard-nosed auditor had died, leaving parochial decisions to others with more flexible attitudes toward the poor, or the parish had succumbed to royal and civic commands to support poor veterans and refugees, as well as domestic sufferers.

Deserving recipients, compared to the casual and stranger poor, included the sick and impotent, at least some of whom were chronologically and functionally aged.[125] Many of the most deserving elderly poor were women, because those who survived childbearing years tended to outlive men. 'Goodwife' was an imprecise title in the sixteenth century, but it suggests an older woman who might eventually work for the parish and collect charity from it. In 1617/18 in St Michael's, the advanced age and infirmity of the poor and mainly female recipients of informal parochial aid is manifest: some certificate-bearers, some foundlings and orphans, widows, goodwives, goodmen. Widow Stowton lacked fuel and needed a 'keeper', Goodman Lewes lacked money and work, Widow Baker was a 'sicke old woman', Goodwife Powell was 'long sick', and Widow Turnor was 'deafe and verie poore'.[126]

Their age and infirmity did not free female, or male, pensioners from oversight and occasionally threats. Parishes attempted to control the behaviour of even the worthy poor. Goody Coke enjoyed her husband's pension, only 'upon hir good behaver'.[127] Griffin Jones sowed discord in his family and parish, breaking the model of the grateful and godly supplicant. He came to St Stephen's vestry with a letter from the Lord Mayor, claiming a £10 pension the parish had already given to his wife.

---

[124] GL, MS 4071/2, fols 24, 26, 47v–48.

[125] Susannah Ottaway, 'The "Decline of Life": Aspects of Aging in Eighteenth-Century England', unpub. Ph.D. diss., Brown University (1998), 17–81; on cultural definition of old age: Lynn Botelho, 'Old age and menopause in rural women of early modern Suffolk' in *Women and Ageing* (Harlow, 2000), pp. 48–52; Peter Stearns, 'Old women: some historical observations' *Journal of Family History*, 5, 1 (Spring 1980), pp. 44–57.

[126] GL, MS 4071/2, f. 37.

[127] GL, MS 4072/1, Part 1, f. 34.

Within a few months the parish promised him a weekly pension of 12d, but first gave him a year's pension 'to redeme his howshoulde stuff out of pawne'. By 1591, however, the vestry had tired of his pleas, giving him 20s to stop asking for a pension. He regained the pension in 1593, only to lose it in 1597 for quarrelling and dragging his son into court. The vestry begged him to be 'godly', to stop this fighting, and granted and withdrew his pension through 1599. The Court of Aldermen kept a poor box in the court to collect 12d fines from people who brought suits without grounds, discouraging the same litigious attitude.[128]

Widows, who were not necessarily aged, could be impoverished by the death of their spouse, the number of their children, or their lack of employment. Despite the apparent 'deservingness' of widows, churchwardens measured their length of residence in the parish in one last test of worthiness. The parish's vestry minutes between 1616 and 1620 listed the poor in receipt of bequests under churchwardens' discretion: 189 gifts to women, in gowns and £17 1s 10d, and 118 gifts to men, in gowns and £10 5s 10d.[129] Many of these individuals were also described in the sequence of recipients from the churchwardens' accounts. Others were other widows, goodwives and goodmen, the aged and impotent poor themselves.

Parochial oversight of the living arrangements of deserving widows, goodwives, goodmen or other pensioners, another aspect of regulation, may have especially burdened poor women. Poor female pensioners needed lodgers to supplement alms, due to the inadequacy of relief or employment in meeting needs, but the city and parishioners cracked down on the practice.[130] Older male and female pensioners often lived in property belonging to the parish, where they sometimes paid reduced rents. St Botolph's vestry, in 1606, outlined new rules for those receiving parish aid: 'the same day it was agreed that noe poore of the p[a]rishe receiving pencon or almes weeklye shall have any pencon or almes payed by the church wardens or overseers for the poore yf they be found to intertaine inmates lodgers or keepe their

---

[128] GL, MS 594/1, fols 11, 12, 21, 38, 5v, 40, 45. CLRO, Rep. 34, f. 21.

[129] GL, MS 4072/1, Part 1, fols 110v–127. On importance of residence, outside London: Barbara Wilkinson, '"The poore of the parish"', *Local Historian*, **16**, 1 (1984), pp. 21–3. On widows as deserving: Brodsky, 'Widows in Late Elizabethan London', pp. 123–4; Erickson, *Women and Property*, pp. 203, 227. The longer the poor remained on relief, the more difficulty they faced leaving it, in advanced age and with decreased opportunities: Wales, 'Poverty, poor relief and the life-cycle', p. 364.

[130] For example: CLRO, Rep. 27, f. 84; Rep. 28, fols 60, 271v. Actions of Privy Council to restrict new building and division of tenements: Ward, *Metropolitan Communities*, p. 17. Work of the aged: Pat Thane, *Old Age in English History: Past Experiences, Present Issues* (Oxford, 2000), pp. 89–114.

children sonnes or daughters eyther married or marriageable within their owne houses & dwellings'.[131] In 1598, St Michael's vestry gave Widow Eyre a house in the churchyard, on condition that 'none shall come into her house during her life to be chargeable to the p[a]rish'. Although this condition did not expressly forbid lodgers, it effectively prevented her from taking in poor, single women who might give birth to children who would be forever chargeable to the parish. Women like Widow Reading in St Michael's needed a nurse during the plague, paid for by the parish, as did Widow Stowton, who needed a 'keeper' during her later sickness.[132]

By restricting inmates and lodgers, parishes, London's government and Parliament confronted the difficulties inherent in London's population growth. Fire, disease, crime, vagrancy and illegitimacy constituted significant social ills and expenses for the growing city. The inadequacy of incomes pieced together through small, seasonal jobs and relief led some poor couples to crime, an illegal parallel to parochial provision of piece-meal employment and relief to the poor. Individual women and wives and husbands together turned to prostitution. The mid-sixteenth-century chronicles described men and women charged with bawdry. Machyn even reported a bawd whipped by a harlot behind a horse, with an 'old prostitute' leading the horse.[133] Churchwardens' accounts demonstrate that the alleys and side streets, with their high population of migratory poor, were prime areas for outbreaks of plague. Inmates and lodgers might also sell their own or stolen goods in pawn, a trade that parishes were supposed to regulate by 1589.[134]

As the vestry minutes of St Botolph and the actions of other parishes made plain, married or marriageable children were not welcome additions to pensioners' households. Children of reproductive age could add their own offspring to the rolls or create some of the same problems blamed on unrelated lodgers. Able-bodied children of pensioners could

---

[131] GL, MS 1453/1, f. 3.

[132] GL, MSS 4072/1, Part 1, f. 76; 4071/2, unfol. [1608/9], f. 37. Beginning of book unfoliated.

[133] Fabyan on banished bawd: *The Great Chronicle of London*, p. 289; Wriothesley on wife who committed adultery with gentleman, and who, with her husband, set their own daughter and 10–11 year-old maidservant in prostitution, *A Chronicle of England*, Vol. II, p. 52; Machyn described a man and woman paraded through London behind a cart, for bawdry, and other cases of bawdry, *The Diary of Henry Machyn*, pp. 98, 104, 107, 111, 112, 161 (whipping by harlot), 242; on bawdry: Gowing, *Domestic Dangers*, pp. 96–7.

[134] See churchwardens' attendance at Commissary Court for not presenting 'shopkepers in the pawne', GL, MS 4071/1, f. 131v.

divert relief meant for the aged and impotent poor – just as bastard-bearers did.[135] In 1585, St Michael's vestry ordered Goody Cherry to remove her married daughter from her house. Later, in 1597, the vestry instructed Goodwife Tompson to 'ride away' three boys, from parish and ward. In 1616, the vestry invited Widow Brayfield to move into Widow Markham's room, but stipulated that she 'should not any longer lodge nor suffer to abide with her in this parish her sonne and his wyfe not eyther of them'. A few weeks later the vestry granted her a weekly pension of 2s 6d, but reminded her to send her son and his wife away. Just as parishes and testators formalized agreements about apprentices and property with bonds and sureties, so they tried contracts to free themselves of poor families. The churchwardens in St Michael's gave £4 to a poor man and his wife, with a bond to release the parish from caring for their children. In another case, the parish simply paid a man 5s to 'avoid' a couple from the parish.[136]

The instances of married children moving in with their parents illustrates that families on the precarious lower rungs of the social ladder altered their living arrangements to meet the needs of elderly parents or of children trying to establish themselves in London. In forbidding marriageable children from rejoining pensioners' households, parish leaders undermined survival strategies of poorer families, both the ageing parent(s) and adult children. Ageing parents often needed their adult children's care and financial support, although details of the elderly's living arrangements are much debated.[137] Parochial pronouncements that poor men and women of marriageable age leave home likely retarded their marriage plans by making it harder to save for independent households. In 1604, stricter regulation of clandestine marriage attempted to discourage the poor from marrying without being settled in independent households, a goal made harder to reach by regulation

---

[135] Elizabeth's 1576 statute (18 Eliz. c.3) *For Setting of the Poor on Work, and for the Avoiding of Idleness* lambasted bastardy and the children left 'to the great Burden of the same Parishes and in defrauding of the Relief of the impotent and aged true Poor of the same Parish', all, incidentally, 'to the evil Example and Encouragement of Lewd Life'. Thanks to Dr Jessica Sheetz for this reference.

[136] GL, MSS 4072/1, Part 1, fols 33, 74, 109v, 110; GL, MS 4071/2. fols 10, 36.

[137] Laslett, 'The traditional English family and the aged in our society' in David D. Van Tassel (ed.), *Aging, Death and the Completion of Being* (Philadelphia, PA, 1979), pp. 97–113; Richard Smith, 'The structured dependence of the elderly as a recent development: some sceptical historical thoughts', *Ageing and Society* 4, 4 (1984), pp. 409–28; David Kertzer, 'Toward a historical demography of aging' in Kertzer and P. Laslett (eds), *Aging in the Past: Demography, Society, and Old Age* (Berkeley, CA, 1995), pp. 363–83; Richard Wall, 'Elderly persons and members of their households in England and Wales from preindustrial times to the present' in D. Kertzer and P. Laslett (eds), *Aging in the Past*, pp. 81–106.

of poorer households and families.[138] The few testamentary bequests for dowry funds could not help many poor women or couples.

Although the actions of the city and parish might have impeded marriages of ordinary and poor people, once made, parishes attempted to cement marriages among the poor. The salutary moral benefits of marriage were augmented by the social advantages of an intact family reliant on each other, rather than on parochial charity. In St Michael Cornhill, in 1613–14, for instance, churchwardens sought the husband of Goodwife Symes, a woman in 'greate wante' who often appeared in lists of the poor receiving testamentary bequests and parochial alms.[139] Finding her husband would keep the couple together and, importantly, would transfer the burden of care from her parish to her spouse.

Although parishes may also have desired to keep families together, abandoned wives and children, on their own, were judged deserving of relief. Edward Howe abandoned his wife Anne in 1591, so St Stephen's vestry gave her 20s.[140] In 1595, St Michael's vestry justified helping a woman and her many poor children because her 'lewd husband' had abandoned them.[141] In 1608–09, the parish began a long stretch of supporting Katherine Locksmith and her children, 'her husband beinge then gone from her'. The payments to the Locksmiths led the church-wardens to appeal to the Lord Mayor and Alderman to reduce the parish's contribution to the poor, out parishes of the city. By 1616, a cobbler from outside the parish kept the children Agnes and John Locksmith, while Joane lived with Goodwife Stamford, one of the usual cast of pensioners and recipients of outdoor relief in the parish. The churchwardens purchased fabric for a winding sheet for Agnes on 22 September 1617 for 18d, and paid 8s 9d for her burial in St Olave in Southwark, and bread, drink and rosemary for those in attendance. In 1618–19, the churchwardens successfully petitioned for John's entrance into Christ's Hospital, and made a series of final payments for shoes and clothing for Joane, suggesting that she entered service.[142]

---

[138] The London elite, who tended to arrange early marriages between their daughters and older men, may have expected the lower orders to do likewise: see Vivien Brodsky Elliott, 'Single Women in the London Marriage Market: Age, Status and Mobility, 1598–1619' in R.B. Outhwaite (ed.), *Marriage and Society: Studies in the Social History of Marriage* (New York, 1981), p. 89; Martin Ingram, 'The Reform of Popular Culture? Sex and Marriage in Early Modern England' in Barry Reay (ed.), *Popular Culture in Seventeenth-Century England* (London, 1985), pp. 144–5.

[139] GL, MS 4071/2, fols 23, 24.

[140] GL, MS 594/1, f. 19.

[141] GL, MS 4072/1, Part 1, f. 63.

[142] GL, MS 4071/2, fols 30v, 33, 37, 40v, 41. The previous year, John was still in petticoats: f. 37. [The beginning of this account is not foliated.]

In contrast to half-hearted efforts to find men who had abandoned their families, parishes often sought, and sometimes found, the mothers of foundlings. Searching for mothers of abandoned children developed as part of an overall pattern of stricter regulation of behaviour, with public discipline of digressions formalized on the parish level.[143] The presence of stocks at church doors, whipping posts nearby, and cages in parishes, reminded parishioners and visitors alike of the conditions of benevolence and the distinction between those deserving and undeserving of parochial aid. Thus, for parishioners, the older women who became pensioners contrasted with the disreputable women who wandered into parishes ready to give birth, or who secretly deposited their children before doorways and on church porches. Infants abandoned in these locations literally brought the issue of poverty into the domestic and religious space of the parish, reminding the wealthy and the comfortable of immorality and distress just around the corner from their homes and churches. Mothers or parents left foundlings at the doors of prominent citizens, such as the Lord Chief Justice in 1598, as if hoping to ensure care for the child.[144]

Not all foundlings were necessarily illegitimate children, but many were probably children born out of wedlock. The strain on parish resources added economic weight to the moral prescriptions about illegitimacy, further stigmatizing poor women. Women could conceal pregnancies from friends and neighbours, but only with some difficulty. Chronicles described the cases of infanticide uncovered by masters and mistresses, neighbours and city authorities. The gossip that circulated in crowded London, especially in the later part of the sixteenth century, enabled parishioners to inform searchers about women suspected of abandoning their children. Although Peter Laslett asserts that 'something like a sub-society of the illegitimacy-prone may have existed over time', these parish records reveal little about apprehended women that would allow proof.[145] Parochial stipulations that marriageable children

---

[143] Attack on illicit sex in 1570s becomes attack on disorderly poor: Slack, *From Reformation to Improvement*, p. 47.

[144] GL, MS 1454, Roll 98. On abandonment and patterns of parochial and institutional care: Fildes, 'Maternal feelings re-assessed', pp. 139–78.

[145] Abandonment and infanticide: *The Diary of Henry Machyn*, p. 298; *Chronicle of the Grey Friars*, p. 62; Mendelson and Crawford, *Women in Early Modern England*, p. 149; Gowing, 'Secret Births and Infanticide in Seventeenth-Century England', *PaP*, 156 (Aug. 1997), pp. 87–115; Peter C. Hoffer and N.E.H. Hull, *Murdering Mothers: Infanticide in England and New England, 1558–1803* (New York, 1981). Using gossip to maintain order: Archer, *Pursuit*, p. 77. Link between prostitution and illegitimacy, the repetition of family names in bastardy cases: Laslett, *Family Life*, p. 107. Cf. Ingram argues that changes in attitudes about sexual morality reflected an 'unexciting process of

leave their parents' home may have increased abandonment as well as retarded marriage plans.

Confinement in bridewells became a way of controlling and of punishing poor, pregnant women. 'Bridewell' originally referred to the house of correction in London, but became the generic term for all such institutions. Parishes petitioned the house of correction to take in poor sick or fallen women in the early seventeenth century and paid for warrants to carry destitute women delivered of children to Bridewell. One parish carried a woman to Bridewell, as she was about to give birth. Occasionally, before pregnancy and its spectre of two poor charges on the parish, churchwardens took pre-emptive action. Targeting poor women, whether old or young enough to bring poor infants on to the parish rolls, developed as poor relief became more formalized.[146] Parishes used their assessed contributions to hospitals to direct patients or inmates to them. Parishes also used cages to punish vagabonds and poor, wandering pregnant women, as in St Botolph's.[147] Cages, like pillories and whipping posts, offered public humiliation, but added other physical discomforts, like dizziness and nausea, to the men and women enclosed in the hanging, swinging contraptions.

In St Michael Cornhill between 1580 and 1620, churchwardens noted 12 abandoned children, in addition to the orphans and fatherless children they supported. The parish never sought fathers, or both parents, and in only three cases did they not seek the mother. In one of those three cases, an uncle deposited the child in the parish, with £5 for his care. Only twice, however, did the seekers hired by the parish find the mother. In 1618–19, the churchwardens paid 4s 'to him that brought word of the childs mother' and spent 6d to send her to Bridewell.[148] The outcome was undoubtedly the one desired by churchwardens: a diligent search, utilizing the gossip of early modern life in London, culminated in the woman's commitment to Bridewell for moral correction and the parish's release from financial responsibility for the poor child. Bridewell often tried to locate the father, with the help of the mother. Confine-

---

adaptation to economic conditions and to modifications in the social structure': 'The Reform of Popular Culture?', p. 159.

[146] Bridewell cases: GL, MS 1454, Roll 96; GL, MS 593/2, f. 137. Roberts believes that parishes recognized a woman as a 'deserving claimant' because of her restricted earning power and economic opportunities, but little evidence of that recognition of cold economic reality surfaces in these sources: Michael Roberts, 'Women and work in sixteenth-century English towns' in Penelope J. Corfield and Derek Keene (eds), *Work in Towns, 850–1850* (Leicester, 1990), p. 96.

[147] GL, MS 1454, Roll 98.

[148] GL, MS 4071/2, f. 24. Later accounts noted the burial of Martin(us) Tickford (elsewhere Titford): f. 28v. See also GL, MS 4071/2, f. 47.

ment and harsh treatment pressured women to divulge their partners' names or to develop more convincing accounts of seduction, shifting responsibility to selected men.[149] St Mary Woolnoth noted only one child, abandoned on the church bench, who was carried to Golding Lane, perhaps to a nurse or to the suspected mother. The churchwardens there, however, may have successfully transferred fiscal responsibility for foundlings from their own accounts to those of the collectors for the poor or of the poor box. St Mary Woolnoth also paid Mr Samwell for 'findinge out the woman that laide the childe in our street lately'.[150]

Over the same period in St Stephen's, at least ten foundlings were left in the small parish, in one case at the door of a prominent citizen. St Stephen's seemed less concerned with locating mothers or parents, its small size and relative wealth enabling it to nurse and train foundlings, as well as orphans. Churchwardens even paid a poor woman 2s 6d for notifying them of a child left in Bucklersbury Street. Twice the parish sought the parents of the children and once sought only the mother of children abandoned near prominent parishioners' doors. In one search for parents, the parish found only the mother, apprehended by two women paid 4s by the churchwardens. The 'yong chyld', Edward Stephens, put into service about four to five years later, was apparently not a newborn since William Dykinsene carried him along to help find his parents. Even as the older man searched for Edward Stephens's parents, the churchwardens laid out 5s for a woman in child bed in 1583.[151] Goodman Payne, for three days in 1584–85, searched alone for 'the mother of a poor childe'. In 1585–86, he went with another woman, carrying the child and seeking the mother.[152] In another case, the parish noted that the mother was sent to Bridewell. In the early seventeenth century, despite discrimination in relief and charity, churchwardens paid a warden to watch 'those that lay childred' in the parish, a reference to a woman's confinement around the birth of a child.[153]

---

[149] Bernard Capp, 'The double standard revisited: plebeian women and male sexual reputation in early modern England', *PaP*, **162** (Feb. 1999), pp. 75–6; Mendelson and Crawford, *Women in Early Modern England*, p. 148; Amussen, *An Ordered Society*, p. 112. Christ's Hospital plan to locate fathers of illegitimate children to support those children and the mothers through churching: Manzione, *Christ's Hospital*, pp. 56–8.

[150] GL, MSS 1002/1B, f. 351v; reference to separate accounts for collection in poor's box: f. 445v; 1002/1A, fols 305–10.

[151] GL, MS 593/2, fols 72, 83–83v. Majority of foundlings were <1 year old, but few were abandoned at birth. In addition, not just infants were abandoned: Fildes, 'Maternal feelings re-assessed', pp. 147–8.

[152] GL, MS 4071/1, fols 124, 125v.

[153] GL, MS 593/2, f. 119, 137. The exact number of foundlings is unclear.

In contrast to the treatment of poor and pregnant women in the small inner-city parish, the situation in St Botolph's, a large, extramural parish, highlights the intersection of population growth and poverty.[154] The vestry of St Botolph's without Aldersgate took a harsher line on pregnant women, passing an order to stem the tide of illegitimate or foundling children falling on parish shoulders at a time of economic constriction. The vestry proclaimed:

> The said daie and yeare [20 June 1596] it is ordered by consent of the whole p[a]rishe that if any inhabitant dwelling within this p[a]rishe doe receave or take into his or her howse any woman with childe, or Inmate whereby any suche woman shalbe delyv[er]ed of childe, whereby any charge may growe to the p[a]rishe as before this tyme is hathe ben very chargeable to the p[a]rishe or if any suche p[er]son shall receave any childe whereby the like charge may growe to the said p[a]rishe, that then every suche p[er]son shall stande charged w[i]th the kepinge of ev[er]y suche woman & childe and shall have ne releif of the p[a]rishe towards the same

The birth of a child on a parishioner's porch seems to have precipitated the severe, and contorted, statement. That child died, and the mother was sent to Bridewell by the churchwardens. Despite the proclamation, the churchwardens continued nursing foundling children, only twice searching for the mothers. Between 1596 and 1607, the parish provided for four foundlings: one who died, another who ran away, an abandoned and possibly older child, and one 'bastard' child. Besides the woman sent to Bridewell after being harboured by a parishioner, searchers never found other mothers. By 1609, the parish needed a loan of £6 13s 4d from the Court of Aldermen for relief of their poor.[155]

The pursuit of mothers of foundlings, and attempts to restrict pregnant women's temporary residence in parishes, attested to the growing preoccupation with women's morality and sexuality or sexual behaviour. Sexual relations between betrothal and the marriage ceremony in the sixteenth and seventeenth centuries seemed a part of popular culture. Although courts upheld expectations of sexual honour, the evidence of sexual activity outside marriage, from parochial accounts, highlights the disparity between prescriptive ideals and real life. A small or relatively stable community exerted pressure on betrothed men and women to fulfil the promise of marriage when pregnancy resulted. With greater mobility, however, partners more easily escaped community pressure

---

[154] The 'burgeoning' numbers of poor in extra-mural parishes: Archer, *Pursuit*, pp. 12–13.

[155] GL, MSS 1454, Rolls 96, 97, 98; 1453/1, f. 4. CLRO, Rep. 29, f. 149v. Increase in abandonment between 1590s and late seventeenth century: Fildes, 'Maternal feelings reassessed', pp. 141–3.

and abandoned their betrothed. Thus, immorality and illegitimacy strained parishes spiritually and financially. Parochial records focused more clearly on the wayward behaviour of disorderly poor women, since they bore the results of their pre-marital sexual activity publicly, as men did not. Middling or 'respectable' men may well have guarded their sexual reputations as diligently as many women did, but the costs of a blemished reputation for poor women were unmistakable. For poorer women, the loss of aid, of the help of a midwife during child-birth, and the uncertain future of their children impinged on their survival.[156]

Exemplary Christian charity and kindness to the poor, even in dis-criminating charity, outlived the formalization of relief by parish and state.[157] Accounts showed simultaneous benevolence and punishment in response to poverty. Expenditures for the burial of abandoned children and the poor exhibited the parish's preoccupation with the salvation of its inhabitants. The rhetoric of distressed preachers, whether about the poor or the ungodliness of most parishioners, served to focus individu-als on their faith and their salvation. Treatment of the poor constituted one factor in London's relative stability, despite rapid social, economic and religious change. The poor more easily became targets of social and moral control because of their dependence on the benevolence of indi-viduals and the parish, in comparison with the pre-Reformation religious houses and fraternities that aided the poor as a part of their duties and services. The poor no longer resembled Christ, but parishioners remem-bered their likeness to Lazarus.

Conclusion

Between 1580 and 1620, centralizing relief and, to a degree, testamen-tary charity in parishes allowed local social and political leaders to experiment with new schemes to inculcate work habits and rewards to alleviate poverty. Socially prominent testators also began to support Christ's Hospital with voluntary gifts, in addition to the assessment for the institution paid in the city. The focus on the problem of poverty – and the distinctions between deserving and undeserving poor – reflected contemporaries' sense that they were enduring a social crisis. The growth

---

[156] Capp, 'Double standard revisited', pp. 79–80; cf. Gowing, *Domestic Dangers*, pp. 111–14. On the withdrawal of help: Mendelson and Crawford, *Women in Early Modern England*, p. 148; Gowing, 'Secret Births and Infanticide,' pp. 100, 103.

[157] Similarly, charitable, Christian practices, especially visiting and aiding the sick, ran afoul of official quarantine orders during plague: Slack, *The Impact of Plague*, p. 232.

of London's population, sporadic economic downturns, and a perception of worsening social conditions contributed to this distress. London shared a grave concern with order with other European cities of the sixteenth and seventeenth centuries. The religious change that encouraged greater discrimination among the poor, along with the demographic change that necessitated it, forced parishes and individual testators to focus on the behaviour of the poor.

Preoccupation with the morality and 'lifestyle' of needy men and women led to gender changes in the provision of charity and relief. Hints of narrowing roles for middling and wealthy women appear in the growing reliance on churchwardens, vestrymen and ministers to identify and to distribute charity among the deserving poor. On the other end of the charitable exchange, the impoverished women who gave birth without husbands or families nearby, who abandoned their children, or who were sent to Bridewell, focused moral scrutiny on women and their biological roles. These twin developments are interrelated: slow withdrawal from public charitable acts distanced respectable women from those of ill fame or sexual reputation. Dame Ramsey makes a notable exception to the trend in these parishes, with her cultivation of a pious and charitable reputation, linked even in death, to the hospital for fatherless children. As Stow related, however, Dame Ramsey made her initial *inter vivos* gift of land she had inherited by the consent of her still-living husband.[158]

Although the poor were evolving into a socially and morally distinct group, rich and poor interacted within the framework of older traditions based on mutual interests. Reciprocal aspects of these social relations weakened, however. Increasingly, the wealthy offered aid in return for deference or material service from the poor. Contemporaries expressed a reluctance to abandon earlier forms of exchange, witnessed by the persistence of doles, mourning processions and casual relief. These hold-overs of private practice from the late medieval or pre-Reformation period attested to the survival of aspects of traditional piety. Bequests to the poor in wills, albeit more often to a list of named and worthy individuals, stressed lingering notions of pre-Reformation charity, as well as 'modern' beneficence to the poor. The conjunction of economic concerns and religious changes made the poor a susceptible target for regulation, but had not yet broken the pious and charitable connection between rich and poor in life, and in death.

---

[158] Morley, p. 141.

CHAPTER SIX

For the most need:
comparative views of reform

London shared a fear of disorder and a tendency towards discrimination in charity with Protestant and Catholic cities in Europe in the sixteenth and seventeenth centuries. Common pressures – inflation, disease, population growth – perceptions of disorder, and religious change led to the separation of the deserving from the undeserving poor and the reform of relief throughout Europe. Material factors help to explain contractions in relief and charity, but social and religious attitudes about the nature of the poor and the purpose of charity also make sense of widespread reform that stretched into the seventeenth century. Differences in the roles of men and women relating to charity and relief, however, distinguished English and Continental practices, as did the English innovations of compulsory rates and workhouses.[1]

The period spanned by England's Reformation, into the early seventeenth century, wrought great changes in the lives of Londoners. The population of London quadrupled between 1500 and 1600 and doubled again by 1650, making intimate knowledge of the lives and reputations of the poor, a pre-Reformation goal as well, more difficult to attain. Charity and poor relief in the city, whether voluntarily supported through last wills or involuntarily paid for through parish rates, showed inhabitants' responses to new problems. Charity survived the Reformation, although altered by it and by social changes in early modern England, but by the late seventeenth century, as Slack argues, it would simply supplement relief.[2] Despite the city's growth and discrimi-

---

[1] On poverty and charity: Cohn, *The Cult of Remembrance*; Kingdon, 'Social welfare in Calvin's Geneva'; Norberg, *Rich and Poor in Grenoble*; Pullan, 'Catholics and the poor in early modern Europe'; Jütte, *Poverty and Deviance*; Hufton, *The poor of eighteenth-century France*; Flynn, *Sacred Charity*; Slack, *Poverty and Policy*; Fideler, 'Poverty, policy and providence'; Heal, *Hospitality*. On 'discernible connections' between 'fluctuations' in charity alongside 'fluctuations' in economy: McCants, *Civic Charity*, p. 16. On relation between moral reform and demographic distress or religious change: Spufford, 'Puritanism and Social Control?' pp. 48ff; Slack, *From Reformation to Improvement*, pp. 32–3, 46–7; McIntosh, *Controlling Misbehavior*, pp. 200–208. English innovations: Slack, *From Reformation to Improvement*, p. 21; McIntosh, 'Local Responses to the Poor', p. 213.

[2] Slack, *Poverty and Policy*, p. 171. See also Archer, *Pursuit*, pp. 168–9.

nation, donors, and the parochial leaders administering rates and bequests attempted to maintain traditional face-to-face almsgiving, since
older notions of obligation and compassion to poor neighbours still
motivated Londoners to give. Parishes and testators hence increasingly
focused on the poor within parochial limits or sheltered in institutional
walls and spent less on the unknown poor scattered throughout the
city.[3]

The pre-Reformation testamentary emphasis on the 'wealth' or 'health'
of donors' souls shifted towards a post-Reformation focus on the 'most
need' of charitable recipients. Although discrimination existed in medieval charity, scrutiny of the poor intensified in the sixteenth century.
This long evolution would end with the concentration on the public
good and the effect of charity on the recipient, rather than the donor,
common to the eighteenth century. Although Jordan argued that
secularization explained this change, '"God mattered"' in the sixteenth
and seventeenth centuries and therefore the involvement of the secular
government cannot alone account for new attitudes. Perhaps the change
encouraged secularization, rather than the other way around.[4] Testators' bequests to the poor and to their business associates, neighbours,
friends and family furthered their pious intentions, without mention of
purgatory or souls' health. Londoners interwove their religious aims
with the needs of their commonwealth and community, often refusing
to separate pious and political or social goals. The events of the sixteenth and seventeenth centuries, despite the doctrinal differences of the
dominant religions, highlighted the connections between piety and political and social order.

Charity and relief, revealed through individuals' last wills and testaments and churchwardens' accounts and vestry minutes, show the
concentric changes in personal lives, in local settings, and in the country
at large. In their response to the religious and economic changes of the

---

[3] Population of 50 000 at 1500; 400 000 at 1650: Finlay, *Population and Metropolis:
The Demography of London, 1580–1650* (Cambridge, 1985), p. 51. Evolution from
voluntarism to obligation: F.G. Emmison, 'Care of the Poor in Elizabethan Essex: Recently Discovered Records', *Essex Review*, 62 (1953), p. 9; charity as a secular concern:
Elfrieda Dubois, 'Almsgiving in Post Reformation England', *History of European Ideas*,
9, 4 (1988), p. 489; survival of 'social economy': John Walter, 'The Social Economy of
Dearth in Early Modern England' in Walter and Roger Schofield (eds), *Famine, Disease
and the Social Order in Early Modern Society* (Cambridge, 1989), p. 127; Paul Slack,
From Reformation to Improvement.

[4] 'Public good': Andrew, *Philanthropy and Police*, p. 5. Secularization: Jordan, *The
Charities of London, 1480–1660*, pp. 22, 49, 68, and throughout; cf. Haigh, *English
Reformations*, p. 285; Sommerville, *The Secularization of Early Modern England*, p.
179. On broader criticisms of Jordan's studies, see Archer, *Pursuit*, pp. 163–5.

sixteenth century, testators turned to familiar social groups, like house-hold and craft, to spread their testamentary bequests. The parish responded in a similar manner, focusing on those linked to it by birth or former service. National leaders – Parliament, monarch, military offic-ers – had their own goals for parochial relief and individual charity, goals which sometimes contradicted local practice. Londoners looked outside the city, and England, for more of their business ventures and potential outlets to ease the burden of poor relief, but they looked to a tighter circle of neighbours, craft brothers and sisters, and family and friends in making their final bequests.

The parish and its sources

By the 1620s, parochial officers performed increasingly demanding administrative tasks, particularly relating to poverty and poor relief.[5] Changes in the sources – in the nature and purpose of churchwardens' accounts and vestry minutes – and the refinement of the duties of parochial officers between 1500 and 1620 reflected the reliance on parishes to administer the developing Poor Law. Accounts and min-utes detailed parish receipts and expenses related to poverty and social order, although not to the exclusion of disbursements relating to religious bequests and complying with Reformation injunctions. Tes-tamentary changes mirrored the new parochial responsibilities in Reformation London, demonstrating the overlap of informal and for-mal solutions to the problem of poverty.

The roles and responsibilities of parishes and their officers had been evolving since their origins in the medieval period, but the religious and social circumstances of the sixteenth and seventeenth centuries wrought particular changes.[6] The late medieval parish obviously played a part in the cultural lives of towns and rural communities, with lay devotions and folk practices lovingly remembered by the likes of Roger Martyn, but the post-Reformation parish continued to shape the social and cultural experiences of the early modern English. Without over-romanticizing the cohesiveness of the late medieval 'community', the early modern years show the loss of traditional cultural practices that once brought parishes together.[7] The course of reform removed tradi-

---

[5] 'The most dramatic transformation in parish operations, however, occurred in the final area to be discussed here, "social relief"': Gibbs, 'New duties', p. 173.

[6] Gibbs, 'New duties', pp. 163–77.

[7] Martyn is often used as a jumping off point for analysis of the Reformation as well as for the compilation of documents pertaining to it: as excerpted in Cressy and Ferrell,

tional parochial duties relating to the remembrance of the souls of the dead and transformed those relating to the commemoration and burial of the dead in a country that officially denied purgatory. Lay piety still centred on the parish, though without the organizations and institutions which once fostered popular devotions to saints and holy figures. Inhabitants of London found new ways or revived forms of old ways both to celebrate 'community' and to accentuate social difference among parishioners.[8] Surviving English pew assessments made obvious the social ranking of seating arrangements: the first numbered pews in St Michael's, for instance, had the highest fees and were occupied by prominent parishioners.[9] The loss of church and chantry property and the expense of renovations throughout the 'Reformations' weakened parishes financially, leaving some wealthier citizens to lead the way in the decoration of churches and in the provision of charity and relief. The donations and bequests related to 'superstitious' purposes that dried up in the Reformation left parishes more reliant on collections and rates over the course of the sixteenth century.[10]

Rates and penalties for moral infractions suggested that community ties had been loosened, to the detriment of older styles of face-to-face charity and voluntary giving, and that social difference was emphasized. Ecclesiastical injunctions and government statutes attempted to substitute newer collections and fines to meet the shortfall precipitated by the end of traditional voluntary and involuntary donations to the church fabric and to the poor. Despite injunctions instructing ministers to encourage testators to replace their gifts to the high altar with those to the parish poor box, however, gifts to the box never approached the testamentary remembrance of forgotten tithes. Parish poor boxes, though, must have drawn lifetime gifts and holiday contributions, since churchwardens' accounts and vestry minutes recorded funds lent or given out

---

Religion and Society, pp. 11–13; Haigh, *English Reformations*, pp. 1–3; 'Introduction' in *The Parish*, p. 7, and footnote 10; Jones, 'Living the Reformations', p. 286. On continued importance of parish church for pious bequests, see also Hickman, 'From Catholic to Protestant', p. 130. Phythian-Adams argues that when the secular half of the calendar triumphed over the sacred half, 'the claims of community ... were yielding first place to class loyalties': 'Ceremony and the citizen', p. 80. On debate over 'community': Tittler, *The Reformation and the Towns*, pp. 13–17; Kowaleski (ed.), 'Vill, Guild, and Gentry'.

[8] See Margo Todd, 'Profane Pastimes and the Reformed Community: The Persistence of Popular Festivities in Early Modern Scotland', *JBS*, **39**, 2 (April 2000), pp. 123–56; Archer, 'Nostalgia', pp. 21–7.

[9] GL, MS 4072/1, Part 1, f. 102v. Scarisbrick on pew hierarchy: *Reformation and the English People*, pp. 173–4.

[10] Pearl discusses the tension between the parishes' fiscal self-government and the city's need to centralize the apparatus of relief: 'Puritans and Poor Relief', p. 214.

of the parish poor box.[11] Boxes also stored the fines collected under a new parochial regime. St Michael's vestry, for instance, fined those who did not sit in their own pews during the service and levied graduated fees for repeated offences. With allowances for those moving 'the more better to heare', the fine enforced new seating plans that trumpeted the parish's social hierarchy, but directed aid to the poor when parishioners transgressed that order.[12] Although new floor plans emphasized social difference, churchwardens ritually diminished difference by using fines for relief.

Shifts in burial practices also signalled an alteration in the relationship between individual parishioners and their parishes. Population growth led to the overcrowding of old burial sites, but a religious critique of contemporary practices also helped to undermine the formerly close bond between parishes and their dead parishioners' bodies. Fewer testators identified the parish of burial and the placement of their grave as the sixteenth century progressed, breaking one of the parish's traditional duties relating not only to remembrance of the dead, but to housing the dead.[13] Crowded burial conditions within parishes and the city as a whole undoubtedly helped to shape this change in practice. In 1589, St Michael's converted its former charnel house, a vault under the south aisle used to store coals, into a burial space. Under a stone, the vestry fitted a 'loope hole w[i]th a planck ov[er] it to let doune a coffen'. Just two years later the vestry proclaimed that no more could be buried in the 'newe vaulte' and further that every new burial should be three feet in the ground. The vestry repeated the order about that vault, or another, in 1607. By 1612 the vestry ordered a register of burial places 'to avoyde anoyances that maye happen in openinge the ground' as the parish struggled to find room for its own dead.[14] Alongside overcrowding of available space, puritan preachers criticized the pompous display inherent in large burial processions and extensive services.[15]

---

[11] Culmination of Poor Law in 1598 (39 Eliz. c.3); Injunctions of 1547 (*VAI*, II, p. 127). Account of 55s 9d out of poor box and its use to set an orphan, born in the parish, into Christ's: GL, MS 1002/1A, f. 261.

[12] GL, MS 4072/1, Part 1, f. 1 (1563); repeated f. 15.

[13] As Kümin writes in his summary of the history of the parish in Europe, 'The *raison d'être* of the local ecclesiastical network was to ensure an adequate administration of sacraments. Baptism and burial stood out as crucial parochial rites, with the cult of the dead often seen as the main spiritual focus of the community': 'The English parish in a European perspective' in *The Parish*, p. 21.

[14] GL, MS 4072/1, Part 1, unfol. and fols 46v, 53, 99, 104v. Harding argues that changes in willmaking and executorship accounted for the change in burial preferences in wills, not necessarily the Reformation: 'Burial Choice and Burial Location', p. 122.

[15] Hickman, 'From Catholic to Protestant', pp. 122–4.

The social pressures of the sixteenth century – London's growth and the perceived worsening of poverty and disorder – also reshaped parochial responsibilities to the living. Rates supported lectures and sermons, maintained and renovated churches and income-generating parochial property, and sustained relief of the poor. The cumulative poor laws, relying on parish implementation and oversight, grew out of local practice and the long-standing association between pious bequests to parishes and the dispersal of charity. These municipal solutions, however, coalesced under churchwardens, men who exercised authority within the parish.[16] Statutory reform shaped early religious change, but the 'vitality' of the parish ensured lay involvement in recasting society in the aftermath.[17] Parochial anticipation of and response to formal proclamations and briefs, as well as informal attitudes about the poor and the alleviation of poverty, illustrates the importance of the parish in meeting social demands.

Thus while the pre-Reformation parish oversaw religious practices and controlled the money behind them, the seventeenth-century parish increasingly implemented social policy and helped maintain order within London. The parish became the mechanism of collection and charity through the developing national Poor Law. The use of rates and fines to the poor box threatened to make charity, for certain 'donors', at worst a punishment and at least an involuntary contribution to the social fabric. Churchwardens recorded the amounts gathered in the poor box, although rarely their provenance, and parishioners relied on churchwardens to oversee both the collection and distribution of the funds. Increased dependence on parochial administration and churchwardens' oversight meant that formal relief and informal charity, even if in line with the expectations and guidance of 'all' or the 'better sort' in parishes, minimized contact between individual donors and the poor. Limiting contact between donors and recipients may have made discrimination in charity easier, allowing judgment without face-to-face refusals.

The parish had long been the principal locus of charity and poor relief, but the wills of these Londoners show that alongside greater discrimination came greater reliance on parishes' schemes for relief. The

---

[16] Slack notes local initiatives alongside the social policies of the central government: 'Poverty in Elizabethan England', *History Today*, **34** (Oct. 1984), pp. 6–7. Role of the parish and churchwardens: Gibbs, 'New duties', p. 173. On financial self-government of parishes: Pearl, 'Puritans and Poor Relief', p. 214.

[17] Barron notes the 'vitality' of parish life before the Reformation and credits that characteristic for the spread of the Reformation, if not its genesis: 'The Parish Fraternities of Medieval London', pp. 36–37.

involuntary assessments and fines directed to the poor slowly altered charitable attitudes. Testators transferred wealth, that at one time would have commemorated Christian souls and celebrated the piety (and social prominence) of individuals and their lineage through endowments and monuments in parish churches and religious houses, to family and associates. Testators focused burgeoning non-pious gifts on their own families, kin, servants, apprentices and craft, not to the larger society, a trend Jack Goody noted in Protestant Europe.[18] The unknown poor, unattached to corporate or familial groups, fell increasingly to the parish's responsibility. Civic proclamations ordering the relief of poorer parishes and post-Reformation hospitals perhaps reflected widespread reluctance to aid the anonymous poor as well as the uneven experience of economic growth in the sixteenth and seventeenth centuries.[19]

By the late sixteenth century, the churchwardens' accounts and vestry minutes demonstrated this preoccupation with issues of order and relief. The selective survival of these records, and their importance in accounting for a parish's financial resources, foster the impression of a crisis in early modern London. Parishes for which records do not survive no doubt similarly concentrated on maintaining order. Other civic records, like those of the Court of Aldermen, pay careful attention to a range of urban ills: poor parishes, overcrowded houses and streets, the poor, and disorder in the city, the latter often blamed expressly on the poor. The churchwardens and 'most part of the parish' that made up the vestries increasingly focused on aged pensioners, foundlings, young men desiring to study divinity at Oxford or Cambridge and poor women. The latter, of child-bearing age, particularly raised the ire of churchwardens who sought to move them out of their parishes.

Changes in record keeping reflect these new parochial responsibilities centred on charity and relief. The contrast between the late fifteenth-century and early seventeenth-century churchwardens' accounts of St Botolph's provides one example of this shift. The roll covering 1496–97 tracked obits and the fees related to the church fabric and the cleanliness of the parish, such as payments to the scavenger, the organ-keeper

---

[18] Less personal and family property was alienated to the church in Protestant areas of Europe: Jack Goody, *The Development of the Family and Marriage in Europe* (Cambridge, 1983), p. 166. Mauss urged modern societies to emulate the Arthurian round table, where all became rich and happy for sharing the 'common store of wealth': *The Gift*, p. 83.

[19] In response to a petition from the churchwardens and overseers of the poor in St Sepulchre's, the Court of Aldermen ordered the officers in St Stephen Walbrook, St Dionis Backchurch, and St Olave's in Hart Street to help relieve the poor in the poorer parish: CLRO, Rep. 32, fols 157–157v. The 1598 Poor Law provided for rating parishes to aid other parishes.

and the person washing the church linens. The accounts concentrated on rents collected for the use of church services and the diligent fulfilment of obit requests. Churchwardens fined parishioners (who were also householders) for not attending the 'yielding up' of the year's account, demonstrating the importance and public airing of record-keeping in the late medieval parish. The roll from 1601–02, on the other hand, detailed payments to the readers, parson and minor officers (clerk and sexton) and recounted the burials of parishioners, but also recorded collection of rates for the poor and maimed soldiers in compliance with Elizabethan statutes. The churchwardens covered the legal costs of ensuring that a legacy left to the poor reached the parish, underscoring how years of fluctuating religious policies that affected provision for the poor made parochial records valuable as legal documents.[20]

Even in the longer and more detailed parochial accounts of the later sixteenth century, however, lifetime giving to the poor remains an elusive category of charity and makes attitudes to the poor less clear. The parish of St Margaret's in Westminster, marked by a wide range of social groups, demonstrates that half of the relief to the poor originated in voluntary, lifetime contributions. The assessed rate within the parish did not suffice to relieve the poor, a problem common to urban parishes.[21] Most indiscriminate or lifetime giving escapes documentation, though local legislation tried to regulate indiscriminate giving and curtail begging and vagrancy. London civic leaders established hours for begging, when the poor could call on rich Londoners in their homes, before finally prohibiting it outright.[22] Practice regarding lifetime bequests or donations might have mitigated the discrimination inherent in parochial relief and testamentary bequests, but parochial and individual practice seemed to parallel one another.

The accounts demonstrate 'community' concerns, moulded by the influence of socially prominent men who served as churchwardens, vestrymen and auditors, and of parsons or ministers with particular

---

[20] GL, MS 1454, Rolls 17, 100. On written and oral traditions: Foster, 'Churchwardens' accounts of early modern England and Wales', p. 85.

[21] St Mary Woolnoth churchwardens referred to a 'man unknowen' who gave money for the poor, possibly a lifetime gift: GL, MS 1002/1B, f. 367. On 'elusive' informal relief: Walter, 'The Social Economy of Dearth', p. 112; Archer, *Pursuit*, pp. 178–9. Cf. Merritt, 'Religion, Government, and Society', pp. 287–8.

[22] In the 1598 statute (39 Eliz. c.3), only the poor who asked for food at appointed times were allowed to beg, a provision not repeated in the 1601 law (43 Eliz. c.2); Slack, *The English Poor Law*, pp. 52–3. On control of begging and focus on residence: Walter, 'The Social Economy of Dearth', pp. 115, 125. Slack shows that the 'dangerous poor' were by definition 'rootless, masterless and homeless': *Poverty and Policy*, p. 91.

religious or social goals. Of their own volition or under the order of the parish in unrecorded sessions or conversations, these officials took greater administrative responsibility for disbursing relief and discriminating among the poor. The tensions within the parish – and the hints of negotiations to resolve ideological conflicts that occurred outside written records – can be seen in the distribution of charity to select strangers and the parochial impotent or aged poor and the occasional audit's condemnation of such an 'evil precedent'.[23] St Stephen's parson attended to converted Protestants and refugees of Catholic and Islamic foes in the early seventeenth century by ordering relief for a 'blackamor' and a number of poor 'Grecians' escaping Ottoman slavery.[24] In other cases, churchwardens fulfilled bequests or mimicked the charity outlined in wills for the deserving poor. An executrix's male representative distributed alms to a group of named poor and held a dinner for other neighbours in a local inn in fulfilment of her husband's final wishes. St Michael's, from about 1605 forward, received a number of bequests from parishioners that the vestry granted to a repetitive list of needy men and women. Similarly, St Stephen's helped a familiar group of widows, men and scholars through the early seventeenth century.[25] The vestry minutes ranged from sketches of decisions to fuller descriptions of petitions and disputes within and between parishes and individuals.

The office of churchwarden changed alongside its records, apparently becoming more onerous since parishioners and officials, both royal and ecclesiastical, expected more careful accounts and parish registers.[26] The office, at least in London, seemed to be linked to one's status within the parish in the late medieval and early modern period. In the 1520s, the illustrious organ-maker John Howe succeeded his father and a business partner in the family firm in the office of churchwarden in St Stephen's, attesting to the family's position in the parish.[27] In the later sixteenth century, the administrative demands of the job became greater. In fact, St Mary's related that one of their churchwardens had been found guilty of negligence regarding his office by a 'spirituall court' and fined 20s. In the 1580s, a churchwarden in St Michael's also served as an alderman's deputy, suggesting that successful office-holders could

---

[23] Schen, 'Constructing the Poor', pp. 454–5.

[24] GL, MS 593/2, fols 106, 120v. Schen, 'Constructing the Poor', pp. 454–5.

[25] GL, MSS 1002/1B, f. 423v; 4072/1, Part 1, fols 95–95v ff.; 593/2.

[26] For example, on the injunctions to keep registers: Coster, 'Popular religion and the parish register', pp. 97–8; Kümin, The Shaping, pp. 243–5.

[27] John How, 1518; John Clymhoo, 1534–35; John How, 1535–36 (accounts did not survive): GL, MS 593/1, unfol. On the Howes, see also Kümin, 'Masses, morris and metrical psalms', p. 223.

progress into positions of greater authority.[28] The greater survival of parochial records after mid-century testifies to the heightened attention to the parchment and paper books under the churchwardens' oversight.[29] The sale of church implements and vestments during Edward's reign often included the names of purchasers and sometimes the names of original donors, to record the source of the items, to prove the church no longer owned them, and to account for money and goods. References to preparations for visitations by bishops and archbishops and to suits over concealed or disputed property after the Reformation, emphasize that churchwardens and parishioners used these sources to make legal and ecclesiastical defences.[30] The power of (some) parishioners to audit accounts yearly, and the audit of all records of collectors for the poor by Christ's governors, also encouraged churchwardens and other parochial officers to collect rates and to act according to the wishes of a wider circle of citizens and parishioners.[31]

In the seventeenth century, parishioners and city inhabitants began to pay fines to remove themselves from consideration for various parochial and civic offices. Parishioners, and strangers or elderly inhabitants, may have wanted to avoid the demands of being churchwarden, but parishes may also have come to see their unwanted appointments as easy fund-raising. St Stephen's collected £10 from Thomas Langton to free him from all offices in the precinct and £10 from Henry Andrews for refusing to serve as churchwarden in the same year.[32] The fines in St Stephen Walbrook could cover the salary of the clerk (£10) or sexton

---

[28] GL, MS 1002/1B, f. 351. Anthony Soda was collector for the poor in 1585 and churchwarden in 1588: GL, MS 4072/1, Part 1, f. 34; Overall, *Churchwardens' Accounts*, p. 177.

[29] On survival of accounts and registers: Foster, 'Churchwardens' accounts of early modern England and Wales', esp. pp. 76–85; Coster, 'Popular religion and the parish register', pp. 98–9.

[30] GL, MS 593/2, fols 17–18. St Stephen's case of concealed property appeared in the accounts of 1559–60, continuing through the 1560s. The wealthy, well-ordered parish could turn back to earlier accounts in their answers and counter-arguments. GL, MS 593/2, fols 48v–50v, 1563/4; Add. Mss. 284, 281, 280. Concealed property related to lights and obits,1559–60: GL, MS 1454, Roll 65; typical visitation expenses: GL, MS 593/2, f. 60; ceiling of 13s 4d on costs of visitation (i.e., dinner): GL, MS 1454, Roll 71.

[31] On Christ's governors' audit of collectors' accounts: Archer, *Pursuit*, p. 160.

[32] GL, MS 593/2, f. 127v. (1616–17). Also GL, MS 593/2, fols 134, 138, and occasional references through 1620s and 1630s. St Botolph's also frequently collected fines, though lower ones (£3 6s 8d., £4 10s) than those gathered in wealthier St Stephen's: GL, MS 1454, Roll 104; GL, MS 1453/1, fols 4v, 6v. See also Kümin, *The Shaping*, p. 245; Scouloudi, *Returns of Strangers*, pp. 34–5. To be excused as collector for the poor: GL, MS 1002/1B, f. 400; to be excused as constable and from sitting on wardmote inquest: GL MS 1002/1B, f. 406.

(£6 13s 4d), though some were granted expressly to the poor. Strangers and those of advanced age avoided parochial offices, like the merchant and stranger Frederick Federigo, who paid £4 towards repairing the church so as not to serve as constable of the parish.[33] The bookseller John Edward paid £3 for not being constable, even though 'hee is lame & impotent' and presumably a poor choice for the office anyway. Later, he found himself in trouble for refusing to serve as churchwarden, relenting only when the parish threatened to treat him as a stranger if he did not take the office. A 74-year-old man gave a 'free gift' of £5 to be excused forever from the office of churchwarden.[34]

The sporadic mention of ongoing suits or disputes, the idiosyncratic nature of accounts compiled by revolving churchwardens of uncertain diligence, and the reactive ways that parishioners used accounts to circumvent potential problems with those outside the parish do offer up warnings about the use of churchwardens' accounts by historians. Accounts give a partial picture despite the appearance of meticulous recording within them. A plague year injunction against the distribution of money to the poor on festivals and eves of holidays, for instance, illustrated a casual custom of informal relief not recorded in formal tabulations of relief and charity. Only the severity of disease and new efforts to combat plague drew attention to the practice and brought it into the accounts.[35] Records can also give an incomplete picture, even a false impression of a parish. St Stephen's operated in debt sporadically in the late 1590s and into the seventeenth century, with parishioners in arrears for clerks' wages and lecture funds, but still paid substantial wages and pensions.[36]

Parishes developed more regular accounting practices while more individuals began to leave wills that survived, making late sixteenth- and early seventeenth-century testaments more available to historians.[37]

---

[33] GL, MS 1002/1B, f. 372v. He was also excused 'during his abode' from serving as churchwarden: GL, MS 1002/1B, f. 413. See also GL, MS 1002/1B, fols 400, 406.

[34] GL, MS 1453/1, fols 3v, 16–16v, 30v.

[35] GL, MS 4072/1, Part 1, f. 60.

[36] GL, MSS 4072/1, Part 1, f. 60; 593/2, f. 90v (debt of £13 13s. 10d.); 593/2, f. 92 (surplus of £3 4s 10d); 593/2, f. 94 (debt of £20 14s 4d); 593/2, f. 95v (surplus of £69 19s 1d). Arrearages did not necessarily include women. Ronald W. Herlan ascribes the lack of women assessed for poor rates in Bristol after 1637 to pre-industrial patriarchalism and 'women's rather inconsequential socio-economic status': 'Relief of the Poor in Bristol from Late Elizabethan Times until the Restoration Era', *Proceedings of the American Philosophical Society*, **126**, 3 (1982), p. 225.

[37] Peter Spufford, 'A Printed Catalogue of the Names of Testators' in in G.H. Martin and Peter Spufford (eds), *The Records of the Nation: The Public Record Office, 1838–1988, the British Record Society, 1888–1988* (Woodbridge, 1990), pp. 167–213.

The practice reflects the growth in wealth in London, the society's greater attention to documentation of property and the facts of the lifecycle, and even the social pretensions of prosperous early-modern Londoners. Testaments, like parochial records, evinced shifting priorities in the city. The content of later testaments necessarily mirrored the post-Reformation doctrine of salvation through faith, rather than through intercession or good works, which in pre-Reformation wills entwined gifts to the poor with endowments for the soul of the testator and his or her friends and relatives, and oftentimes 'all Christian souls'. The testaments bridging Edward's radical reforms, Mary's restoration and Elizabeth's early years manifest uncertainty, and offer fewer idiosyncratic donations or preambles, while gradually directing more bequests to the poor. After 1580, however, the uncertainty of those middle years had 'settled', at least officially and in public testaments, into a pattern that emphasized help to the poor alongside greater bequests to friends, family and company members.

The peculiarities of London?

That London was an urban area – and a large and rapidly growing one – also helps to explain the parochial changes, not to mention the course of reform of religion and poor relief there. The peculiarities of London are important to bear in mind, but should not cause us to dismiss the historical lessons to be gleaned from this particular case. London's policies and inhabitants' actions, compared with those uncovered in studies of smaller towns and rural areas in England and on the Continent, show peculiarities and commonalities. London's humanist social policy, imitating the directives that established medical schools, created sumptuary legislation, and controlled vagrancy on the Continent, developed slowly over the sixteenth and seventeenth centuries in response to unique local and common problems.[38]

Parochial service and individual charity may have helped to paper over social and pious differences. Although the development of a more rigid social hierarchy may have been common in sixteenth- and seventeenth-century England, London's social and economic circumstances set the city apart. The mantle of parochial offices allowed citizens without vast fortunes to shape local policies of relief, as when the

---

[38] In particular, these represent Wolsey's efforts to 'put England on a par with other Renaissance states': Slack, *The Impact of Plague*, p. 201. Brigden on humanist city: 'Religion and Social Obligation', p. 71. See also Martha C. Skeeters, *Community and Clergy: Bristol and the Reformation, c.1530–c.1570* (Oxford, 1993), pp. 1–3.

reform-minded William Winthrop acted as collector for the poor before ultimately casting himself on the benevolence of the parish.[39] In other cases, like that of Sir Martin Bowes, social status buttressed the parochial influence of a man whose religious views ran towards traditional ones. For the zealous reformer and the mere conformist, service to the parish may have helped to smooth over potential religious controversies. Those areas outside London where ideals of hospitality may have survived longer enabled gentry or noble families and individuals to assume greater charitable control than they appeared to exercise in London. The 'shared outlook' of different social groups in Havering weakened after the medieval period, for example, resulting in greater social control by the elite. By 1620, a few powerful families exercised greater control over relief than churchwardens, even though parish authority had characterized sixteenth-century relief.[40] In seventeenth-century Norfolk, gentry largesse and voluntary contributions from lower down the social scale outpaced formal relief, although informal and formal relief were interrelated.[41]

On the other hand, London's characteristics, especially its size and restless growth, limited the folk traditions that commonly marked village life and helped to negotiate social difference. London parishes relied less on communal fundraising through these traditions to maintain the church and parish, outside services for the dead and remembrance of them and the acquisition of property, than did parishes elsewhere in England before the Reformation.[42] Thus lay parishioners in smaller towns and rural areas may have had more control over or even interest in their parishes' practices and groups. London's closeness to the national government no doubt 'encouraged' speedy conformity to directives regarding parochial worship, entertainments and property.[43] The lack of help ales in London also meant that aid from peers, a third way

---

[39] Wrightson and Levine, *Poverty and Piety in an English Village*, p. 43. Bremer suggests that Winthrop's financial support of reform may have contributed to his own collapse: 'William Winthrop', pp. 12–13.

[40] McIntosh, *A Community Transformed*, pp. 1–2, 287.

[41] Wales, 'Poverty, poor relief and the life-cycle', p. 359.

[42] Mediation of difference through voluntary gatherings and through charity: Rosser, 'Going to the Fraternity Feast: Commensality and Social Relations in Late Medieval England', *JBS*, **33**, 4 (Oct. 1994), pp. 430–46; Elaine Clark, 'Social Welfare and Mutual Aid in the Medieval Countryside', ibid., pp. 381–406. French emphasizes the greater involvement of lay parishioners in the diverse activities used for fundraising in rural parishes: 'Parochial fund-raising', p. 117. See also Alexandra F. Johnston and Sally-Beth MacLean, 'Reformation and resistance in Thames/Severn parishes: the dramatic witness' in *The Parish*, pp. 182–3; Brown, *Popular Piety*, p. 91; Bennett, 'Conviviality and Charity', pp. 19–24.

[43] Johnston and MacLean, 'Reformation and resistance', p. 196.

between the charity of the wealthy and the benevolence of the parish, had less of a chance to develop.[44] After the Reformation, London parochial officers collected rates, but rural parishes may not have.[45]

In addition to the limited opportunities for parishioners to join together despite differences, the perception of economic crisis weakened notions of mutual benefit among parishioners. London inhabitants believed that poverty was a worsening problem in their city, as seen in the estimated number of poor put forth by a former renter warden from Christ's, in which he emphasized the deserving.[46] Actually, they shared this impression with the inhabitants of smaller towns and rural areas throughout England. In their study of Terling, Wrightson and Levine found worsening poverty until the late seventeenth century.[47] McIntosh, Slack and Beier found an increase in poverty through the sixteenth century. No wonder parishes attempted to conceal property to conserve resources and rents for their myriad needs.[48] The response of London and other municipalities may have insulated England from upheaval, with well-organized loan and work schemes.[49] These forms of relief drew on local practice, including 'socially beneficial' schemes that had not been widespread in the sixteenth century. Statutory relief and private charitable bequests followed a parallel course into the seventeenth century in response to the problem of poverty.[50] London was not the only urban

---

[44] Bennett, 'Conviviality and Charity', p. 23.

[45] Bennett, 'Conviviality and Charity', p. 23; Slack, *Poverty and Policy*, p. 170.

[46] Three hundred fatherless children, 200 sore or sick, 350 poor men 'overburdened' with children, 400 aged men and women, 650 decayed householders and 200 idle vagabonds: Howes, 'Familiar and Frendely Discourse' in *TED*, Vol. 3, p. 418.

[47] Also 'increased social regulation, new forms of dependency and public humiliation and, for the most part, exclusion from an elite culture that was not only novel but aggressive': Wrightson and Levine, *Poverty and Piety in Terling*, p. 184.

[48] Marjorie McIntosh, 'Local responses to the poor in late medieval and Tudor England', *Continuity and Change*, 3, 2 (Aug. 1988), p. 210; increase in intensity of poverty and numbers of the poor through the sixteenth century: Slack, *Poverty and Policy*, p. 39; Beier, *Masterless Men*, p. 16. Farnhill, 'Religious policy and parish "conformity": Cratfield's lands in the sixteenth century' in *The Parish*, p. 218.

[49] On insulation from social revolution: Ronald W. Herlan, 'Relief of the Poor in Bristol from Late Elizabethan Times until the Restoration Era', *Proceedings of the American Philosophical Society*, **126**, 3 (1982), p. 212; on the law-abiding character of the British nation and its strong Constitution: E.M. Leonard, *The Early History of English Poor Relief* (New York, 1965), orig. 1900, p. vii.

[50] Change in charitable bequests toward the 'socially beneficial': McIntosh, *A Community Transformed*, pp. 276–9; 'setting the poor to work' had been noted in early studies: Emmison, 'The Care of the Poor in Elizabethan Essex', p. 27, and 'Poor Relief Accounts of Two Rural Parishes in Bedfordshire, 1563–1598', *Economic History Review* 3 (1931), p. 111; private charity followed the trends in parochial relief, especially regarding the provision of work: Ethel Hampson, *The Treatment of Poverty in Cam-*

area with puritan leanings that precipitated social control in seventeenth-century relief, for example the 'new zeal' of a 'Puritan oligarchy' in place after 1630 in Stratford-upon-Avon resulted in similar attempts to regulate morality and help the poor. Towns throughout England, including the city of London, experimented with municipal storehouses and work-houses more extensively in the seventeenth than the sixteenth century, when the shortcomings of the new relief system became apparent.[51]

Although all of England shared in the perception of worsening poverty, London's demographic growth created problems peculiar to the city. The migration that fuelled the city's growth between 1500 and 1620 strained parochial and civic resources and stoked ill-will toward 'vagrants'. As the largest city in England, London attracted people looking for work, especially as wages in London outpaced those in the countryside by the early seventeenth century. Howes noted that London was pestered not by its own poor: 'London can not relieve England'.[52] Extramural parishes saw great growth – and poverty – and certain parishes in the city's walls, especially by the river, experienced greater demands on poor relief. In 1580, as the period of rapid growth in London began, the Privy Council attempted to stop new building and the subdivision of houses.[53] Churchwardens and vestries limited parochial responsibility for inmates and lodgers to curtail the numbers of dependent poor. St Botolph's restricted married or marriageable children lodging with parents, hoping to cap the swelling of the roster of the parochial poor. The vestry in St Michael's threatened to stop renting

---

bridgeshire, 1597–1834 (Cambridge, 1934), p. 28; strength of local practice: Carol Moore, 'Poor Relief in Elizabethan England: A New Look at Ipswich', Proceedings and Papers of the Georgia Association of Historians, 7 (1986), pp. 98–119.

[51] J.M. Martin, 'A Warwickshire Market Town in Adversity: Stratford-upon-Avon in the Sixteenth and Seventeenth Centuries', Midland History, 7 (1982), p. 35; Slack on 'Godly Cities', in From Reformation to Improvement, pp. 29–52. For example outside London: Slack, 'Poverty and Politics in Salisbury, 1597–1666' in Peter Clark and Slack, Crisis and Order in English Towns, 1500–1700: Essays in Urban History (Toronto, 1972), pp. 180–83.

[52] Finlay, Population and Metropolis, pp. 7, 63; Rollison, 'Exploding England', p. 10. Beier sees migration and vagrancy as distinct, yet related: Masterless Men, p. 29; Rollison sees vagrancy laws as the attempt to control migration created by market contractions: 'Exploding England', p. 12, TED, Vol. 3, p. 425.

[53] Jones, 'London', p. 125. The estimated population of London in 1550 (70 000) meant that a great increase occurred over the next fifty years for the population to reach 200 000: Finlay, Population and Metropolis, p. 51; also see Slack on higher incidence of plague in suburbs after 1580, not during the 1563 plague, as a result of population growth and the actions of the Privy Council: The Impact of Plague, pp. 159, 207. Harding, 'Burial of the plague dead in early modern London', pp. 53–64, on-line at http://www.ihrinfo.ac.uk/cmh/epiharding.html

to individuals who entertained inmates or lodgers, again including grown children living with parents. In 1573, they warned that 'all suche Inmates as are received into the Tenements of the Churche shall presentlye be avoyded, or ellse the Tenants themselves for to be avoyded'.[54]

Evidence from churchwardens' accounts suggests that the apparent labour shortage had begun to improve by the early seventeenth century, but as population continued to rise so did unemployment. Even if contemporaries, or later historians, overstated the 'crisis' of the 1590s, those fearful contemporaries helped to shape parochial and testamentary practice.[55] London's hospitals showed signs that un- or underemployment was a problem in the city by the seventeenth century. Christ's held 926 children by 1641, of whom just 103 were placed as apprentices, discharged or died. Bridewell, with its assortment of 711 vagrants and wandering soldiers, clothed some poor to be sent beyond the seas and found occupations, arts, work and labours for only 170.[56]

Abandoned children and orphans became a matter of parish concern because fewer families needed the service of 'almschildren' in the seventeenth century than they had in the early sixteenth century, when wealthy households gained domestic servants by taking in these young charges. Towns throughout England found homes and employment for abandoned, orphaned and poor children. The abandoned children found in inner city parishes may have been the offspring of migrating parents, or of adult children living with poor, disabled or aged parents. St Michael's paid Goodman Hallye 12d to care for a child left in Sir Harper's entry, the doorsteps of prominent citizens providing, perhaps, a relatively safe place for abandonment if parents thought the child might be taken in as an eventual servant or that an influential man could get a child admitted to Christ's.[57] St Botolph's, outside the walls, attempted to prevent the births of poor infants in parochial bounds so as not to be held 'chargeable'. The careful perambulation of borders resurrected the shell of an older festive tradition in parishes, but also marked the limits of parochial responsibility for the poor, for abandoned children, or for the maintenance of shared conduits or pumps.

Even in the early seventeenth century, churchwardens described children placed in service in the old language of quasi-familial relations,

---

[54] GL, MSS 1453/1, f. 3; 4072/1, Part 1, fols 16v–17.

[55] Cf. Rappaport's 'decade of exceptional hardship': *Worlds*, pp. 378–9 and 'the reality of a *perceived* crisis in the 1590s': Archer, *Pursuit*, pp. 9–14.

[56] 'A Psalme of Thanksgiving'.

[57] See Sharpe, 'Poor children', *passim*; Ben-Amos, 'Women apprentices', pp. 232–33; Fildes, 'Maternal feelings', *passim*. Overall, *Accounts of the Churchwardens*, p. 158; Finlay, *Population and Metropolis*, p. 153. On power of influence in admissions: Manzione, *Christ's Hospital*, pp. 139–40.

despite the contractual nature of the arrangements. St Botolph's, for instance, placed a child born in the parish with a cordwainer in St Bartholomew the Great, who pledged 'to make him his adopted Child'. Apprenticeship agreements show that the placement of foundlings or orphans with individual masters was made binding by churchwardens who did not want to resume care of the child later. The vestry of St Michael's in 1593 transferred all responsibility for an orphaned girl to William Hammon, in return for his promise to discharge the parish of all future costs relating to the child.[58] Although parishes tried to set the poor to work or to apprentice abandoned or orphaned children to masters in and around London, work and apprentice schemes required greater centralization and only flowered after the 1620s.[59]

High migration magnified the symptoms of urban distress and potential disorder in London, giving common problems unique characteristics in the city. London's leaders reluctantly adopted policies that controlled the economy, although Hugh Alley pleaded for greater consideration during inflationary times for those who lived close to poverty. Howes blamed the 'myserable covetousnes' of landlords of alley tenements who exacted and raised 'greate' rents for their 'fylthie houses' for the high cost (and low standard) of living for the city's poor, seemingly asking for voluntary rent control.[60] Civic leaders experimented with urban reorganization somewhat more readily, although not so quickly as other European leaders.[61] The link made by contemporaries between plague, vagrancy, poverty and suburban disorder has already been well drawn. Overcrowded houses and neighbourhoods facilitated the spread of sickness, possibly fomented criminal activity, and even made the spread of fire easier, so churchwardens prohibited boarding of lodgers and inmates. In the 1560s, the Dutch congregation debated how best to care for the infected, but London parish leaders remained inactive despite the severity of the 1563 outbreak.[62] Churchwardens restricted trade in second-hand clothes, particularly of the plague dead, sensing some link

---

[58] GL, MS 1453/1, f. 5. Overall, *The Accounts of the Churchwardens*, p. 183. Sharpe describes the apprenticeship as 'a system similar to present-day fostering': 'Poor children as apprentices', p. 255.

[59] Pearl, 'Puritans and Poor Relief', pp. 214–15; cf. post-1620 centralizing solutions outside London: Slack, 'Poverty and Politics in Salisbury', pp. 180–83.

[60] *Hugh Alley's Caveat* (1598); *TED*, Vol. 3, p. 427.

[61] Slack, *The Impact of Plague*, pp. 192–5, 200–202. In sixteenth-century Venice, new evangelical religious societies and Orders attended to the problem of poverty, motivated by concern for the salvation of the souls of the poor and for fear of disease: Brian Pullan, *Rich and Poor in Renaissance Venice: The Social Institutions of a Catholic State, to 1620* (Cambridge, MA, 1971), pp. 216–21.

[62] Slack, *The Impact of Plague*, pp. 205–6.

between clothes and the disease. St Michael's vestry allowed Goodwife Asheton to sell clothes against the wall of a building rented by the church, as long as she did not sell anything that came from those infected with the plague. Later outbreaks changed usual charitable practices, as when St Michael's vestry allowed churchwardens to distribute alms on a case-by-case basis, rather than only on the eves of festivals, as custom dictated.[63] The developing 'social geography' of London, noticeable by the 1625 plague, suggests that suburban parishes became overwhelmingly poor and their environments worsened. Simultaneously, the wealthier parishes within the centre of the city became cleaner and less likely to suffer the ravages of disease.[64]

London's size made the enforcement of policies to segregate the plague-stricken more difficult. Officials marked the homes of the visited sick and confined a small number to pesthouses in the mid-sixteenth century.[65] St Michael's vestry noted two infected houses in July 1603, after the burial of the first plague victim at the end of June, and uttered a series of decrees to meet the problem. St Michael's built a shed to adjoin the pesthouse in the outbreak, coping with the problem of plague on the most local level, the parish. The shed sheltered those sick with the plague and living in Harp Alley, with its cluster of poor dwellers, and elsewhere in the parish. The vestry also allowed the visited 4d daily and paid for the burial of poor plague victims. In addition, they paid the sexton 6d daily to look for the sick and vagrants 'not to be suffered to wand[e]r about the stretes', fearing for the spread of disease by the infected not confined to houses. The Book of Orders in 1666 for the city of London further stipulated the removal of the sick to pesthouses, sheds and huts for the survival of others in the family.[66]

Policies meant to alleviate London's problems may have created social systems peculiar to the city. In particular, parochial and royal efforts to curb lodging, and children's co-residence with parents, disrupted traditional practices of the ageing, and the ageing poor, to piece together a

---

[63] GL, MS 4072/1, Part 1, fols 25, 60. Discussion of the theories about the transmission of disease and the relation to those theories to the trade in second-hand clothes: see Slack, *The Impact of Plague*, pp. 11–12.

[64] In addition to the growing social divergence in cities and towns, Slack points to 'flight' from cities to country estates by wealthier town-dwellers to explain the social distribution of plague and disease: *The Impact of Plague*, pp. 152–3, 165–7.

[65] Slack, *The Impact of Plague*, pp. 204, 5. Carpenter paid for building pesthouses in St Michael Cornhill in 1563: GL, MS 4071/1, f. 75v.

[66] GL, MS 4072/1, Part 1, f. 90; burial of first plague victim in June: GL, MS 4061. Slack, 'The Response to Plague in Early Modern England: Public Policies and Their Consequences' in John Walter and Roger Schofield (eds), *Famine, Disease and the Social Order in Early Modern Society* (Cambridge, 1989), p. 172.

livelihood.[67] Historians debate the nature of the elderly's living arrangements, especially whether or not they lived in reconstructed nuclear families. London's concern to prevent widespread fire and crime and to discriminate against the able-bodied poor outweighed consideration of the elderly's living companions. Churchwardens, aldermen and even parliamentary members modified harsh rules to accommodate the living arrangements of some poor women and men, however. Considerations, like the reputations of certain inhabitants and their resources, identified worthy poor exempted from strict regulations. St Michael's vestry, in 1587, allowed Peter Cutler, a former clerk, to have his daughter and her husband with him in the house he rented from the parish, as long as he spent money improving it. By contrast, in 1616, the vestry warned Widow Brayfield to send her son and his wife out of her room and out of the parish, or else she would lose her pension. The difference between the cases of the widow and the man hinged on the money he could spend on improvements to the parish's tenements, and the nearly thirty years separating the decisions, during which time strains on parochial resources grew. Brayfield's greater dependence on the parish meant that officials could order her to follow rules, even though she was a 'deserving' woman. Similarly, as Cutler aged, losing his position in the parish and possibly outliving his daughter, the son-in-law was ordered to leave in 1599.[68] Utter dependency changed the pensioners' relationship with the parish.

New policies altered traditional living arrangements, but a newer capitalist economy also contributed to novel pressures in the lives of the poor. London's economy left the city's poor with the problem of adjusting to inflation, a problem not necessarily shared by those in the country or smaller urban areas where the poor relied less on cash gifts than on gifts in kind. The prevalence of alms in money in sixteenth- and seventeenth-century London may have added to the economic pinch felt by the needy. Parochial relief in this form, rather than in bread or food, and in contrast to wages in kind paid by some employers outside

---

[67] Laslett, 'The traditional English family', pp. 97–113; Smith, 'The structured dependence of the elderly as a recent development', pp. 409–28; Kertzer, 'Toward a historical demography of aging', pp. 363–83; Wall, 'Elderly persons and members of their households', pp. 81–106. German 'sleeping houses' provided by older women, older couples and widows: Merry Wiesner, 'Making Ends Meet: The Working Poor in Early Modern Europe' in Kyle C. Sessions and Phillip N. Bebb (eds), *Pietas et Societas: New Trends in Reformation Social History*, Volume IV, Sixteenth Century Essays and Studies (Ann Arbor, MI, 1985), p. 84.

[68] GL, MS 4072/1, Part 1, fols 38, 80v, 110; Cutler had retired in 1592/93, when he only worked a quarter: GL, MS 4071/1, f. 144. Wales points out that in the seventeenth century, parishes assumed that paupers were single and responsible only for themselves: 'Poverty, poor relief and the life-cycle', p. 364.

London, left recipients to cope with price fluctuations.[69] As early as the beginning of the sixteenth century, the city also experimented with municipal granaries to aid the poor, like the gentry in the countryside who made grain available below market price, although testamentary and parochial charity often provided money and left the poor to buy in the market.[70] Ceremonial gifts or doles of bread survived the Reformation in London, notably the pre-Reformation benefaction of the Percivales and the post-Reformation bequest by Bowes, but the city's puritan-leaning religious climate cast suspicions on these endowments that mimicked traditional, indiscriminate, Catholic doles. Indeed, the fracas at Lady Mary Ramsey's dole reminded all of the potential misrule that could unleashed by a restless mob of poor women and men.[71] Parishes provided coals to the poor, especially on Easter and Christmas eves, but unevenly recorded their purchase and distribution. Inflation through the sixteenth century and a few bad harvests tested the resilience of the London economy and the ability of parishes to confront poverty. In arguing that historians have exaggerated the threat of famine and extent of poverty, John Walters emphasizes the survival of a 'social economy' that sheltered most poor from the full onslaught of dearth that market fluctuations would suggest.[72] Service in London may have insulated poor children and young adults employed in shops and households from the effects of poor harvests, but we have already seen that many children could not secure those positions. Howes even claimed that children procured from the countryside were turned out when the work ran out, or were treated so poorly they ran away.[73]

London's local concerns reflected demographic and economic pressures, especially as parochial and civic leaders realized that poor relief could not satisfy all those in need, nor could some parishes even collect sufficient rates to support their own poor. Civic leaders responded to problems within and around the city with mandates to support new charitable institutions and to force wealthier parishes to support poorer ones. Collectors for the poor gathered rates to cover pensions and to see

---

[69] On day employment that included meat and drink: Walter, 'The Social Economy of Dearth', p. 100.

[70] Walter, 'The Social Economy of Dearth', p. 118; Pearl, 'Puritans and Poor Relief', pp. 228–9.

[71] The alderman Richard Goddard in 1604, explaining why he did not want a dole, said, 'for I conceive that to be but a popish imitation of such as were desirous after their death to have their soul prayed for': Hickman, 'From Catholic to Protestant', p. 124. Nicholas Bourman, *An Epitaph*, sig. Bv.

[72] Walter, 'The Social Economy of Dearth in Early Modern England', pp. 82–3.

[73] See discussion of service as 'refuge of the children of the poor': Walter, 'The Social Economy of Dearth', p. 97. *TED*, Vol. 3, p. 430.

needy parishioners and vagrants admitted to post-Reformation hospitals and Bridewell. Significant portions of these collections, however, directly financed the hospitals of London, especially Christ's.[74] The Court of Aldermen experimented with redistributing the city's wealth by requiring better-off parishes to supplement poorer parishes' collections for the poor. Although St Stephen's was not one of the wealthiest parishes in the mid-seventeenth-century assessment, the Court recognized the wealth in certain households in the small parish and ordered it to contribute to St Sepulchre's. The parish withheld, however, collections for poor parishes for its own poor in 1611. The crown also occasionally mandated that towns in crisis receive part of wealthier parishes' rates. St Mary Woolnoth, for instance, raised a collection for the town of Uttoxeter.[75]

Besides local concerns, parochial and civic leaders faced mandates that originated in the national concerns of Parliament and crown. Orders from national leaders cast broader concerns as parochial responsibilities. National needs intersected, and clashed, with local goals in charity and poor relief, adding to strains on local relief and even contradicting local efforts to discriminate between the deserving and undeserving poor. St Stephen's, besides answering the Court of Aldermen's call to help troubled parishes, granted benevolences and one-time gifts to refugees, maimed soldiers and individuals or towns suffering loss by fire or disaster, some of whom carried certificates from the Queen or King.[76] These casualties of wars against Catholic and Ottoman foes or of financial risk-taking in legitimate trade and in piracy gained the sympathy of national leaders interested in checking Spanish or Turkish imperial and merchant power.

Charity, and the Christian's duty to aid the poor, remained a central facet of religious and social life, regardless of distinctions between rural and urban areas. Pre-Reformation charity largely concentrated on what effect giving had on the donor, while post-Reformation charity to a greater degree focused on the behaviour of the poor and what effect accepting charity had on the poor. Elizabeth's 1559 injunctions promised that Christ 'will mercifully reward the same [donor] with everlasting life',

---

[74] See the account of George Samwell and Richard Brock, collectors for the poor in Christ's in 1588–89 to see the simultaneous support of the poor there and within the parish from the same collection: GL, MS 1002/1A, f. 261v.

[75] CLRO, Rep. 32, fols 157–157v; GL, MSS 594/1, f. 75; 1002/1B, f. 324.

[76] Refugees and maimed soldiers: Schen, 'Constructing the Poor', pp. 453–5. Fires in 1606, in Woking, co. Surrey (5s 5d); Burwell in co. Cambridge (6s 8d); Kennington in co. Lambeth (4s 2d); New Branford in co. Middlesex (4s 9d); Greenwich: GL, MS 594/1, fols 57–8.

coming close to preserving the traditional notion of 'good works'.[77] The Elizabethan homilies justified refusing charity to the idle poor, but reminded the wealthy not to withhold their 'great store of moth-eaten apparel' or 'heaps of gold and silver' and refuse to 'help and succour the poor, hungry, and naked Christ, that cometh to your doors a begging'. The theme of greedy rich men and women hoarding their worldly wealth became a standing grievance, helped no doubt by Stow's criticism of the same. Henry Arth described 'poore makers', after delineating the sins of the poor, who wore proud apparel, wasted meat and drink, collected exorbitant rents, were usurers and 'corn-mongers', succumbed to their own vices, and generally abused 'God's benefits'.[78] The deserving poor had a right to charity and relief and the wealthy had an obligation to give. Importantly, reminders of compassion and obligation still figured in the pleas from parochial leaders and individuals in need of assistance. Despite religious change, the notion of a moral community, and the apparatus to see alms distributed, persisted in sixteenth- and seventeenth-century London.[79] Thus, St Botolph's churchwardens attempted to restrict their responsibility for poor foundlings or children born to mothers from outside the parish and threatened to refuse repairs of communal water pumps, but in the end they met these costs. Disputes over customary 'rights' in parochial records centred on maintaining status despite age, as in widows fighting to maintain their usual seats in church, or despite lifecycle changes, like seeking considerations in rent or employment after long residence in or service to a parish. Although parochial evidence did not restate a 'right' to charity, instead highlighting the good order achieved by relief, the remembrance of the poor and attempts to identify the deserving among them suggests that an older 'right' lingered.[80]

---

[77] Somers, p. 69. Dubois, 'Almsgiving in Post Reformation England', p. 493; importance of charity in Calvinist thought: Paul Fideler, 'Discussions on Poverty in Sixteenth Century England', unpublished Ph.D. thesis, Brandeis University, History of Ideas, 1971, pp. 218–19.

[78] See 'An Homily against Idleness', *Sermons, or Homilies*, p. 445 and 'An Homily of Alms-Deeds, and Mercifulness towards the Poor and Needy', ibid., p. 334. Complaints of hospital governors using alms for themselves: Somers, p. 86. Henry Arth, 'Provision for the Poore', 1597 in *TED*, Vol. 3, pp. 451–2. On Stow's 'timeless' lament: Archer, 'Nostalgia', p. 23.

[79] Common 'vocabulary' of sermon and government decree: Walter, 'The Social Economy of Dearth', p. 122; Fideler, 'Discussions of Poverty', p. 243. The 'moral economy' would in fact survive into the eighteenth century: Thompson, 'The Moral Economy of the Crowd'. McIntosh found that the administrative apparatus in place and the autonomy of parishes before the Reformation played more important roles in relief after the Reformation: 'Local Responses to the Poor', p. 212.

[80] See Archer on lack of 'right' to relief in later Tudor and early Stuart London: *Pursuit*, p. 97.

Protestant and Catholic charity

The earliest Reformation critics derided Catholic charity for its indiscriminate care of the impotent and the able-bodied poor, not to mention its inadequacy in the care of the 'true' poor, as opposed to monks, nuns and clerics living under voluntary vows of poverty, obeyed or not. These reformers argued that discriminate relief would better serve the poor. Protestant donors hastened to distinguish themselves from Catholics by trying to restrict indiscriminate almsgiving and begging, although even late medieval churchgoers scorned the beggar, while aiding the poor and sick.[81] Despite contemporary enthusiasm to distinguish between Catholic and Protestant charity, however, modern historians have noted similarities in spite of doctrinal differences. Catholics and Protestants discriminated in charity, especially by the later sixteenth century, and emphasized common elements of social control and civic humanism. The motivations and piety of donors, the morality of the poor, and the effect of charity on recipient and giver concerned sixteenth-century Europeans, whether Protestant or Catholic. Post-Reformation English and Catholic Reformation charity shared similar tendencies to differentiate among the poor, exercise social control, and effectively separate rich and poor.

Despite varied religious views and practices, Catholics and Protestants encountered common demographic problems and cultural anxieties. Population pressures and disease, like plague, encouraged changes in charity and poor relief. The material pressures experienced in London, and in many other European towns and cities, led city leaders to experiment with centralized charity and relief. Catholic and Protestant reform revamped notions of responsibility and questioned the appropriateness of indiscriminate giving.[82] Coupled with the widespread fear of disorder in sixteenth-century Europe, these factors precipitated greater formalization of and discrimination in relief. Yet Protestants and Catholics followed slightly different policies to combat poverty. Catholic Reformation charity relied on large endowments linked to lay devotional piety, essentially decentralized, while English charity and relief developed under a national poor law overseen by the secular government and financed by taxation, centralized.[83]

---

[81] Rubin, *Charity and Community*, p. 98.

[82] Decline of support for hospitals, monasteries and parish churches and dramatic increase in bequests left for revitalized confraternities focused on burials and charity directed to deserving poor, not indiscriminate, mendicant targets: Cohn, *Death and Property*, pp. 162–5. Attack on mendicant orders as part of reform of relief: McCants, *Civic Charity*, p. 7.

[83] On this essential distinction, see Jütte, *Poverty and Deviance*, pp. 100–142.

In founding new institutions to help the poor, many times in the buildings once used by Catholic religious houses or hospitals, the English drew on Catholic and Protestant examples from the Continent.[84] Italian city-states had begun the transition from 'scattered, smaller institutions' to 'large general hospitals' in the late fourteenth century, under clerical influence.[85] London's testators, however, slowly adopted these homes for orphaned children, houses of correction and hospitals for the sick and impotent. As a result, the condition of and support for the London hospitals seemed to lag behind those of institutions elsewhere in Europe in the sixteenth and seventeenth centuries. An Italian visitor criticized most London hospitals for being small and in poor condition, though not Christ's Hospital.[86] The puritan Robert Crowley blamed the lack of hospital space and beds in 1550 on the lordly houses that stood where hospitals for the poor should have been. A comparison of the estimated beds available in medieval hospitals in and around London with those of the Reformation Sts Thomas and Bartholomew shows that the hospitals, besides Christ's, did not initially serve far greater numbers after the Reformation.[87] The number of inmates and pleas for money implied deterioration in care in the London hospitals generally, which were unable to attend to their inmates or to take in as many impoverished men, women and children as would have entered.[88] As parishes found in attempting to relieve their own, Christ's had difficulty caring for poor children at a time when city inhabitants perceived worsening poverty and increasing abandonment.

Testators' reasons for reluctantly supporting and endowing institutions may illustrate an important difference between English and some Continental charity. William Temple, one-time ambassador to The Hague, remarked in 1673 about the United Provinces that 'Charity seems to be very National among them, though it be regulated by Orders of the Country, and not usually mov'd by the common Objects of Compas-

---

[84] Foundation of Savoy on model of 'new' Italian hospitals and emulation of Holland in mid-seventeenth century: Slack, *From Reformation to Improvement*, pp. 19, 78. The officials of Santa Maria Nuova corresponded with Henry VIII in 1536 about hospital administration: Gavitt, *Charity and Children*, p. 299.

[85] Gavitt, *Charity and Children*, pp. 10–11.

[86] Described in Archer, *Pursuit*, pp. 156–7; Slack, *From Reformation to Improvement*, p. 25

[87] 'Crowley on Almshouses and Beggars, 1550' in *TED*, Vol. 2, p. 405. About 420 beds in medieval period, with 220 in the two post-Reformation hospitals, and 550–650 children in Christ's in 1580s and 1590s: summarized in Archer, *Pursuit*, pp. 154, 156.

[88] On the hospitals in general, see lengthy discussion in Archer, *Pursuit*, pp. 154–63, especially deterioration in care, p. 156. Shortcomings of municipal hospitals in mid-seventeenth century: Pearl, 'Puritans and Poor Relief', p. 214.

sion'.[89] The English may have seen the benevolence of the large hospitals of Renaissance and later commercial cities as less personal and direct than charity administered through parishes, even if that relief were supplied through involuntary rates mandated by the national government. Traditional compassion could temper the desired efficiency of parochial relief and charity. English commentators emphasized the personal and national value of being 'moved' by the plight of the poor to give speedily and readily, as 'John Downame' urged in a treatise of 1616 that sprang from his lectures to the Company of Haberdashers. The puritan lecturer Downham and John Howes, former renter for Christ's, warned against misusing money to indulge in vices and entreated people to care for the poor, to be 'richer in good workes'. Howes warned, 'Surely god can not but be angrie with vs, that will suffer our Christian Bretheren to die in the streates for wante of relyefe, and wee spende and consume our wealthe and our wytte in searching out of Harlotts, and leave the worckes of faythe and mercie vndone'.[90]

Although observers reminded inhabitants and citizens to remember the poor and even to anticipate their needs, practice in the city rested upon parochial administration. Perhaps London Protestants saw a resemblance between institutional charity and pre-Reformation monastic almsgiving that they wished to avoid. Institutions housing the poor may have undermined the discriminate giving exercised by testators and churchwardens, who tended to help the poor 'known' to them by name and reputation. Testators consistently aided those connected to them by parish, household or craft, rather than the 'unknown' poor of the city. Relying on reputation allowed greater discrimination, but also maintained the semblance of face-to-face charity among neighbours. Protestant cities that experimented with poor relief in the early sixteenth century centralized efforts in local communities, through the common chest.[91] The importance of endowments for charitable institutions in England, and the civic overtones of those endowments, would be more apparent in the later seventeenth and eighteenth centuries than in the sixteenth century.

London's largest institution, Christ's Hospital, enjoyed some testamentary and, more significantly, co-ordinated civic and parochial funding that dated back to the citizens' petition for its foundation to serve fatherless children. The Hospital ran in debt for all but two years

---

[89] Quoted in McCants, *Civic Charity*, p. 10.

[90] 'Downame', *TED*, Vol.3, pp. 14, 17, 23 (quote from p. 23); Howes, *TED*, Vol.3, p. 442.

[91] After 1610, a decline in 'face-to-face contact' in company charity: Ward, *Metropolitan Communities*, pp. 82–3. Jütte, *Poverty and Deviance*, pp. 105–12.

between 1585 and 1602, and in 1591 briefly halted new admissions. In the midst of a mid-decade accounting crisis, observers charged the hospital with favouring the fatherless children of aristocratic officials and courtiers, tension that Archer believes 'represented a weakening of the bond between the hospital and the parishes'. Despite the imprimatur of respectability and the potential benefits to individual and civic pride from a well-run hospital overseen by some of London's most influential men, Christ's could not meet the needs of the poor or continue to discriminate between orphaned and illegitimate children.[92]

Other European institutions for children similarly wrestled with the problem of accommodating illegitimate and legitimate children, a potentially thorny moral dilemma with implications for charitable support. Historians have noted the attack on illicit sex in the later sixteenth and early seventeenth centuries, as well as the gender crisis reflected, in part, by the moral diatribes against promiscuity, sex outside of marriage and adultery.[93] Early modern hospitals regularly differentiated between and often segregated legitimate and illegitimate children. The *Ospedale degli Innocenti* in Florence was overcrowded by 1552, leading to a discussion about banning the entrance of legitimate children, unlike Christ's efforts to ban the illegitimate. The majority of inmates in that institution were the offspring of servants and slaves.[94] Amsterdam had the *Burgerweeshuis* for legitimate children and the *Aalmoezeniersweeshuis* for illegitimate children, while London did not have two distinct houses to separate children. The inhabitants of London had chosen to care for fatherless children, though the alleged aristocratic commandeering of admissions rankled the city, and not until the eighteenth century would institutions confront illegitimacy and abandonment head on.[95]

Although Temple would later comment upon the impersonal nature of Dutch charity, London's reliance on centralized administration of relief may also have diminished the closeness between the well-off and the poor, or miserable. Hence Downham and Howes exhorted readers to think of the poor and redirect spending from consumption to charity.[96]

---

[92] Archer notes that despite reluctance to admit illegitimate children, by the end of the sixteenth century 10 per cent of the inmates were illegitimate: *Pursuit*, pp. 157–61.

[93] Amussen, 'Gender, Family and the Social Order, 1560–1725'; Underdown, 'The Taming of the Scold'; Slack, *From Reformation to Improvement*, p. 47.

[94] Gavitt, *Charity and Children*, pp. 301, 20.

[95] Both Thomas Coram's Foundling Hospital (founded in 1739 for preservation and education of abandoned and illegitimate children) and the Lock Hospital (founded in 1746 for the treatment of venereal disease) did not list female subscribers, however, since the taint of impropriety hung over them: Andrew, *Philanthropy and Police*, pp. 72–3.

[96] Although historians point to the mid-seventeenth century and later in the birth of a consumer society, wills in this database show growing wealth and the accumulation of

The economic trends of the long sixteenth century affected cities through-out Europe and seemed to highlight common unease about worldliness and wealth. Political and religious uncertainty reshaped ritual brother-hood in Florence, seen in the sixteenth-century confraternities that introduced hierarchy, status, honour and rank into what had been mutual organizations cutting across neighbourhood and class lines. The Venetian *Scuole Grandi*, becoming 'worldly and ostentatious' and less 'penitential', separated the orders of rich and poor, analogous to the stricter social hierarchy formulated in London. The *Scuole Grandi*, though, helped poor men and women who were not singled out as frequently by English testators or parishes, the *poveri vergognosi*, or those of noble origins who had fallen on hard times, and poor maidens needing dowries.[97]

Unlike in Catholic Reformation cities and towns, no lay fraternities or devotions increased charity or reinforced a personal relationship between privileged and needy inhabitants of London. Puritans like Downham could encourage the Haberdashers to extend beneficence to all, 'yet chiefly to those *who are of the houshould of faith*', without having lay groups to identify and bring the pious together. Instead, donors could only judge godliness by attendance at services and reports on morality, potentially no more than an indication of outward con-formity.[98] The loss of religious guilds in England compelled the sick and elderly poor to draw on parochial relief in addition to informal help from family, rather than subsist with the help of fraternities.[99] London hospitals depended on parochial rates and the benevolence of elite citizens or aristocratic patrons, not on the lay organizations frequently affiliated with institutions in Catholic Reformation countries. The Board of Governors for Christ's and the other hospitals depended upon the oligarchic and rising middling sort of citizens to serve in leadership capacities, as in other countries, but seemed to limit roles for women, a

---

goods. Contemporary prescriptive literature chastised extravagant spending on leisure activities, indulgences and vices. Discussion of emergent consumerism of mid-seven-teenth century: Robert S. Duplessis, *Transitions to Capitalism in Early Modern Europe*, p. 112.

[97] Weissman, *Ritual Brotherhood* (New York, 1982), p. 198. The *Scuole Grandi* 'lost their penitential character and had become increasingly worldly and ostentatious': Pullan, *Rich and Poor*, p. 186.

[98] John Downham, *The plea of the poore, or a treatise of beneficence and almsdeeds*, printed by Edward Griffin for Ralph Mabbe (London, 1616), STC 7146, sig. B. Original emphasis. Arth includes irregular attendance at services in the 'sins of the poor': *TED*, Vol. 3, p. 451.

[99] Absence of recorded charity noted by McRee, 'Charity and gild solidarity', pp. 195–225; cf. Barron's suggestion that charity was informal: 'The Parish Fraternities of Medieval London', p. 27; Schen, 'Strategies of poor aged women and widows', p. 18.

departure from the practice of some other countries or cities. Members of women's confraternities of the Orphans and Madelines in Grenoble, for instance, styled themselves '"like perfect mothers to the poor"'. Through these French Catholic confraternities, members provided charity, sought the conversion of souls, and mortified and mastered their own flesh. The Daughters of Charity helped to treat disease and alleviate poverty by nursing in homes and parishes and, later, in institutions.[100] Importantly, the Daughters gave the elite married Ladies an outlet for charitable activity, through their patronage of the unmarried, poorer Daughters, and enabled working women to combat poverty and illness, fulfilling professional and pious ambition.

Even without confraternities, other Protestant countries and cities saw the establishment of charitable institutions that utilized the leadership of lay women and men. Men's service to charitable institutions furthered their political ambitions while women's service reflected, and buttressed, the social and political achievements of their husbands, fathers and brothers. Although laywomen often performed gendered work, they used their positions to secure their own status, to solidify family standing or to exercise patronage. The Amsterdam *Burgerweeshuis* relied on regents and regentesses, though the latter concentrated on domestic duties and the former made policy and budget decisions. The regents were politically and economically elite, while those managing the home for illegitimate children did not share this profile. In eighteenth-century Rotterdam, the mothers, wives and especially widows of prominent male citizens played central roles in institutional charities as regentesses, who fulfilled traditional responsibilities relating to 'keeping house' and hiring and supervising staff and servants.[101]

Women in sixteenth- and early seventeenth-century London, by contrast, had fewer opportunities for public charitable roles and even began to lose some older forms of control over money and alms in the city.[102]

---

[100] Norberg, *Rich and Poor in Grenoble*, p. 26. The Daughters concentrated on helping the sick, pregnant women, and people with venereal disease and avoided helping the able-bodied poor: Susan Dinan, 'A Nursing Vocation: the Hospital Work of the Daughters of Charity in Seventeenth-Century France', unpublished paper, presented at the Eleventh Berkshire Conference on the History of Women, June, 1999.

[101] McCants, *Civic Charity*, pp. 90, 102. Marybeth Carlson, 'Overseers and the Overseen: Women's roles in administering poor relief in Eighteenth-Century Rotterdam', unpublished paper presented at the Eleventh Berkshire Conference on the History of Women, June, 1999.

[102] I do not mean to suggest that women's work was not essential to the running of medieval or Reformation hospitals or to the operation of the parish. Women acted as nurses, housekeepers, and, poorer women with their husbands, as part of couples hired to oversee an almshouse. The titled roles, however, and opportunities for professionalization along the lines of the Daughters, are not present. See Willen, 'Women in the Public Sphere'.

Lady Ramsey's poet explained his epigram celebrating her bequests so 'that thou shouldst not cleane forgotten be', perhaps recognizing that without leadership in life her merits might go unremarked, or the deaths of paupers remembered instead.[103] In London, women did not serve in feminized administrative posts in hospitals, in the office of churchwarden or vestryman, or in membership or more official capacities as they had once done in parochial guilds. Pre-Reformation fraternities, obits and services often included disbursements for the poor that could have been administered by a female officer or executrix, or outlined by a female testator. By the early seventeenth century, parish officials, from churchwardens to collectors for the poor, oversaw the relief of the deserving poor within the parish. Parochial officials gained greater discretion over testamentary bequests left to parishes and over relief more generally. In 1616, a citizen and goldsmith attended a vestry on behalf of an executrix in order to give the churchwardens money from a bequest that was directly handed out to the poor.[104]

The taint of immorality and disorder hanging on the poor could reflect on the women who helped them, perhaps figuring in contemporaries' attitudes about female charity. The 'Maydens of London' developed an argument about face-to-face charity in answering accusations of thievery set out in Hake's lost pamphlet. The figure of Mother B. was undeserving in Hake's pamphlet, even a bawd, as Jones argues. The maidservants argued that Hake would mistakenly urge mistresses to support beggars (implicitly the idle poor) through the poor box rather than the hard-working poor who still came begging at the doors of the well-to-do. They describe Mother B. instead as a poor older woman in want of bread and meat who came knocking for a bit of food or a candle end so as not to stumble about her dark house.[105] The 1598 Poor Law allowed begging for food in parishes of residence, possibly a reflection of practice as much as a prescription. The domestic roles of women, whether servants or mistresses of households, may have led them to retain some older habits of hospitality and face-to-face charity, especially as they might still judge the morality and worthiness of the poor who came to their doors. With the passage of the final Poor Law, however, the sanction for such begging, and one form of women's almsgiving, was removed.

In the semi-private execution of non-pious bequests and the public allotment of pious ones, women's roles were diminishing. London women

---

[103] Bourman, 'Epitaph', sig. B2. Bourman might also have emphasized her humility by explaining his purpose in writing about her or have simply played the familiar refrain of charitable acts going unappreciated (and not imitated).

[104] GL, MS 1002/1B, f. 423v.

[105] A letter, sig. Biiij-Biiijv; Jones, 'Maidservants of London', pp. 29–30.

had fewer opportunities to disburse charity through pious devotions, since even the percentage of husbands electing their widows as future executrices declined. We cannot, however, access the private conversations of men and women about testamentary plans. Did husbands order certain pious practices, or did husbands and wives reach agreements about the best use of pious bequests? The residue left by most pre-Reformation testators for deeds of pity and charity for souls' remembrance varied in value and depended on the wisdom of the executors (executrices) and/or the parish or craft officers left in charge of the amounts. Assumptions about women's piety may have reassured those who still left their residues and estates to the charitable oversight of women after the Reformation, despite parallel doubts about women's intellectual ability and moral rectitude.[106]

Women's testamentary bequests slowly diverged from their male friends and family members, but differed in key areas relating to reformed doctrine. Men in London gave more frequently to institutions and men while women gave more to women, perhaps showing that men funded the institutions in which they had served, or once aspired to govern.[107] London women restricted their bequests to the morally upright earlier than men did and dropped their bequests for burial sermons, perhaps at the behest of puritan preachers. Thus, women's charity and piety reflected assumptions about the maintenance of public order though private moral reform and showed, by the absence of women's commemoration in burial sermons, their adherence to reform. For a brief stretch of the early Catholic Reformation, Italian women followed a unique pattern of pious giving, focusing on pious devotions that were significantly different from those practised by Italian men. In his study of Siena after the Council of Trent, Samuel Cohn has found that women constituted the 'vanguard' of Catholic reform, as more women wrote wills and the size of their bequests rose dramatically in the late sixteenth century and remained high through the seventeenth century. Women played a primary role in the early funding and support for new devotions; '"conversion" of men came at least a generation later'. On the other hand, Kathryn Norberg found no difference between the giving of men and women in France, where religious confraternities devoted to the piety of women and their welfare existed.[108]

---

[106] Willen, 'Godly women', p. 563.

[107] In pious bequests from men and women to institutions, or 'unisex' targets, z-scores of 14.54 (1580) and 10.76 (1601). In those to men, 34.44 (1601) and 29.37 (1620). In those to women, 63.48 (1580) and 156.57 (1601), with more from women in this last category.

[108] Cohn, *Death and Property*, pp. 198–201, quote p. 199; Norberg, *Rich and Poor in Grenoble*, p. 120.

London women's charitable roles, outside vestry deliberations over the deserving poor or the administration of hospitals, mirrored the roles of women in Reformation religion. Lyndal Roper has argued that the Reformation promulgated a 'theology of gender' that was 'domesticated' through the 'politics of reinscribing women within the "family"'.[109] Willen refers to the 'spiritualised household' that rested upon 'spiritual egalitarianism', by which 'godliness tempered patriarchy'.[110] Although the family cannot be circumscribed within a 'private' sphere that would not have been recognizable in the sixteenth century, the language of household spirituality and governance laid the foundation for later arguments about women's private roles.[111] We have no easy answer, however, to the vexing question of whether women were 'better off' with Protestant or Catholic reform, partly because Catholic devotion, and especially recusancy in England, also depended on the household.[112] Elite status enabled women to patronize puritans and recusants, and justified their judgment of the morality of poorer women (and men), while low status forced women to conform to prevailing religious doctrine in London and to work and compete for limited charity and relief.

The lack of women's devotions or guilds in Protestantism and the limited opportunities for English women's guiding roles in institutions or in parishes may reflect the hold of patriarchy within reformed religion. Even under Mary, however, no new or revived devotions or guilds created lay outlets especially for women. New devotional societies could give women in other countries alternatives, like the Italian women of the sixteenth century who elected burial in the homes of women's confraternities, bypassing the constraints on burial location previously imposed by the male line.[113] English women seemingly chose by which husband finally to rest, but could not choose an all-female resting place in Protestant churches. In the mid-seventeenth century, the proliferation of prophesying, petitioning, and otherwise exceptionally behaving women, especially in London, has been seen variously as a rejection of the Reformation's strictures and of the prevailing gender order.[114]

---

[109] Roper, *The Holy Household*, pp. 1, 3.

[110] Willen, 'Godly Women', pp. 564–5, 580.

[111] Roper, *The Holy Household*, pp. 1, 3. Willen, 'Godly Women', pp. 564–5, 580. Cf. Carlson's argument about the 'failure of the English Reformation to share in the dramatic transformation of the status of marriage': *Marriage and the English Reformation*, p. 3. Wiesner warns against seeing the sixteenth-century family as private, or separate from the 'public realm of politics and economic life': 'Beyond women and the family', pp. 316–17.

[112] Willen, 'Godly Women', pp. 564, 577–8.

[113] Cohn, *Death and Property*, p. 202.

[114] Sects as reaction to the Reformation: Scarisbrick, *Reformation and the English*

The centralization of charity and relief depended upon agents accept-able to prevailing notions of female subordination and to emerging ideals of religious households, but also succoured the poor who con-formed to developing ideas of 'worthiness'. London's hospitals could not meet the needs of all of the deserving poor, but they helped to cement attitudes about who the worthy were. Concerns about the harm to women's reputations, from charitable giving to certain poor persons, and the fear that vice could be encouraged by alleviating its dire conse-quences shows the tenuousness between 'deserving' and 'undeserving'. Religious reform and demographic pressure throughout Europe placed impoverished people, young and old, under increasing scrutiny, in the widespread attempts to alleviate poverty. Institutions, rates and social experiments demonstrated a slow movement away from individual to municipal responsibility for the poor in the later sixteenth century that gradually altered charitable practices and motivations. The transition from personal interaction and moral obligation towards formalized and potentially impersonal municipal relief certainly had its roots in the late medieval period, but the developments of the sixteenth century has-tened the transition.

Assessments of the worthiness of the poor relied on churchwardens' observation of their behaviour and knowledge of their reputations, the length of residence in the parish, and, especially for stranger poor, their religious affiliation or experience. The discrimination that labelled certain men and women 'undeserving' and the use of poor employees to exert social control were common to European charity in the sixteenth century. Continental hospitals and lay organizations employed poor women and men in the oversight of other recipients of charity and relief, like the Florentine confraternities that hired poor or 'working class' men to dis-tribute grain and to patrol taverns, fashioning the working class 'as the instrument of its own regulation'.[115] Norberg places the assault on popu-lar culture under the rubric of stern 'paternalism', espoused by men and women in the Company of the Holy Sacrament in Grenoble. She per-ceives greater cruelty in charity of the seventeenth century as charitable groups practised organized, deliberate social control.[116] St Botolph's paid men to watch alehouses and other places of entertainment during services

---

People, p. 39; temporary transcendence of strict gender roles through religious practice: Mack, *Visionary Women*, p. 49.

[115] This policy enforced 'social and moral orthodoxy on the working class, using the working class as the instrument of its own regulation': Weissman, *Ritual Brotherhood*, pp. 204–5.

[116] Norberg, *Rich and Poor in Grenoble*, pp. 26, 65. Safley argues against reducing charitable motives to paternalism or something sinister: *Charity and Economy*, p. 288. A desire to exert control behaviour and morality can, however, coexist with compassion.

and to bring strangers there to morning and evening prayer.[117] Exceptions to this tendency towards social control are apparent in Italy and Spain, however. Christopher Black does not see a consistent trend to social control in charity in Italy, despite an elaborate schema of the types of poor in society and a fear, noticeable from the late fifteenth century, of the idle poor. In Spain, traditional relief continued, without denial of charity for immorality or improper behaviour.[118]

The discriminating charity that attempted to curb disorder in sixteenth- and seventeenth-century Europe especially affected female recipients, but in England leaders stopped short of implementing radical policies to keep women out of poverty. Women in receipt of charity fell under parochial or confraternal control, whatever their ages. Poorer women became pariahs to local English churches as they wandered poor, possibly pregnant, and unattached through parishes. Jodi Mikalachki has noted the bind for women, who involuntarily became vagrants, and then could not support themselves through casual work.[119] The behaviour and morality of women, as potential burdens on the parish, became increasingly important to decisions about relief and charity.[120] In their efforts to encourage economic self-sufficiency or to prevent illegitimacy, however, churchwardens and civic leaders did not turn to a social policy once popular in medieval Europe and in Renaissance Italy: dowries for poor maidens.[121] London testators and parishes paid scant attention to poor maidens' dowries, although settling these women in marriages would have planted the responsibility for their children more squarely with the married fathers.[122] As Wiesner has pointed out, Lutheran theology arguably elevated marriage and the status of women, and dowry funds would have enabled more women to marry. This Lutheran change seems not to have taken firm hold in England, however, between the lack of change in marriage law and the

---

[117] GL, MS 1453/1, f. 3v.

[118] Black, *Italian Confraternities*, p. 144; Flynn, *Sacred Charity*, pp. 110–12.

[119] Mikalachki, 'Women's Networks and the Female Vagrant', pp. 56–7.

[120] 'Strange women were particularly vulnerable' to accusations in church courts: Carlson, *Marriage and the English Reformation*, p. 154.

[121] Black, *Italian Confraternities*, pp. 178–83; unsuccessful English attempts to provide dowries for poor girls: Carlson, *Marriage and the English Reformation*, p. 117. On sixteenth-century decline in gifts to poor maidens' dowries, contrasted with popularity of dowries over small and indiscriminate gifts to the poor in Christ in the fifteenth century: Cohn, *Death and Property*, pp. 165, 29.

[122] The portioning of daughters did not bankrupt English families, allowing them to avoid establishing more institutions or 'funds' to serve this social need for middling families. Cf. Julius Kirshner and Anthony Molho, 'The Dowry Fund and the Marriage Market in Early *Quattrocento* Florence', *Journal of Modern History*, 50, 3 (Sept. 1978), pp. 403–38.

noted practice of husbands to forbid their widows to remarry, despite the social and Christian benefits of marriage.[123]

Duty to the poor and repugnance with the idle, coexisted in medieval and early modern Europe. The poor's status did degrade over time, however, as they became more explicitly a burden on parishes, using up involuntary contributions made to the parish chest, rather than reminding inhabitants of death, purgatory and good works. As Marcel Mauss argued, the inability to reciprocate gift-giving lowered the status of the recipient.[124] The presence of poor men and women in post-Reformation burial processions and funeral services illustrated the power of patronage more than pious repayment of charity. In fact, sextons were expected to hire the parish's 'own' poor to 'yearne mony' at burials, admitting that the once idealized mournful procession had become another piece of the economy of makeshifts and offset low wages earned elsewhere.[125] The reiteration of an older language of mutual benefit and obligation in the Poor Law, in tracts about poverty, and in homilies shows the conscious effort to preserve charity and compassion despite reform of relief. Relief or charity did not redistribute income or property, but preserved the existing social order and fostered deference. The 'humbell thancks', offered by a young scholar at Cambridge in 1588 in a letter to the parish that provided his exhibition, deferentially expressed the lowly student's gratitude to his patrons.[126] Even the veterans of war, many of whom returned home disfigured and impoverished by their years of service, were not seen simply as the rightful recipients of national relief, as the statute for the relief of maimed (deserving) and vagrant (undeserving) soldiers demonstrated.[127]

---

[123] Wiesner notes that contributions to dowries may have been disparaged for their resemblance to traditional 'good works': 'Beyond women and the family', p. 320; Carlson, *Marriage and the English Reformation*, p. 180. Newberie's defence of the custom of London complained about husbands' strictures on widows, even though one could avoid sin and live a 'sociable Christian life' in marriage: *A Breefe Discourse*, p. 36.

[124] Mauss, *The Gift*, pp. 41–2.

[125] Warning to sexton Edward Tittle in St Michael's to be of good behaviour and to prefer the poor of his parish in hiring for burials. GL, MS 4072/1, Part 1, f. 89. (1603) 'Economy of makeshifts' coined by Hufton, *The poor of eighteenth-century France*, pp. 69–127. On link between capitalism and charity: Safley, *Charity and Economy*, p. 20.

[126] GL, MS 594/1, f. 12. Pullan, *Rich and Poor*, p. 229. In fact, McCants sees charitable institutions serving middling social groups, like the *Burgerweeshuis*, as being as essential to 'civic harmony' as those helping the very poor: *Civic Charity*, p.104. Charity's usefulness in fixing social rank and 'palliating the worst consequences of an unbalanced distribution of wealth': Safley, *Charity and Economy*, pp. 29–30.

[127] *TRP*, Vol. 3, pp. 46–8; 35 Eliz. c. 4. Geoffrey L. Hudson, 'Disabled Veterans, the State and Philanthropy in England, 1585–1680', p. 1 and handout; paper presented at the North American Conference on British Studies, October 1998, at Boulder, Colorado.

As in other Protestant countries, English leaders attempted to centralize poor relief in parishes and in foundations that survived in part
through the collection of involuntary rates that were sometimes compelled from wealthy parishes and their inhabitants. Testamentary charity
followed a similar pattern of centralizing, in churchwardens' hands,
and of imposing increasingly strict definitions of the deserving and
undeserving poor. Yet while the mode of relief is arguably a Protestant
style, with the special English additions of rates and eventually the
workhouse, the impetus for the reform of poor relief and charity came
from Catholics and Protestants across Europe. Regardless of doctrinal
differences, Protestants and Catholics sought to make relief and charity
more efficient and to exercise some form of social control over the poor,
to remake the idle into the industrious and to reform vices.[128]

Conclusion

Widespread fear of disorder and attempts to regulate the poor and
poverty marked the policies of Reformation and Catholic Reformation
countries alike. Protestant English efforts resembled those on the Continent, and London's actions looked similar to those of other locales in
England. Across religious lines, the participation of lay people in pious
devotions and in charity and relief became more formalized. Churchwardens' accounts and vestry minutes illustrate the problem of
demographic growth, the perception of worsening poverty in Reformation London, and the measures taken with limited parochial resources.
Population pressure necessitated and justified stricter regulation of the
poor to combat plague, disease, illegitimacy, crime, fire and overcrowding. Parochial leaders balanced discrimination with deeply held ideas of
obligation towards the poor, persisting from the medieval period. Within
England, aspects of the conditions in London, especially the city's size
and the lack of a landed nobility to offer traditional hospitality, created
some differences between the city and outlying areas. In efforts to
develop municipal aid schemes and to centralize relief, however, smaller
towns and rural communities resembled London.

The changes in relief contributed to, as well as drew on, the development of the parish as an administrative unit, without fully displacing its

---

[128] Jütte sees three principal areas of overlap between Catholic and Protestant poor
relief reform, in 'the enhanced role of the state', 'increasing rationalization, bureaucra-
tization and professionalization of relief work', and the use of 'education' for removing
'social evils' or 'reducing poverty in the next generation': *Poverty and Deviance*, pp.
101–3.

traditional role in the social and religious lives of parishioners. Religious services and burials were still fixed on the parish, but parochial officers increasingly centred on accounting for collections and expenditures relating to poor relief. Parochial leaders, as well as testators and other officials, split the poor into distinct categories of 'deserving' and 'undeserving', although these categories shifted. For middling and elite women, changes connected to the Reformation decreased their public participation in the parish and in public or formal charity and emphasized their household roles. In connection with demographic changes and hardening views of the poor, poor women became more vulnerable to prescriptions about morality. An emphasis on the 'most need' of worthy recipients rather than the 'health' or 'wealth' of donors' souls created and facilitated centralized relief and charity. Attempts first to control the numbers of poor legitimately calling on the parishes for relief and, second, to monitor those receiving aid, reflected parishes' incentive to protect funds, to limit indiscriminate charity, and to reform the able-bodied poor into productive workers.

Conclusion

In the sixteenth century, testators and parishioners responded to demographic, social, economic and religious changes that swept through the city of London. Charity to and relief of the poor shaped the wills and the churchwardens' accounts of the pre-Reformation and Reformation city. Some pious bequests maintained the church fabric, while others principally maintained the social fabric of the parish and the city at large. Before the abolition of purgatory and the destruction of shrines and images, testators and parishioners regularly supported elements of traditional Catholic services and devotions. Giving to the poor increased as testators redirected bequests away from the churches, in reflection of their uncertainty regarding religious change or of their whole-hearted adoption of the 'new ways'. The old benefactions linked to purgatory and prayers for souls, often including bequests for the parish fabric and the poor, were no longer viable.

Giving to the poor focused on the parish and on certain parochial traditions or duties, most specifically having to do with death and burial. Before the Reformation, the poor figured as significant actors in burial processions and continued to wear the gowns provided for the occasion in their everyday lives. Pre-Reformation testators asked for prayers from the poor, as well as from family, friends and members of the church. Following the Reformation, the poor continued to escort bodies to graves. After 1580, however, testators heeded developing notions of appropriate godly burials and began to shorten their processions.

The dichotomy between deserving and undeserving poor, having its roots in the medieval period, became increasingly significant as parishes assumed greater responsibilities in relief. Religious doctrine, economic spasms and new local and national needs contributed to the refinement of categories of worthiness. Poor women especially experienced difficulties, as migration and vagrancy became prominent social problems and abandonment and illegitimacy taxed parochial resources more sharply. Although giving increased to the poor as testators and parochial leaders sought new outlets for their piety, the bequests left to family, friends and neighbours grew at a faster pace.

The new ways presented challenges to the inhabitants of early modern London. On the one hand, charity continued to be extolled as an important sign of faith and humility. Yet charity was no longer connected to requests for prayers for souls or to the good works that formerly insured salvation. Further, popular pre-Reformation targets of bequests like fraternities or shrines, that often directly or indirectly aided the worthy poor, became objects of ridicule and disdain. Puritan preachers discouraged vainglorious burial processions, indiscriminate doles, and even suspected funeral sermons of perpetuating the old ways, although all of these areas could relieve the poor. Women in particular responded to new religious ideas and altered their final bequests, but in doing so diminished their own opportunities to augment their and their families' reputations. As reform took hold in the city, women struggled to maintain influence in civic and parochial practice, most notably through their charity.

The Reformation took hold in London by the later sixteenth century, though not without disputes or at least negotiations. Prominent men, like Sir Martin Bowes and Philip Gunter, found ways of keeping their reputations and positions through the vagaries of religious change, despite their private beliefs. Women supported reform and reaction by directing their charity to certain poor men and women and by embracing elements of religious doctrine that can be discerned through their last wills. Going to church in London in the 1570s was a different experience than it had been in the 1530s, partly because parishioners sat in new pews, listened to endowed preachers and lecturers, and participated in the formation and implementation of new social and religious policies.

Bibliography

Manuscript Sources

A   Corporation of London Record Office

CLRO Rep.	Repertory Books, Court of Aldermen

B   Public Record Office

Probate 11/12–136	Wills and Administrations, Prerogative Court of Canterbury, 1500–1620

C   Guildhall Library

MS 9051/2–6	Wills and Administrations, Archdeaconry Court, 1549–1627
MS 9171/9–20	Wills and Administrations, Commissary Court, 1517–1603

Churchwardens' Accounts

Add. MS 292	Account of Churchwarden, 1587–8, St Stephen Walbrook
Add. MS 207	Account of Churchwarden, 1592–3, St Stephen Walbrook
MS 593/1	St Stephen Walbrook (1474–1538)
MS 593/2	St Stephen Walbrook (1549–1637)
MS 593/3	St Stephen Walbrook (1577–81)
MS 593/4	St Stephen Walbrook (1637–1748)
MS 1002/1A	St Mary Woolnoth (1539–99)
MS 1002/1B	St Mary Woolnoth (1599–1641)
MS 1454, Rolls 1–105	St Botolph Aldersgate (1466–1636)
MS 4071/1	St Michael Cornhill (1455–75, 1547–1608)
MS 4071/2	St Michael Cornhill (1608–1702)

Vestry Minutes

MS 1453/1	St Botolph Aldersgate (1601–57)
MS 4072/1	St Michael Cornhill (1563–1646/47)
MS 594/1	St Stephen Walbrook (1587–1614)

Other

MS 1005/1	Register of Charitable Donations, St Mary Woolnoth (1523–1812)
MS 4083	Ancient Abstract Book of Deeds, Evidences, Muniments, St Michael Cornhill, compiled 1696 and later
MS 90/2–7	Miscellaneous Materials, St Michael Cornhill
MS 3103	Deeds, Property, Inventory, St Stephen Walbrook
MS 1506/1–5	Indenture Records
Add. MSS. 217	Indenture, Edward Stephens
MS 15, 361	Skidmore Legacy, St Botolph Aldersgate

Parish Registers

MS 7635/1	St Mary Woolnoth
MS 8319/1	St Stephen Walbrook
MS 4061	Register of Christenings, Marriages and Burials, St Michael Cornhill, 1546–1657, deaths 1546–1653
MS 4062	Register General, St Michael Cornhill, 1558–1654

Printed Primary Sources

Archer, I., C. Barron, V. Harding (eds), *Hugh Alley's Caveat: The Markets of London in 1598*, London Topographical Society, Publication No. 137 (London, 1988).

Awdelay, J., *The fraternitye of uacabondes* (London, 1575, 2nd edn) STC 994.

Basing, P. (ed.), *Parish Fraternity Register: Fraternity of the Holy Trinity and SS. Fabian and Sebastian in the Parish of St. Botolph without Aldersgate*, London Record Society, 18 (London, 1982).

Bourman, N., *An Epitaph upon the decease of the worshipfull Lady Mary Ramsey, late wife unto Sir Thomas Ramsey Knight, sometime Lord Maior and Alderman of the honorable Cittie of London. Whereunto is annexed certaine short epigrams, touching the mortalitie of man. Published by the consent of the executors. Written by N.B.* (London, R. R[ead], 1602) STC 3415.

A Breefe Discourse, declaring and approuing the necessarie and inviola-

ble maintenance of the laudable Customes of London, printed by Henrie Midleton for Rafe Newberie (London, 1584) STC 16747, reprinted New York, 1973.

Brinkelow, H., *The Complaint of Roderick Mors*, No. 500, The English Experience (New York, 1973).

————, *The Complaint of Roderick Mors and The Lamentacyon of a Christen against the cytye of London*, Early English Text Society, J. Meadows Cowper (ed.), (London, 1874).

Brooke, J.M.S. and A.W.C. Hallen (eds), *The Transcript of the Registers of the United Parishes of S. Mary Woolnoth and S. Mary Woolchurch Haw, in the City of London, from their Commencement 1538–1760* (London: Bowles & Son, 1886).

Cressy, D. and L. Ferrell (eds), *Religion and Society in Early Modern England: A Sourcebook* (London, 1996).

Darlington, I. (ed.), *London Consistory Court Wills, 1492–1547*, London Record Society, 3 (London, 1967).

Downame, J., *The plea of the poore, or a treatise of beneficence and almsdeeds* (London, 1616, printed by Edward Griffin for Ralph Mabbe), STC 7146.

Fabyan, R., *The Great Chronicle of London*, A.H. Thomas and J.D. Thornley (eds) (London: George W. Jones at the Sign of the Dolphin, 1938), orig. 1516.

————, *The New Chronicle of England and France*, Henry Ellis (ed.), (London, 1811).

Foxe, J., *The Second Volume of the Ecclesiasticall Historie, Containing the Acts and Monuments of Martyrs* (London, 1610).

Frere, W.H. and W. McClure Kennedy (eds), *Visitation Articles and Injunctions of the Period of the Reformation* (3 vols, Alcuin Club, 1910).

Gough, R., *The History of Myddle*, D. Hey (ed.) (Harmondsworth, 1981).

Hall, E., *Hall's Chronicle: containing the history of England, during the reign of Henry the Fourth, and the succeeding monarchs, to the end of the reign of Henry the Eighth, in which are particularly described the manners and customs of those periods. Carefully collated with the editions of 1548 and 1550* (London, 1809).

Hughes, P.L. and J.F. Larkin (eds), *Tudor Royal Proclamations* (3 vols, New Haven and London, 1969).

Humphery-Smith, C.R. (ed.) *The Phillimore Atlas and Index of Parish Registers* (Sussex: Phillimore & Company, Ltd, 1984).

Kitching, C.J., *London and Middlesex Chantry Certificate, 1548*, London Record Society, 16 (London, 1980).

A letter sent by the Maydens of London, to the vertuous Matrones &

Mistresses of the same, in the defense of their lawfull libertie. Answering the Mery Meeting by us Rose, Iane, Rachell, Sara, Philumias, and Dorothie, Henry Binneman for Thomas Hacket, London, 1567, STC 16754.5.

London, Court of Common Council, Committee in Relation to the Royal Hospitals, *Memoranda, References, and documents relating to the royal hospitals of the city of London* (London, 1836).

Maitland, W., *The History and Survey of London, From Its Foundation to the Present Time* (London, 1756).

Newes from Vienna the .5. day of August .1566. of the strong towne and Castell of Jula in Hungary, printed by John Awdelay (London, 1566) STC 24716.

Nichols, J.G. (ed.), *Chronicle of the Grey Friars of London*, Camden Society, vol. 53 (London, 1852).

————, *The Diary of Henry Machyn, citizen and Merchant-Taylor of London. From* AD *1550 to* AD *1563*, Camden Society, vol. 42 (London, 1848).

Overall, W.H. (ed.), *The Accounts of the Churchwardens of the Parish of St Michael Cornhill, in the City of London, from 1456 to 1608* (London, 1871).

Page, W. (ed.), *Victoria County History: London* (Folkestone and London, 1974).

A Psalme of Thanksgiving – to be sung on Monday in Easter Holy-days at St Mary's Spital for founders and benefactors (by children of Christ's Hospital), London: R. Oulton, 1641. TT E.669.f.4 [5].

A Relation of the Island of England, c. 1500, Camden Society, Vol. 37, (London, 1847).

Schofield, J. (ed.), *The London Surveys of Ralph Treswell*, London Topographical Society, Publication No. 135 (London, 1987).

Scouloudi, I., *Returns of Strangers in the Metropolis 1593, 1627, 1635, 1639: A Study of an Active Minority*, Quarto Series of the Huguenot Society of London, Vol. 57 (London, 1985).

Sermons, or Homilies, Appointed to Be Read in Churches in the Time of Queen Elizabeth, of Famous Memory. In two parts, the first American from the last Oxford Edition (New York, 1815), Early American Imprints, no. 34346.

Somers, Baron J., *A Collection of Scarce and Valuable Tracts* (London, 1809).

Stow, J., *A Survay of London*, written 1598, increased 1603, William J. Thoms (ed.) (London, 1876).

————, *A Survay of London*, (*London under Elizabeth: A Survey*), Henry Morley (ed.) (London, 1890).

Strype, J., *A Survey of the cities of London and Westminster: containing the original, antiquity, increase, modern estate and government of those cities. Written at first in the year MDXCVIII. By John Stow, citizen and native of London* (2 vols, London, 1720).

Tanner, T., *Notitia Monastica: Or, an account of all the abbies, priories, and houses of friars, heretofore in England and Wales; and also of all the colleges and hospitals founded before AD 1540* (London, 1744).

Tawney, R.H. and E. Power, *Tudor Economic Documents* (3 vols, London, 1951).

Thirsk, J. and J.P. Cooper (eds), *Seventeenth-Century Economic Documents* (Oxford, 1972).

Waterton, E., *Pietas Mariana Britannica: a history of English devotion to the Most Blessed Virgin Marye Mother of God: with a catalogue of shrines, sanctuaries, offerings, bequests and other memorials of the piety of our forefathers* (2 vols, London, 1879).

Wright, P.D.D. (ed.), *The New and Complete Book of Martyrs; or, An Universal History of Martyrdom: Being Fox's Book of Martyrs, revised and corrected* (2 vols, New York, 1794).

Wriothesley, C., *A Chronicle of England During the Reigns of the Tudors, from AD 1485 to 1559*, 2 vols, W.D. Hamilton (ed.), Camden Society (London, 1875–77).

Printed Secondary Sources

Abbott, M., *Life Cycles in England, 1560–1720: Cradle to Grave* (London and New York, 1996).

Amussen, S.D., 'Gender, Family and the Social Order' in A. Fletcher and J. Stevenson (eds), *Order and Disorder in Early Modern England* (Cambridge, 1985), 196–217.

———, *An Ordered Society: Gender and Class in Early Modern England* (Oxford, 1988).

Andrew, D.T., *Philanthropy and Police: London Charity in the Eighteenth Century* (Princeton, 1989).

Andrews, K.R., *Trade, plunder and settlement: Maritime enterprise and the genesis of the British Empire, 1480–1630* (Cambridge, 1984).

Archer, I., *The Pursuit of Stability: Social Relations in Elizabethan London* (Cambridge, 1991).

———, 'The nostalgia of John Stow' in D.L. Smith, R. Strier and D. Bevington (eds), *The Theatrical City: Culture, Theatre and Politics in London, 1576–1649* (Cambridge, 1995), 17–34.

Aston, M., 'Segregation in church' in W.J. Sheils and D. Wood (eds), *Women in the Church* (Oxford and Cambridge, MA, 1990), 237–94.

————, *The King's Bedpost: Reformation and Iconography in a Tudor Group Portrait* (Cambridge, 1993).

Aston, M. and E. Ingram, 'The Iconography of the *Acts and Monuments*' in D. Loades (ed.), *John Foxe and the English Reformation* (Aldershot, 1997), 66–142.

Attreed, L., 'Poverty, payments, and fiscal policies in English provincial towns' in S.K. Cohn and S. Epstein (eds), *Portraits of Medieval Living: Essays in Memory of David Herlihy* (Ann Arbor, MI, 1996), 325–48.

Baillie, H., 'Some biographical notes on English church musicians, chiefly working in London (1485–1569)', *Royal Musical Association Research Chronicle*, **2** (1962), 18–57.

Barron, C., 'The Parish Fraternities of Medieval London' in C.M. Barron and C. Harper-Bill (eds), *The Church in Pre-Reformation Society: Essays in Honour of F.R.H. Du Boulay* (Woodbridge, Suffolk, 1985), 13–37.

Barron, C. and A.F. Sutton (eds), *Medieval London Widows 1300–1500* (London, 1994).

Beaver, D.C., *Parish Communities and Religious Conflict in the Vale of Gloucester, 1590–1690* (Cambridge, MA, 1998).

Beier, A.L., *Masterless Men: The Vagrancy Problem in England, 1560–1640* (London and New York, 1985).

Ben-Amos, I.K., 'Women apprentices in the trades and crafts of early modern Bristol', *Continuity and Change* **6**, 2 (1991), 227–52.

————, *Adolescence and Youth in Early Modern England* (New Haven and London, 1994).

Bennett, J., 'Conviviality and Charity in Medieval and Early Modern England', *PaP*, **134** (Feb. 1992), 19–41.

————, 'Women's history: a study in continuity and change', *Women's History Review*, **2**, 2 (1993), 173–84.

————, 'Reply', *PaP*, **154** (Feb. 1997), 235–42.

Berlin, M., 'Civic Ceremony in Early Modern London', *Urban History Yearbook 1986*, 15–27.

Bestor, J.F., 'Marriage Transactions in Renaissance Italy and Mauss's *Essay on the Gift*', *PaP*, **164** (Aug. 1999), 6–46.

Bindman, D., *Hogarth* (London, 1981).

Binion, R., *After Christianity: Christian Survivals in Post-Christian Culture* (Durango, CO, 1986).

Black, C.F., *Italian Confraternities in the Sixteenth Century* (Cambridge, 1989).

Botelho, L., 'Old age and menopause in rural women of early modern Suffolk' in *Women and Ageing* (Harlow, 2000), 43–65.

Botelho, L. and P. Thane (eds), *Women and Ageing in British Society since 1500* (Harlow, 2001).

Boulton, J., *Neighbourhood and Society: A London Suburb in the Seventeenth Century* (Cambridge, 1987).

Bremer, F.J., 'William Winthrop and Religious Reform in London 1529–1582', *London Journal* **24**, 2 (1999), 1–17.

Brigden, S., 'Youth and the English Reformation', *PaP*, **95** (May 1982), 37–67.

————, 'Religion and Social Obligation in Early Sixteenth-Century London', *PaP*, **103** (May 1984), 67–112.

————, *London and the Reformation* (Oxford, 1989).

Brodsky Elliott, V., 'Single Women in the London Marriage Market: Age, Status and Mobility, 1598–1619' in R.B. Outhwaite (ed.), *Marriage and Society: Studies in the Social History of Marriage* (New York, 1981), 81–100.

Brodsky, V., 'Widows in Late Elizabethan London: Remarriage, Economic Opportunity and Family Orientations' in L. Bonfield, R.M. Smith and K. Wrightson (eds), *The World We Have Gained: Histories of Population and Social Structure* (Oxford, 1986), 122–54.

Brown, A., *Popular Piety in Late Medieval England: The Diocese of Salisbury, 1250–1550* (Oxford, 1995).

Brown, K.M., '"Changed ... into the Fashion of Man": The Politics of Sexual Difference in a Seventeenth-Century Anglo-American Settlement' in C. Clinton and M. Gillespie (eds), *The Devil's Lane: Sex and Race in the Early South* (New York and London, 1997), 39–56.

Burgess, C., 'Late Medieval Wills and Pious Convention: Testamentary Evidence Reconsidered' in M. Hicks (ed.), *Profit, Piety and the Professions in Later Medieval England* (Gloucester, 1990), 14–33.

————, 'Shaping the Parish: St Mary at Hill, London, in the Fifteenth Century' in J. Blair and B. Golding (eds), *The Cloister and the World: Essays in Medieval History in Honour of Barbara Harvey* (Oxford, 1996), 246–86.

Burgess, C. and B. Kümin, 'Penitential Bequests and Parish Regimes in Late Medieval England', *Journal of Ecclesiastical History*, **44**, 4 (Oct. 1993), 610–30.

Burke, P., *Popular Culture in Early Modern Europe* (New York, 1978).

————, 'Popular Culture in Seventeenth-Century London' in B. Reay (ed.), *Popular Culture in Seventeenth-Century England* (London and Sydney, 1985), 31–58.

Capp, B., 'The double standard revisited: plebeian women and male sexual reputation in early modern England', *PaP*, **162** (Feb. 1999), 70–100.

Carlson, E.J., *Marriage and the English Reformation* (Oxford, 1994).

Carrier, J.G., *Gifts and Commodities: Exchange and Western Capitalism since 1700* (London and New York, 1995).

Carroll, W.C., *Fat King, Lean Beggar: Representations of Poverty in the Age of Shakespeare* (Ithaca and London, 1996).

The Catholic Encyclopedia (1913). This is available on-line through New Advent on <http://www.newadvent.org/cathen/>.

Clark, A., *Working Life of Women in the Seventeenth Century* (London, 1982), orig. 1919.

Clark, E., 'Social Welfare and Mutual Aid in the Medieval Countryside', *JBS* 33, 4 (Oct. 1994), 381–406.

Clark, P., 'The migrant in Kentish towns 1580–1640', Clark and Slack (eds), *Crisis and Order in English Towns, 1500–1700: Essays in Urban History* (Toronto, 1972), 117–63.

Clark, P., 'The Alehouse and Alternative Society' in D. Pennington and K. Thomas (eds), *Puritans and Revolutionaries: Essays in Seventeenth-Century History Presented to Christopher Hill* (Oxford, 1978), 47–72.

Clark, P. and P. Slack (eds), *Crisis and Order in English Towns, 1500–1700: Essays in Urban History* (Toronto, 1972).

Clay, R.M., *The Medieval Hospitals of England* (New York, 1966), orig. 1909.

Cohn, S.K., *Death and Property in Siena* (Baltimore, MD, 1988).

————, *The Cult of Remembrance and the Black Death: Six Renaissance Cities in Central Italy* (Baltimore, MD, 1992).

Cole, R.G., 'Pamphlet Woodcuts in the Communication Process of Reformation Germany' in K.C. Sessions and P.N. Bebb (eds), *Pietas et Societas: New Trends in Reformation Social History, Essays in Memory of Harold J. Grimm*, Vol. IV of Sixteenth Century Essays & Studies (Ann Arbor, MI, 1985), 103–22.

Collinson, P., *The Religion of Protestants* (Oxford, 1982).

————, *The Birthpangs of Protestant England: Religious and Cultural Change in the Sixteenth and Seventeenth Centuries* (New York, 1988).

Coster, W., 'Popular religion and the parish register 1538–1603' in *The Parish*, 94–111.

Cox, J.C., *Churchwardens' Accounts: From the Fourteenth Century to the Close of the Seventeenth Century* (London, 1913).

————, *The English Parish Church* (London, 1914).

————, *Pulpits, Lecterns, and Organs in English Churches* (London, 1915).

Craig, J. and C. Litzenberger, 'Wills as Religious Propaganda: The Testament of William Tracy', *Journal of Ecclesiastical History*, 44, 3 (1993), 415–31.

Crawford, P., *Women and Religion in England 1500–1720* (London and New York, 1993).

Cressy, D., *Bonfires and Bells: National Memory and the Protestant Calendar in Elizabethan and Stuart England* (Berkeley and Los Angeles, CA, 1989).

———, *Birth, Marriage and Death: Ritual, Religion and the Life-Cycle in Tudor and Stuart England* (Oxford, 1997).

Cross, C., *Church and People, 1450–1660: The Triumph of the Laity in the English Church* (Atlantic Highlands, NJ, 1976).

———, 'The Development of Protestantism in Leeds and Hull, 1520–1640: The Evidence from Wills', *Northern History*, **18** (1982), 230–8.

———, 'The religious life of women in sixteenth-century Yorkshire' in W.J. Sheils and D. Wood (eds), *Women in the Church*, Studies in Church History, **27** (Oxford, 1990), 307–24.

Cunningham, C., 'Christ's Hospital: Infant and Child Mortality in the Sixteenth Century', *Local Population Studies*, **18** (1977) 37–40.

Davies, C.S.L., 'Slavery and Protector Somerset; the Vagrancy Act of 1547', *Economic History Review*, 2nd series, **19** (1966), 533–49.

Davies, M., 'Thomasyne Percivale, "The Maid of the Week" (d. 1512)' in C.M. Barron and A.F. Sutton (eds), *Medieval London Widows 1300–1500* (London, 1994), 185–207.

———, 'The Tailors of London: Corporate Charity in the Late Medieval Town' in R. Archer (ed.), *Crown, Government and People in the Fifteenth Century* (New York, 1995), 161–90.

Davis, N.Z., 'City Women and Religious Change' in *Society and Culture in Early Modern France* (Stanford, CA, 1975 edn, 1965 orig.), 65–95.

———, 'The Sacred and the Body Social in Sixteenth-Century Lyon', *PaP*, **90** (Feb. 1981), 40–70.

———, 'Poor Relief, Humanism, and Heresy' in *Society and Culture in Early Modern France* (Stanford, CA, 1987), 17–64.

Dickens, A.G., *Lollards and Protestants in the Diocese of York, 1509–1558* (London, 1959).

———, *The English Reformation* (New York, 1964).

Dubois, E., 'Almsgiving in Post Reformation England', *History of European Ideas*, **9**, 4 (1988), 489–95.

Duffy, E., 'The Godly and the Multitude in Stuart England', *Seventeenth Century*, **1**, 1 (1986), 31–55.

———, *The Stripping of the Altars: Traditional Religion in England, 1400–1580* (New Haven and London, 1992).

———, 'The parish, piety, and patronage in late medieval East Anglia: the evidence of rood screens', in *The Parish*, 133–62.

Emmison, F.G., 'Poor Relief Accounts of Two Rural Parishes in Bedfordshire, 1563–1598', *Economic History Review*, **3** (1931), 102–16.

———, 'The Care of the Poor in Elizabethan Essex: Recently Discovered Records', *Essex Review*, **62** (1953), 7–28.

Erickson, A.L., *Women and Property in Early Modern England* (London and New York, 1993).

Everitt, A., 'The English Urban Inn 1560–1760' in Alan Everitt (ed.), *Perspectives in English Urban History* (New York, 1973), 91–137.

Farnhill, K., 'Religious policy and parish "conformity": Cratfield's lands in the sixteenth century' in *The Parish*, 217–29.

Febvre, L., 'The Origins of the French Reformation: A Badly-Put Question?' in Peter Burke (ed.), *A New Kind of History* (London, 1973), 44–107.

Felch, S., 'Shaping the reader in the *Acts and Monuments*', in D. Loades (ed.), *John Foxe and the English Reformation* (Aldershot, 1997), 52–65.

Fideler, P.A., 'Poverty, policy and providence: the Tudors and the Poor' in Fideler and T.F. Mayer (eds), *Political Thought and the Tudor Commonwealth* (London and New York, 1992), 194–222.

———, '*Societas, Civitas* and Early Elizabethan Poverty Relief' in C. Carlton, R.L. Woods et al. (eds), *State, Sovereigns and Society in Early Modern England: Essays in Honour of A.J. Slavin* (New York, 1998), 59–70.

Fildes, V. (ed.), *Women as Mothers in Pre-Industrial England: Essays in Memory of Dorothy McLaren* (London and New York, 1990).

Finlay, R., *Population and Metropolis: The Demography of London, 1580–1650* (Cambridge, 1985).

Finucane, R.C., *Miracles and Pilgrims: Popular Beliefs in Medieval England* (New York, 1995), orig. 1977.

———, 'Sacred Corpse, Profane Carrion: Social Ideals and Death Rituals in the Later Middle Ages' in Joachim Whaley (ed.), *Mirrors of Mortality: Studies in the Social History of Death* (New York, 1981), 40–60.

Fletcher, A., *Gender, Sex and Subordination in England, 1500–1800* (New Haven and London, 1995).

Flynn, M., *Sacred Charity: Confraternities and Social Welfare in Spain, 1400–1700* (Ithaca, NY, 1989).

Foster, A., 'Churchwardens' accounts of early modern England and Wales: some problems to note, but much to be gained' in *The Parish*, 74–93.

Foyster, E., 'A Laughing Matter? Marital Discord and Gender Control in Seventeenth-Century England', *Rural History* **4**, 1 (1993), 5–21.

French, K., '"To Free Them from Binding": Women in the Late Medieval English Parish', *Journal of Interdisciplinary History*, **27**, 3 (Winter 1997), 387–412.

————, 'Parochial fund-raising in late medieval Somerset' in French et al., *The Parish*, 115–32.

————, 'Maidens' lights and wives' stores: Women's parish guilds in late medieval England', *SCJ*, **29**, 2 (Summer, 1998), 399–425.

————, *The People of the Parish: Community Life in a Late Medieval English Diocese* (Philadelphia, PA, 2001).

French, K., G. Gibbs and B.A. Kümin (eds), *The Parish in English Life, 1400–1600* (Manchester, 1997).

Frye, S. and K. Robertson (eds), *Maids and Mistresses, Cousins and Queens: Women's Alliances in Early Modern England* (Oxford and New York, 1999).

Gavitt, P., *Charity and Children in Renaissance Florence: The Ospedale degli Innocenti, 1410–1536* (Ann Arbor, MI, 1990).

Gibbs, G., 'New duties for the parish community in Tudor London' in *The Parish*, 163–77.

Gillis, J.R., *For Better, For Worse: British Marriages, 1600 to the Present* (New York and Oxford, 1985).

Gittings, C., *Death, Burial and the Individual in Early Modern England* (London and Sydney, 1984).

————, 'Urban Funerals in Late Medieval and Reformation England' in Steven Bassett (ed.), *Death in Towns: Urban Responses to the Dying and the Dead, 100–1600* (Leicester, London, New York, 1992), 170–83.

Goldberg, P.J.P., 'Women's Work, Women's Role, in the Late-Medieval North' in Michael A. Hicks (ed.), *Profit, Piety and the Professions in Later Medieval England* (Gloucester, 1990), 34–50.

Goody, J., *The Development of the Family and Marriage in Europe* (Cambridge, 1983).

Gowing, L., *Domestic Dangers: Women, Words, and Sex in Early Modern London* (Oxford, 1996).

————, 'Secret Births and Infanticide in Seventeenth-Century England', *PaP*, **156** (August 1997), 87–115.

Graves, C.P., 'Social space in the English medieval parish church', *Economy and Society*, **18**, 3 (August 1989), 297–322.

Griffiths, P., *Youth and Authority: Formative Experiences in England, 1560–1640* (Oxford, 1996).

Haigh, C. (ed.), *The English Reformation Revised* (Cambridge, 1987).

————, *English Reformations: Religion, Politics, and Society under the Tudors* (Oxford, 1993).

Hampson, E.M., *The Treatment of Poverty in Cambridgeshire, 1597–1834* (Cambridge, 1934).

Hanawalt, B., *Growing Up in Medieval London: The Experience of Childhood in History* (New York, 1993).

Harding, V., '"And one more may be laid there": The Location of Burials in Early Modern London', *The London Journal*, **14**, 2 (1989), 112–29.

———, 'Burial Choice and Burial Location in Later Medieval London' in S. Bassett (ed.), *Death in Towns: Urban Responses to the Dying and the Dead, 100–1600* (Leicester, London, New York, 1992), 119–35.

———, 'Burial of the plague dead in early modern London', in J.A.I. Champion (ed.), *Epidemic Disease in London* (London Centre for Metropolitan History Working Papers Series, No. 1, 1993), 53–64, on-line at http://www.ihrinfo.ac.uk/cmh/epiharding.html

Harris, B., 'A new look at the Reformation: aristocratic women and nunneries 1450–1540', *JBS*, **32** (1993), 89–113.

Hazlitt, W.C., *The Livery Companies of the City of London: Their Origin, Character, Development, and Social and Political Importance* (New York and London, 1969), orig. 1892.

Heal, F., *Hospitality in Early Modern England* (Oxford, 1990).

Herbert, W., *The History of the Twelve Great Livery Companies of London* (2 vols, Newton Abbot, 1968), orig. published by author at the Guildhall Library, London, 1834–1837.

Herlan, R.W., 'Relief of the Poor in Bristol from Late Elizabethan Times until the Restoration Era', *Proceedings of the American Philosophical Society*, **126**, 3 (1982), 212–28.

Hickman, D., 'From Catholic to Protestant: the changing meaning of testamentary religious provisions in Elizabethan London' in N. Tyacke (ed.), *England's Long Reformation* (London, 1998), 117–39.

Hill, B., 'Women's history: a study in change, continuity or standing still?', *Women's History Review*, **2**, 1 (1993), 5–22.

Hill, C., 'William Perkins and the Poor' in *Puritanism and Revolution: Studies in the Interpretation of the English Revolution of the Seventeenth Century* (London, 1958), 215–38.

Himmelfarb, G., *The Idea of Poverty: England in the Early Industrial Age* (New York, 1985).

Hoffer, P.C. and N.E.H. Hull, *Murdering Mothers: Infanticide in England and New England, 1558–1803* (New York, 1981).

Holderness, B.A., 'Widows in pre-industrial society: an essay upon their economic functions', in R.M. Smith (ed.), *Land, Kinship and Life-Cycle* (Cambridge, 1984), 423–43.

Houlbrooke, R., *Church Courts and the People During the English Reformation, 1520–1570* (Oxford, 1979).

Hufton, O.H., *The Poor of Eighteenth-Century France, 1750–1789* (Oxford, 1974).

Hughes, A., 'Introduction' to 'Anglo-American Puritanisms', *JBS*, **39**, 1 (Jan. 2000), 1–7.

Hutton, R., 'The Local Impact of the Tudor Reformations' in C. Haigh (ed.), *The Reformation Revised* (Cambridge, 1987), 114–38.

———, *The Rise and Fall of Merry England: The Ritual Year 1400–1700* (Oxford and New York, 1994).

Ingram, M., 'The Reform of Popular Culture? Sex and Marriage in Early Modern England' in B. Reay (ed.), *Popular Culture in Seventeenth-Century England* (London, 1985), 129–65.

Johnson, R.C., 'The transportation of vagrant children from London to Virginia, 1618–1622' in H.S. Reinmuth (ed.), *Early Stuart Studies: Essays in Honor of David Harris Willson* (Minneapolis, MN, 1970), 137–51.

Johnston, A.F. and S.-B. MacLean, 'Reformation and resistance in Thames/Severn parishes: the dramatic witness' in French et al., *The Parish*, 178–200.

Jones, A.R., 'Maidservants of London: Sisterhoods of Kinship and Labor' in S. Frye and K. Robertson (eds), *Maids and Mistresses, Cousins and Queens: Women's Alliances in Early Modern England* (Oxford and New York, 1999), 21–32.

Jones, E., 'London in the Early Seventeenth Century: An Ecological Approach', *The London Journal*, **6**, 2 (Winter 1980), 123–33.

Jones, G.S., *Outcast London: A Study in the Relationship between Classes in Victorian Society* (Oxford, 1971).

Jones, N., 'Living the Reformations: Generational Experience and Political Perception in Early Modern England', *Huntington Library Quarterly*, **60**, 3 (1999), 273–88.

Jordan, W.K., *The Charities of London, 1480–1660: The Aspirations and the Achievements of the Urban Society* (London, 1960).

———, *Philanthropy in England, 1480–1660: A Study of the Changing Pattern of English Social Aspirations* (Westport, CT, 1978).

Jütte, R., *Poverty and Deviance in Early Modern Europe* (Cambridge, 1994).

Keene, D., *The Walbrook Study: A Summary Report*, Social and Economic Study of Medieval London c. 1100–1666, London University, Institute of Historical Research, 1987.

Kent, J.R., 'Population Mobility and Alms: Poor Migrants in the Midlands during the Early Seventeenth Century', *Local Population Studies*, **27** (1981), 35–51.

Kertzer, D., 'Toward a historical demography of aging' in Kertzer and Peter Laslett (eds), *Aging in the Past: Demography, Society, and Old Age* (Berkeley, CA, 1995), 363–83.

Kingdon, R.M., 'Social Welfare in Calvin's Geneva', *American Historical Review*, **76**, 1 (1971), 50–69.

Kirshner, J. and A. Molho, 'The Dowry Fund and the Marriage Market in Early *Quattrocento* Florence', *Journal of Modern History*, **50**, 3 (Sept. 1978), 403–38.

Kisby, F., 'Music and Musicians of Early Tudor Westminster', *Early Music*, **23**, 2 (1995), 223–40.

———, 'Royal Minstrels in the City and Suburbs of Early Tudor London: Professional Activities and Private Interests', *Early Music*, **25**, 2 (1997), 199–219.

Kisby, F. (ed.), *Music and Musicians in Renaissance Urban Communities* (Cambridge, 2001).

———, 'Books in London Parish Churches, c. 1400 – c. 1603' in C. Barron and J. Stratford (eds), *The Church and Learning in Late Medieval Society: Essays in Honour of Barrie Dobson*, Proceedings of the Harlaxton Symposium (Grantham, forthcoming).

Kitching, C.J., 'The Quest for Concealed Lands in the Reign of Elizabeth I', *TRHS*, 5th series, **24** (1974), 63–78.

Klapisch-Zuber, C., *Women, Family, and Ritual in Renaissance Italy* (Chicago, 1987).

Knowles, D., *The Religious Orders in England* (3 vols, Cambridge, 1961).

Kowaleski, M. (ed.), 'Vill, Guild, and Gentry: Forces of Community in Later Medieval England', *JBS* **33**, 4 (Oct. 1994).

Kreider, A., *English Chantries: The Road to Dissolution* (Cambridge, MA, 1979).

Kümin, B., *The Shaping of a Community: The Rise and Reformation of the English Parish, c. 1400–1560* (Aldershot, 1996).

———, 'Masses, Morris and Metrical Psalms: Music in the English Parish c.1400–1600' in F. Kisby (ed.), *Music and Musicians in Renaissance Urban Communities* (Cambridge, 2001), 216–41.

Kunze, B.Y., *Margaret Fell and the Rise of Quakerism* (Stanford, CA, 1994).

Lake, P. and D. Como, 'Orthodoxy and Its Discontents: Dispute Settlement and the Production of "Consensus" in the London (Puritan) "Underground"', *JBS*, **39**, 1 (Jan. 2000), 34–70.

Laslett, P., *Family Life and Illicit Love in Earlier Generations: Essays in Historical Sociology* (Cambridge, 1977).

———, 'The traditional English family and the aged in our society' in

D.D. Van Tassel (ed.), *Aging, Death and the Completion of Being* (Philadelphia, PA, 1979), 97–113.

Leonard, E.M., *The Early History of English Poor Relief* (New York, 1965), orig. 1900.

Levin, C., *The Heart and Stomach of a King: Elizabeth I and the Politics of Sex and Power* (Philadelphia, PA, 1994).

Lewis, S., *Topographical Dictionary of England*, 7th ed. (London, 1848).

Litzenberger, C., 'St Michael's, Gloucester, 1540–1580: the cost of conformity in sixteenth-century England' in French et al. (eds), *The Parish*, 230–49.

————, *The English Reformation and the Laity: Gloucestershire, 1540–1580* (Cambridge, 1997).

Liu, T., *Puritan London: A Study of Religion and Society in the City Parishes* (Newark, DE, 1986).

Loach, J., *Parliament and the Crown in the Reign of Mary Tudor* (Oxford, 1986).

Loades, D.M., *Mary Tudor: A Life* (Oxford, 1989).

————, (ed.), *John Foxe and the English Reformation* (Aldershot, 1997).

MacDonald, M., *Mystical Bedlam: Madness, Anxiety, and Healing in Seventeenth-Century England* (Cambridge, 1981).

Mack, P., *Visionary Women: Ecstatic Prophecy in Seventeenth-Century England* (Berkeley, CA, 1992).

Maltby, J., *Prayer Book and People in Elizabethan and Early Stuart England* (Cambridge, 1998).

Manley, L., 'Of Site and Rites', in D.L. Smith, R. Strier and D. Bevington (eds), *The Theatrical City: Culture, Theatre and Politics in London, 1576–1649* (Cambridge, 1995), 35–54.

Manzione, C.K., *Christ's Hospital of London, 1552–1598: 'A Passing Deed of Pity'* (Selinsgrove, PA and London, 1995).

Marsh, C., 'In the Name of God? Will-making and faith in early modern England' in G.H. Martin and P. Spufford (eds), *The Records of the Nation: The Public Record Office, 1838–1988, the British Record Society, 1888–1988* (Woodbridge, 1990), 215–49.

Martin, J.M., 'A Warwickshire Market Town in Adversity: Stratford-upon-Avon in the Sixteenth and Seventeenth Centuries', *Midland History*, 7 (1982) 26–41.

Mauss, M., *The Gift: The Form and Reason for Exchange in Archaic Societies* (New York, 1990), orig. 1950, trans. Mary Douglas.

McCants, A., *Civic Charity in a Golden Age: Orphan Care in Early Modern Amsterdam* (Urbana and Chicago, 1997).

McClendon, M.C., 'Discipline and punish? Magistrates and clergy in early Reformation Norwich' in E.J. Carlson (ed.), *Religion and the*

English People 1500–1640: New Voices, New Perspectives, Sixteenth Century Essays and Studies, Vol. 45 (Kirksville, MO, 1998), 99–118.

———, 'A Moveable Feast: Saint George's Day Celebrations and Religious Change in Early Modern England', *JBS*, 38, 1 (Jan. 1999), 1–27.

———, 'Religious toleration and the Reformation: Norwich magistrates in the sixteenth century' in N. Tyacke (ed.), *England's Long Reformation* (London and Bristol, PA, 1998), 87–115.

McIntosh, M.K., 'Local responses to the poor in late medieval and Tudor England', *Continuity and Change*, 3, 2 (Aug. 1988), 209–45.

———, *A Community Transformed: The Manor and Liberty of Havering, 1500–1620* (Cambridge, 1991).

———, *Controlling Misbehavior in England, 1370–1600* (Cambridge, 1998).

McRee, B.R., 'Charity and gild solidarity in late medieval England', *JBS* 32, 3 (1993), 195–225.

Mendelson, S.H., 'Stuart Women's Diaries and Occasional Memoirs' in M. Prior (ed.), *Women in English Society 1500–1800* (London and New York, 1985), 181–210.

———, *The Mental World of Stuart Women: Three Studies* (Brighton, 1987).

Mendelson, S. and P. Crawford, *Women in Early Modern England, 1550–1720* (Oxford, 1998).

Mikalachki, J., 'Women's Networks and the Female Vagrant: A Hard Case' in S. Frye and K. Robertson (eds), *Maids and Mistresses, Cousins and Queens: Women's Alliances in Early Modern England* (Oxford and New York, 1999), 52–69.

Moisà, M., 'Debate: Conviviality and Charity in Medieval and Early Modern England', *PaP*, 154 (1997), 223–34.

Mollat, M., trans. by A. Goldhammer, *The Poor in the Middle Ages: An Essay in Social History* (New Haven and London, 1986), orig. 1978.

Moore, C., 'Poor Relief in Elizabethan England: A New Look at Ipswich', *Proceedings and Papers of the Georgia Association of Historians*, 7 (1986), 98–119.

Morgan, D.A.L., 'The house of policy: the political role of the late Plantagenet household, 1422–1485' in D. Starkey, D.A.L. Morgan, J. Murphy, P. Wright, N. Cuddy and K. Sharpe (eds), *The English court: from the Wars of the Roses to the Civil War* (London and New York, 1987), 25–70.

Mullaney, S., *The Place of the Stage: License, Play, and Power in Renaissance England* (Ann Arbor, MI, 1997), orig. 1988.

Munkhoff, R., 'Searchers of the dead: Authority, marginality, and the interpretation of Plague in England, 1574–1665', *Gender and History*, **11**, 1 (April 1999), 1–29.

Norberg, K., *Rich and Poor in Grenoble, 1600–1814* (Berkeley, CA, 1985).

Norland, H.B., *Drama in Early Tudor Britain, 1485–1558* (Lincoln, Nebraska and London, 1995).

O'Day, R., *The Longman Companion to the Tudor Age* (London and New York, 1995).

Owen, D., *English Philanthropy: 1660–1960* (Cambridge, MA, 1964).

Ozment, S., *Magdalena and Balthasar: An Intimate Portrait of Life in Sixteenth-Century Europe Revealed in the Letters of a Nuremberg Husband and Wife* (New Haven and London, 1989), orig. 1986.

Palliser, D.M., 'Popular Reactions to the Reformation during the Years of Uncertainty, 1530–70' in C. Haigh (ed.), *The English Reformation Revised* (Cambridge, 1987), 94–113.

Pearl, V., 'Puritans and Poor Relief: The London Workhouse, 1649–1660' in D. Pennington and K. Thomas (eds), *Puritans and Revolutionaries: Essays in Seventeenth Century History Presented to Christopher Hill* (Oxford, 1978).

———, 'Change and Stability in Seventeenth-century London', *The London Journal*, **V**, 1 (May 1979), 3–34.

———, 'Social Policy in Early Modern London' in H. Lloyd-Jones, V. Pearl, B. Worden (eds), *History and Imagination: Essays in Honour of H.R. Trevor-Roper* (London, 1981), 115–31.

Pelling, M., 'Healing the Sick Poor: Social Policy and Disability in Norwich 1550–1640', *Medical History*, **29**, 2 (1985), 115–37.

Pemberton, W., 'The System of Briefs Illustrated from Leicestershire Records', *Local Historian*, **15** (May 1983), 345–54.

Phythian-Adams, C., 'Ceremony and the Citizen: The Communal Year at Coventry, 1450–1550', in P. Clark and P. Slack (eds), *Crisis and Order in English Towns 1500–1700: Essays in Urban History* (Toronto, 1972), 57–85.

———, 'Urban Decay in Late Medieval England' in P. Abrams and E.A. Wrigley (eds), *Towns and Societies: Essays in Economic History and Historical Sociology* (Cambridge, 1978), 159–185.

———, *Desolation of a City: Coventry and the Urban Crises of the Late Middle Ages* (Cambridge, 1979).

Pogson, R.H., 'Revival and reform in Mary Tudor's Church: A question of money', *Journal of Ecclesiastical History*, **25**, 3 (July 1974), 249–65.

Pounds, N.J.G., *A History of the English Parish: The Culture of Religion from Augustine to Victoria* (Cambridge, 2000).

Prior, M. (ed.), *Women in English Society 1500–1800* (London and New York, 1985).

Pullan, B., *Rich and Poor in Renaissance Venice: The Social Institutions of a Catholic State, to 1620* (Cambridge, MA, 1971).

———, 'Catholics and the Poor in Early Modern Europe', *TRHS*, 5th Series, **26** (1976), 15–34.

Questier, M., *Conversion, Politics and Religion in England, 1580–1625* (Cambridge, 1996).

Rappaport, S., *Worlds within Worlds: Structures of Life in Sixteenth-Century London* (Cambridge, 1989).

Reddaway, T.F., 'The London Goldsmiths *circa* 1500', *TRHS*, 5th series, **12** (1962), 49–62.

Roberts, M., 'Women and work in sixteenth-century English towns' in P.J. Corfield and D. Keene (eds), *Work in Towns, 850–1850* (Leicester, 1990), 86–102.

Rollison, D., 'Exploding England: the dialectics of mobility and settlement in early modern England', *Social History*, **24**, 1 (Jan. 1999), 1–16.

Roper, L., *The Holy Household: Women and Morals, in Reformation Augsburg* (Oxford, 1989).

Rosenthal, J., 'Aristocratic Widows in Fifteenth-Century England' in B.J. Harris and J.K. McNamara (eds), *Women and the Structure of Society: Selected Research from the Fifth Berkshire Conference on the History of Women* (Durham, NC, 1984), 36–47.

Rosser, G., *Medieval Westminster, 1200–1540* (Oxford, 1989).

———, 'Going to the Fraternity Feast: Commensality and Social Relations in Late Medieval England', *JBS*, **33**, 4 (Oct. 1994), 430–46.

Rowlands, M.B., 'Recusant Women 1560–1640' in M. Prior (ed.), *Women in English Society*, 149–80.

Rubin, M., *Charity and Community in Medieval Cambridge* (Cambridge, 1987).

———, *Corpus Christi: The Eucharist in Late Medieval Culture* (Cambridge, 1991).

Safley, T.M., *Charity and Economy in the Orphanages of Early Modern Augsburg* (Atlantic Highlands, NJ, 1997).

Salerno, A., 'The Social Background of Seventeenth-Century Emigration to America', *JBS*, **19**, 1 (Fall 1979), 31–52.

Scarisbrick, J.J., *The Reformation and the English People* (Oxford, 1984).

Schen, C.S., 'Women and the London Parishes, 1500–1620' in *The Parish*, 250–68.

———, 'Constructing the Poor in Early Seventeenth Century London', *Albion*, **32**, 3 (Fall 2000), 450–63.

————, 'Strategies of Poor Aged Women and Widows in Sixteenth-Century London' in L. Botelho and P. Thane (eds), *Women and Ageing in British Society since 1500* (Harlow, 2001), 17–25.

Schofield, J., 'Medieval parish churches in the City of London: the archaeological evidence', in French et al. (eds), *The Parish*, 35–55.

Seaver, P., *The Puritan Lectureships: The Politics of Religious Dissent, 1560–1662* (Stanford, CA, 1970).

Sharpe, P., 'Poor children as apprentices in Colyton, 1598–1830', *Continuity and Change*, **6**, 2 (1991), 253–70.

Skeeters, M.C., *Community and Clergy: Bristol and the Reformation, c. 1530–c. 1570* (Oxford, 1993).

Slack, P., 'Poverty and Politics in Salisbury, 1597–1666' in P. Clark and P. Slack (eds), *Crisis and Order in English Towns, 1500–1700: Essays in Urban History* (Toronto, 1972), 164–203.

————, 'Poverty in Elizabethan England', *History Today*, **34** (Oct. 1984), 5–13.

————, *The Impact of Plague in Tudor and Stuart England* (Oxford, 1985).

————, *Poverty and Policy in Tudor and Stuart England* (London, 1988).

————, 'The Response to Plague in Early Modern England: Public Policies and Their Consequences' in J. Walter and R. Schofield (eds), *Famine, Disease and the Social Order in Early Modern Society* (Cambridge, 1989), 167–87.

————, *The English Poor Law, 1531–1782* (Cambridge, 1995).

————, *From Reformation to Improvement: Public Welfare in Early Modern England* (Oxford, 1999).

Smith, J.T., *English Gilds* (London, 1870).

Smith, R., 'The structured dependence of the elderly as a recent development: some sceptical historical thoughts', *Ageing and Society* **4**, 4 (1984), 409–28.

Sommerville, C.J., *The Secularization of Early Modern England: From Religious Culture to Religious Faith* (Oxford, 1992).

Spufford, M., *Contrasting Communities: English Villages in the Sixteenth and Seventeenth Centuries* (Cambridge, 1974).

————, 'Puritanism and Social Control?' in A. Fletcher and J. Stevenson (eds), *Order and Disorder in Early Modern England* (Cambridge, 1985), 41–57.

Spufford, P. 'A Printed Catalogue of the Names of Testators' in G.H. Martin and P. Spufford (eds), *The Records of the Nation: The Public Record Office, 1838–1988, the British Record Society, 1888–1988* (Woodbridge, 1990), 167–213.

Stearns, P., 'Old women: some historical observations', *Journal of Family History*, **5**, 1 (Spring 1980), 44–57.

Stone, L., *The Family, Sex and Marriage in England 1500–1800* (New York, 1979).

Strocchia, S.T., *Death and Ritual in Renaissance Florence* (Baltimore and London, 1992).

Tate, W.E., *The Parish Chest: A Study of the Records of Parochial Administration in England* (Cambridge, 1969).

Terpstra, N., 'Confraternal Prison Charity and Political Consolidation in Sixteenth-Century Bologna', *The Journal of Modern History*, **66**, 2 (June 1994), 217–48.

Thane, P., *Old Age in English History: Past Experiences, Present Issues* (Oxford, 2000).

Thomas, E.G.. 'Pauper Apprenticeship', *Local Historian*, **14**, 7 (1981), 400–406.

Thomas, K., *Religion and the Decline of Magic* (New York, 1971).

———, *Man and the Natural World: Changing Attitudes in England, 1500–1800* (Oxford, 1983).

Thompson, E.P., *The Making of the English Working Class* (New York, 1966).

———, 'The Moral Economy of the Crowd in the Eighteenth Century', *PaP*, **50** (1971), 76–136.

Thomson, J.A.F., 'Piety and Charity in Late Medieval London', *Journal of Ecclesiastical History*, **16**, 2 (Oct. 1965), 178–95.

Thorndale, W., 'The Virginia Census of 1619', *Magazine of Virginia Genealogy*, **33** (1995), 155–70.

Tittler, R., 'Money-lending in the West Midlands: the activities of Joyce Jefferies, 1638–49', *Historical Research*, **67**, 164 (Oct. 1994), 249–63.

———, *The Reformation and the Towns in England: Politics and Political Culture, c. 1540–1640* (Oxford, 1998).

Todd, B.J., 'The remarrying widow: a stereotype reconsidered' in M. Prior (ed.), *Women in English Society 1500–1800* (London and New York, 1985), 54–92.

Todd, M., 'Profane Pastimes and the Reformed Community: The Persistence of Popular Festivities in Early Modern Scotland', *JBS*, **39**, 2 (April 2000), 123–56.

Tyacke, N., 'Popular puritan mentality in late Elizabethan England' in P. Clark, A.G.R. Smith and N. Tyacke (eds), *The English Commonwealth, 1547–1640: Essays in Politics and Society* (New York, 1979), 77–92.

———, 'Anglican Attitudes: Some Recent Writings on English Religious History, from the Reformation to the Civil War', *JBS*, **35** (April 1996), 139–67.

Tyacke, N. (ed.), *England's Long Reformation 1500–1800* (London and Bristol, PA, 1998).

Underdown, D., *Revel, Riot and Rebellion: Popular Politics and Culture in England 1603–1660* (Oxford, 1985).

———, 'The Taming of the Scold: the Enforcement of Patriarchal Authority in Early Modern England' in A. Fletcher and J. Stevenson (eds), *Order and Disorder in Early Modern England* (Cambridge, 1985), 116–36.

Unwin, G., *The Gilds and Companies of London* (London, 1938).

Usher, B., '"In a Time of Persecution": New light on the secret Protestant congregation in Marian London' in D. Loades (ed.), *John Foxe and the English Reformation* (Aldershot, 1997), 233–51.

———, 'Backing Protestantism: The London Godly, the Exchequer and the Foxe Circle' in D. Loades (ed.), *John Foxe: An Historical Perspective* (Aldershot, 1999), 105–34.

Valbuena, O., 'To "Venture in the Rebels' Fight": History and Equivocation in Macbeth', *Renaissance Papers* (1994), 105–22.

Valenze, D., *Prophetic Sons and Daughters: Female Preaching and Popular Religion in Industrial England* (Princeton, 1985).

Van Gennep, A., *Rites of Passage* (Chicago, 1960), orig. 1908.

Von Friedeburg, R., 'Reformation of Manners and the Social Composition of Offenders in an East Anglian Cloth Village: Earls Colne, Essex, 1531–1642', *JBS*, **29**, 4 (October 1990), 347–85.

Wabuda, S., 'Shunamites and nurses of the English Reformation: the activities of Mary Glover, niece of Hugh Latimer' in W. J. Sheils and D. Wood (eds), *Women in the Church*, *Studies in Church History*, **27** (Oxford, 1990), 335–44.

———, 'Equivocation and Recantation During the English Reformation: The "Subtle Shadows" of Dr Edward Crome', *Journal of Ecclesiastical History*, **44**, 2 (April 1993), 224–42.

———, 'Bishops and the Provision of Homilies, 1520 to 1547', *SCJ*, **25**, 3 (1994), 551–66.

———, 'Revising the Reformation', *JBS*, **35**, 2 (1996), 257–62.

Wales, T., 'Poverty, Poor Relief and the Life-Cycle: Some Evidence from Seventeenth-Century Norfolk' in R.M. Smith (ed.), *Land, Kinship and Life-Cycle* (Cambridge, 1984), 351–404.

Wall, R., 'Elderly persons and members of their households in England and Wales from preindustrial times to the present' in D. Kertzer and P. Laslett (eds), *Aging in the Past*, 81–106.

Walter, J., 'The Social Economy of Dearth in Early Modern England' in

W. and R. Schofield (eds), *Famine, Disease and the Social Order in Early Modern Society* (Cambridge, 1989), 75–128.

Wandel, L.P., *Always Among Us: Images of the Poor in Zwingli's Zurich* (Cambridge, 1990).

Ward, J.P., *Metropolitan Communities: Trade Guilds, Identity, and Change in Early Modern London* (Stanford, CA, 1997).

Watt, T., *Cheap Print and Popular Piety, 1550–1640* (Cambridge, 1991).

Weber, M., *The Protestant Ethic and the Spirit of Capitalism* (New York, 1958).

Weissman, R.F.E., *Ritual Brotherhood in Renaissance Florence* (New York, 1981).

White, B., *The Origins of American Slavery: Freedom and Bondage in the English Colonies* (New York, 1997).

Whiting, R., *The Blind Devotion of the People: Popular Religion and the English Reformation* (Cambridge, 1989).

Wiesner, M., 'Making Ends Meet: The Working Poor in Early Modern Europe' in K.C. Sessions and P.N. Bebb (eds), *Pietas et Societas: New Trends in Reformation Social History*, Volume IV, Sixteenth Century Essays and Studies (Ann Arbor, MI, 1985), 79–88.

———, 'Beyond Women and the Family: Towards a Gender Analysis of the Reformation', *SCJ*, **18** (1987), 311–21.

———, *Gender, Church, and State in Early Modern Germany* (London and New York, 1998), Series: Women and Men in History.

Wilkinson, B., '"The poore of the parish"', *Local Historian*, **16**, 1 (1984), 21–3.

Willen, D., 'Women in the Public Sphere in Early Modern England: The Case of the Urban Working Poor', *SCJ*, **19**, 4 (1988), 559–75.

———, 'Godly Women in Early Modern England: Puritanism and Gender', *Journal of Ecclesiastical History*, **43**, 4 (October 1992), 561–80.

Williamson, M., 'The Role of Religious Guilds in the Cultivation of Ritual Polyphony in England: the Case of Louth, 1450–1550' in F. Kisby (ed.), *Music and Musicians in Renaissance Urban Communities* (Cambridge, 2001), 242–70.

Wilson, J., 'A Catalogue of the "unlawful" books found in John Stow's study on 21 February 1568/9', *Journal of Recusant History*, **20** (1990–91), 1–30.

Wright, J., 'The World's Worst Worm: Conscience and Conformity during the English Reformation', *SCJ*, **30**, 1 (1999), 113–33.

Wrightson, K. and D. Levine, *Poverty and Piety in an English Village: Terling, 1525–1700* (New York, 1979).

Wunderli, R.M., *London Church Courts and Society on the Eve of the Reformation* (Cambridge, MA, 1981).

Unpublished Dissertations and Papers

Carlson, M., 'Overseers and the Overseen: Women's roles in administering poor relief in Eighteenth-Century Rotterdam', unpublished paper presented at the Eleventh Berkshire Conference on the History of Women, June, 1999.

Dinan, S., 'A Nursing Vocation: the Hospital Work of the Daughters of Charity in Seventeenth-Century France', unpublished paper, presented at the Eleventh Berkshire Conference on the History of Women, June, 1999.

Fideler, P., 'Discussion of Poverty in Sixteenth Century England', unpublished Ph.D. thesis, Brandeis University, History of Ideas, 1971.

French, K., '"Where, Oh Where, Have the Lay Women Gone?"', unpublished paper presented at the American Historical Association Annual Meeting, 1997.

Hudson, G.L., 'Disabled Veterans, the State and Philanthropy in England, 1585–1680', paper presented at the North American Conference on British Studies, October 1998, at Boulder, Colorado.

Kisby, F., 'Urban Cultures and Religious Reforms: Parochial Music in London, c. 1520–c. 1580', presented at Leeds Medieval Conference, July 1998.

Merritt, J.F., 'Religion, Government, and Society in Early Modern Westminster, c. 1525–1625', unpublished Ph.D. thesis, Royal Holloway and Bedford New College, University of London, 1992.

Ottaway, S., 'The "Decline of Life": Aspects of Aging in Eighteenth-Century England', unpublished Ph.D. dissertation, Brown University, 1998.

Page, D.B., 'Uniform and Catholic: Church Music in the Reign of Mary Tudor (1553–1558)', unpublished Ph.D. dissertation, Brandeis University, 1996.

Index